# Recreating Europe

Since the fall of Communism, countries such as Hungary and Poland have experienced a spectacular transformation into democracies with market economies. Ten countries in Central Europe have now applied for membership of the European Union, which they regard as the final step on the road back to the heart of Europe. For the European Union, this enlargement provides a significant challenge to its capacity for change and flexibility. In this book an academic with wide experience in policy-making in the European Union and Central Europe investigates the relationship between the European Union and countries of Central Europe as it is today. He examines the detail of the Association Agreements, and provides the first analysis of their operation in key areas like trade and competition policy. Part III of the book considers the costs and benefits of enlargement and investigates the key problems in both East and West, including the CAP, EU Structural Funds, budgetary policy and migration. Finally, the book investigates alternative strategies for enlargement.

ALAN MAYHEW is Visiting Professor at the Catholic University of Leuven, and Professor at the College of Europe, Natolin. He previously held a number of posts within the European Commission, most recently being responsible for economic relations with Central and Eastern Europe in the Directorate General for External Economic Relations. He also served as an adviser to the Polish government on European integration in 1996–7 and has advised other governments in the region.

# Recreating Europe

*The European Union's Policy towards*
*Central and Eastern Europe*

Alan Mayhew

CAMBRIDGE
UNIVERSITY PRESS

*HF*
*1532.935*
*.E852*
*M39*
*1998*

PUBLISHED BY THE PRESS SYNDICATE OF THE UNIVERSITY OF CAMBRIDGE
The Pitt Building, Trumpington Street, Cambridge CB2 1RP, United Kingdom

CAMBRIDGE UNIVERSITY PRESS
The Edinburgh Building, Cambridge, CB2 2RU, United Kingdom
http://www.cup.cam.ac.uk
40 West 20th Street, New York, NY 10011–4211, USA   http://www.cup.org
10 Stamford Road, Oakleigh, Melbourne 3166, Australia

First published 1998

Printed in the United Kingdom at the University Press, Cambridge

Typeset in Plantin 10/12pt [CE]

*A catalog record for this book is available from the British Library*

*Library of Congress Cataloging in Publication data*
Mayhew, Alan.
Recreating Europe: the European Union's policy towards Central and
Eastern Europe / by Alan Mayhew.
    p.    cm.
Includes bibliographical references and index.
ISBN 0 521 63086 X (hardback). – ISBN 0 521 63897 6 (pbk.)
1. European Union countries – Foreign economic relations – Europe, Eastern.
2 Europe, Eastern – Foreign economic relations – European Union countries.
3. European Union countries – Foreign economic relations – Europe, Central.
4. Europe, Central – Foreign economic relations – European Union countries.
5. European Union countries – Economic policy.   I. Title.
HF1532.935.E852M39   1998
337.4047–dc21   97–38835   CIP

ISBN 0 521 63086 X hardback
ISBN 0 521 63897 6 paperback

# Contents

## Part III   Making enlargement a reality

# Maps and figures

# Tables

# Preface

The enlargement of the European Union to include the countries of Central and Eastern Europe is the final step in the reintegration of the continent after almost half a century of forced division. This process did not begin in the revolution of 1989 but in the courageous actions of ordinary people fighting Soviet domination over three decades. The workers' uprising in East Germany in 1953, the Hungarian revolution of 1956, the Czech Spring of 1968 and the long series of Polish revolts from Poznan in 1956 through to the triumph of Solidarity in the June 1989 elections were all steps in the destruction of a system which negated the fundamental European values of democracy, freedom of the spirit and basic human rights.

Seven years after the Polish election, the enthusiasm for this last step appears unbroken in much of Central and Eastern Europe. In Western Europe on the other hand, the supportive political statements of the early 1990s have given way to a questioning of the whole process of enlargement. Initial enthusiasm has turned to fear of change, fear of unemployment and increased competition and fear of immigration, in an economic climate in much of the European Union characterised by slow growth.

Yet it is one of the themes of this book that the whole of Europe wins from wider integration. For Central and Eastern Europe it means that for the first time it is anchored in a democratic union of nations rather than floating dangerously between East and West. As importantly, it means that the region's major markets in Western Europe cannot be closed. For the European Union there are gains politically, from the security point of view and in the economy. More importantly enlargement will perhaps shake the European Union into tackling some of the problems which are afflicting it. In politics and economics the signs of crisis in Western Europe are everywhere. Some see the answer in closing off the Union in a highly protected state, which will demonise the foreigner and where enlargement has no real place. This is the recipe for both moral and economic decay, leading to the destruction of the immense benefits of European integration. It is only through increased openness that peace, prosperity and the integration of the Continent can be achieved. Enlargement, with all the changes that this process will force on Western Europe, may be an important element in transforming the European Union into a political, moral and economic force for international peace and development.

But these great issues are only the framework for the longer-term development of the Continent. An understanding of the current relationship requires a profound knowledge of the legally binding agreements which exist between the two regions and how they are managed. It is the detail which is important for the average person. When can I legally set up in business in the United Kingdom? Can I practise as a doctor in Germany? Can I buy land in Estonia? What documentation must I have to export to the Union? This detail is determined today principally by the Association Agreements between the countries of Central Europe and the European Union. They form the basis for the detailed day-to-day decisions which have to be taken in the relationship between the two partners.

This book attempts to analyse both the current situation resulting from the Association Agreements and their implementation and the problems and opportunities of enlargement in the future. It tries to explain the detail of the current and future relationship rather than to stick to the political high ground of generalities. It is important to know what the Association Agreements say about the right of establishment or the procedure for following up a dumping complaint. The impact of enlargement on the Union's GATT commitments are crucial to any discussion of enlargement.

Part I considers the development of relations between the Central and Eastern European (CEE) countries and the Union from the early 1980s through to the present. This background material is important to an understanding of the position of both sides today. It explains the feeling of rejection which many of the reformers in Central Europe experienced in the early 1990s, as they realised that their countries would not have an automatic right to membership of the Community. It also explains the cautious attitude which the Community adopted towards the region: immensely proud of the achievement of the internal market but chastened by the experience of Maastricht and the need to move quickly to re-establish the credibility of the Union.

Part II analyses in detail the Association Agreements. This is not simply a description of what the Association Agreements say, although each chapter starts from this point. The chapters seek to analyse the impact of the Association Agreements and to point to areas where these

Agreements could be improved. Chapters 3, 4 and 5 on trade, creating the market economy and on financial assistance are particularly detailed, but these are the areas which impact every day on people in both regions. It is important to understand why the Agreements state what they do, and how and in what direction they may change.

Part III considers the question of the next enlargement from the basis of an understanding of the Association Agreements. The key problems for enlargement are treated in detail, notably agriculture, the Structural Funds and the whole question of how the Union can operate with 25 or more members (chapters 9–11). In each case the problems are discussed and possible solutions proposed. These solutions are gathered together in chapter 15 on the strategies for accession.

Enlargement will be the key development in the European Union in the coming years. It is fundamentally a political process, leading to overcoming some of the remaining divisions of the Second World War and the period of Soviet domination. As a political process, the decisions on enlargement will be political. The theme of this book is not, however, political; it is essentially economic. Unless the economic preparation for accession – including the creation of a supportive market economy legal framework and the continuation of reform in the associated countries as well as changes in Union policies – is not undertaken, the political decisions cannot be made.

The process of enlargement will change both the Union and the countries which join. At the end of the first decade of the next century, if enlargement takes place, the Union will be larger and undoubtedly more complex. If there is more flexibility in new policy-making, it will also be a much more diverse Union. This does not mean that it will be weak – indeed, if the necessary institutional and policy reforms are carried out, it will be stronger and more acceptable to its citizens. For the CEE countries, accession to the Union means the end of the road which started in internal revolts of their citizens and passed through the glory days of the overthrow of Soviet domination and the difficult transition process. For Europe as a whole, the coming decade will in many ways determine whether the Continent can remain prosperous, peaceful and united, or whether it descends into economic decline or worse.

ALAN MAYHEW
*Brussels*

# Acknowledgements

My thanks are due to so many friends and colleagues, who have shared my interests in economic systems and economic transition in Central and Eastern Europe over many years, that I cannot mention them all here. Studies in Germany, at the Universities of Münster and Göttingen, stimulated my early interest in questions of the division of Europe and the impact of central planning in the DDR. Teaching at Birkbeck College at the University of London gave me access to colleagues with similar interests and allowed me to travel for the first time in Central and Eastern Europe and to discuss with academics from the region.

I would particularly like to thank my friends at the Economic University of Poznan, Renata Stawarska and Bogdan Gruchman and at the University of Gdansk, Andrzej Stepniak, Anna Zielinska and Krystyna Gawlikowska-Hueckel, all of whom showed remarkable courage and clear-sightedness in the 1980s and whose hospitality in the worst years of that decade was wonderful.

The months in 1991 spent as adviser to the Polish Prime Minister, Jan-Krzysztof Bielecki, to whom my personal thanks are due, were some of the most interesting and instructive. During this period I met and worked with many of the figures in the Solidarność Government, whose enthusiasm and determination were exceptional. Anna Fornalczyk, then Head of the Anti-Monopoly Office, Henryka Bochniarz, formerly Industry Minister and now head of NICOM and Jacek Saryusz-Wolski, from 1991 to 1996 Plenipotentiary for European Integration in the Polish Government and now Vice-Rector of the College of Europe were among these pioneers. Since 1996 as adviser again to the Polish Government, I have gained enormously from contact with many old friends. I would particularly like to thank Marek Belka and Pawel Samecki, respectively Minister and Under-Secretary at the Ministry of Finance and Danuta Hübner and Jarek Pietras, respectively Secretary of State for European Integration and Under-Secretary at the Committee of European Integration. Jan Kulakowski, the first Ambassador of Poland to the European Union and his wife Sophie have been good friends and a mine of information; I have also benefited from the wealth of knowledge and experience of Andrzej Byrt, formerly trade minister and now Polish Ambassador in Germany. Numerous other colleagues in and out of government have helped me generously with their time and friendship; to name just a few, Marek Tabor, Andrzej Harasimowicz, Ewa Osniecka, Piotr Kotelnicki, Jan Kluk, Pawel and Kasia Kastory

Endre Juhasz, one of the wisest men I have worked with and now Hungary's Ambassador to the European Union, János Martony, Peter Gottfried and András Inotai have all helped me to understand Hungarian policy and outlook. Pawel Telicka, Josef Kreuter and my former colleague Jean-Luc Delpeuch have done the same for the Czech Republic, Clyde Kull for Estonia, Dalia Grybauskaita for Lithuania, Boris Ciselj for Slovenia and many others from Central Europe for their own countries.

I owe an enormous debt of gratitude to my academic colleagues and friends; Christian Kirchner and his colleagues at the Humboldt University in Berlin, Marvin Jackson and Joep Konings at the Leuven Institute for Central and East European Studies (LICOS), Helen Wallace and Alasdair Smith at Sussex, colleagues and students at the Economics University of Poznan, the University of Gdansk and at the College of Europe Natolin campus in Warsaw.

At the European Commission in Brussels I was very lucky in being able to work with colleagues who were intelligent, experienced and enthusiastic. Catherine Day, Rita Hemschemeier, Robert Verrue, Pablo Benavides, Jean-Claude Morel, Michael Leigh, Jerome Vignon, Karen Fogg, Mark Franco, Amir Naqvi, Pierre Mirel, Tom Garvey, Graham Avery, Michael Emerson, Vittoria Alliata and Graham Meadows are just a few of many from whom I have learned much.

At the Commission I had the opportunity to work closely with many colleagues in national governments of EU Member States, especially in London, Bonn and Paris. Again I had the great fortune to work with highly motivated and intelligent officials. Participating in the preparation of the European Councils of Copenhagen and Essen with these officials and with colleagues from the Community institutions was a fascinating experience.

I would especially like to thank Hans-Friedrich von Ploetz, Wilhelm Schönfelder, Gerhard Rambow, Sigrid Selz, Bernhard Zepter and Walter Kittel in Bonn, Claude-France Arnaud and Jean-Luc Delpeuch in Paris, Stephen Wright, Andrew Kahn, Bill Stow, Emyr Jones Parry, Richard Jones and many others in London. I would also like to pay tribute to the work of the British Know-How Fund, which has been a model for efficient, effective and unbureaucratic assistance to the CEE countries.

Above all I would like to thank my family, who have put up with years of my travelling in Central and Eastern Europe and elsewhere, as well as the writing of this book.

# Glossary

| | |
|---|---|
| AMO | Anti-Monopoly Office (in associated countries). |
| AMS | Aggregate Measure of Support (GATT Agriculture Agreement). |
| BSI | British Standards Institution. |
| CAP | Common Agricultural Policy. |
| CBSS | Council of the Baltic Sea States. Potentially important and valuable discussion shop for Baltic countries. |
| CEFTA | Central European Free Trade Area. Agreement to create free trade in Central Europe in parallel with the Association Agreements. |
| CEI | Central European Initiative. Inspired by Italy to discuss problems of Central Europe. |
| CET | Common External Tariff. |
| CFSP | Common Foreign and Security Policy. |
| CIS | Commonwealth of Independent States. |
| CMEA | Council for Mutual Economic Assistance. FSU-dominated economic coordination organisation in Central and Eastern Europe, dissolved in 1991. Also known as COMECON. |
| COM | European Commission. Executive body of the Union. Has quasi-exclusive right of policy proposal to Council and Parliament. Implements Union policy and programmes. Has only a limited role in Union foreign policy and justice and home affairs. Far more powerful than a normal civil service. |
| COREPER | EU Committee of the Permanent Representatives of the Member States. Prepares agenda of Council meetings. |
| Council | EU Council of Ministers. Takes decisions on Union matters and makes policy. The most powerful decision-making institution of the European Union. |

| | |
|---|---|
| Council of Europe | Strasbourg-based Europe-wide organisation specialising in non-economic issues, notably human rights, democracy and culture. |
| CSFR | Former Czech and Slovak Federal Republic. |
| DDR | Former East Germany. |
| DIN | Deutsche Industrie Norm (German Standards Institute). |
| EBRD | European Bank for Reconstruction and Development. London-based bank created by industrialised countries in 1990 to finance the transition of the CEE and FSU economies. The European Union and its Member States hold over half of the bank's capital. |
| EC | European Community. |
| ECE | Economic Commission for Europe. |
| ECJ | European Court of Justice. Final legal arbiter on EC law. Deals with cases started in the ECJ and referred to it by national courts. Attached to the ECJ is a Court of First Instance which hears cases brought by private parties. |
| ECOFIN | EU Council of Economy and Finance Ministers. |
| ECSC | European Coal and Steel Community. |
| EEA | European Economic Area. |
| EEC | European Economic Community. |
| EFTA | European Free Trade Area. |
| EIB | European Investment Bank. Exists to further economic development by providing loan finance for projects inside and outside the Community. Major lender to CEE countries. Loans covered by 100% guarantee on Community budget. |
| EMU | European Monetary Union. |
| EP | European Parliament. Has co-decision-making role with the Council in certain areas. Real power in spending the 'free margin' of the budget and progressively in overseeing work of Commission. |
| ERDF | European Regional Development Fund. |
| ERM | Exchange Rate Mechanism. |
| ERP | European Recovery Programme (Marshall Fund). |
| Eurofer | European Association of Iron and Steel Producers. |
| European Council | Meetings of heads of state and governments of the 15 Member States to discuss policy; held every six months. |

| | |
|---|---|
| European Court of Auditors | Audits Community revenue and expenditure and produces annual report and many sectoral reports. Has grown in importance with increase in size of Community budget. |
| FDI | Foreign direct investment. |
| fob | Free on board. |
| FSU | Former Soviet Union. |
| FTA | Free trade area. |
| G7 | Group of 7 industrialised countries. |
| G24 | Group of 24 countries providing assistance to the CEE transition countries |
| GATS | General Agreement on Trade in Services (GATT). |
| GATT | General Agreement on Trade and Tariffs. Spearheaded liberalisation since the end of the 1940s. |
| GDP | Gross domestic product. |
| GNP | Gross national product. |
| GSP | General System of Preference (GATT). |
| IBRD | International Bank for Reconstruction and Development – World Bank. Washington-based Bretton Woods institution responsible for medium- and long-term lending to CEE countries. |
| IFI | International Financial Institution (IMF, World Bank, etc.). |
| IGC | Inter-Governmental Conference. Conference of EU Member States to discuss changes in the Union Treaty. Current IGC started in March 1996 and ended mid-1997. |
| IMF | International Monetary Fund. Washington-based Bretton Woods institution responsible for coordination of policy between member governments and the granting of conditional short-term balance of payments lending. |
| LIBOR | London Inter-Bank Offered Rate – base interest rate for interbank landing. |
| MFA | Multifibre Arrangement. |
| MFN | Most favoured nation. |
| NATO | North Atlantic Treaty Organisation. Main Western defence alliance. Many of the associated countries have also asked to join. |
| NGO | Non-governmental organisation. |
| NIS | Newly independent states (of FSU). |
| NTB | Non-tariff barrier. |

| | |
|---|---|
| OECD | Organisation for Economic Cooperation and Development. The club of advanced industrial nations. Mainly devoted to discussion of mutual problems but has developed specific fields of action (e.g. the regulation of use of export credits). |
| OPT | Outward processing traffic (Textile Arrangement). |
| OSCE | Organisation for Security and Cooperation in Europe. Created 1972 and led to Helsinki Final Act in 1975. Objective is to secure peace and stability in Europe. |
| PCA | Partnership and Cooperation Agreement. |
| PHARE | EU assistance programme for Central and Eastern Europe. |
| PPS | Purchasing power standard. |
| QR | Quantitative restriction. |
| RTA | Regional trade area. |
| SME | Small and medium-sized enterprise. |
| SOE | State-owned enterprise. |
| TAIEX | Technical assistance information exchange office (EU Commission). |
| TENs | Trans-European Networks. |
| TRIPS | Trade-Related Aspects of Intellectual Property Rights (GATT). |
| UNPROFOR | United Nations Protection Force (Bosnia). |
| VAT | Value added tax. |
| VER | Voluntary export restraint (GATT). |
| Warsaw Pact | Now dissolved CEE military alliance dominated by the Soviet Union. |
| WEU | West European Union. European pillar of the Atlantic Alliance. Objective to develop European defence identity. |
| WTO | World Trade Organisation. Organisation responsible for negotiating and policing international trade. Created 1995. Incorporated the GATT. |

*Map 1* A political map of Europe

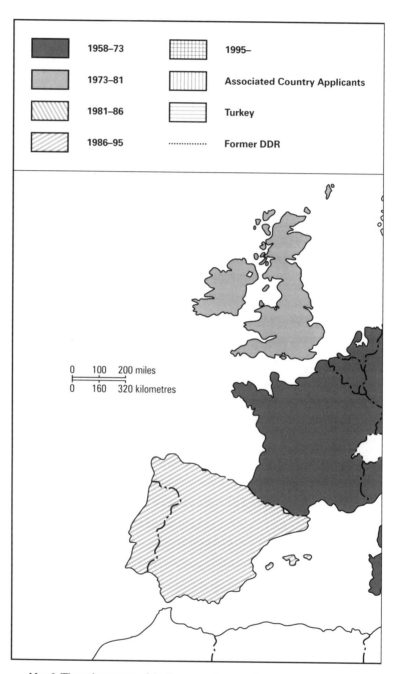

**Legend:**

- 1958–73
- 1973–81
- 1981–86
- 1986–95
- 1995–
- Associated Country Applicants
- Turkey
- Former DDR

Scale:
0   100   200 miles
0   160   320 kilometres

*Map 2* The enlargement of the European Community

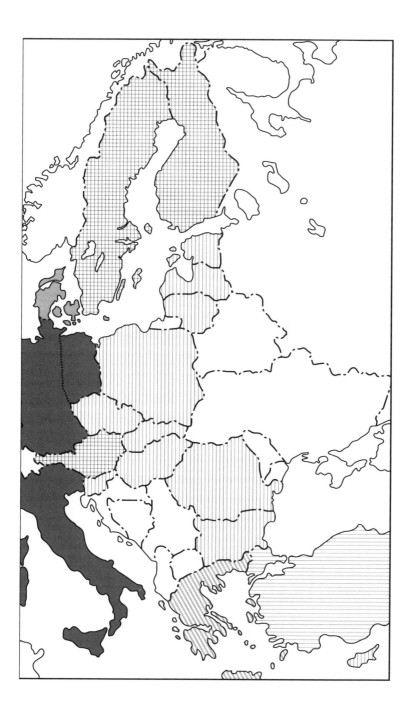

*Part I*

# Background

# 1     From the overthrow of Soviet domination to integration with the European Union

## Central Europe, an integral part of European history

Since 1989 the question of the boundaries of Europe has become one of the favourite topics of seminars throughout Europe and the United States. It seems strange that such a question should be put. Did the fact that Hungary involuntarily became part of the Communist bloc for almost 50 years mean that it was no longer part of Europe? When it reasserted its independence in the 1980s, was it rejoining Europe?

For many in Western Europe in 1989, their experience stretched only over the period when Western Europe enjoyed peace and growing prosperity, and Central and Eastern Europe was locked up behind the 'iron curtain'. This sort of myopia was never shared by the citizens of Central and Eastern Europe, who could not bring themselves to feel that the Yalta division of Europe was a normal condition of the Continent. When considering the background to discussions about the future enlargement of the European Union to the countries of Central and Eastern Europe (CEE) it is important to remember the historical ties which bind Europe together.

The great doyenne of German journalism, Marion Gräfin Dönhoff, writing in her book *Kindheit in Ostpreußen* (1988) tells how her family migrated in the fourteenth century from the Ruhr area of Westfalia to the Livland (modern Estonia and Latvia), before settling in East Prussia.[1] She relates how part of her family became Polish and served the Polish kings in highest office, while another part remained German and created the line of which she, through war, eventually became head. But the most interesting part of her story is the degree to which it was possible for a German to take high office in Lithuania, for a Pole to serve the Order of Teutonic Knights; there was no division of Europe at this period.

The impact of the French Revolution was felt throughout the Con-

---

[1] Marion Gräfin Dönhoff, *Kindheit in Ostpreußen* (Berlin: Siedler Verlag, 1988).

tinent (and beyond) and its influence can be seen clearly in the attempts of the nobility in Hungary to liberalise the constitution and to develop the idea of Hungarian nationhood, which led in the end to the Revolution of 1848. The French Revolution was also the inspiration behind the first Polish Constitution of 3 May 1791, which however preceded the French Constitution by six months. But this Constitution was also lengthily discussed amongst political circles in the United Kingdom, where the positive opinion of Edmund Burke was used in the political debate in Poland.[2] The Constitution, which includes references to Europe clearly placing Poland within the heart of the Continent, shows a degree of tolerance which owes much to the liberal ideas of France at this period. In paragraph 1, the Constitution defines the Catholic religion to be the religion of the Polish state, but then affirms that the most important Christian rule is the love of one's neighbour and therefore establishes that religious freedom in all forms will be practised in the state.

But the integration of Europe East and West before the Second World War was not only political and administrative; Europe was also integrated economically. This fact can be demonstrated through the use of economic statistics as well as through the records of individual companies, which produced and traded throughout the whole region. That the Czech Republic had a higher GDP *per capita* than Austria because of its important mechanical industries and its pan-European trade is now an oft-quoted fact which is worth repeating. But one could also draw the same conclusion from the literature of the period. In Władysław Remont's novel *The Promised Land* (*Ziemia obiecana*), written in 1899 and made famous in the film by Andrzej Wajda, the integrated nature of the Łódz textile industry, with its markets in Russia and its three groups of owners and workers – the Germans, the Poles and the Jews – is clearly demonstrated.

If we look at trade flows in the inter-war period we see the same phenomenon: Central Europe lived in an integrated system with what is now the European Union. If we take 1928 as one of the last times that there was freer trade in Europe before the arrival of dictatorship, we see a trade pattern similar to that of today – with, for instance, 55% of total Polish trade being with the States which today make up the Community, over 60% in the case of Bulgaria.

But the history of Europe since the Second World War was marked by a forced division of the continent decided by the Allied leaders meeting

---

[2] Warsaw University Library, *Lord Burke do Polaków; pismo z angielskiego przełożone* (1791).

in Yalta in 1944, certainly against the will of the peoples of Central Europe who suffered the consequences of this division for the next 45 years. As Timothy Garton Ash in his book *In Europe's Name* notes, 'the "Yalta" division of Europe [is] distinguished from previous divisions of Europe by its historical arbitrariness, its absoluteness, the asymmetrical roles of partly extra-European, nuclear-armed superpowers, and the congruence of military, political and economic differences'.[3]

While being quite 'arbitrary and absolute' and totally unjust and immoral from most points of view, this division came to be accepted in Western Europe, outside Germany, as inevitable. Indeed many statesmen seemed to regard the division as a guarantee for peace and prosperity. In the 1980s, as reforms in the communist centrally-planned systems became more general (without, however, reforming the basic political one-party system or giving democratic rights to citizens) it became commonplace in intellectual circles to argue that the reforming communist system was an acceptable alternative to the capitalist market economy system of Western Europe. This feeling, by no means general, was the opposite of that developing to the East of the 'iron curtain', where citizens were becoming more convinced that the corrupt and inefficient system of one-party rule and central planning, held together by the power of the Soviet army, must be swept away.

It is true to say that the countries of Central Europe freed themselves from Communism through their own efforts and largely without more than the moral support of the Member States of the European Community. It is also true to say that there was probably little more at the political level which the Community or the United States could have done to help, other than standing firm against further Soviet aggression outside the Soviet bloc. But the level of support for dissident groups, intellectuals and workers' protests was also much lower than one could have expected from governments committed to the restoration of democracy and human rights. And no effective steps were taken to show the Soviet Union that its treatment of the Hungarian uprising or the Czechoslovak 'Spring' were unacceptable or to show real displeasure at the way the numerous revolts of the Polish workers and intellectuals were put down by the national militias. Essentially the peoples of Central Europe freed themselves, at great cost and with practically no outside assistance, from Communist rule.

In 1989 and 1990, however, political leaders throughout the Western world in their 'Sunday' speeches proclaimed how the brave peoples of

---

[3] Timothy Garton Ash, *In Europe's name: Germany and the divided continent* (London: Jonathan Cape, 1993).

Central Europe would be helped by the old democracies.[4] These
peoples were the more astonished then to find that they were not
immediately taken into the European Community and given adequate
assistance to rapidly overcome the disastrous economic situation which
the final death-throws of the Communist system had produced, a
system which, through their own efforts, they had brought to its knees.
The leaders of the new countries soon realised that the division of
Europe which had been decreed at Yalta had been accepted and to some
extent internalised by Western leaders. They now had to fight to
persuade them that the division of Europe was an historical anomaly.

## Official relations between the European Community and Central Europe, 1970–89

At the official level, the period between 1970 and 1989 was marked by a
steady but irregular progress in the relationship between the European
Community and its Member States and the Council of Mutual Economic Assistance (CMEA) and its members, as these latter introduced
economic reforms into their systems. Throughout much of this period
there were similar policies on both sides of the European divide: both
the European Community and the CMEA sought to arrange agreements
between themselves and the individual Member States on the other side,
while shunning relations with each other. For the Soviet Union, the
European Community was the economic arm of NATO and for most of
the 1960s and 1970s was treated accordingly.

A fundamental technical problem which made relations difficult was
the fact that the two organisations had very different powers and areas of
competence. Whilst the European Community consisted of free and
independent democracies, which were gradually, albeit sometimes grudgingly, pooling their sovereignty in order to have more influence in the
world and to improve economic efficiency, the CMEA consisted of
countries which *de facto* had very limited freedom, but where sovereignty
was not pooled, and where cooperation between partners took place on
an ad hoc basis. The CMEA had no common commercial policy or
external tariff. It was only to 'assist the Member countries . . . in the
preparation, coordination and the implementation of joint programmes
. . . for the expansion of trade and . . . services among the Member
countries . . . [and] between them and third countries'. These programmes were therefore carried out by the Member States themselves,

---

[4] Jacques Delors, President of the European Community, warned leaders not say things in
their Sunday speeches which they had no intention of carrying out during the week.

not by the CMEA. That the CMEA had an international role is certain, but it was a very different organisation from the European Community.

Whilst at the national level agreements of various quality were made in the 1960s and 1970s, especially after the start of Chancellor Brandt's 'Ostpolitik', it was only at the beginning of the 1970s that the first attempts were made at general agreements between the two blocs. With the 'communitarisation' of national commercial policy in the European Community, it became necessary to replace national agreements with CMEA Member States by Community agreements. In December 1969, the European Community decided that its Common Commercial Policy would apply to the CEE countries in the same way that it was applied to other third countries.

In May 1974 the EC Council offered to negotiate trade agreements with each of the Member States of the CMEA and later in the same year it agreed to continue to offer Most Favoured Nation (MFN) treatment to these countries. However these offers were rejected or completely ignored by the CMEA countries, which considered that they would weaken the organisation while strengthening the EC's bargaining position. The Community was then forced, by the expiry of bilateral agreements, to introduce autonomous measures to regulate trade with the CEE countries in early 1975. This autonomous regime formed the basis of most trade throughout the 1970s and 1980s.

The only exceptions to this general freezing of trade relations between the two parts of Europe were the bilateral arrangements made with the most independent of the CEE countries, Yugoslavia and Romania. A non-preferential agreement was signed as early as 1970 with Yugoslavia followed by a five-year agreement in 1973 and a cooperation agreement in 1980. Yugoslavia benefited from Generalised System of Preference (GSP) treatment as early as 1971. Romania also enjoyed GSP treatment and it signed a cooperation agreement with the Community in 1980. This agreement instituted a joint committee on trade matters between the partners, an extremely important institutional development. It should also not be forgotten that the European Community and its Member States had a common framework for trade through their membership of the GATT, of which Romania, Hungary, Poland and Czechoslovakia were also members. Sectoral agreements with the European Community were also permitted by the CMEA, where this was economically advantageous to Member States and where the overall position of the CMEA was not put at risk. This led to textile agreements based on the Multifibre Agreement (MFA), agreements on trade in steel products following the Davignon steel industry rationalisation plan for the Community (1977) and further agreements on trade in lamb and goat meat. As far as the CMEA was concerned, in order to save face, the bilateral global agreement between Romania and the Community was considered to be a sectoral agreement.

Although reform of the economic system in the CMEA countries was being carried out throughout the 1970s and 1980s, and notably in Hungary, further developments in relations had to await the arrival of Gorbachev, who in May 1985 made it clear that it was time for the Soviet Union to recognise the existence of the European Community. One month later the CMEA secretary Sychev wrote to President Delors suggesting that relations between the two institutions should be established through a common declaration rather than through treaty negotiations. In September, the CMEA produced the first draft of such a declaration. At the same time the CMEA cleared the way for bilateral agreements between the European Community and individual CMEA Member States. One of the main reasons that the negotiation of the common declaration took so long was the refusal of the CMEA side to accept the 'Berlin clause', which regulated the geographical scope of the agreement.[5] In the end the common declaration was not signed until June 1988. By this time diplomatic relations had been agreed between the Community and the Soviet Union, the DDR, Bulgaria and Czechoslovakia, but long before this negotiations had also started with both Hungary and Czechoslovakia to conclude bilateral agreements. Undoubtedly relations had developed most favourably with Hungary which had shown the greatest interest in bilateral agreements with the Community. After concluding a textile agreement in 1978, Hungary had several exploratory discussions with the Community which eventually led ten years later to the signing of a cooperation agreement in September 1988. This agreement swept away all quantitative restrictions (QRs) in trade in industrial goods, invited the partners to move towards trade liberalisation, laid down safeguard provisions and made it clear that counter-trade should not be used in bilateral trade relations. The trade liberalisation measures were spread out in three phases over the ten-year life of the treaty, which also provided the framework for economic and trade cooperation and set up a joint committee to manage and arbitrate the agreement.

---

[5] The treatment of Berlin created a problem in all agreements between the European Community and the CEE countries and the Soviet Union. The 'Berlin declaration' of the Federal Republic of Germany in the EEC Treaty stated that the EEC Treaty was equally applicable to Land Berlin. The Soviet Union was always keen to refuse this clause in international agreements. The problem was solved in the Hungarian textile agreement with a unilateral declaration of the Hungarian side on the 'four-power' status of Berlin.

The Hungarian agreement marked a new phase in the relationship between the European Community and the CEE countries. Before the agreement was signed and especially immediately afterwards, the degree of contact between the parties at all levels increased significantly. The first joint committee was held in December 1988 in Budapest, agricultural discussions on concessions were held in early 1989 and less formal contacts were frequent. This reflected the fact that Hungary was already well advanced in economic reforms and realised that the system of central planning had already more or less broken down. The privileged position of Hungary was certainly a tribute to its government and its negotiators, and was partly reflected in the flow of inward investment after the removal of the communist government. An agreement with Czechoslovakia was signed in December 1988.

Cooperation agreements were also negotiated with Poland, Bulgaria and Romania in 1989 and 1990. With the revolutions in Central Europe following the Polish Round Table discussions and Solidarność's triumph in the June 1989 election, these agreements had very short active lives and were soon overtaken by the demand for new types of agreement, which paid tribute to the new quality of relationships between free and sovereign countries.

The considerable improvement in relations between the European Community and the CMEA and their respective Member States which took place in the second half of the 1980s obviously owes much to the policies of 'perestroika', followed by President Gorbachev. In a speech to the Council of Europe in early July 1989 he emphasised the importance of cooperation between the countries in the Common European House. He quoted Victor Hugo's famous words: 'the day will come when you France, you Russia, you Italy, you England, you Germany and you all the nations of the continent will join in a higher union and constitute the European fraternity, without losing your distinct qualities and your glorious individuality.'

However in the same speech, Gorbachev attacked the West, which saw the conflict between two totally different systems of society as the major problem for further European integration. He maintained that it was not necessary to overcome socialism to create the European 'house'. He went on to say:

the attachment of European States to different systems of society is a fact. And the recognition of this historical fact, the respect for the sovereign right of each people to freely choose its own social system, constitutes a primary condition for normality in Europe. The social and political organisation of the different countries has undergone changes in the past and this process can continue. But it is up to the peoples to decide and to make their choice. All interference in the internal affairs of these countries, each attempt to limit their sovereignty, whether allies or friends or any other state, are not admissible.

For the countries in Central Europe, in mid-1989, these words seemed like the height of hypocrisy. They were still governed by one-party systems, elected in sham elections, they were still part of the CMEA system, which guaranteed economic decline and many of them still had Soviet troops on their territories. In spite of the movement which had entered the relationship between Central and Eastern Europe and the European Community after 1985, this therefore did not satisfy the peoples of Central Europe, who were still not free. The desire to escape from the system of communist rule increased even as the system attempted to reform itself ever more quickly and with a singular lack of success.

As well as these 'push' factors, there were many 'pull' factors in the 1980s which made the European Community more and more attractive to the countries of Central Europe. The period from 1985 to 1990 certainly marked a high point of prestige for the Community as the completion of its internal market was achieved, the final barriers to the freedom of movement of goods, services, capital and labour were swept away and important institutional developments, like the Single European Act, which increased majority voting in the Council of Ministers, took place. The Community enjoyed renewed growth, industry restructured and became more competitive on world markets and people began to talk of Europe as the new power which would outrun both the United States and Japan in the twenty-first century. To the peoples of Central Europe, impoverished by years of central planning and deprived of all democratic rights, the attraction of a free and prosperous European Community was, and remains today, immense.

As the Communist system began to crumble, first in Poland and Hungary, then in the DDR, eventually reaching the Soviet Union itself, the Europeans of Central Europe naturally turned their attention to joining a Community which was free and prosperous. By then, however, many West Europeans had become accustomed to equating Europe with the European Community and were not prepared to share their prosperity: 45 years had obliterated centuries of common history. Timothy Garton Ash quotes the British Foreign Minister, probably one of the more enlightened foreign ministers at that time, looking back in December 1989 and saying that this was the system 'under which we've lived quite happily for forty years'.[6]

---

[6] Garton Ash, *In Europe's name*, p. 2.

## Development of relations after 1989

It is astonishing that the Member States of the Community and the Community institutions appeared unprepared and without any well developed strategy for tackling the results of the collapse of Communism. It had been obvious since the end of the 1970s that the centrally-planned economies were in a terminal decline which could be arrested only by fundamental market economy reforms, and since the triumph of Gorbachev, change had also become possible on the political level. This unpreparedness underlines a major problem for EU foreign policy: that there is no real capacity to predict crises and no forward contingency planning for them.

When the peoples of the region took power from the communists, the reaction of Community politicians was extremely enthusiastic. All the Community's leading politicians queued up to visit the region and gave speeches welcoming the new democracies into the European family of nations. Especially in Central Europe, which had been unwillingly separated from Western Europe by the Yalta agreements, these speeches were interpreted as promises of rapid integration into Western European structures and markets.

The reality was different. As it became clear that integration into the structures of the European Union was the objective of the CEE countries, the enthusiasm of the Member States rapidly declined. There were various reasons for this: the fear of a dilution of the existing level of integration in the European Union and of a slowing of integration in the future; uncertainties over the course of reform to the East and preoccupations with other problems such as the reunification of Germany. However perhaps the main reason was that enthusiasm (which is costless) rapidly gave rise to the need for economic concessions, as trade within the former CMEA broke down. This is a reminder that the European Union today still remains essentially an economic union based upon the assumption that it is in each Member State's economic interest to be a Member. Member States consistently oppose foreign policy measures which they consider will not bring them additional economic advantage

The European Union's relations with Central and Eastern Europe also illustrate the problems of constructing consistent policy when the members' traditional spheres of interest differ so largely. Both geography and history play roles in complicating foreign policy development. The most consistent supporters of enlargement to the East are the countries which are geographically close to the region: Germany, Austria and the Nordic countries. These are also the countries which are historically most closely linked with Central Europe. The peripheral, and especially the Mediterranean Member States, are at best neutral to enlargement, but are extremely concerned about security problems and migration in the Mediterranean region. The extreme difference in views between France, Germany and the United Kingdom on the Yugoslav conflict, on the Middle East and on relations with African countries are also due in part to historical causes.

Geography and history also play a role in the importance given to the political objectives of Russia in determining the relationship with the associated countries in Central Europe. There has been a long tradition in German foreign policy (and indeed in US and to a lesser extent in other EU Member States' policy) to allow Russia to exert a major influence on the EU's relations with Central and Eastern Europe. There is nothing strange in this, but there is a question on the degree to which this influence may be used to slow down or even prevent the integration of certain democratic and independent countries (e.g. the three Baltic countries) into the European Union. The associated countries have suffered throughout their history from such neglect of their own legitimate interests by the West European powers and it would appear that there is a good chance that they will suffer in the future as well.

Relations with the associated countries have also revealed the fault lines in the European Union between countries such as the Netherlands and the United Kingdom (and, on some issues, Germany) which have a liberal approach to economic policy and those which have a more protectionist policy with a larger role for the state such as France and Spain. These differences have been particularly obvious in the retention by the European Union of an unacceptably high level of protectionism in agriculture, in the face of large trade balance surpluses in favour of the Union, but they have also been obvious in more obscure areas such as rules of origin or rules on establishment. These differences will re-emerge in the negotiations for accession.

Overall, however, the policy of the European Union was supportive to the challenges of reform, especially in the first years after 1989, even though it left much to be desired. The answer to the question of whether there was any clear overall strategy governing this policy and whether there is any clear policy today is much less clear.

### Policy planning and the revolution in Central Europe

The historic changes which culminated in the year of peaceful revolution, 1989, came as something of a surprise to many politicians and policy makers in Western Europe and the United States. They were in fact a surprise to many of the groups working for reform in CEE countries themselves. There was no well-thought-out strategy in Western Europe to cope with the new situation. In most administrations, the staff working on the 'state-trading countries' in 1989 were few in number and without much political influence. There were not many think-tanks worrying about the future of Central Europe. The situation was different to that prevailing, for instance, at the end of the Second World War when, although the challenge was enormous, people had had several years to consider what would be necessary after it was over. Not only was there no strategy to deal with the challenge of reform in Central and Eastern Europe, there was also no strategy to tackle the complicated problems suddenly posed by reunification in Germany.

The unpreparedness can be measured by considering official and unofficial documents at the time. At the European Council in Rhodes in December 1988 the heads of state and government produced a declaration on the role of the Community in the world.[7] While expressing the wish to 'overcome the division of our Continent', the steps proposed were extremely general (develop the Conference on Security and Cooperation in Europe (CSCE), promote disarmament in Europe and promote the respect of human rights). While more positively expressing determination to develop political dialogue between East and West, the declaration still mentions the previous summer's agreement with the CMEA as a major step forward. At the Madrid Summit six months later, it is even more surprising to see that Central and Eastern Europe does not figure amongst the main points of the agenda and in the Conclusions of the Presidency is treated summarily in a chapter entitled 'Political cooperation'. This Summit came after the Polish elections and after Gyula Horn, the Hungarian Foreign Minister, had ordered the removal of the border controls between Hungary and Austria. This unpreparedness became even clearer when the chance to reunite the divided Germany presented itself.

During the events of 1989 and 1990, and indeed through to the independence of the Baltic countries in 1992, it is clear that Western leaders were always slightly behind events, at least as far as understanding their real significance was concerned. A clear example of this is the frequent insistence by Western politicians that the countries of the region should maintain the CMEA organisation, even though this organisation symbolised economic servitude and maintained a trade in goods of unacceptable quality and technical inferiority.

---

[7] European Council, Declaration on the international role of the European Community, Conclusions of the Presidency, Rhodes (December 1988).

In spite of the lack of policy planning, the reaction of the Community was, however, commendably rapid in the area of assistance to reform.

### First reactions: assistance

The first coordinated Western response came in the G7 Summit meeting in Paris in July 1989, which was convened in the follow-up to both the precipitous developments in Poland and Hungary and the human rights violations in China. In the Declaration of the Summit on East–West relations, the G7 leaders stated that 'we offer the countries of the East the opportunity to develop balanced economic cooperation on a sound commercial basis consistent with the security interests of each of our countries and with the general principles of international trade'.[8] On Poland and Hungary, the G7 stated that 'each of us is developing concrete initiatives designed to encourage economic reforms, to promote more competitive economies and to provide new opportunities to trade'. On assistance in particular, the Summit agreed to call a meeting of all interested countries to support the reforms in Poland and Hungary and asked the Commission of the European Communities to take over responsibility for this coordination: this marked the birth of the G24 process in which 24 donor countries agreed to coordinate their assistance.

As far as the European Community itself was concerned, an informal Summit of Heads of Government was called by the French Presidency in Paris in November 1989 to consider the Community's response to the challenge of revolution in the East. By this time the opening of the inner-German border and the fall of the Berlin Wall were clearly indicating if not immediate reunification, then at least a major change in the relationship between the Federal Republic and the DDR. The Summit agreed to look at a series of further measures to support reform, including the creation of the European Bank for Reconstruction and Development (EBRD – a French government initiative which was destined to play a significant role in the transition in Central and Eastern Europe) and the opening up of Community programmes in education, training and technology. It underlined the importance of the Polish Stabilisation Fund and balance of payments support for Hungary, subject to agreements between these two countries and the International Monetary Fund. President Mitterrand stressed that the Summit has been about 'solidarity and unity; unity . . . tomorrow why not with those who feel able to integrally associate themselves with the

---

[8] G7 Declaration, Summit of the Arch, Paris (July 1989).

disciplines which we impose on ourselves?'.[9] This sentence appeared to be a clear indication that membership of the Community was on offer, when certain conditions were met. At the Summit in Strasbourg in December the European Council could already welcome the progress towards the reunification of Germany and could also point to an impressive series of measures taken to support reform in Poland, Hungary and the Czech and Slovak Republics.[10] The European Council could report on the creation of the EBRD. It could also confirm that the Community's Member States were to contribute over half of the $1 billion Stabilisation Fund to support internal convertibility in Poland and that it was necessary to make a balance of payments loan of the same magnitude available to support reform in Hungary. It further reinforced its commitment to the coordination of assistance through the G24 process.

In a special Declaration on Central and Eastern Europe, the heads of state and government noted again that the developments in the region meant that 'the division in Europe can be overcome . . . whether in the security area, in economic and technical cooperation or in the human dimension'. In the same Declaration the Council looked forward to the reunification of Germany, in the context of East–West dialogue and cooperation, and in the perspective of European integration. It also stated that it was

ready to develop richer and closer relationships based on an intensification of the political dialogue and cooperation in all areas with the USSR, and the other countries of Central and Eastern Europe and with Yugoslavia, once it was clear that these countries had embarked on a reform course.

The European Council was followed immediately by the creation of the PHARE programme (the French acronym for Poland and Hungary Assistance to Economic Restructuring), adopted by the Council on 18 December 1989.[11] This grant programme was intended to implement economic aid measures 'primarily to support the process of reform in Poland and Hungary, in particular by financing or participating in the financing of projects aimed at economic restructuring'.[12] With an immediate allocation of ECU300 million this was a significant response

[9] Declaration of President Mitterrand at the meeting of heads of state and government, Paris (18 November 1989).
[10] European Council, *Conclusions of the Presidency*, Strasbourg (December 1989).
[11] Council regulation 3906/89 (18 December 1989) on economic aid to the Republic of Hungary and the Polish People's Republic. *Official Journal*, L 375, 23.12.1989. PHARE is the EU's grant aid programme for Central and Eastern Europe and by far the most significant source of grant assistance. It is dealt with extensively in chapter 5 of this book.
[12] Quotation from Council Regulation (EEC) no. 3906/89.

by the Community to the challenges of reform. Not only were funds made available by the Community but the Member States also responded with major allocations. Germany, the United Kingdom, France, the Netherlands and the Nordic countries especially made an effort to make knowledge transfer available for the transition.

By the end of 1989 the assistance effort was in full swing and a structure for the coordination of assistance had been established. Through 1990 this effort continued as more countries were added to the list of states receiving help from the G24. G24 assistance was extended to the DDR, Czechoslovakia, Yugoslavia and Bulgaria at the G24 Ministers' meeting in July 1990; Romania had to wait another six months before being admitted, owing to the unclear situation following the May 1990 elections. In September 1990, the European Community extended the PHARE programme to cover Bulgaria, Czechoslovakia, the DDR, Romania and Yugoslavia. An additional ECU200 million were also added to PHARE's 1990 budget, bringing total spending up to ECU500 million.

The first response was therefore an assistance response, as was to be expected and was indeed required. Poland's first Solidarność government inherited a catastrophic economic situation, with rampant inflation and food shortages and was determined to introduce a radical reform programme. Hungary, while in a less precarious situation since it had been reforming steadily since 1968, nevertheless required support for the necessary transformation of the economy. Romania and Bulgaria were in very difficult situations and required immediate help.

Early on in the transformation process, there were many calls for a new 'Marshall Plan' for Central and Eastern Europe. However the assistance effort in Central Europe had a completely different character to that of the Marshall Fund and was incomparably less effective. The Marshall Plan had dealt with a situation where market economies had been devastated by war; in Central and Eastern Europe there was economic destruction, but as a result of a planned rather than a market economy. The systemic challenge to the latter was therefore far greater than that faced by the Marshall Plan. The Marshall Plan had also had the advantage that there was only one donor with no coordination problems; the G24 assistance coordination effort was a relative failure because of a total lack of willingness of donors to coordinate their action. The Marshall Plan had also had a greater volume of assistance, a higher grant component and tougher conditionality. The major problem now was a much lower level of political will.

No serious evaluation has been made of the effectiveness of the aid effort. The Polish Stabilisation Fund, even though it was never drawn down, and the early balance of payments assistance, certainly had an important influence on the success of reform. Grant aid in general, however, did not make a significant contribution to the transition; the lack of coordination between donors meant that resources were wasted through duplication.

The European Community's own assistance effort was concentrated in the PHARE programme, which had substantial budgetary funds from the start – ECU500 million in 1990 and ECU775 million in 1991. PHARE finance, however, amounts to roughly only ECU10 per year for each person in the CEE countries.

The balance of the aid effort for Central Europe is certainly less rosy than the donors pretend, but sometimes better than some of the over-hasty judgements from governments in the region. It is clearly not through aid, however, that the CEE countries will succeed in their reforms; such success will come through trade and other economic relations and through appropriate macroeconomic policies.

*Trade and economic cooperation*

Far more important than aid were the macroeconomic and microeconomic policies applied by governments and the development of trade and other economic relations with the 'West'. The end of the 1980s saw a series of negotiations between the Community and individual CMEA countries to establish stronger trade relations. These negotiations led to the signing of agreements on trade and economic cooperation between the Community and Hungary (September 1988), Poland (September 1989), Czechoslovakia and Bulgaria (May 1990) and Romania (October 1990).

These agreements reaffirmed the commitment to granting each other MFN treatment in accordance with the GATT and the protocols of accession to GATT of the individual countries. They abolished, over a period of four years, the QRs which had governed trade under the GATT protocols. The agreements included strong safeguard clauses, and for anti-dumping purposes these countries were still dealt with as state-trading countries under the Community anti-dumping regulation.[13]

As a response to the revolutions after 1989, the Community rapidly improved on the terms of the trade agreements by offering GSP, leading

---

[13] Safeguards and anti-dumping procedures are trade policy measures designed to protect domestic business from unfair trade practices of third countries. They are also used as instruments of protectionist trade policies. They are dealt with extensively in chapter 3 of this book.

to more generous export conditions for agricultural produce, and by increasing export possibilities in textiles. The transition period for the abolition of QRs was also removed, so that from early 1990 no QRs remained, at least as far as Hungary and Poland were concerned. The initial response was adequate in the sense that the CEE countries were hardly affected in their redirection of exports by the trade restrictions still imposed by the Community. The total break-up of the old COMECON trading system became clear only at the end of 1990, leading to the disastrous collapse of regional trade the following year. In 1990, however, Polish exports to the Community rose by over a third in nominal ECU terms, while Hungarian exports rose by 16% over the previous year.

The conclusion which can be drawn from the earliest phase of relations between the Community and the CEE democracies in 1989 and 1990 is that in terms of both aid and market opening the EC's response can be considered to have been adequate to support the immediate needs of reform, but could hardly be characterised as generous or far-sighted.

### German reunification

The rapid changes east of the Oder were very soon matched by enormous changes in the DDR and progress towards reunification. This is not the place to consider the reunification process in detail, but it is worth considering the impact which it had on the relationship between the European Community and Germany on the one hand, and the CEE countries on the other.

From August 1989, when DDR citizens began to seek refuge in Embassies of the Federal Republic in Budapest, Prague and Warsaw, it was clear that major changes in the direction of more democracy and a higher level of contact between the 'two Germanies' was going to result. With the opening of the inner-German border on 9 November 1989 and the publication of Helmut Kohl's ten-point plan for reunification at the end of the same month, it was obvious that some form of unification was in sight, though as late as the Informal Council meeting in Dublin at the end of January 1990 it was not clear to the Ministers, including Hans-Dietrich Genscher, what exact form this unification would take. Reunification finally took place on 3 October 1990.

In a very short time between April and September 1990 the necessary administrative work was accomplished to bring the DDR into the Community as part of the Federal Republic. However, major decisions on relations with Central and Eastern Europe were not taken again until the end of 1990, when the Rome European Council considered a series of financial decisions.

As important as moving the Central Europeans down the agenda, reunification led to, or perhaps coincided with, a more restrictive attitude on the part of the Member States. The Member States in 1990 realised that the countries of Central Europe were looking for more than assistance money and slightly easier trading regimes. Their precarious political situation – with a destabilised Russia to the East, with potential in-region conflicts where large minority populations were present – led them to look for a much closer association with the Community. For the leading thinkers in these countries, it had been clear from the beginning that there was no alternative to accession; 'third ways', politically or economically, led to nowhere or to chaos. As this thinking became clear, Community leaders became nervous; leading politicians expressed their strong reserve about any thought of accession, and when the idea of association for Central Europe began to be discussed, many made it clear that this was something for the longer term. German reunification was not necessarily the main reason for this increased reserve, but the political and financial strain put on the Community by German reunification was certainly a factor.

German policy towards the CEE countries was affected at least in four ways by the problems of reunification:

- Firstly reunification naturally absorbed an enormous proportion of the energies of political and economic actors in
  Germany. There are many indicators of this. German investment in CEE countries was lower than that of other third
  countries, even though Germany is a direct neighbour and,
  through its trade links, dominates the regional economy. By the
  end of 1992, for instance, committed capital in Poland from
  Germany was less than that of the Netherlands and a tenth of
  that committed by the United States. Germany was also often
  barely represented in discussions on the development of the
  relationship between the European Community and Central
  Europe. This was particularly noticeable at lower levels, where
  the demands made on German government officials by reunification simply meant that international meetings had sometimes
  to be sacrificed. Finally, whereas German service providers
  (consultants, advisers, and so on) might normally have been
  expected to flood into Central and Eastern Europe, in fact
  Germany was greatly under-represented, because of the enormous amount of work which was required in the New Bundesländer.

- Secondly, reunification absorbed enormous financial resources, and indeed is still doing so today. While Germany consistently contributed more to G24 assistance than the other 11 Member States together, nevertheless the financial strain of reunification set a clear limit to German financing of CEE development, and will continue to do so for years to come.

- Thirdly, the potential competition from CEE countries for the New Bundesländer made the German government perhaps slightly less ready to open markets than might otherwise have been the case. In 1992, for instance, the German government resisted an increase in the tariff quota for imports of television tubes from Poland (produced by Thomson, the French company, in one of their investments near Warsaw), in order to protect a Samsung plant which had just been attracted to the former DDR. In spite of this perhaps marginal effect, however, Germany remained consistently one of the most liberal countries with respect to imports from Central Europe.

- Fourthly, and perhaps most importantly, reunification once again reinforced the natural German predilection to negotiate with Russia over the heads of all the countries lying between. Reunification was possible only because of the success of a consistent Ostpolitik, which was always privileging relationships between the two major powers. The negative side of this was that Germany was frequently prepared to neglect the interests of CEE countries for the sake of its relationship with Moscow. As Timothy Garton Ash underlines, Germany was one of the least enthusiastic supporters of the Lithuanian revolution for fear of annoying Russia, even though at this time Russia was almost at its weakest point.[14]

The reunification of Germany was clearly one of the triumphs of freedom and democracy over tyranny. It certainly ranks as one of the greatest achievements of the 'West' in the post-war period. It was also a great triumph for the German political class and for German diplomacy. Those West European politicians who seemed disappointed that 'there were no longer two Germanies' were short-sighted and fundamentally anti-democratic. It is however a simple fact that the pain and joy of reunification made the situation for CEE countries somewhat more difficult and led to a certain loss of enthusiasm for enlargement from the Member States of the Community.

---

[14] Garton Ash, *In Europe's name*, pp. 378ff.

### The Association (Europe) Agreements

The superficial facts would clearly not appear to support the claim that the Member States of the Community became less positive about the relationship with Central Europe through 1990 as they had been after the first enthusiasm of the revolution. For it was in 1990 that the foundations for the Association Agreements with these countries were laid, and it is these agreements which form the fundamental legal basis of the relationship today. The idea of offering associated status to the newly emerging democracies in Central Europe began to be discussed at the end of 1989. A further deepening of institutional relations had already been mentioned at the Strasbourg European Council in December 1989.[15] It was discussed by Foreign Ministers meeting in Dublin at the end of January 1990, where it appears that the British government introduced the point in the discussion leading up to the Council meeting. At this meeting, Frans Andriessen, the Commissioner in charge of foreign relations, could already give an outline of the contents of such an agreement. The idea had also been discussed between President Delors and the Polish Prime Minister, Tadeusz Mazowiecki, early in 1990.

The idea of offering Association Agreements based on Article 238 of the Treaty to Czechoslovakia, Hungary and Poland was indeed a major step forward in the quality of relations between the Community and these countries. Association meant not only that there would be a formal legal basis for a close relationship between the partners but also that a process of political dialogue would be started, which would allow Ministers from both sides to discuss matters of common interest on a regular basis. It would also establish common institutions, notably the Association Council, Association Committee and the Association Parliamentary Committee. These would ensure close cooperation with the Community. For the three countries concerned association was an important way of locking into the Community and was a clear step on the road to accession.

The European Council meeting in Dublin in April 1990 gave its agreement to the idea of negotiating Association Agreements.[16] It took the rest of 1990 to prepare the mandate for negotiation, which was adopted by the Council only in December 1990. The fact that the preparation in the Commission and in the Council took so long can largely be attributed to the fact that these agreements, although

---

[15] See p. 15 above.
[16] European Council, *Conclusions of the Presidency*, Dublin (June 1990).

following the model of Association Agreements with other third countries, were unique in that they dealt with countries in transition. The objections to the negotiating mandate proposed by the Commission were relatively minor, but it is worth noting that already at this stage the Mediterranean Member States were demanding that the level of financing for the Mediterranean should be at least as high as that for Central and Eastern Europe.

Following the adoption of the mandate by the Council on 18 December 1990, it took a whole year to finalise the negotiation and sign the agreements, the signature taking place on 13 December 1991. During the negotiations, it soon became clear to the negotiators from the three partner countries that they were in a different quality of negotiation to that which they were used to having with the World Bank or even the IMF. The negotiation of the Association Agreements relatively rapidly became hard-nosed trade bargaining, in which the Community side had relatively clear objectives on what it wanted to get out of the negotiations. The impact on the negotiators from the CEE side, some of whom had no previous experience of dealing with the Community, was quite marked. They faced the problem that it was important to get a relatively quick agreement because of the precarious economic and strategic position in which they found themselves; the population had also been led to expect a rapid conclusion to the negotiations. On the other hand while the Community was offering an asymmetric agreement, with faster import liberalisation on the Community than on the CEE side, the degree of market opening on offer in agriculture, iron and steel, textiles and certain other 'sensitive' goods was unsatisfactory. The problem of agriculture led to a virtual breakdown of negotiations over the summer 1991, in spite of the coup attempt in Moscow, which one would have thought would have lead to a greater degree of flexibility on the Community side. The Commission had been forced to go back to the Council in April 1991 in order to get improvements to the negotiating mandate in six areas, where the negotiations had shown that the mandate was too restrictive. Some improvement was made, but the negotiations broke down again over imports of live cattle, where the French government refused to accept a somewhat higher import quota for live animals and meat, even though the proposed improvements were very limited.

The refusal by the Community to agree to stating in the agreement that it was the joint objective of both parties to work towards accession made a considerable impact on the partner governments. The fact that the Community was not prepared to accept even a vague declaration about future accession made many people in these countries wonder if they were following a mirage in their determination to join the Community.

The Association Agreements, which were called 'Europe Agreements' in order to underline their importance, in several respects mark a turning point. They represent a big step forward in formalising relations and creating the institutional framework within which it has subsequently been possible to deepen relations. They were a further step on the road to trade liberalisation in industrial products and as far as trade was affected they imposed Community competition and state- aid rules on the three countries. Perhaps the most important role of the agreements was to make sure that the associated countries did not turn to massive protection once the initial liberalisation euphoria had passed. In ensuring a reasonably liberal trade policy and laying down some of the fundamental building blocks of the market economy, they have certainly been valuable. They did, however, also have a negative impact on relations.

They marked the end of the phase where the response of the Community to the needs of Central Europe was invariably positive. By the end of 1991, with deep recession and the imminent problem of the Maastricht Treaty marking the beginning of the crisis of public acceptability of the Community in most Member States, it was already clear to the Czechs, Hungarians and Poles that they were now in a different world; one where they could no longer assume that the Community was acting in their favour and where they would have to vigorously defend their rights. The insistence of the Community on treating the sensitive sectors much less liberally, even though these were the sectors where the three countries could most easily export in order to finance the reform, showed that the agreements were not aimed at helping them over the difficult second stage of the reform, where public support was bound to weaken. And the refusal from the Community side to accept any declaration on accession also reduced the credibility of the reformers in all countries, but especially in Hungary and Poland.

*The Copenhagen European Council, June 1993: the common objective of accession*

The signing of the Association Agreements at the end of 1991 was the beginning of a very long ratification process in the 12 Member State Parliaments. For Hungary and Poland this process was concluded exactly two years later on 13 December 1993. The agreement with the Czech and Slovak Federal Republic was never ratified owing to the break-up of the country, which took place peacefully on 1 January 1993.

Those parts of the agreements which were of Community responsibility (essentially the trade aspects) were, however, put into immediate effect with all three countries in March 1992. The interim agreements established joint committees, which were responsible for the implementation of these trade aspects until ratification of the Association Agreements. The joint committee meetings immediately led to an increase in contacts between the three countries' institutions and those of the Community, which had an important impact on the quality of relations. These growing contacts also allowed difficult trade problems to be resolved in quiet and constructive ways out of the glare of publicity.

With the signing of the three agreements with the 'Visegrád' group of countries, attention was turned to Romania and Bulgaria which had also started on their own reform programmes. The negotiations with these countries were concluded extremely rapidly, partly because the countries themselves wanted to conclude quickly and partly because it was obviously difficult to depart in any major way from the agreements with the Visegrád countries. The agreement with Romania was signed at the beginning of February 1993 and that with Bulgaria in March 1993.

The decision to offer Association Agreements to these two countries was an important step. It clearly underlined the policy of the Community to offer such agreements to all the countries of Central Europe which set out on the course of reform. Each country would have the same opening deal from Brussels, and each would then make its own way towards deeper integration depending on its own progress. For the Visegrád countries it marked the end of their special relationship with the Community, a relationship which they had assumed would lead to rapid accession. For the Community, too, it meant that the fast track to accession, which had seemed to exist for the Visegrád countries and which seemed to have been supported by the more liberal Member States, was no longer open. The decision to open negotiations with Romania and Bulgaria paved the way for later agreements with the three Baltic countries and with Slovenia. The Association Agreements lost their very special meaning and became important but standard agreements with the Community's European partners in Central and Eastern Europe.

An enormous amount of thought was given at this time to the question of the future European architecture. The negotiations which led to the Maastricht Treaty in December 1991 and the questions thrown up in the process about the construction of Europe over the longer term led to many proposals being put on the table. The idea of a European Confederation was proposed by President Mitterrand, various arrangements of concentric circles with different degrees of integration were considered; the relationship between the Community and the EFTA countries seemed to some to be an interesting model for the Central Europeans.

One of the most conclusive statements on the European architecture was made by the EFTA states themselves, when five of them, Austria (in 1989), Finland (in March 1992), Norway (in November 1992), Sweden (in July 1991) and Switzerland (in May 1992) applied for membership of the European Union in spite of having all the advantages of the European Economic Area Agreement (EEAA). For them it was clear (though apparently not for the Norwegian or Swiss electorates) that close economic integration without membership and therefore the power to influence decisions was second best to membership itself. This message was not lost on the associated countries in Central Europe, all of which persisted in proclaiming accession as one of the most important elements of their reform policies.

The question of future enlargement of the Community was extensively dealt with at the Lisbon European Council in June 1992, where an important paper on the subject from the Commission was attached to the Presidency conclusions and therefore had the tacit approval of heads of state and government.[17] The conclusions of Lisbon were written in a way that clearly pointed to accession for the associated countries: 'As regards relations with Central and Eastern Europe . . . cooperation will be focused systematically on *assisting their efforts to prepare the accession to the Union which they seek* [author's italics]'. Although the 'they' was clearly intended to show that there was still no Community agreement on the principle of accession, this statement cleared the way for the Commission to return to the Council with a proposal that the Community should also agree to the objective of accession for Central Europe.

The Commission's own paper to the Lisbon Summit spelled out the main questions concerning enlargement: deepening and widening should go on together and deepening the degree of integration should not suffer at the hands of enlargement. New members must take over the *'acquis communautaire'* but this could be accompanied by temporary derogations and transitional periods; enlargement must not put in doubt common policies and especially the developing Common Foreign and Security Policy (CSFP); and the Community's effectiveness must be protected. For the associated countries of Central Europe it talked almost in a matter of fact way about accession as if it was already agreed as a common objective. It proposed that a calendar should be estab-

[17] European Council, *Conclusions of the Presidency*, Lisbon (June 1992).

lished for the adoption of the Community's *acquis*, that trade concessions agreed to in the Association Agreements should be further improved and that the review of the Association Agreements planned for five years after their entry into force should be brought forward. These proposals, not adopted by the Council, attempted to move the degree of integration on in one very large step.

On the basis of these ideas the Commission made a report to the following European Council in Edinburgh in December 1992 entitled 'Towards a new association with the countries of Central and Eastern Europe'.[18] This document, which was barely discussed at a Summit overshadowed by the question of Community finance, stated that 'The European Council should now confirm that it accepts the goal of eventual membership in the European Union for the countries of Central and Eastern Europe when they are able to satisfy the conditions required'. The document went on rightly to underline the real significance of such a declaration:

By offering this perspective, the Community will provide encouragement to those pursuing reform and make the short-term economic and social consequences of adjustment easier to bear. This perspective will also provide a stimulus to investment and discourage excessive nationalism.

The document went on to indicate certain conditions which would have to be met by acceding countries and suggested that it was, however, impossible to give a timetable for accession.

Beyond accession, the paper suggested ways both to make the most of the existing Association Agreements and to go beyond them. 'Making the most' of the Europe Agreements included reinforcing political dialogue through its multilateralisation (following on from the first multilateral meeting between the Visegrád countries and the Community Member States in London in October 1992), in a very general way improving market access for the Central Europeans, setting up special sub-committees of the Association Committees to consider specific ways to promote the approximation of laws and improving the operation of the PHARE programme. 'Going beyond' the Europe Agreements concentrated on the idea of moving towards a European Political Area. Here the idea which later became known as the 'structured dialogue' was launched. Dialogue should not be limited to the Association Councils, but there should be a multilateral structured dialogue, where ministers from the associated countries would be invited not only to European Councils and Foreign Affairs councils but also to sectoral

---

[18] European Council, *Conclusions of the Presidency*, Edinburgh (December 1992) and European Commission (1993).

councils on such things as transport or agriculture. It also raised the possibility that countries in Central and Eastern Europe could be associated with particular policies, in which they would participate in the relevant Council or Commission meetings. Although in many areas this paper was relatively vague, it marked an important advance in Commission thinking. The Edinburgh European Council asked the Council of Ministers to give early consideration to the Commission's proposals, with a view to taking decisions at the Copenhagen Summit in June 1993.

The Danish Presidency was obviously a favourable moment for pushing further advances in the Community's relationship with the associated countries through the Council.[19] The Commission prepared a proposal for decision for the Council, which took up several of the elements of the Edinburgh Summit paper but went further in specifying concrete trade concessions to be made to the associated countries. This paper, called 'Towards a closer association with the countries of Central and Eastern Europe', contained four chapters of measures: towards a European Political Area, improving market access, making assistance more effective and furthering economic integration.

The most important proposal was contained in the first part on moving towards a European Political Area – that 'the European Council should confirm in a clear political message, its commitment to membership of the Union for Europe Agreement signatories when they are able to satisfy the conditions required'. This was the great achievement of Copenhagen. Interestingly, it was hardly discussed by the Member States and certainly not disputed in the many hours of discussion and negotiation leading up to the Summit. The explanation of this show of unanimity is difficult, given that probably a majority of countries were not totally in favour of accession, at least in the near term. On the other hand once the conditions for membership of the Union are met (see chapter 6 of this book), the Treaty of Rome is clear that countries can become members of the Union. Further resistance to such a general statement on accession was therefore not only bad politics but was also not in the spirit of the Treaty.

The Commission's proposal also included the creation of the structured relationship, which had already been advanced in the Edinburgh paper, with the proposal to hold joint Council meetings and to expand cooperation in the area of justice and home affairs. There was also the proposal 'to establish an Action Committee for Central and Eastern Europe to make recommendations on other means to create a structured

---

[19] For the results of the Copenhagen European Council, see European Council, *Conclusions of the Presidency*, Copenhagen (June 1993).

relationship between partners in Central and Eastern Europe and the European Union'. While this last proposal was not accepted by the Council, the remaining proposals were agreed with remarkably little resistance.

The proposals on improving market access were, however, contested strongly: European political cooperation was not perceived to cost Member States much money, whilst market opening could lose votes! The Commission's arguments for its rather modest proposals were that trade opening was vital to support the reforms in Central Europe, that the Union was already running a large trade surplus with the region (understandable in the context of its rapid economic growth) and that improving market access to Central Europe would also help Community producers.

By this time, trade relations between the Union and several of the associated countries were becoming very difficult and causing major political friction. This was particularly the case in agricultural trade, where measures which were seen as minor in the Union were making headline news in Poland and Hungary. The imposition of minimum prices on cherries from Hungary and Poland, considered in the Union to be a trivial and entirely political measure, led to massive ill-feeling in Central Europe where it was considered to be the real response of the Union to these countries' needs, as opposed to the fine words of the declarations of European Summits.

The total value to the associated countries of the measures proposed by the Commission was negligible, but politically the additional unilateral concessions, in increasing asymmetry in the Association Agreements, were significant, and were intended to fight the damage being done to the political relationship between the partners in areas such as agriculture and anti-dumping. Nevertheless, the negotiation of these measures in the Council proved to be extremely difficult and several of the Commission's proposals were lost in the negotiation, weakening the whole package.

The Commission also proposed to improve the allocation of assistance to Central Europe, to intensify the work on the approximation of laws to those of the Union and to open up certain Community programmes to the participation of the Central Europeans. An important decision was taken at Copenhagen to use PHARE resources to support the development of infrastructure in Central Europe financially, part of the general move to shift assistance towards investment. These proposals were agreed in slightly amended form by the Copenhagen European Council.

Copenhagen marks an important further logical step in the development of relations between the Union and the associated countries of Central and Eastern Europe. However the practical economic and trade stance of the Community was rather negative, in spite of the overall rapid move towards free trade in industrial products, essentially because of its attachment to agricultural protection and anti-dumping and safe-guard measures. In Central Europe and with many non-partisan ob-servers in Western Europe, the view began to take hold that the Union was very reluctant to open its markets in all areas which could remotely be called sensitive or to agree to anything which would cost real financial resources. The progress in the political area, this view maintained, was due to the fact that political cooperation was a relatively costless activity and that negotiations on accession could be delayed a very long time (e.g. Turkey). In other words, the proliferation of small trade disputes was beginning to undermine a fundamentally unflawed global political approach strategy.

As in the past, too, it was becoming clear that the driving force in the Community was the European Commission and that several Member States were rather unwillingly being dragged along. This was not the first time that this had been the case; the completion of the internal market had been proposed by President Delors and piloted by Lord Cockfield in a way that had the Member States catching their breath. Nevertheless with the difficult debate over Maastricht still in full swing, significant reticence on the part of certain Member States was an important warning for the future.

### *A strategy for the preparation of accession: the Essen European Council*[20]

While the associated countries obviously approved of the decisions of the Copenhagen Summit, the offer of accession lacked credibility for two main reasons. Firstly the offer mentioned no timetable for member-ship and mentioned only general criteria, which could not easily be turned into concrete objectives for the CEE countries to aim at. Secondly the attitude of the Community on trade issues indicated that there were powerful forces which were protectionist and against acces-sion. In order to keep some dynamism in the process of integration with the associated countries, it quickly became clear that new steps would have to be taken to reinforce the credibility of the common objective of accession. The next major and necessary steps were therefore prepared by the German Presidency at the end of 1994, a Presidency which could

[20] European Council, *Conclusions of the Presidency*, Essen (December 1994).

be expected to be particularly favourable to the enlargement of the Union.

The logical next step was to attempt to point the way from Copenhagen to accession. This would not only be important for policy planning in both the Community and the associated countries, it would also add considerably to the credibility of the accession pledge. There were perhaps four main elements which the Essen European Summit needed to tackle in any realistic accession strategy: how to implement properly the structured relationship decided in Copenhagen, how to support the acceleration of economic growth rates in Central and Eastern Europe, how to help the associated countries to prepare to adopt the Community *acquis* and finally how to change existing Community policies to make accession possible. The possible proposals were discussed first in a Seminar held amongst Commissioners in March 1994 at the instigation of President Delors, then informally with the associated countries, at a very early stage with the German government and with a large number of experts in areas such as trade policy. There was, however, considerable resistance to any decrease in agricultural protectionism and to reductions in protection afforded by the trade instruments of the Community. The very idea of helping to bring these countries into the internal market of the Community also met with considerable resistance. The same fate befell the idea of turning the PHARE assistance programme into a type of Structural Fund, where the countries receiving the assistance would be responsible for its implementation and where the assistance could be used for investment purposes.

The Commission forwarded two proposals to the Council in July, which were then discussed over a six-month period up to the Essen Summit in December 1994. Many of the original proposals were lost in the negotiation and more would have been lost but for the powerful leadership of the Presidency. The Essen Strategy as it has become known, was certainly a major step on the road to preparing for accession but it was almost as important for what it did not as for what it did include. Essen marks an important step in the political logic followed by the Community since the changes in 1989. The Association Agreements laid down the essential legal relationship; Copenhagen underwrote the objective of accession to the Union; Essen designed a strategy for the associated countries to follow in achieving this goal.

The Essen strategy can be measured against the four elements mentioned above as necessary to promote accession:

- Essen did indeed lay down in considerable detail the way in which the structured relationship should function. A strict

annual timetabling of enlarged Councils to be approved by the
Council Presidency at the beginning of each year was established. It was agreed that the heads of government of the
associated countries would be invited once a year to European
Council meetings and twice a year to Foreign Affairs Councils.

- The possibility for the associated countries to cooperate with
  the Union more closely under the CFSP was opened up by the
  Council in its report of 7 March 1994, and in the practical
  guidelines issued in October 1994. This report established the
  principle of the associated countries being aligned with certain
  statements, demarches and joint actions in the context of CFSP.
  It also proposed that in order to facilitate cooperation, the
  associated countries should appoint shadow European corre-
  spondents.

- As to fostering economic growth in Central Europe, and
  notably in the trade area, Essen was a failure. On agriculture, so
  important to Central Europe where it contributes roughly 8%
  of GDP and employs around 20%–25% of the working population, the European Council could write only that it acknowl-
  edged that 'agriculture represents a key element of this
  strategy', but it could not take any concrete decisions to
  improve even marginally access to the EU market. All that
  Essen offered was a

  study of alternative strategies for the development of relations in the
  field of agriculture between the EU and the associated countries with a
  view to a future accession of these countries . . . in the second half of
  1995.

  The Commission was also asked to write reports on the effects
  of Community-subsidised exports on agriculture in these countries, and also on why certain quotas open to the associated
  countries were not being fully used.

- In the area of commercial policy instruments, too, little progress
  was made. There is no doubt that the Community's anti-
  dumping regulation is sometimes used as an instrument of
  industrial policy by industrial interest groups in the Union.
  There have been astonishing misuses of the instruments, and
  regulatory capture is a phenomenon not limited to the EU's
  regulators. Here again only minor improvements were agreed to
  by the Council in Essen. The Council could also only agree a
  strategy on the cumulation of rules of origin, which essentially
  described the present situation as future strategy and put off the

consideration of the full cumulation of origin to the distant future.

The only gleam of light, in an otherwise gloomy chapter of Essen was that it was decided that up to 25% of the PHARE programme could be used for infrastructure investment. This decision meant that well over 50% of the programme could be used for all forms of investment.

Essen was considerably better on how to help the associated countries prepare for accession. The essential part of the strategy consisted of steps to prepare the associated countries to enter the EU's internal market. Three areas are important – competition policy, control of state aids and the *acquis communautaire* in the internal market area. In the first two areas the Union promised assistance, and this is being given. In the third area the Essen strategy promised a White Paper to assist the associated countries to adopt the necessary *acquis*. While being a somewhat dangerous element for an accession strategy, the White Paper exercise was carried out exceedingly efficiently by the European Commission with great professionalism and sent to the European Council meeting in Cannes in June 1995.[21]

The final criterion, that of considering how Community policies might change to prepare for accession, was almost totally absent from Essen. There was once again a simple request for the Commission to submit 'a detailed analysis . . . on the impact of enlargement in the context of the current policies of the Union and their development'. Indeed, there was considerable resistance amongst Member States to the very notion that Community policies might have to be changed.

Finally, Essen underlined that one of the very important conditions which would determine accession was that the applicant countries must not bring unresolved problems of the treatment of minorities or unresolved frontier problems into the EU with them. This was also linked to the question of intra-regional cooperation, which was given such importance in the strategy. In order to deal with these problems the French government promoted the idea of a Pact for Stability which involved all the associated countries and led to some new agreements between them on the problems of the treatment of minorities. Most notable amongst these agreements was that between Hungary and Slovakia. The work on the pact also led to negotiations between Hungary and Romania, which yielded an agreement in late 1996. Responsibility for the Pact for Stability was handed over to the Organisation for Security and Cooperation in Europe (OSCE) after the Paris Conference in March 1995.

---

[21] European Commission (1995d).

The Essen strategy marked a logical extension of EU policy towards the CEE countries and a further important step on the route to accession. Once again however, the credibility of the common objective of accession was not fully established, largely because of the inability of the Union to show further concrete steps in the trade area and notably in agriculture, but also because there was no timetable or objective criteria by which the associated countries could judge themselves or be judged.

### Enlargement: the scope of the Association Agreements and the position of Russia

The Danish Presidency in 1993 was particularly interested in supporting the newly emerging democracies of Estonia, Latvia and Lithuania, which had fought to free themselves from the Soviet Union and had achieved independence in August–September 1991. Trade and economic and commercial cooperation agreements with the three countries were negotiated in 1992 and entered into force in February and March 1993. At Copenhagen, the European Council declared itself already dissatisfied with these agreements and asked the Commission to prepare to negotiate free trade agreements (FTAs) with the three countries. In addition it also declared itself in favour of offering the Baltic States Association Agreements 'as soon as the necessary conditions have been met'. The FTAs were then negotiated in 1994, becoming subsequently an integral part of the Association Agreements which were signed in June 1995. In addition to the three Baltic States, an Association Agreement with Slovenia, one of the most advanced and prosperous of the Central European countries, was also negotiated and initialled by the summer of 1995.[22]

Once the Association Agreements spread beyond the first three Central European countries, they grew to be seen as the normal contractual relation between the Union and the CEE countries which could be considered to be potential members of the Union. By June 1995, there were ten associated countries, each with essentially the same type of agreement, all interested in joining the Union.[23]

The perspective of enlargement led to two types of introspection in the European Union: on the value of association when there are many

---

[22] The signing of the agreement with Slovenia was held up by an Italian veto because of the bilateral dispute between the two countries. This unsavoury problem was resolved with the change in Government in Italy in Spring 1996.

[23] Hungary, Poland, Czech Republic, Slovak Republic, Romania, Bulgaria, Estonia, Latvia, Lithuania and Slovenia.

associated countries (put another way, the future European architecture with 27 or 28 members) and on the role which Russia seeks to play in the region. The first question will be dealt with later in this book. The second question, posed at the time of the negotiation of Association Agreements with the three Baltic countries, was raised simultaneously in Bonn, Brussels and Washington.

The three countries, absorbed by the Soviet Union in 1940 following agreement with Hitler were granted their independence in 1991 only grudgingly and after bloodshed in Lithuania. While Russia recognised their independence, there appear to be many forces in Russia which have not really accepted it. There are objective difficulties which cause problems for the Russian government, most noticeably the treatment of the large Russian populations in Latvia and Estonia. The European Union has brought considerable pressure to bear on these two countries to improve the treatment of these minorities, in which Russia takes a keen and justifiable interest. A further problem is the existence of the Kaliningrad exclave, which means that Russian supplies have to cross Lithuania or Poland and Belarus to reach mainland Russia.[24] The remaining border disputes seem now, however, to be well on the way to being solved.

Even during the struggle for independence certain Western statesmen were warning the Baltic countries against provoking Russia by demanding independence. There appears to be some agreement that the defence of the Baltic countries from Russian attack is impossible and therefore that entry into NATO is not to be considered. This makes closer integration with the European Union even more important for Estonia, Latvia and Lithuania. The discussion over the negotiation of Association Agreements was resolved in favour of opening negotiations, and these agreements were signed in mid-1995. However the strong reserve expressed by some politicians in the West raises the question of the influence which Russia will have in the future, not only on the extension of NATO but also on possible future enlargement of the European Union, and not only to the Baltic countries but also to the other associated States.

The question is not whether the Russians will try to influence the future enlargement of NATO and the European Union; this is their own natural self-interest. It is whether they will be given a voice in future decisions by the European Union. The Union will listen very carefully to what Russia is saying before taking crucial decisions about the future

---

[24] In Spring 1996, for instance, there was great indignation in Poland when, without consultation, it was announced that the Russian and Belarus Presidents had agreed that there should be a 'corridor' through Poland linking Belarus to Kaliningrad.

shape of Europe. But what influence will this voice have? Will the traditional political reaction of looking straight from Berlin, Paris and London towards Moscow without worrying about what lies between re-appear or will there be a more balanced approach to relations with Central and Eastern Europe? The proposal of the Commission to open negotiations with Estonia in its 'Agenda 2000' package is a clear attempt to clarify this issue.[25]

The policy of the Union with respect to Russia is therefore of great importance for successful future enlargement of the Union to Central Europe. Successful reform and democratisation in Russia (and indeed in the Ukraine) is an important criterion for economic development and political stability in the CEE countries. Bilateral agreements between Member States and Russia and the Partnership and Cooperation Agreement (PCA) with Russia at the Union level together with Community assistance programmes and attempts to draw Russia closer to many aspects of Community affairs are all important for creating an environment in which the Union can enlarge eastwards.[26]

### The Cannes and Madrid European Councils

The Essen strategy and the GATT agreement provided a major work programme for the Community in 1995. Perhaps the most important task was the writing of the White Paper on the preparation of the associated countries to enter the internal market of the Community. This was approved by the European Council meeting in Cannes in June 1995.[27] In providing an overview of the most important Community legislation which the associated countries should take over into their own legislation, the White Paper provided an important new guide for future work. It also provided a shock to many associated countries through the obvious complexity of the task before them.

Many of the other proposals of the Essen strategy were implemented, or at least a start was made on their implementation, during the year. However there was to some extent a loss of dynamic in the whole process as implementation took over from conception, as the two southern presidencies concentrated more on the Mediterranean area than on Central and Eastern Europe and as, at the end of the year, the

---

[25] European Commission (1997a).

[26] PCAs have been signed with several countries of the former Soviet Union: Russia, Ukraine and Moldova concluded in 1994; with Belarus, Kazakstan and Kyrgyzstan signed in 1995 and initialled with Armenia, Azerbaijan and Georgia. They do not hold out any prospect of accession to the Union but include agreements on trade, competition policy, investment and democracy and human rights.

[27] European Council, *Conclusions of the Presidency*, Cannes (June 1995).

implementation of the Dayton Peace Agreement in Bosnia grabbed the headlines and some of the resources.

The most important revelation of the Madrid European Council in December 1995 was that the leadership in the process of preparing accession had moved from the Commission to the Member States. Bearing in mind what was said above this is not necessarily a positive sign for enlargement. It was Chancellor Kohl of Germany who pushed the Madrid Summit into making concrete and important decisions on the preparation of enlargement. While his proposals to treat enlargement in stages, starting with the Visegrád countries, were not agreed to by the other Member States, the pressure exerted by Germany led to the Council asking the Commission to prepare the opinions on the member-ship applications of all the applicant countries. This important step kept the process of preparing enlargement on track for the rest of 1996. Madrid also asked for papers to be prepared on the overall impact of enlargement on the Union and on the impact of enlargement on the financial perspective post-1999. It finally expressed the hope that the preliminary stage of the negotiations for membership could be accom-plished at the same time as negotiations with Cyprus and Malta begin (six months after the end of the Inter- Government Conference (IGC)). On agriculture, the Commission brought a new approach to the joint problems of preparing the CAP for the next century and of preparing for accession. Its proposals to the Madrid European Council marked a clear step forward in strategic thinking.

### After Madrid: 'Agenda 2000', the Commission Opinions and differentiation

On the Union side, 1996 and the first half of 1997 were taken up largely with the preparation of the Commission's Opinions on the membership applications of the associated countries. The Madrid Summit request that the Opinions be made available after the end of the IGC led the Commission to prepare an extremely detailed questionnaire, which was sent to all the applicant countries, in order to ascertain how far they had advanced in the adoption of the Community *acquis*.

This exercise allowed politicians in the Union to push Central European accession and its challenges to the back of their agendas. Instead of reflecting on strategies for enlargement, politicians were able to plead that there was little that could be done until the Commission had completed its Opinions. With major crises in the economy, on monetary union and the lack of progress in the IGC, this meant that enlargement had slipped out of many governments' view. This situation led to some drift, with statements coming out of Brussels suggesting that enlargement might take place 'in the years after 2000'.

The completion of the opinions in July 1997, together with reform proposals for Union policies (the 'Agenda 2000' package) has brought the Commission and the politicians back into play on enlargement.[28] 'Agenda 2000' is being discussed in the Council and decisions on opening negotiations in 1998 will be taken at the Luxembourg European Council meeting in December 1997. Unless there is a serious problem with the progress of preparations for monetary union, it does appear probable that negotiations with at least the five countries proposed by the Commission will start in Spring 1998.[29] A worry persists however that, with still unresolved economic and political problems inside the existing Union and very little serious preparation at Member State level, some governments in the Union will push for further delays in the start of negotiations. Even if negotiations start on time, unless the interested Member States exert clear and strong leadership, enlargement may not happen and the Union will have committed an immense breach of faith and turned its back on an opportunity to enhance prosperity, peace and stability on the European Continent.

In the associated countries the preparation of accession continues to be a major objective of government. The policy distance which most countries must travel to reach the Union is large, and up to now the populations of these countries have not really been told what the consequences of accession will be. The amount of work still to be completed was underlined by the Commission Opinions presented in July 1997. Accession remains at the top of the list of most countries' foreign policy but there are signs of a first fatigue in the realisation of this objective, especially faced with waning enthusiasm in the Union itself. On the other hand, the most promising signs are that economic development is progressing well in many of the associated countries to the point where the Czech Republic, Hungary and Poland have already become members of the OECD. Output growth in several countries is two or three times that of the Union itself and there is little sign of a break in this trend or of macroeconomic instability.

## Conclusion

It is clear that, while far from perfect, Community policy has not been marked by pure drift. Policy has evolved over the last eight years in a consistent and relatively clear way. Progress has been marked by

---

[28] European Commission (1997a).
[29] The Czech Republic, Estonia, Hungary, Poland and Slovenia (in addition to Cyprus).

compromise but sufficient core policy has been saved at each step to take the integration process forward. The main problem has been the discrepancy between policy development on the one hand and concrete steps in the economic area, and notably in trade policy, on the other. Still today, however, faced by numerous internal crises, there are signs that the Union has no clear policy on enlargement. The 'Agenda 2000' package presented by the Commission shows one way of reaching accession. It still has to be seen whether these proposals are followed, equally or more persuasive policies are decided in their place, or whether the Union drifts towards crisis through lack of reform courage and lack of common interest.

*Part II*

# Association

# 2 The Association Agreements and their Institutions: the legal framework

## Introduction

The Association Agreements (Europe Agreements) are the basic legal instruments of the relationship between the European Union and the associated countries of Central Europe. The other texts which have been produced by European Councils or elsewhere have real legal meaning only when they are incorporated into the Association Agreements. Whenever there is a dispute between the parties, it is always resolved by reference to the agreements and through the procedures established by them.

## The Association Agreement negotiations

For the drafting and negotiation of the first agreements with Czechoslovakia, Hungary and Poland in 1990–1, the European Union was able to assemble a wide range of experienced officials and experts. The draft agreements were prepared by the Commission with the cooperation of all the Commission specialised services, each responsible for its own articles in the agreements. They were submitted to the Member States which eventually agreed them in Brussels in the Council. The result of this long process was the draft negotiating mandate approved by the Council at the end of 1990 and the draft agreement prepared by the Commission for the beginning of 1991.

On the side of the CEE countries in 1991 there was considerable experience in international trade negotiations, because these countries were members of the GATT and they had also had experience of negotiating with the Community in the second half of the 1980s. In the other more complex areas, there was a real lack of skilled experts. Subjects such as competition policy or the treatment of state aid were subjects dealt with by only a few academics and even fewer lawyers before 1989. Liberalisation of services, problems of establishment and the niceties of the CAP were all relatively new subjects for the Czechs,

Hungarians and Poles. In these areas, the need for thorough analysis of the implications of association for the process of transition conflicted with the political need for a quick agreement. The agreements with the Community were seen as important from economic, political and security points of view. The Soviet Union still existed, but was breaking up. Soviet soldiers were still present in several of the CEE countries and in East Germany, and the situation in Russia was still unstable, as demonstrated by the attempted coup in Moscow in August 1991. The economic transition would be a sufficiently difficult process that it was important to create stability in the political and security sphere. The negotiators on the CEE side were therefore under pressure to complete the negotiations as quickly as possible, even at the cost of somewhat less favourable results.

The three partners in 1991 did not exploit their joint negotiating muscle to the full, though after the first rounds there were coordination meetings between the three ambassadors. Coordination was difficult between three countries, which had been forced to live together in the CMEA system for so long; it is, however, clear that if they had coordinated certain positions, they would have obtained somewhat better agreements than the ones which were finally signed.[1]

Finally it is interesting to note that there was no real attempt on either side before or during the negotiations to seriously estimate the impact of the agreements on the transition process or to look at what terms of agreement would have best served the transition. It is true that this would have been a very complex matter in 1991. The outline of the transition was relatively clear, but the detail was very muddy. The shift of trade flows from being mainly towards the East to being mainly with the European Union was in full swing. Exogenous variables could be established with more certainty than endogenous relationships. Nevertheless it is astonishing that so little serious work was done on the impact of the Association Agreements on the transition.

The negotiations with the remaining associated countries, in 1992–3 with Romania and Bulgaria and in 1995 with the three Baltic countries and Slovenia were completed far more quickly. In each case, the reason was mainly one of time pressure coming from political and security implications and because it was not possible for the Community to radically alter the later agreements with respect to the earlier ones. In each case, minor differences exist between the agreements; only in the case of Estonia is there a major difference. The Estonian agreement sees

---

[1] With more coordination it might have been possible to have obtained shorter transition periods for sensitive product exports to the European Union, or even to have achieved a financial protocol.

no consistent asymmetrical treatment in favour of that country; indeed, on the right of establishment there is asymmetry in favour of the Community.

The one-sided nature of the negotiating balance of forces does not mean that the agreements are necessarily bad. One of the roles of such agreements was to try to maintain as liberal a trading environment in the associated countries as possible, at a time where changes in the system were forcing many economic interests to search for government protection. The agreements have played this role relatively well. The agreements have also set up important institutional links between the parties through the creation of the Association Councils and the Association Committees. They permitted the establishment of associated country businesses in the Community to an extent which shocked several Member State governments during the ratification process. They are not, however, ideal agreements to support the transition to democracy and the market economy. Indeed, at one changeover in government between a reforming party and a post-Communist party, the leader of the reformists could put some of the blame for the loss of the election on the Association Agreements and the trade restrictions coming from them.[2]

## Legal base of the Association Agreements

The Association Agreements are mixed agreements, based on articles 238 and 228 (3) of the Treaty establishing the European Community.[3] The fact that they are mixed agreements, including some items which are the responsibility of the Community and others which are the responsibility of the Member States, means that the agreements must be ratified by all Member State Parliaments, by the European Parliament and by the European Council.

This led to much consternation in Central and Eastern Europe, because the ratification by all Member State Parliaments usually takes around two years to obtain. The first agreements, for instance, were signed in December 1991 but came fully into force only in February 1994. However, those parts of the agreements which are Community competence, notably the trade areas, do not need to await ratification before being implemented. These parts therefore have always been collected in an interim agreement and implemented by both sides soon

---

[2] Prime Minister Suchocka, speaking after the loss of the Polish election in 1994.

[3] Article 238 of the Treaty is the general article which allows the Community to negotiate Association Agreements with third countries, while article 228 (3) formally establishes the necessity of obtaining the assent of the European Parliament.

after the negotiations have finished. The first interim agreements, based on article 113 of the Treaty, came into force on 1 March 1992.[4] The interim agreements themselves establish joint committees, forerunners of the Association Committees, which meet regularly to discuss matters arising from the application of the interim agreements.

Other legal arrangements have been made within the Union itself to decide on the way in which power on the Union side is shared out between the Council and the Commission and the way in which trade protection measures are decided. Such arrangements can make an important difference to the impact which the agreements have, because although they affect only one party to the agreement, this is by far the stronger party. These specific measures are dealt with below.

## Structure of the Association Agreements

All the Association Agreements with the CEE states have the same structure, though the most recent ones have been adapted to changes which have been decided since 1991 and which have been introduced into the older agreements through additional protocols (see figure 2.1).

### The Preamble

The Preamble to the agreements states the reasons why the parties are making the agreement, lists past agreements which need to be taken into consideration, and makes other remarks of a general nature. It underlines the common values of the two parties and the common commitment to strengthening political and economic freedoms and to the CSCE process and the implementation of the Helsinki Final Act. It recognises the progress which the country in question has made towards democracy and the market economy. The Preamble sees the agreement as a step to establishing a system of stability in Europe based on cooperation; however, only the CEE party is recognised as having membership of the European Union as its goal. The Preamble and the 'general principles' are the only places that some conditionality is brought into the agreement in that full association is linked with progress towards reform. This conditionality has never been applied, and there is no mechanism for applying it, except through putting it on the agenda of the Association Council or Committee. It underlines the

[4] Article 113 of the European Union Treaty establishes the rules which govern the common commercial policy. The Common Commercial Policy, defined by articles 110–115, establishes this policy as a Community responsibility, where decisions are taken at the Community level, without requiring the approval of national legislatures.

- The Preamble
- Objectives of the agreement
- Title I: general principles of the agreement
- Title II: political dialogue
- Title III: free movement of goods
    Chapter 1: industrial products
    Chapter 2: agriculture
    Chapter 3: fisheries
    Chapter 4: common provisions (trade protection instruments)
- Title IV: movement of workers, establishment, supply of services
    Chapter 1: movement of workers
    Chapter 2: establishment
    Chapter 3: supply of services
    Chapter 4: general provisions
- Title V: payments, capital, competition and other economic provisions, approximation of laws
    Chapter 1: current payments and movement of capital
    Chapter 2: competition and other economic provisions
    Chapter 3: approximation of laws
- Title VI: economic cooperation
- Title VII: cooperation in the prevention of illegal activities[5]
- Title VIII: cultural cooperation
- Title IX: financial cooperation
- Title X: institutional, general and final provisions

There follow 12 or 13 *Annexes* relating mainly to the trade chapters and listing individual products and rates of duty.

These are followed by important *Protocols*, which are fully part of the agreements and which cover specific areas such as trade in textiles, European Coal and Steel Community (ECSC) products, processed agricultural goods, rules of origin, specific transitional arrangements for trade with Spain and Portugal, mutual assistance in customs matters. Finally there are the joint declarations which were made during the negotiations and which help to interpret the articles of the agreement.

*Figure 2.1* The structure of the Association Agreements

importance of free trade (apparently not in agriculture!) and of complying with the rules of the GATT. The later agreements also include references to the World Trade Organisation (WTO), to the Partnership for Peace agreement and to the Essen Council Pre-Accession Strategy.

It is interesting to compare the Preambles of the earliest agreements with those of the later ones (Baltics or Slovenia). Apart from the obvious changes to adapt to events between 1991 and 1995 (such as the

---

[5] Not included in agreements prior to 1995.

Copenhagen and Essen Summits), there have been subtle changes in language proposed by the Union and not contested by the other party. This is particularly clear in the trade field. In the agreement with Poland and Czechoslovakia in 1991, the commitment of both parties to free trade was stated clearly and simply. In the latest agreements the wording is not at all precise: there is reference to the commitment to liberalise trade based on GATT and WTO principles and a reference back to the FTA negotiated in 1994 (but which does not guarantee free trade!).

### The objectives of the agreement

The objectives of the agreements take up some of the points made in the Preamble; they give a certain marker against which to measure performance. In the case of the agreement with Lithuania, the objectives are as follows:

- to provide an appropriate framework for the political dialogue between the Parties allowing the development of close political relations
- to establish gradually a free trade area between the Community and Lithuania covering substantially all trade between them
- to promote the expansion of trade and the harmonious economic relations between the Parties and so to foster dynamic economic development and prosperity in Lithuania
- to provide a basis for economic, financial, cultural and social cooperation and cooperation in the prevention of illegal activities, as well as for the Community's assistance to Lithuania
- to support Lithuania's efforts to develop its economy and to complete the transition into a market economy
- to provide an appropriate framework for the gradual integration of Lithuania into the European Union. Lithuania shall work towards fulfilling the necessary requirements in this respect
- to set up institutions suitable to make the Association effective.

The objectives cover the most important elements of any strategy towards the full integration of the countries into the European Union. There are two points worth noting. The first is that the language on trade is very measured. An FTA will be established gradually and will cover only 'substantially all trade between them'. The second point is that in providing an appropriate framework for the gradual integration of Lithuania into the European Union, 'Lithuania shall work towards fulfilling the necessary requirements in this respect'. There is apparently no question of the Union adjusting any of its policies to facilitate accession. This is a matter to which we shall return later.

*General principles and the transition period*

The general principles of the agreement establish that respect for democratic principles and human rights and the principles of the market economy constitute the essential elements of the agreement. They lay down that in the economic reform area, there will be regular examination of progress made. This possibility has not really been seriously implemented; the Association Committees always have economic reform on their agendas, but the discussion is usually very general and consists of an exchange of information between the two sides on the economic situation of each party.

The general principles also cover the question of the 'transition period'. The Association Agreements are concluded for unlimited periods, nevertheless it was thought wise to introduce the concept of a transition period. The transition period serves two purposes. It is a period allowed for legal adaptations to be made in areas where immediate change is not possible or not desired – it is used, for instance, in the chapters on establishment, payments and public procurement. On the other hand, the end of the transition period is considered to be a good moment to take stock of the agreement and to consider whether it needs any modification. The pre-1995 agreements were all concluded with a ten-year transition period from the time the agreements entered into force. As it does not apply to the trade chapters, however, it is not very significant, especially as some of the associated countries may be members of the Community before the transition period is over.

The latest agreements contain very different transition periods. There was real competition between the three Baltic countries to reduce the transition period to a minimum. In fact, there is no general transition period at all in the Estonian agreement, though in individual articles of the agreement there are specific transition periods mentioned. In the case of Latvia and Lithuania, there is a general transition period which is not linked to the entry into force of the agreement but is tied to a precise date, 31 December 1999 (the transition period for the Czech Republic ends in the year 2005!). However this general transition period is subordinated to specific transition periods mentioned in individual articles. While the transition period was really suggested by the Union to take account of the time required to complete the transition, the three Baltic States considered it to be a mechanism through which they would be held back from joining the other associated countries in the preparation for accession. In the Estonian case, it was also considered to be contrary to the liberal economic policy which the country was running.

### Political dialogue

The chapter on political dialogue comes at the beginning of the agreement and appears also in the Preamble. It is seen by both parties to be of considerable significance. Whereas the first agreements emphasise the bilateral nature of political dialogue which takes place in the Association Council, the later agreements with the three Baltic countries and Slovenia emphasise the multilateral political dialogue approved by the Copenhagen and Essen European Councils.

In general, neither the bilateral nor the multilateral dialogue has worked particularly well, largely for technical, time availability, reasons. Indeed in 'Agenda 2000' the Commission proposes abolishing the structured dialogue and replacing it by ad hoc meetings arranged by the Union. This downplays a process that has been very important for the associated countries, even though frequently frustrating. It has allowed ministers to sit at the table with EU ministers to discuss not just foreign affairs but also first-pillar Community issues. At the technical level, groups of officials meeting on both second- and third-pillar issues have often been very successful. And in the foreign policy area, it has allowed the associated countries to join the European Union on several occasions in common positions in international fora (for instance, on the extension of the UNPROFOR mandate in Croatia and on the prolongation of the non-proliferation treaty).

### The four freedoms, titles III –V

The articles on the four freedoms (movement of goods, services, capital and labour) form the core of the Association Agreements. It is in these chapters that their main economic impact lies, regulating as they do both the degree of liberalisation in trade and certain characteristics of market reform in the associated countries (competition policy, for instance).

The articles on the free movement of goods are broken down into three separate sections on industrial products, agricultural products and fisheries. The opening to this part of the agreement states clearly that the Community and the associated country shall gradually establish an FTA during the transitional period. In the case of Estonia, the agreement simply says that

the Community and Estonia establish a free trade area upon entry into force of the Agreement on Free Trade and Trade-Related Matters on 1 January 1995, in accordance with the provisions of this Agreement and in conformity with those of the General Agreement on Tariffs and Trade (GATT) and the World Trade Organisation (WTO).

It is interesting to note that this can only apply to industrial goods and that therefore the agreements equate trade with industrial products trade. The final part of this title is given over to 'common provisions', essentially the commercial policy measures governing the trade chapters. It is in this final part that one finds the rules for implementing contingent protection, which will be referred to extensively later.

Title IV deals with three areas which are economically closely related: the movement of workers, the right of establishment and the supply of services. The supply of services, unlike the supply of goods, is often connected to the movement of workers. This is true for transport, for construction but also for financial services. The right of establishment, which under certain conditions allows self-employed persons and undertakings to enjoy the right of non-discriminatory national treatment when taking up or pursuing activities in the other party's territory, is also obviously closely related to the movement of workers. The freedom to supply many services (construction and transport, for instance) depends on the supplying company being able to use its own workers in the market being supplied; strict limitation on the mobility of workers in the agreements therefore restricts the value of the liberalisation of services and indeed establishment.

Title IV also has its own specific safeguard clauses. The provisions of the chapters on establishment and the supply of services are subject to limitations justified on grounds of public policy, public security or public health. They also do not apply to 'activities which in the territory of each Party are connected, even occasionally, with the exercise of official authority'. In most agreements there are derogations granted to the associated country for certain periods. These derogations normally affect the right of EU citizens and companies to purchase land or property.

Title V covers a variety of areas vital to the functioning of the market economy. The first of these is payments and capital movements. The objective of the agreement is to ensure that administrative measures will not be put in the way of payments linked to the current account of the balance of payments and to gradually move towards free movement of capital on the capital account. These provisions also guarantee to investors from the other party that they will be able to repatriate their capital whether from profits or liquidation of assets. This should be seen as an important link into the freedom of establishment rules discussed above.

Chapter II of title V deals with competition policy, the control of state aids, the protection of intellectual property and public procurement policy, four of the main supports of the market economy system. On competition policy and the control of state aids the agreement is very precise, setting deadlines for the introduction of the necessary legislation. In the other two areas the agreement is less restrictive but attempts to encourage the associated countries to adopt Community rules or to join international agreements.

The final chapter of title V concerns the approximation of laws. It goes little beyond re-stating that the approximation of laws is vital for the economic integration of the associated country and the Union and that the Union will provide technical assistance to promote this objective.

All of the chapters on the four freedoms must be read together with the relevant Annexes and Protocols, which determine to which products or services the articles refer. The Protocols include specific arrangements for textiles and clothing and steel and coal and rules governing origin.

### Economic and cultural cooperation

Title VI on economic cooperation is an extremely long listing of areas where the two parties agree to cooperate. Generally these articles are considered to be in favour of the associated country, as they are essentially offering assistance to economic reform and integration. The areas covered by the title are very wide and include most of the areas necessary for the associated country to prepare for accession. They range from industrial cooperation, through investment promotion, energy, education and training, transport, telecommunications, tourism, promotion of small and medium-sized enterprises (SMEs) to economics and drugs. Title VIII deals separately with cultural cooperation. This is a reflection of the generally held view that culture is uncontroversial and does not cost much; therefore it is important!

Title VII, which exists only in the newest agreements, covers cooperation in the prevention of illegal activities. This is an area which has become extremely important to the Member States, which feel that integration with the associated countries leaves them open to both increased illegal immigration and also to new forms of crime, including mafia-style activities involving drugs, the smuggling of nuclear materials and the stealing of (high-value) motor cars. This has become a priority area for the home affairs ministries of all the Member States, and especially those nearest to the frontiers of the associated countries.

### Financial cooperation

The short chapter on financial provision, dealt with extensively below in chapter 5, is important to the agreement, for without a financial input from the Union it is clear that many parts of the Association Agreements would not be implemented. The three countries negotiating in early 1991 expected to be offered a Financial Protocol, as with previous Association or cooperation agreements, where the Protocol specifies exactly how much finance will be made available over a given period. This system was not accepted by the Community, however. The result is a brief title listing the available forms of finance, the PHARE grant aid, the European Investment Bank (EIB) development loan assistance and balance of payments assistance.

## Institutional provisions: the Institutions of Association

The final part of the agreement lays down the mechanisms which are to be used in its implementation. These institutional provisions are very significant for the whole accession preparation process and will be dealt with extensively here.

### What the Association Agreements say

The agreements establish the Institutions of Association, the mandate of these institutions, the process for resolving disputes within the agreements and the general responsibilities of the parties to the agreement.

The agreements create three institutions, the Association Council, the Association Committee and the Parliamentary Association Committee.

### The Association Council

The Association Council is the body which supervises the implementation of the agreement. It is established at Ministerial level and usually meets once each year. It is the responsible body for the performance of numerous functions throughout the agreement:

- it is the location of the bilateral political dialogue
- it is officially the framework within which all litigation in trade and other economic and commercial matters takes place
- it takes decisions on a wide range of trade and commercial issues
- it is responsible for developing all those areas in the agreements which were not adequately developed at the time of negotiation of the agreements.
- and 'it shall examine any major issues arising within the framework of the agreement and any other bilateral or international issues of mutual interest'.

The members of the Association Council are the members of the European Council, the European Commission and the government of the associated country. Normally this is at Foreign Minister level. The Presidency of the Council rotates between the Community and the associated country, usually on an annual basis. On the Community side, the Association Council is presided over by the Minister representing the Council Presidency, and therefore rotates every six months.

### The Association Committee

The Association Council is assisted by the Association Committee, where all matters for the Council are prepared and where most of the work is done. This Committee is usually presided over by the junior minister or the senior civil servant responsible for European integration on the associated country side and by the European Commission civil servant responsible for relations with that country on the Community side. The Presidency of the Committee is an area of some jealousy between the Member States of the Community and the Commission. The Commission President of the Association Committee is therefore always watched closely by the Member States.

The Association Council determines the methods of working of the Committee. Normally the Committee does not make decisions, but the Council can delegate its decision-making powers to the Committee if its wishes.

The Association Council can establish any other special committee to help it in its work and it approves the rules of procedure of such bodies. Practically this possibility has been used to create *sub-committees of the Association Committee* which specialise in particular parts of the agreement and which report to the Council via the Association Committee. The number and scope of such sub-committees varies from agreement to agreement but there are some which are more or less standard such as those on agriculture, transport, economic policy, approximation of laws, competition policy, ECSC matters and customs. The members of these sub-committees are specialists in charge of these issues in the associated country and in the Commission and the Member States at the civil servant level.

### The Association Parliamentary Committee

At the parliamentary level, the agreements create an Association Parliamentary Committee consisting of members of the Parliament of the associated country and of the European Parliament. This institution is created by the Parliaments, which make their own rules of procedure. The only point determined by the agreements is that the presidency rotates between the two Parliaments and that the Parliamentary Committee can make proposals to the Association Council. In fact, the parliamentarians operate more or less separately from the other institutions of the agreement.

### Disputes resolution procedure

The agreements also set out the procedures of the Association Council for taking decisions. If the Council cannot reach a decision by the agreement of both sides, then the agreements disputes resolution procedure is applied. Each party nominates one arbitrator and the Association Council nominates a third. The decision is then taken by majority of the three arbitrators. This procedure could prove extremely difficult, given that there is unlikely to be easy agreement over the nomination of the third arbitrator.

The workings of the Association Council and its arbitration procedures are extremely important in that these decisions will take precedence over the law of both parties. Neither party should therefore go lightly into the disputes resolution procedure, as the prospect is fraught with difficulty and risks, leading to a deterioration of relations between the two sides.

The remaining articles of the agreements underline essential conditions for their functioning:

- natural and legal persons of one party are guaranteed access to the courts and the administration of the other party in order to defend their rights, both their individual rights and their property rights
- nothing in the agreement should endanger the security of the parties
- the arrangements for the implementation of the agreements should not lead to any discrimination between the Member States or between the nationals or companies of the parties; this also means that products imported from the associated country should not enter a Member State on more favourable conditions than the same product from another Member State
- if either side feels that the other party has failed in an obligation under the agreement, it can 'take appropriate measures'; it must inform the Association Council but it does not have to have the agreement of the Council: this obviously leaves an important escape clause open to both sides in the event of a deterioration of relationships, and does not encourage constructive conflict resolution
- the agreements are concluded for an unlimited period and can be renounced by one side notifying the other of its denouncement; the agreement then ends six months after this notification.

*The Association Councils*

The objectives of the Association Councils go well beyond the role determined by the Association Agreements. The objective of the Council is also to bring together the political leadership of both parties in order to foster an atmosphere of good cooperation, if not of friendship. There is no better way of avoiding problems than if the ministers on both sides know and have confidence in each other. Unfortunately, the Association Council meetings have not in general been successful. This is mainly a problem of time, though it is certain that some Member States have also shown a marked lack of enthusiasm in discussing with ministers from the associated countries. Frequently the 'real' ministers have left the Council Chamber when the Association Councils begin. Decisions, some of them important, have been prepared in the Association Committee and are only formal points on the Association Council agenda, and the agenda points have frequently been agreed and rehearsed on the Community side in order to avoid any free discussion.

To some extent the Association Councils' role has been usurped by the structured relationship, discussed earlier. As it has become clear that bilateral political dialogue is being replaced by multilateral political dialogue, so part of the content of the Association Councils has been lost. With ten Association Councils established for the associated countries together with the extended multilateral structured relationship, without considering the numerous other similar institutions with other countries in the Mediterranean Basin, Latin America and Asia, it is difficult to imagine a practical way of giving the Association Councils more content. In reality, the Community finds it difficult to deal with the current situation where there are ten countries which are neither in the Community nor simple third countries. This suggests that the only real solution to the problem of the Association Councils is for these countries to become Members!

*The Association Committee: the workhorse of the agreements*

Most of the work generated by the Association Agreements is dealt with by the Association Committee. The Committee normally meets at least once a year, but it can be called into session whenever required. It is presided over alternately by both sides, each presidency lasting a year. Each side has a secretary of the Committee who keep in regular contact and who are responsible for producing a first draft of agendas and the minutes of the Committee. At the Committee level, contacts between officials on both sides are relatively intense and normally friendly, something valuable in itself.

The typical agenda of an Association Committee (see figure 2.2) consists of four main blocks:

- political and economic developments in the European Union and the associated country
- trade and trade-related issues
- other cooperation issues, such as PHARE or questions of economic cooperation
- reports from sub-committees.

The core of the proceedings is constituted by the trade and trade-related issues because it is here that there is usually conflict and a need to apply the rules of the Association Agreements. The other points on the agenda are usually treated as relatively routine and consensual. They are considered useful to counter any hostility coming from the trade part of the agenda!

The Association Committee is an important learning institution for both sides in the preparation of accession. The Committee meets alternately in Brussels and the capitals of the associated countries. When it meets in Brussels, it is possible for a large number of Member State, Council and Commission officials to take part while in the associated countries there are often up to 50 civil servants of the associated country present. The preparation for the sessions and the sessions themselves provide the opportunity both for learning about each other's problems and getting to know officials of the other side.

*The impact of the Association Committee on policy: the example of trade negotiations*

Although in a book on enlargement and the future of the European architecture it may seem irrelevant to descend to the detail of how the Association Committees operate, this is not the case. The Association Committees, especially in the trade area, deal with problems which have an impact on the economy of both the associated countries and the Union, but which also have an important impact on public opinion and on the image of the accession process in both parties.

It is worth considering a moment how such committees are prepared on the Union side. There will be at least four separate actors involved:

- economic agents, usually from the business community in the Union who are affected by a measure taken by the associated country
- the national government representing the affected company
- the Council of Ministers, firstly represented by the relevant

---

**1 Opening statements**

**2 Approval of agenda**

**3 Developments in the European Union and in the associated country since the previous meeting**
   3.1 National elections in the associated country
   3.2 Developments in the European Union
   3.3 Economic situation in the associated country
   3.4 Economic situation in the European Union

**4 Trade and trade-related issues**
   4.1  Trends and prospects for bilateral trade
   4.2  Adaptation of the Europe Agreements following EU enlargement and the end of the Uruguay Round
   4.2.1 Agricultural and processed agricultural products and fisheries; levels of duty resulting from the Uruguay Round and application in a preferential agreement
   4.2.2 Other sectors
   4.2.3 Procedure
   4.3  Implementation of competition rules
   4.4  Infant industry clause and application
   4.5  Quality control on imports of consumer goods into the associated country
   4.6  Lorry drivers
   4.7  Imports of EC spirits
   4.8  Exchange of views on the steps to be taken to arrive at a mutual recognition of qualifications and diplomas
   4.9  Agreement on equivalency (veterinary and phyto-sanitary issues)

**5 Cooperation**
   5.1 Financial cooperation
   5.2 PHARE
   5.3 Infrastructure and regional cooperation
   5.4 Opening of Community programmes

**6 Strategy for accession**
   6.1 Discussion of White Paper on the internal market

**7 Reports of sub-committees**

---

*Figure 2.2* A typical agenda of an Association Committee

working group of diplomats, which deals with all the Community problems arising in the context of the Association Agreements and later by the COREPER (the Committee of Permanent Representatives of the Member States), which deals with problems which cannot be resolved at a lower level and which prepares points for the agenda of the ministerial councils

- the European Commission, which presides over the Association Committee, prepares the draft of the agenda and investigates the substance of the complaint.

A trade case on the Union side is born when problems are raised by economic operators in the Community or in the associated country and brought to the attention of the European Commission, whether directly or through one of the Permanent Representations (Embassies) of the Member States in Brussels. Alternatively the associated government itself might notify the Community of measures it intends to take. The EU secretary of the Association Committee will generally ask the opinion of the relevant service in the Commission (often, for instance, the Directorate General for Industry or for Agriculture). If it is confirmed that there is a problem and that the associated country appears to have broken the letter or the spirit of the Association Agreement, the matter will probably be notified unofficially first to the secretary of the Association Committee of the associated country. The matter will also be brought to the attention of the Member State representatives in the Council, where it will be discussed by diplomats who may or may not have instructions from their capitals. If the answers coming from the associated country do not seem to be satisfactory, discussions will ensue between the two sides, where it is usually the officials of the Commission who take the lead. Eventually, and often after many months, a deal will probably be done which is confirmed by the Association Committee and sent for formal decision to the Association Council. In cases where agreement is impossible, the arbitration process can be started.

Such procedures have many problems associated with them. Firstly they reduce trade negotiations to a level of detail which makes no sense in any economic system. Association Committees negotiate over an extra few tons of fish imports or about transferring an unfilled quota for chicken legs to an over-filled quota for chicken breasts. There is never any consideration of the overall macroeconomic situation or even of the real interest of the European Union (not to speak of the interest of Europe); as with anti-dumping procedures it is the very narrow interests of often very small sectors which are allowed to drive policy.

A further problem on the Union side is that policy towards Central Europe is often driven more by quarrels between the Member States of the Union than by the substance of the dispute or of the needs of trade development between the parties to the agreement. This is often the case, for instance, in the negotiation of agricultural 'concessions' for the Central Europeans, where the protectionist northern Member States will often refuse additional access for the associated countries in products where they themselves are major producers, but will happily make concessions in Mediterranean products. Germany has in the past usually refused any improvement in import quotas for live animals but has been happy to grant increases for tomatoes. In such cases, the Mediterranean Member States naturally demand the same treatment for tomatoes as for live animals, although they would be happy to agree to improvements in both. In such discussions, the needs of the associated countries are usually forgotten in the enthusiasm for Community infighting.

Such discussions can have very negative impacts on the CEE economies and on public opinion in the region. Whereas such internal fights do not interest the West European media, they are major stories in the press of the associated countries. It is extremely difficult for the population in these countries to understand that, with their combined GDP being the size of that of the Netherlands, an extra 1,000 tons of chicken exports risks pushing the EU economy into crisis! It also suggests to popular opinion that the Community is incapable of rising above self-interest.

These methods of working are of course the way in which negotiations on trade take place everywhere, including in the GATT. It is however unfortunate that these same methods are applied to countries to which the Union has offered, under certain conditions, membership and countries which are undergoing major structural change.

### The sub-committees of the Association Committee

Sub-committees of the Association Committee have been created for several specific parts of the Association Agreements. These sub-committees consist of those responsible for particular areas of policy and experts in those areas in both parties. They are important because they bring together specialists rather than diplomats and therefore key technical areas of difficulty in the agreements can be tackled and solutions found. Inside the Commission they are usually presided over by the responsible line Directorate General and in the associated countries by the respective technical ministry. The sub-committees cannot make decisions, but they do report to the Association Committee after each meeting and can make recommendations.

In the case of the Czech Association Committee for instance nine sub-committees were established (see figure 2.3). These sub-committees can be used to further the process of integration in a relatively unpoliticised environment and can be very effective.

The economic policy sub-committee, which has proved a considerable success and is taken very seriously by both sides, could develop a process of monitoring economic reform and those areas of the *acquis*

| | |
|---|---|
| 1 Customs cooperation | 6 Industrial standards and |
| 2 Transport issues | conformity assessment |
| 3 Agriculture | 7 Economic policy issues |
| 4 Approximation of legislation | 8 Competition and state aids |
| 5 Science and technology | 9 Contact group on ECSC matters. |

*Figure 2.3* Sub-committees established in the Czech Association Agreement

which are related to economic policy. Such surveillance could help the associated countries keep their reform on track and clarify the objectives for membership. Similar procedures could be used in the other areas covered by the sub-committees.

### The Parliamentary Association Committee

The Parliamentary Association Committee comprises members of the national Parliament of the associated country and members of the European Parliament. A delegation is officially appointed in the European Parliament for each Association Agreement or for groups of agreements. The parliamentarians involved are usually people with particular interests in the associated countries in question, while on the associated country side, the delegations tend to consist of parliamentarians with interests in the integration process. Given the relatively high level of motivation, these meetings can be important for deepening the understanding of issues between the parties. The Parliamentary Association Committees can send resolutions or declarations to the Association Councils for consideration.

The relatively limited contact of parliamentarians with the integration process, at least on the Union side, is regrettable. It leads to integration being seen as a very technical matter. It is to be hoped that such contacts between Parliaments can be intensified in the future.

# 3 Trade and the Europe Agreements

## Introduction

Trade is frequently considered to be the most important element of the relationship between the CEE countries and the European Union. It is obvious that for the associated countries, exports provide resources to finance the transition and imports provide the capital and know-how to make economic development possible. Other things being equal, both the Union and the associated countries should try to remove all obstacles to trade in order that it should reach an optimum level. But trade not only brings prosperity, it also brings conflict. Since the signing of the Association Agreements, almost all the Association Committees with Hungary and Poland have been dominated by contentious trade issues, which have frequently soured relations.

This chapter looks at what the Association Agreements say on trade, as amended by subsequent decisions, and how the discussions in the Association Committees have dealt with trade conflict. It also looks at the data on trade to see the reality rather than the rhetoric of trade discussions. It traces trade policy developments and the institutions of trade policy. It considers the techniques of trade protection in the light of the Uruguay Round and dwells at length on the problems of contingent protection. Trade in agriculture, however, is dealt with in chapter 9 on that sector. Finally, it suggests ways to liberalise trade further, on the road to accession.

## What the Association Agreements say

The Association Agreements state that the Community and the associated country will gradually establish an FTA over a period of ten years (six for Lithuania and Latvia and immediately for Estonia) from the entry into force of the agreement. While this may be an important statement for the purposes of acceptability as a preferential agreement under the GATT, it is essentially correct only for industrial goods.

The first essential element in the agreements is the standstill clause, which from the day before the date of entry into force of the (interim) agreement does not allow in general any increase in protection on either side of the agreement. The basic duties in force on that day (or lower ones if agreed subsequently in the GATT context) form the basis of the agreement.

### Industrial goods

Industrial goods are divided into three groups in the agreements: textiles and clothing, ECSC products and other industrial products. The first two groups are dealt with in separate Protocols.

For industrial goods, the Association Agreements detail the reductions in customs duties, QRs and charges equivalent to duties as well as of export restrictions. Reductions in protection are treated asymmetrically, with a more rapid reduction on the side of the Community than on the side of the associated country (except in the case of Estonia, where free trade is implemented immediately on both sides). Whereas following the Copenhagen and Essen Summits the Community applies the same treatment to all associated countries, the rules applied by the latter vary somewhat, depending on the outcome of the individual negotiations. In table 3.1 the agreements with Hungary and Poland are illustrated. While the Community has adopted a position of free trade for imports from both these countries as from 1 January 1995, Hungary and Poland also move towards complete liberalisation of imports from the Community within a ten-year period, but it is immediately obvious that there are wide differences in the rate of liberalisation depending on the particular interests of each country. In the most liberal case, that of Estonia, mutual free trade was agreed as from 1 January 1995. Latvia and Lithuania also have shorter transition periods to free trade than the other associated countries.

As far as clothing and textile products are concerned, the relevant protocol of the Association Agreement deals only with customs duties and refers to a separate Textiles Protocol with respect to QRs. Taking into account the Copenhagen decisions, customs duties on imports to the Community were to be eliminated within five years of the entry into force of the first interim agreement, in other words at the beginning of January 1996. At the same time duties on imports of outward processed goods were abolished on entry into force of the agreement. For Community exports to Hungary, the same regime of duty reduction as for other industrial products was adopted.

Table 3.1 *The timing of the elimination of trade barriers for industrial products (excluding textiles and ECSC products)*

| Measure | European Union | Hungary | Poland |
|---|---|---|---|
| Customs duties on imports[a] | General : at entry into force | Annex IV in two years (three stages) | Annex IVa entry into force |
| | Annex IIa: in one year (2 × 50%) | Annex V in nine years (in seven stages from January 1995– January 2001) | IVb (cars) reduced over seven years (1 January 2002) with reduced duty-free tariff quota |
| | Annex IIb: in two years[b] | General: in five years (1 January 1997) | General: reduction over seven years (1 January 1999) |
| | Annex III: in three years[c] | | |
| QRs and equivalent effects on imports | At entry into force | In nine years for Annex VIa products (40% by January 1997); opening of quotas | At entry into force except Annex V: used vehicles in ten years Certain petroleum oils and gases: five years |
| Charges equiv. to duties on imports | Entry in force | Over five years (January 1997) | Entry in force |
| Exports | Duties: over five years QRs: entry into force | Duties and QRs over five years | Duties over five years QRs: entry into force except petroleum (five years) |

*Notes*:
[a] Industrial products are split into several different Annexes in the agreements. The trade in goods in each Annex is liberalised to a different timescale, with protection being kept longest for 'sensitive' goods.
[b] Originally four years (5 × 20%), reduced to two years at the Copenhagen Summit.
[c] Originally five years (no duties up to tariff quota or ceiling) reduced to three years at the Copenhagen Summit.

The bilateral agreement on QRs was concluded with Hungary in December 1992 as part of the negotiations with all trading partners in the Multifibre Agreement (MFA). Similar agreements have been made with other associated countries. This agreement, forced on all the associated countries by the Community (as well as the other industrialised countries), determines in great detail how the QRs will be operated and policed. It of course excludes outward processing traffic in both directions.[1] However, article 1 of these agreements and an exchange of letters confirms that all quantitative restrictions and equivalent measures will be abolished on 1 January 1998, unless the Uruguay Round results in a longer period having to be agreed. As this was not the case, this is the date on which free trade in imports into the Community will begin. At that date only relatively low customs duties in the associated countries will affect goods in the clothing and textile areas.

ECSC products are treated in a second protocol in the agreements. This foresees the immediate abolition of QRs on both sides for steel products from the entry into force of the agreement. The Community agreed to eliminate customs duties originally over five years for the first agreements, though this was reduced to four years at Copenhagen; customs duties were finally removed for all the associated countries on 1 January 1996. The associated countries negotiated longer periods for the elimination of duties ranging from seven years (Poland) up to nine years (Hungary and Czechoslovakia). Duties and QRs on coal and coal products were eliminated rather rapidly, except in the case of Hungary which negotiated lengthy transition periods. The Community eliminated these barriers to trade in general in one year with the exception of specific products and regions (Germany and Spain), where certain duties and QRs were not eliminated until 1 January 1996.

While the agreements are relatively liberal in terms of eliminating duties and QRs in steel, they include in the ECSC Protocol specific rules on competition policy and state subsidies. The provisions state that agreements between undertakings, abuse of dominant position and public aid in any form are incompatible with the agreement. Any dispute arising from anti-competitive behaviour of the giving of state aids is to be judged on the basis of practice in the Community. However for the first five years of the agreement, the associated country can grant public aid for restructuring purposes, leading to the viability of firms and aiming at a global reduction of capacity.

While there is a procedure involving the Association Council in the case of disputes over competition or state aids in steel, each side is allowed to take measures unilaterally to counter the perceived breaches of the agreement after 60 days at the latest. This gives considerable room to use these clauses for protectionist purposes. Given that the five-year period allowed for restructuring aid may be somewhat short, especially in the light of low inward investment, problems with the

---

[1] Outward processing traffic (OPT) is a scheme where EU textile producers can export unprocessed materials to a third country, have the materials processed in that country, and reimport them into the EU free of duty.

application of these rules may well continue in the second five-year period.

On industrial products, therefore, the Association Agreements led to free trade as far as imports into the Community were concerned by the end of 1994, with minor exceptions in clothing and textiles and ECSC products – minor because these restrictions have now disappeared. Barriers are still maintained by the associated countries in many areas but practically all barriers are to be eliminated by 1999 and the final ones will disappear in 2002. It is not duties and QRs which are the main problem in goods trade, but on both sides contingent protection measures and on the side of the associated countries the exceptions which have been made and which allow the standstill arrangement to be set aside for a certain number of years.

### Agriculture

As has been mentioned several times above, the Association Agreements are not at all liberal in the areas of agriculture or processed agricultural products. This is a major drawback for the associated countries, where agriculture is not a marginal part of the economy as in Western Europe, but often employs some 25% of the working population and contributes near to 10% of GDP. Indeed, the successful restructuring of agriculture may be seen in certain countries as the key to the success of the whole reform process. Or put another way, success in the reform of the macroeconomic, financial, industrial and service areas might be put at risk if the reform of the agricultural sector was not successful.

The 'concessions' of the agreement vary in detail from country to country but generally they are similar across all the associated states. They consist of levy reductions on very limited quantities of certain poultry and pig products, reductions of duty on some meat, vegetable and fruit products (the entry of several of which is however restricted by minimum price arrangements), a tariff quota shared between some of the associated countries for the import of certain categories of live bovine animals, levy and duty reductions on small quantities of poultry, eggs and some meats, and duty reductions on very small quantities of a wider range of products. None of these concessions makes trade significantly more liberal. Indeed, when the specific agricultural commercial defence mechanism in the agreement is taken into consideration, the degree of liberalisation becomes insignificant. If the (very limited) concessions granted by the agreements are deemed to cause serious disturbance in the markets of the other partner, the aggrieved party can take immediate measures to halt imports.

Copenhagen brought a minimal improvement in these already very limited concessions in a unilateral way; the Community agreed to bring forward by six months certain of the tariff concessions agreed to in the Association Agreements. Essen brought no improvements, only the promise of studies. At the beginning of 1995, the Community attempted to agree minimal additional concessions: a roughly 10% increase in quotas was finally agreed in mid-1997. The Association Agreements then do not improve the situation of the associated countries much beyond that of any other third country. These rules governing agricultural trade have been somewhat changed by the Uruguay Round Agreement. Unfortunately this has not led to any major liberalisation.

The final mention of agriculture in the agreements is contained in the section on common provisions and states that 'without prejudice to the concessions granted under article . . . , the provisions of paragraph 1 and 2 [standstill arrangements] shall not in any way restrict the pursuance of the respective agricultural policies of [Hungary] and the Community or the taking of any measures under such policies'. In other words, in spite of the agreement to reduce certain duties and increase quotas and to introduce a standstill on duties and quantitative restrictions, each side can take decisions which deviate from the agreement as part of the pursuance of their respective agricultural policies. This was clearly negotiated to allow the CAP to evolve without any constraint being imposed by the agreements. Indeed when one of the associated countries tried to use this possibility, the Community claimed it could not because the country had no agricultural policy at all!

Agriculture will be dealt with at length in later chapters of this book. It remains one of the most critical areas for the accession of the associated countries.

*Commercial policy measures in the agreement: safeguards, anti-dumping and anti-subsidy measures* [2]

Apart from the specific agricultural safeguard clause mentioned above, there are several other elements of commercial defence instruments contained in the agreements:

- a general safeguard clause where the increase in imports causes or threatens to cause serious injury to domestic producers or

[2] Safeguard clauses give a party the right to not respect a trade liberalisation agreement when its vital interests are affected, although it may still have to introduce safeguard measures according to agreed rules; anti-dumping measures give a party to an agreement the right to penalise goods coming from a trade partner if these goods are being sold into its market at a lower price than they are sold on the trade partner's market; anti-subsidy measures are similar but apply when a foreign competitor is receiving state subsidies.

serious disturbance in any sector of the economy or in any region of one of the parties

- a specific safeguard clause allowing the associated country to raise customs duties on imports coming from the Community under certain circumstances; these are infant industries and sectors undergoing restructuring or facing serious difficulties, especially when these difficulties produce important social problems
- an anti-dumping clause (the associated countries have been treated as market economies for anti-dumping purposes since the agreements were made)
- in some agreements a safeguard clause applied to exports in case of a serious shortage or threat of shortage in the exporting country or where re-exports leads to products going to a third party against which the original exporting party maintains exporting restrictions
- specific safeguard clauses exist in the area of state aids, both generally and in the case of ECSC products, and in the rules on establishment
- the usual clause on restrictions on the grounds of public morality, public policy and public security.

The agreements lay down how these restrictions on trade should be applied.

The procedure for implementing the general safeguard clause, the anti-dumping procedure and, where applicable, the export safeguards, includes the following steps:

- notification to the Association Council, with appropriate information, in all three cases
- in the case of the general safeguards and the export safeguards, if the Association Council has not taken a decision within 30 days of the matter being referred to it, the plaintiff may adopt appropriate measures
- in the case of anti-dumping, the Association Council must be informed as soon as the other party initiates an investigation; again, if the Association Council does not take a decision within 30 days, the importing party may introduce measures.

But in exceptional circumstances appropriate measures can always be taken immediately by the aggrieved party.

The specific safeguard for the associated countries is limited in scope and application in several ways. Firstly the customs duties must not be increased above 25% ad valorem and there must still be an element of preference for the Community in the customs schedule of the associated country. Secondly the total value of the imports affected by the measure must not exceed 15% of the total imports from the Community. The measures may not be applied for a period longer than five years unless agreed to by the Association Council and they must cease by the end of the transition period. Finally these measures cannot be introduced for imports for which all duties and QRs were removed more than three years beforehand. Normally the phasing out of these measures should start at the latest after two years, and should be completed in equal annual reductions. In this case the Association Council is also informed and, at the request of the Community, consultations may be held. In spite of the results of the consultations, the associated country can take the measures, as long as it submits a schedule for phasing them out.

In the final institutional articles of the agreement, the rules under which the Association Council can reach a decision are laid down. If the Association Council cannot resolve a dispute, the matter can be put to arbitration. In this case, each party appoints one arbitrator and the Association Council appoints a third, the majority decision of the three arbitrators being binding.

It can hardly be said that these rules for the implementation of safeguards or anti-dumping are very constraining. On the one hand, both parties can always implement measures within 30 days of notification, and, *in extremis*, immediately. The associated country can introduce additional duties without the agreement of the Community at all. If the objective of the agreements is to prevent government from providing additional protection or maintaining existing protection to its domestic clients, the Association Agreements are not perfect instruments.

### Origin and Pan-European free trade

The final area which is of considerable importance in the agreements is that of rules of origin. Rules of origin, giving each product a 'nationality', are necessary to determine the conditions under which the product can enter the market of the importing country. The preferential terms of the agreements are applied only to products which when imported from an associated country are considered to have origin in that country. These rules are to be found in the Origin Protocol of the Association Agreements. Apart from a group of products which have total origin in the country, such as live animals born and raised there, the Protocol consists of an extensive list of products with their harmonised customs system number and the rules of origin applying to that product. For instance, in the manufacture of office machines the value of all non-originating materials used must not exceed 40% of the ex-works price of the product. The rule that 60% of the value of the product must be derived from value added in the associated country is the most common rule applied in the agreements.

The European Union has a general scheme of rules of origin applied to MFN trade and to which the newly agreed rules of the WTO following on from GATT 1994 will apply. But the GATT rules do not and will not apply to preferential agreements such as the Association Agreements, which will continue to have their own specific rules.

In a strange logic the rules of origin for preferential agreements are stricter than the general rules of origin. Therefore although the customs duties are lower in these preferential agreements than for MFN trade, it is more difficult for products to obtain origin under the Association Agreements. It is also clearly more difficult for small economies to establish origin for their exports than larger, more complex economies. For a country like Slovakia with a small economy and a concentration in certain sectors resulting from its past membership of both the Czech and Slovak Republic and the CMEA, it is probable that many of its exports to the Community will consist of materials and parts bought in from other countries and therefore not counting towards establishing Slovakian origin. It is easier for products to obtain origin in larger economies like that of Germany or the United States, where most of the value added is likely to be produced inside the state.

In order to privilege regional economic integration, it is possible to 'cumulate' rules of origin. This effectively means that origin can be obtained for a product not simply through value added in the exporting country, but by adding the value derived from inputs coming from other countries in the region. There are basically three forms of cumulation – bilateral, diagonal and full.

- *bilateral cumulation* exists when there is an agreement between two partners that products originating in the partner country shall be considered as having origin in the exporting country; if the Czech Republic exports a product to the Community which includes parts imported into the Czech Republic from the Community, then these parts are considered to be of Czech origin
- *diagonal cumulation* exists when, in a group of three or more countries using identical rules of origin, the exporting partner can use inputs originating in its partner countries as originating value added in its calculation of origin; in the case of the Visegrád countries, Slovakia may produce an export to the Community which includes parts originating in the Czech

Republic, and for the calculation of origin these parts will be considered as having Slovak origin

- *full cumulation* exists when inputs coming from partner countries in the zone of cumulation but not necessarily qualifying as originating in those countries are counted as originating in the exporting partner.

In order to help the associated countries, the diagonal cumulation of rules of origin between the four original Visegrád signatories of Association Agreements and the Community was agreed to. This meant, for instance, that materials used as inputs in the Czech Republic but originating in any of the other Visegrád countries could also be considered as originating in the Czech Republic, as long as their value did not exceed that of the value added in the Czech Republic itself. One of the conditions for schemes of origin cumulation to operate, however, is that the partners adopt the same system of origin for trade within the region affected by the cumulation. This means that not only must the rules be the same between each Visegrád country and the Community, but also between the Visegrád countries themselves – i.e within the Central European Free Trade Area (CEFTA) organisation. The latter condition posed many problems and therefore diagonal cumulation of rules of origin did not operate within the Community–CEFTA region until relatively recently.

Cumulation of rules of origin is an important incentive for developing regional trade and opens wider location choices to businesses establishing in the region. This does, however, mean that rules of origin are not purely technical arrangements but are an important part of commercial policy – in other words, they can be part of the commercial defences erected by trading partners. Obviously with very restrictive rules of origin an FTA can become a rather illiberal arrangement.

The importance of rules of origin was recognised by the Copenhagen Summit, which invited the Commission to make a study of the cumulation of rules of origin and to make proposals to the Council on cumulation between the associated countries, the Community and EFTA. This study was translated by the Commission into three sectoral studies. The results of the three studies, the terms of reference of which included the impact of cumulation on employment, investment decisions and transfer of production facilities, were generally favourable to the cumulation of rules of origin, arguing that this would improve the competitivity of EU enterprises. Only the study on textiles raised some doubts about the potential negative effects on direct employment.

The strategy proposed by the Community at the Essen Council was in three stages, but without a timetable:

- The first step was to streamline and simplify the diagonal cumulation with the Visegrád countries, which had existed since 1991 but had not been implemented because of technical problems in the Visegrád countries themselves; diagonal cumulation would then be extended to include Bulgaria and Romania.
- In the second stage, diagonal cumulation was to be introduced between the European Community, the associated countries and the EFTA countries. Given that EFTA now has only Switzerland, Norway, Iceland and Lichtenstein as members, this would not be a major move; it would, however, raise the problem of introducing no-drawback clauses into the Association Agreements to avoid circumvention.[3]
- The third stage would then be the move to full cumulation in all agreements leading to one Europe as far as origin is concerned. The Commission's paper includes a revealing phrase: 'this would result in a truly free trade area without artificial origin barriers.' But unfortunately the paper ends with the phrase:

> before moving to the third stage a thorough evaluation of the sectoral and regional consequences on European industry of introducing full cumulation would be carried out, taking into account the first two stages. This evaluation would cover a representative cross-section of European trade and industry and might lead to limited sectoral exceptions. Furthermore, there are major practical difficulties with introducing full cumulation at this stage, and it must remain a longer term option.

A more supportive policy would be to simplify rules of origin by harmonising those applying to preferential agreements and non-preferential agreements, and to move to full cumulation as quickly as the purely technical problems allowed. These would both help business throughout Europe, and therefore improve the functioning of the European economy.

However the Union has made very significant and barely recognised strides to liberalise trade in Europe through the completion of the first and second stages of the Essen strategy. As from 1 July 1997 pan-

---

[3] 'Drawback' is the process by which an exporter can claim reimbursement of taxes and duties paid on imported materials used in the production of the export. In the absence of a no-drawback clause in FTAs, exporters therefore have a competitive advantage over domestic producers on the import market, the domestic producers not being able to reclaim taxes and tariffs paid. The Association Agreements do not include no-drawback clauses while the EEA agreement (and most other agreements) does. Obviously mixing the no-drawback rules in a region with diagonal cumulation could lead to tariff-induced disturbances if the tariffs have a more than negligible level.

European diagonal cumulation of rules of origin has been achieved, covering the associated countries, the EEA countries and the European Union. This is a major achievement which will help firms in all parties to the agreement. As far as the associated countries are concerned a limited amount of no-drawback has been introduced into the Origin Protocol of the Europe Agreements in order to avoid distortions and there are still one or two bilateral agreements to be signed. However this breakthrough means that the 'hub and spoke' arguments proposed by Richard Baldwin today have far less validity.[4]

### The pattern of trade

Trade is usually strongest amongst geographical neighbours. This is common sense, verified by statistics, and geography is indeed one of the variables of the gravity model approach to estimating potential trade flows. It is to be expected therefore that associated country trade with the European Union will be more intense than that with the United States or Japan. But it also suggests that trade with Germany will be more important than that with Spain within the Union.

   For 45 years prior to 1989 trade had been totally managed through the CMEA system. Geography still played a part in the planning of production and trade but simply reinforced the linkages between the CEE countries and the Soviet Union; trade with the European Union played a relatively small part in total trade. The changes which took place after 1989 led to a large change in the directions of trade for the associated countries from East to West. This is often seen as a somewhat abrupt and artificial shift in trade patterns; that this was not the case and that it was quite a natural response to a more open trading environment is demonstrated by a brief look at trading patterns in the 1920s, the last time that a more open trading environment existed.

#### Trade in the inter-war years

In 1928 Czechoslovakia, Poland, Bulgaria, Romania and Hungary exported between 70% and 80% of total exports to the countries of the present European Union.[5] Trade with the other associated countries was, however, far more important than it is today, generally around 20% of total trade. At that time trade with the Soviet Union was negligible, as was that with the rest of the world. For the Baltic countries, almost all

[4] Baldwin (1994).    [5] Baldwin (1994).

their trade at this period was with the current European Union, mainly with Germany and the United Kingdom. As markets for West European countries, the associated countries were also far more important at this period than they are today. Exports of goods to the Visegrád countries made up approximately 13% of total German goods exports in 1928, whereas today (1995), though on a sharply rising trend, they are only 5.5%. Roughly a third of Austrian exports went to the Visegrád countries (the Austro-Hungarian empire had been dissolved only ten years earlier), while in the case of Switzerland it was slightly less than 10%.

Such comparisons are very dangerous. The countries themselves occupy different areas today than they did in the 1920s and their relative wealth is completely different. Czechoslovakia in 1928, for instance, was one of the most highly developed industrial countries while the Soviet Union was in only the first phase of its industrial development. Nevertheless these comparisons clearly demonstrate that the reversal of trade flows after 1989 was not abnormal.

### Trade flows under CMEA

Under the CMEA system, the countries of Central Europe were forced into patterns of trade which were geared to meet the needs of the Soviet Union, although the CMEA never developed into an internal trading system which allocated exports and imports to each of its members. However table 3.2, taken from Kornai's book *The socialist system* (1992) illustrates the degree of concentration of trade within the socialist bloc.[6]

Tables 3.2 and 3.3 clearly show the abrupt turnaround in trade after the Second World War. The European socialist countries traded principally with developed capitalist countries in 1938 (75% of exports, 72.4% of imports), whilst in 1958 only 20% of their export and import trade was with these countries and over 70% was with the socialist countries. After 1958, however, there was a steady increase in trade with the developed capitalist economies as the socialist governments struggled to keep their peoples happy with Western consumer goods and to import technology from the West. By 1980 over one-third of the European socialist countries' trade was with the West, only just over half being with the socialist countries.

With the Communist system putting emphasis on quantitative output goals rather than quality or reliability, exports of the East European

---

[6] Kornai (1992).

Table 3.2 *Export structure of socialist countries, by main markets, 1938–80*

| Exporting countries | | Shares by importing countries (%) | | |
|---|---|---|---|---|
| | | Socialist | Developed capitalist | Developing capitalist |
| All Socialist countries | 1938 | 11.0 | 73.9 | 14.1 |
| | 1958 | 69.8 | 19.5 | 9.2 |
| | 1970 | 59.4 | 24.5 | 16.1 |
| | 1980 | 47.6 | 33.9 | 18.5 |
| of these: | | | | |
| European socialist | 1938 | 12.7 | 75.0 | 11.0 |
| | 1958 | 70.6 | 20.8 | 6.9 |
| | 1970 | 62.7 | 24.1 | 13.2 |
| | 1980 | 52.0 | 32.6 | 15.4 |
| Asian socialist states | 1938 | 3.1 | 69.0 | 28.6 |
| | 1958 | 65.7 | 12.7 | 21.6 |
| | 1970 | 22.1 | 28.8 | 49.1 |
| | 1980 | 13.7 | 43.7 | 42.6 |
| Soviet Union | 1958 | 71.8 | 17.5 | 10.7 |
| | 1970 | 57.8 | 21.2 | 21.0 |
| | 1980 | 45.3 | 36.1 | 18.6 |

*Source*: Kornai (1992).

Table 3.3 *Import structure of socialist countries, by main markets, 1938–80*

| Importing countries | | Shares by exporting countries (%) | | |
|---|---|---|---|---|
| | | Socialist | Developed capitalist | Developing capitalist |
| All Socialist countries | 1938 | 15.6 | 73.6 | 10.8 |
| | 1958 | 72.1 | 20.7 | 7.2 |
| | 1970 | 58.1 | 31.1 | 10.8 |
| | 1980 | 47.0 | 39.3 | 13.7 |
| of these: | | | | |
| European socialist | 1938 | 20.1 | 72.4 | 7.7 |
| | 1958 | 74.1 | 19.4 | 6.5 |
| | 1970 | 62.6 | 27.7 | 9.7 |
| | 1980 | 51.3 | 35.2 | 13.5 |
| Asian socialist states | 1938 | 8.0 | 76.0 | 16.0 |
| | 1958 | 61.6 | 27.0 | 11.0 |
| | 1970 | 24.4 | 56.5 | 19.1 |
| | 1980 | 18.6 | 66.2 | 15.2 |
| Soviet Union | 1938 | 12.5 | 78.6 | 7.5 |
| | 1958 | 77.4 | 14.9 | 7.7 |
| | 1970 | 58.6 | 26.2 | 15.2 |
| | 1980 | 44.7 | 39.4 | 15.9 |

*Source*: Kornai (1992).

Table 3.4 *Main imports into the European Community from Bulgaria, Hungary, Poland and Romania, 1987 (% of total)*

|  | Bulgaria | Hungary | Poland | Romania |
|---|---|---|---|---|
| Live animals | 7.4 | 15.3 | 13.4 | – |
| Vegetables | – | 7.7 | 5.3 | – |
| Prepared foods | 9.7 | – | – | – |
| Mineral products | 18.2 | – | 18.4 | 37.0 |
| Textiles | 12.8 | 16.2 | 11.0 | 17.2 |
| Base metals | 14.5 | 10.3 | 11.7 | 6.9 |
| Chemicals | 8.3 | 8.2 | – | 4.2 |
| Wood | – | – | – | 3.5 |
| Vehicles/transport | – | – | 5.3 | – |
| Machinery | – | 10.2 | – | – |
| Misc manufactures | – | – | – | 11.3 |
| % total of main sectors | 70.8 | 67.8 | 65.1 | 80.0 |

*Source*: EUROSTAT.

socialist countries to the Western developed countries were always concentrated on raw materials, raw or processed agricultural goods and low value manufactured goods. This comes out clearly in table 3.4, showing Community imports from certain associated countries in 1989. Roughly 20% of Hungary's, Poland's and Bulgaria's exports were made up of agricultural products, between 10 and 20% of all countries' exports were textiles and around 10% base metals. Minerals were important for Romania (37%), Poland (18.4%) and Bulgaria (18.2%), and chemical exports for Hungary, Bulgaria and Romania. Imports from the Community at this time were largely of machinery and consumer goods.

The structure of the economy which developed under the socialist system, and which is reflected in these trade statistics tells us only a limited amount about the comparative advantage of these countries. Market prices and factor prices were distorted and had little to do with the allocation of resources, which was determined mainly by bureaucratic control. Nevertheless it was impossible to radically change the installed physical capital of these countries after 1989, so that the sectors in which the countries exported to the European Community in 1987 were clearly going to be the important sectors also after the revolution. It would be essential for the CEE countries at least to maintain these exports to generate the resources necessary to pay for the high level of imports which were required to re-tool the economy.

For the European Community, merchandise trade with the associated countries prior to 1989 was minimal. In 1987, for instance, trade
with Poland, Hungary, Czechoslovakia, Romania and Bulgaria made
up just 2.9% of total extra-Community imports and 2.6% of exports.
For Germany, the most active trader with the region, goods exports to
these countries were only a little less than 2% of total exports, or 4% of
extra-EC exports. Most trade was cumbersome and unreliable, being
dependent on the state monopoly of foreign trade. The extreme
restriction on the use of hard currency also meant that imports were
strictly rationed.

### Trade flows in the period of transition

#### Development of trade after 1989

The European Union's trade with Central Europe had stagnated in the
mid-1980s as the communist regimes desperately tried various reforms
in order to keep their people happy or, as in the case of Romania, ran
policies which limited trade considerably. It was only in 1989 that trade
began to grow again.

Tables 3.5 and 3.6 show for the Community (EU-12) the growth of
imports and exports of goods with CEE countries between 1988 and
1996. They show a substantial jump in trade in 1989 and again in 1991.
The intermediate year 1990 showed very modest growth owing to the
rigours of the macroeconomic stabilisation policy and the rapid decline
of state-owned enterprises (SOEs). Export growth since 1992 overall
has been steady at a high rate of over 20% per year, reflecting the
renewed growth of the CEE economies (with the exception of
Hungary). Imports, on the other hand, were affected by the recession in
the Community in 1993, though growth of imports into the Community
was again significant in 1994 (+29%) and 1995 (+25%). The recession,
together with the impact of rising export prices from the associated
countries, led to a quasi-stagnation of associated country exports
(imports of the European Union) in 1996 (+4.8%).

The result of this more or less sustained growth in trade since the
revolutions at the end of the 1980s is that today Central Europe
accounts for a considerably larger part of the Community's trade than in
1987. In 1996 10.2% of the Community's extra-EU (EU-15) exports
went to Central Europe, while 8.1% of imports came from the region.
The respective figures for Germany were 6.7% of its total exports and
6.4% of its imports (15.3% of extra-exports and 15.5% of extra-
imports). While these figures show remarkable growth, EU trade with
the associated countries is still less than that with Switzerland.

Table 3.5 *Growth rates of EC imports from Central Europe, 1989/88–1996/95, EU-12 (%)*

|  | 1989/88 | 1990/89 | 1991/90 | 1992/91 | 1993/92 | 1994/93 | 1995/94 | 1996/95 |
|---|---|---|---|---|---|---|---|---|
| Estonia | – | – | – | – | 90.6 | 47.7 | 62.9 | 37.5 |
| Latvia | – | – | – | – | 32.5 | 19.8 | 18.0 | 17.8 |
| Lithuania | – | – | – | – | 45.1 | 14.6 | 17.5 | 17.7 |
| Poland | 14.8 | 33.7 | 20.5 | 14.0 | 7.1 | 20.1 | 21.9 | 0.5 |
| Czechoslovakia | 15.7 | 7.3 | 24.3 | 23.6 | 8.3 | – | – | – |
| Czech Rep. | – | – | – | – | – | 31.5 | 23.5 | 7.0 |
| Slovak Rep. | – | – | – | – | – | 61.4 | 39.6 | 8.3 |
| Hungary | 19.9 | 13.4 | 23.5 | 10.0 | −0.9 | 25.4 | 32.0 | 9.3 |
| Romania | 14.1 | −37.0 | −7.6 | −4.3 | 20.4 | 48.7 | 30.1 | 4.6 |
| Bulgaria | 15.0 | 9.8 | 29.0 | 20.4 | 5.0 | 41.2 | 31.5 | −7.6 |
| Slovenia | – | – | – | – | – | 27.8 | 10.7 | −1.5 |
| Central Europe | 15.9 | 7.3 | 24.3 | 23.6 | 8.5[a] | 29.1 | 24.9 | 4.8 |

*Note:* [a] Including Estonia, Latvia, Lithuania, Slovakia and Slovenia
*Source:* EUROSTAT.

Table 3.6 *Growth rates of EC exports to Central Europe, 1989/88–1996/95, EU-12 (%)*

|  | 1989/88 | 1990/89 | 1991/90 | 1992/91 | 1993/92 | 1994/93 | 1995/94 | 1996/95 |
|---|---|---|---|---|---|---|---|---|
| Estonia | – | – | – | – | 67.3 | 47.1 | 46.2 | 31.0 |
| Latvia | – | – | – | – | 81.4 | 56.6 | 28.8 | 18.6 |
| Lithuania | – | – | – | – | 111.7 | 51.0 | 14.5 | 43.7 |
| Poland | 43.1 | 11.4 | 79.3 | 3.5 | 22.3 | 8.5 | 24.7 | 32.2 |
| Czechoslovakia | 9.8 | 9.3 | 46.4 | 64.1 | 16.6 | – | – | – |
| Czech Rep. | – | – | – | – | – | 30.5 | 27.7 | 20.1 |
| Slovak Rep. | – | – | – | – | – | 46.8 | 50.1 | 23.0 |
| Hungary | 26.9 | −3.7 | 21.2 | 16.5 | 22.3 | 23.8 | 10.0 | 15.0 |
| Romania | 12.1 | 78.2 | 8.4 | 39.4 | 25.2 | 14.1 | 34.2 | 15.6 |
| Bulgaria | 5.0 | −38.8 | 14.0 | 7.9 | 21.1 | 26.4 | 17.2 | −18.5 |
| Slovenia | – | – | – | – | – | 20.0 | 19.1 | 3.5 |
| Central Europe | 23.4 | 4.6 | 46.1 | 25.2 | 22.5[a] | 21.0 | 23.9 | 20.2 |

*Note:* [a] Including Estonia, Latvia, Lithuania, Slovakia and Slovenia
*Source:* EUROSTAT.

Table 3.7 *Direction of merchandise exports in 1996 (ECU million)*

| | France | BLEU | Neth | Germ. | Italy | UK | Irel. | Dk | Greece | Port | Spain | Sweden | Finland | Austria | total | %trade |
|---|---|---|---|---|---|---|---|---|---|---|---|---|---|---|---|---|
| Estonia | 35 | 35 | 66 | 237 | 62 | 65 | 9 | 64 | 2 | 2 | 10 | 208 | 875 | 10 | 1681 | 2.7 |
| Latvia | 38 | 48 | 85 | 321 | 63 | 91 | 11 | 70 | 4 | 1 | 11 | 163 | 185 | 13 | 1102 | 1.7 |
| Lithuania | 77 | 59 | 92 | 560 | 122 | 95 | 14 | 125 | 4 | 4 | 36 | 115 | 123 | 25 | 1451 | 2.3 |
| Poland | 1624 | 928 | 1148 | 8567 | 2683 | 1532 | 137 | 653 | 60 | 25 | 487 | 842 | 466 | 639 | 19791 | 31.3 |
| Czech | 995 | 559 | 552 | 7256 | 1365 | 839 | 102 | 159 | 36 | 14 | 280 | 288 | 194 | 1267 | 13906 | 22.0 |
| Slovak | 280 | 110 | 157 | 1927 | 543 | 124 | 16 | 42 | 14 | 13 | 86 | 53 | 52 | 547 | 3964 | 6.3 |
| Hungary | 580 | 396 | 397 | 4372 | 1195 | 413 | 63 | 86 | 42 | 44 | 192 | 228 | 146 | 1747 | 9900 | 15.7 |
| Romania | 438 | 150 | 151 | 1520 | 1307 | 248 | 15 | 40 | 136 | 17 | 85 | 60 | 23 | 235 | 4425 | 7.0 |
| Bulgaria | 135 | 58 | 81 | 546 | 294 | 102 | 8 | 24 | 246 | 7 | 24 | 65 | 26 | 99 | 1716 | 2.7 |
| Slovenia | 707 | 167 | 160 | 1624 | 1524 | 146 | 12 | 34 | 10 | 3 | 138 | 77 | 28 | 707 | 5338 | 8.4 |
| Total | 4910 | 2510 | 2888 | 26929 | 9158 | 3655 | 387 | 1296 | 554 | 131 | 1350 | 2098 | 2119 | 5288 | 63275 | 100 |
| % of total | 7.8 | 4.0 | 4.6 | 42.6 | 14.5 | 5.8 | 0.6 | 2.1 | 0.9 | 0.2 | 2.1 | 3.3 | 3.4 | 8.4 | 100 | |

Table 3.8 *Direction of merchandise imports in 1996 (ECU million)*

| | France | BLEU | Neth | Germ. | Italy | UK | Irel. | Dk | Greece | Port | Spain | Sweden | Finland | Austria | total | % trade |
|---|---|---|---|---|---|---|---|---|---|---|---|---|---|---|---|---|
| Estonia | 36 | 36 | 137 | 158 | 19 | 137 | 3 | 58 | 1 | 3 | 4 | 232 | 299 | 3 | 1128 | 2.4 |
| Latvia | 53 | 42 | 330 | 251 | 15 | 240 | 15 | 58 | 1 | 7 | 9 | 139 | 28 | 3 | 1190 | 2.5 |
| Lithuania | 64 | 83 | 93 | 379 | 61 | 204 | 5 | 84 | 2 | 18 | 43 | 56 | 27 | 16 | 1136 | 2.4 |
| Poland | 936 | 413 | 800 | 6301 | 1063 | 730 | 58 | 550 | 79 | 27 | 208 | 463 | 219 | 371 | 12217 | 26.0 |
| Czech | 463 | 300 | 296 | 5931 | 596 | 458 | 31 | 104 | 83 | 22 | 123 | 147 | 80 | 1060 | 9694 | 20.6 |
| Slovak | 164 | 96 | 123 | 1778 | 453 | 96 | 9 | 28 | 29 | 8 | 48 | 40 | 30 | 484 | 3386 | 7.2 |
| Hungary | 486 | 328 | 371 | 4023 | 987 | 527 | 13 | 56 | 75 | 11 | 223 | 143 | 59 | 1406 | 8708 | 18.5 |
| Romania | 371 | 125 | 189 | 1136 | 1128 | 228 | 3 | 14 | 113 | 8 | 96 | 40 | 5 | 118 | 3575 | 7.6 |
| Bulgaria | 118 | 70 | 76 | 399 | 408 | 127 | 1 | 19 | 287 | 11 | 113 | 14 | 7 | 45 | 1696 | 3.6 |
| Slovenia | 575 | 70 | 95 | 1890 | 855 | 131 | 4 | 37 | 20 | 16 | 39 | 46 | 18 | 449 | 4245 | 9.0 |
| Total | 3267 | 1563 | 2509 | 22249 | 5584 | 2877 | 142 | 1009 | 689 | 131 | 906 | 1320 | 772 | 3955 | 46975 | 100 |
| % of total | 7.0 | 3.3 | 5.3 | 47.4 | 11.9 | 6.1 | 0.3 | 2.2 | 1.5 | 0.3 | 1.9 | 2.8 | 1.6 | 8.4 | 100 | |

*Source:* Eurostat

*The directions of trade*

Germany dominates Community trade with the associated countries (tables 3.7 and 3.8). 47% of all imports into the Community from the associated countries in 1996 were imported by Germany and 43% of Community exports to the region were German. With total trade with the EU-15 at between 60% and 70% of the trade of the associated countries, Germany alone on average accounts for between 25 and 30% of their total world trade. With the exception of Estonia, Germany is the largest EU trade partner of every single associated country, even those like Bulgaria and Romania which are further away and often thought to be the 'clients' of other Member States. Italy, with around 13% of total trade is second, while France, the Netherlands and the United Kingdom have between 5% and 7% each. It should be noticed that the 'cohesion countries' in the Community (Greece, Spain, Portugal and Ireland) are all small traders with Central Europe, though in individual cases, such as Greek–Bulgarian trade, small concentrated flows may be important.

The Community Member States do have stronger trade relations with some of the associated countries than with others, reflecting geography and history. Austria's trade with Hungary is of course determined by both history and geography, and much the same might be said for Swedish and Finnish trade with the Baltic countries. Denmark's trade is concentrated on Poland and the Baltic countries, while Greek trade is heavily regional, concentrating on Bulgaria and Romania.

Sweden, Finland and Austria, which became members of the European Union in 1995, are all significant traders with the associated countries. Austria alone contributes about 8% of total EU trade with Central Europe. Finland totally dominates the Community trade with Estonia, with over half of EU exports to that country and one-third of imports.

*The commodity structure of trade*

In terms of the commodity structure of trade, an analysis of the 1995 trade flows shows strong concentration in certain sectors in both exports to the EU and imports from it (tables 3.9 and 3.10).

The exports of the associated countries to the European Union are dominated by three sectors: textiles; iron and steel and base metals; and machinery and electrical equipment. In 1996 they made up 47.4% of total exports. Four other sectors contributed between 5% and 9%: mineral products and oil; vehicles and transport equipment; miscellaneous manufactures; and wood products. These seven sectors contrib-

Table 3.9 *Commodity structure of Associated Country trade with the European Union, 1996: Exports - sectors contributing over 5% of total exports (EU-15 imports)*

|  | EU88 | EU92 | EU95 | Poland | Hung | Czech | Rom |
|---|---|---|---|---|---|---|---|
| Animal products | 8.4 | 5.2 |  |  | 5.0 |  |  |
| Mineral products/oil | 14.5 | 8.9 | 6.5 | 8.8 |  | 5.3 |  |
| Chemicals | 6.8 | 5.8 |  |  |  | 5.0 |  |
| Plastics and rubber |  |  |  |  |  | 5.9 |  |
| Wood/wood products |  |  | 5.0 | 5.2 |  |  |  |
| Textiles | 13.6 | 16.1 | 14.7 | 15.5 | 11.0 | 8.9 | 33.9 |
| Footwear |  |  |  |  |  |  | 10.6 |
| Iron/steel, base metals | 14.0 | 16.6 | 13.4 | 13.8 | 9.4 | 14.8 | 15.5 |
| Machinery,electrical equip. | 7.5 | 10.0 | 19.3 | 12.8 | 36.3 | 22.5 | 8.9 |
| Vehicles, transport equip. |  | 5.6 | 8.7 | 10.0 | 6.1 | 10.7 |  |
| Miscellaneous manufactures | 5.5 | 5.8 | 6.4 | 9.1 |  | 6.5 | 9.2 |
| Total % of these sectors | 70.3 | 74.0 | 74.0 | 75.2 | 67.8 | 79.6 | 78.1 |
| No. of sectors >5% | 7 | 8 | 7 | 7 | 5 | 8 | 5 |

*Source*: EUROSTAT.

Table 3.10 *Commodity structure of associated country trade with the European Union, 1996, imports, sectors contributing over 5% of total imports (EU-15 exports)*

|  | EU88 | EU92 | EU95 | Pol. | Hun. | Czech. | Rom. |
|---|---|---|---|---|---|---|---|
| Prepared foodstuffs |  |  |  |  |  |  | 5.0 |
| Chemicals | 15.8 | 9.5 | 9.1 | 9.7 | 9.1 | 8.7 | 8.7 |
| Plastics | 8.4 | 5.0 | 6.0 | 6.7 | 5.6 | 6.4 |  |
| Textiles | 9.6 | 10.8 | 9.7 | 9.7 | 9.3 | 6.0 | 20.3 |
| Iron/steel, base metals | 7.1 | 5.3 | 7.4 | 6.9 | 7.2 | 9.0 | 5.9 |
| Machinery, electrical equip. | 29.5 | 28.0 | 30.1 | 27.4 | 37.1 | 34.4 | 28.8 |
| Vehicles, transport equip. |  | 11.1 | 11.5 | 13.0 | 9.2 | 11.3 | 6.1 |
| Total % of these sectors | 70.4 |  | 73.8 | 73.4 | 77.5 | 75.8 | 74.8 |
| No. of sectors >5% | 5 | 6 | 6 | 6 | 6 | 6 | 6 |

*Source*: EUROSTAT.

uted almost three-quarters of total exports. While from country to country there is a different range of exports, the three main sectors are common to all the main associated countries. At present the three Baltic states have a somewhat different structure, with very large exports of oil and other mineral products (37% of Latvia's and 16% of Lithuania's exports to the European Union), reflecting their importance as storage locations for Russian oil. Estonia and Latvia also have very large exports of wood and wood products (16% and 19%, respectively).

In 1996, imports from the European Union were even more concentrated, six sectors contributing 74% of the total. Machinery and electrical equipment dominated, making up 30% of total imports from the European Union. This was followed by vehicles, with 11.5%. Chemical and textile (mainly OPT) imports contributed around 10% each and plastics and iron and steel both around 6% of imports from the European Union.

A comparison with the structure of trade in 1988, before the revolution, and 1992 shows that there has been no major restructuring in foreign trade, though important shifts are taking place. Whereas associated countries' exports to the European Union in 1988 were more heavily concentrated in mineral products and oil and in live animal exports, imports featured a higher proportion of chemicals and plastics, but vehicle imports were only 3% of total imports from the European Union. Nevertheless the same sectors dominated both exports and imports in 1988 as in 1992 and 1996. The only sectors which have been added have been the vehicle sector in imports and exports and wood products in exports to the European Union and the only sectors to disappear from the table are live animals and chemicals in 1996.

Over this period of some eight years, however, certain significant changes are observable. The steady increase in textile exports from the European Union to the associated countries is a clear result of the development of the outward processing business. This is reflected in the fact that both textile imports and exports have risen as a percentage of total trade, which itself has risen sharply over the period. Whether this is a very positive development for the textile industry in Central Europe in the long run can be questioned. On the one hand, it produces cash flow to finance investment in the businesses of Central Europe, on the other it avoids the need to transfer technology from the European Union to the associated countries, which would be the result of inward investment in the textile sector. This growth was stopped in 1996, however, probably reflecting recession in the Union and rising costs in the associated countries.

There has also been an important increase in exports of machinery and electrical equipment from the associated countries, accounting for 36% of total exports to the European Union in the case of Hungary and 23% from the Czech Republic. Added to this is the increase in the share of vehicle exports from 4% in 1988 to almost 9% in 1996. In value terms these increases in export share are very significant as exports were expanding rapidly over this period. These two sectors accounted for exports to the European Union of just ECU1,200 million in 1988, ECU 3,100 million in 1992 and ECU13,000 million in 1996 (this data excludes the Baltic countries and Slovenia). While still being dwarfed by the value of imports of these sectors from the European Union, these figures point to a strong development of higher-value exports and a growth in intra-industry trade.

Two points are of considerable importance for the analysis of trade in the context of both the Association Agreements and the future prospects for accession. The first is the fact that the economies of the associated countries are still heavily dependent on exports in the 'sensitive sectors' of the EU economy. Resources to finance the further restructuring of the economy will have to be partly earned from a continued growth in these exports. The second is that exports of investment goods from the Union to the associated countries remain at a high level and are likely to create a growing demand component for EU industry.

*The visible trade balance*

The visible trade balance has been a major point of political discussion between the Union and the associated countries over the past few years, on account of the overall deficit of the associated countries. The subject merits depoliticization. The recent large trade deficits recorded in some of the associated countries require domestic economic policy measures, however, if financial stability is to be maintained.

The associated countries included in Table 3.11 had a combined trade deficit with the European Union (EUR-12) of ECU4,846 million in 1994, ECU5,636 million in 1995 and ECU12,842 million in 1996. In each year the most important deficit was that of Poland, followed by those of the Czech Republic and Hungary, as might be expected. Latvia was the only country to show a surplus in EU trade in all three years, while Slovakia showed a small surplus in 1994. The only EU country to be in deficit in both years was Portugal, but the deficit was small. The United Kingdom ran a slightly larger deficit in 1994 but again at ECU198 million it was almost negligible, and as for most EU countries the UK surplus in 1996 was considerable (ECU778 million). Germany had a surplus of around ECU1,500 million in both 1994 and 1995 but

Table 3.11 Bilateral visible trade balance, European Union and associated countries, 1994–6 (ECU million)

| | Poland | | Czech Rep. | | Hungary | | Romania | | Bulgaria | | Ass. States[a] | |
|---|---|---|---|---|---|---|---|---|---|---|---|---|
| | 1994 | 1996 | 1994 | 1996 | 1994 | 1996 | 1994 | 1996 | 1994 | 1996 | 1994 | 1996 |
| France | 167 | 688 | 336 | 533 | 105 | 94 | 82 | 67 | 0 | 16 | 707 | 1,643 |
| BLEU[b] | 189 | 515 | 170 | 260 | 105 | 69 | −14 | 25 | −25 | −12 | 446 | 947 |
| Neth. | 295 | 347 | 131 | 256 | 161 | 26 | 4 | −38 | 19 | 5 | 436 | 379 |
| Ger. | 212 | 2,266 | 601 | 1,325 | 520 | 349 | 122 | 384 | 184 | 147 | 1,563 | 4,681 |
| Italy | 710 | 1621 | 157 | 769 | 179 | 208 | −24 | 179 | −11 | −114 | 1,489 | 3,574 |
| UK | 46 | 803 | 101 | 381 | 3 | −114 | −28 | 20 | 17 | −26 | −198 | 778 |
| Ire. | −7 | 79 | 28 | 70 | 27 | 50 | 2 | 12 | 4 | 7 | 53 | 244 |
| Dk. | −28 | 103 | 37 | 54 | 57 | 30 | 20 | 25 | 5 | 5 | 112 | 287 |
| Greece | 18 | −19 | −32 | −46 | −6 | −33 | 0 | 24 | 81 | −41 | 42 | −135 |
| Port. | −15 | −3 | −10 | −8 | 10 | 33 | −3 | 9 | 1 | −4 | −31 | −1 |
| Spain | 135 | 280 | 44 | 158 | 69 | −31 | −25 | −11 | −22 | −88 | 227 | 445 |
| EU-12 | 1,722 | 6,680 | 1,563 | 3,752 | 1,230 | 681 | 136 | 696 | 253 | −105 | 4,846 | 12,842 |
| Swe. | | 379 | | 140 | | 85 | | 19 | | 51 | | 776 |
| Fin. | | 248 | | 114 | | 86 | | 18 | | 19 | | 1,348 |
| Aust. | | 268 | | 207 | | 341 | | 118 | | 54 | | 1,333 |
| EUR-15 | | 7,574 | | 4,213 | | 1,192 | | 850 | | 20 | | 16,300 |

Notes:
[a] Includes the three Baltic states, Slovakia and Slovenia.
[b] BLEU = Belgium and Luxembourg.
Source: EUROSTAT.

this grew to almost ECU4,700 million in 1996, while the Italian surplus almost reached ECU2,000 million in 1995 and was over ECU3,500 million in 1996.

Table 3.11 also shows bilateral trade balances for the three new EU Member States for 1996. All three have significant trade surpluses with the associated countries; together they increased the overall EU-12 surplus by over 27% in 1996, with the Austrian and Finnish surpluses being not far short of that of France.

It is quite natural that the associated countries, in the middle of a massive restructuring of their economies and many of them with economic growth rates twice that of the Union, should run deficits. These countries must import machinery and new technology in order to raise their potential output and their future exports. The worry is not in the existence of a deficit but whether it is occasioned by a burst of consumer goods' imports rather than investment goods, and at what level of trade the deficit occurs. The Polish deficit in 1993, for instance, was associated not only with a downturn in economic activity in the Community, but also with increased domestic absorption following an acceleration of public sector pay and a decline in the household savings rate. Domestic absorption is a matter for domestic macroeconomic policy. The deficit, however, should also be associated with the highest level of trade possible; in other words, to support the expected high level of imports, the associated countries will need to be able to achieve real growth in exports to the European Union. The size of the trade and current account deficits of some of the associated countries in 1996 and the first half of 1997 do, however, give rise to concerns about their financial stability. The Czech crisis in 1996 and early 1997 has been the most dramatic sign but the situation in Poland and Slovakia is worrying, too. Domestic economic policy measures are called for to raise savings in the economy. But of course further trade opening on the part of the European Union would also help.

The visible trade balance is only part of the balance of payments story. Many of the associated countries are also deeply indebted; this applies particularly to Bulgaria, Hungary and Poland. The servicing of the debt, even where it has been re-scheduled or partly forgiven, will remain a major burden for the medium and long term. The problems posed by the combination of the visible and invisible trade account and the debt transfers was neatly summed up in an OECD economic survey of Poland:[7]

Even after the debt reduction and rescheduling agreements with both the

_____

[7] OECD (1994a), p. 146.

London and Paris Clubs, Poland will remain a heavily indebted country with significant servicing commitments. At the same time, imports can be expected to exhibit an underlying tendency to increase faster than GDP, quite independently of the level of domestic absorption, as the economy is integrated into the world economy. Under these circumstances it is important that exports grow rapidly and domestic absorption remains restrained. The key question for policy will be to judge the current account deficit which would be sustainable and the degree to which foreign borrowing opportunities should be utilised. The decision will need to be influenced by the rate of return which can be earned on foreign savings (borrowings) and this will in turn depend on progress in establishing corporate behaviour oriented towards profitability.

Another reason to be careful in discussing the trade balance is that in some cases the level of unrecorded transactions may distort the statistics considerably. As an example, the unrecorded transactions with German citizens at markets inside the Polish border in 1993 were estimated to have equalled that year's recorded trade deficit of Poland with the European Union. More recently, however, these revenues have fallen with the strong real appreciation of the Zloty against the German Mark. It should be also noted that there are major differences in the statistics used by the Union (and used here) and the statistics coming from the statistical offices of the associated countries.

It is worth concluding that the deficit does not justify the associated countries from protecting against imports, but it also makes any EU protection against imports from the associated countries, including agricultural imports, extremely difficult to justify on economic grounds.

### Trade potential between the associated countries and the European Union

Trade between these two areas is growing rapidly. An important question is what is the level of trade likely to be when it has reached some sort of equilibrium level. This question has been investigated essentially by two methods: the first uses historical data from periods when trade management was less intense and the second uses various versions of gravity models.[8]

Almost all of the estimates of potential trade between the European Union and the associated countries show that actual trade is below what it should normally be. This general finding has, however, been questioned in an article by Gros and Gonciarz (1994), who conclude that 1992 trade data do not indicate any remaining CEE trade potential.[9]

The work which attempts to estimate potential trade from adjusted

[8] See Baldwin (1994) for an excellent summary of this work.
[9] Gros and Gonciarz (1994).

bilateral trade shares from 1928 and potential total trade flows suggests that potential exports to the EU-12 in 1988 were between three and four times the level of actual trade in 1988.[10] While the assumptions made in this model are heroic, it is intuitively plausible that trade patterns should return to something like the patterns when trade was last 'free', if adjustments are made for changes in relative economic performance in the intervening years. This estimate was based on pre-reform statistics, which complicates the situation considerably. Interestingly, however, the results are similar to those obtained by Baldwin and others using gravity models. Between 1988 and 1994 exports to the EU-12 did in fact grow in real terms by around 230%. This model would suggest that there is still considerable growth possible.

Gravity models work on the basis that trade is a function of size and distance. Size in this case is measured usually by GDP *per capita*. Richard Baldwin estimated the gravity equation on data from 1979 to 1988. His results show that potential exports in 1989 were between 1.2 and 5.2 times greater than actual exports, with an average for the five largest associated countries in 1989 of just under 3. Again, the gravity model has many problems associated with it, not least that it abstracts from most of the factors which are normally considered in trade equations, such as relative price, relative factor endowments, commercial policy and the trade regime, product differentiation and so on. And estimating using 1979–88 data intuitively suggests that the model might not tell us much about the situation in the medium run after the revolution. Nevertheless gravity models have proved themselves powerful instruments of analysis and prediction in the past. If Baldwin's results are to be believed, there would still be scope for future growth beyond the normal expansion of trade in coming years.

One area which is generally ignored in the discussion of potential trade flows is the development of foreign investment in the associated countries. Foreign investment flows to the associated countries have been far below what was generally expected, except in the case of Hungary. This certainly reflects the uncertainty factors linked to the transformation, the depressed state of domestic demand in the early years of reform and the attention paid in Germany to the development of the New Bundesländer. Many of these constraints are now in the process of being reduced in importance and with the current differences in the levels of wage costs and the prospect for stronger domestic demand, foreign investment should continue to rise strongly, although this will depend partly on the trade policy stance of the European

---

[10] Collins and Rodrik (1991).

Community. With increased foreign investment, trade should also rise considerably.

The result of these inconclusive attempts to look at the scope for further trade expansion suggests that there is room for export growth from the associated countries but that it should not be over-estimated. Essentially for growth in trade to continue in excess of the growth in world trade beyond the 1995 level, economic growth must remain strong in the European Union and the associated countries, thereby expanding the latter's capacity to supply exports. The growth in domestic and foreign investment in new plant and improvements in areas such as quality control and design will be crucial.

### Intra-regional trade

The European Union has always put considerable emphasis on the need to stimulate regional cooperation and regional trade within Central and Eastern Europe. The reasons behind this insistence were primarily political. The EU Member States of the Union want to see that the countries which are going to join are able to cooperate with each other. This subject has often been viewed with suspicion by the CEE countries. Some have thought that it was a crude attempt to force them back into some CMEA Mark II. Indeed, this suspicion was reinforced early on in the reform when certain leading Western politicians appeared to support a slowing down of the reforms and an artificial prolongation of the life of the CMEA. Fortunately, these ideas had no impact on the reformers in Central Europe who were not interested in keeping a system which produced shoddy goods for export to guaranteed markets.

Much nonsense has been talked about both the regional trade patterns before the revolution and the potential for trade development since. During the heyday of the CMEA system most trade was intra-CMEA trade, though, as was seen above, by 1980 the proportion of European socialist countries' trade with the CMEA area had fallen to only just over half of total trade. However, even in the 1980s trade was generally totally managed in the sense that even the trade with the capitalist world was determined centrally and was a response to certain internal problems in the region rather than an attempt to develop a dynamic foreign trade sector. The internal CMEA trade was largely with the Soviet Union rather than with other CMEA countries. The economic structures of each country reflected partially this geographic pattern of specialisation, but also the strong tendency towards autarky.

Under the new trading system which was introduced on 1 January 1991 under pressure from the Soviet Union, convertible currencies and world market prices were to replace the transferable rouble and CMEA prices, and trade between individual enterprises replaced inter-governmental agreements. Intra-CMEA trade collapsed dramatically, sending great shock-waves through the economic systems of all affected countries. Intra-regional trade amongst the CSFR, Hungary, Poland, Bulgaria and Romania collapsed from around $37,000 million in 1989 to $29,000 million in 1990, $21,000 million in 1991 and to only $3,000 million in 1993.[11] These figures probably over-state the magnitude of the decline due to problems of estimating the true flows in 1989 and 1990; nevertheless the real pain of the decline was evident everywhere in 1991 where producers in agriculture and industry saw markets they had relied on for decades disappear almost overnight. The scale of the decline for individual countries is shown in Table 3.12. This shows that trade within the CMEA bloc was very severely reduced between 1989 and 1992, with the major trade losses in Hungary and Poland clearly occurring in 1991. Interestingly, trade between the CEE socialist countries themselves declined more rapidly than that between these countries and the Soviet Union, though the differences are within the range of statistical error (table 3.13). These tables demonstrate further that while exports within the region declined, they did so from a very low 1989 level. No one should think therefore that stimulating regional trade will be any sort of solution to the economic problems of the region, although with high investment intra-industry trade should develop. Nevertheless, trade is beneficial, and every attempt should be made to develop trade integration in the region further.

The analysis by Richard Baldwin of the negative impact on the associated countries, leading to the hub and spoke trade arrangement, is certainly valid here. Baldwin points out that where a major hub, like the European Union, which dominates the economy of a region through its high purchasing power, has bilateral trade arrangements with a number of peripheral countries (the associated countries), but these countries do not have free trade amongst themselves, the location of economic activity in the hub will be favoured. A business choosing a location for a new plant and which narrows down its choice to the Union or the Czech Republic is faced with the situation that if it locates in the Union it can export (at the end of the transition period) freely anywhere within the Union or to any associated country, while if it locates in the Czech Republic it can export freely to the European Union but is faced by trade barriers if it wants to export to the other associated countries. There is therefore a bias in favour of a location in the European Union,

[11] Rudka and Mizsei (1995).

Table 3.12 *Export declines in CEE trade, 1989–93*

| | Exports ($million) | Annual growth of exports to East Europe and FSU (%) | | | | |
|---|---|---|---|---|---|---|
| | 1992 | 1989 | 1990 | 1991 | 1992 | 1993[b] |
| *CSFR* | | | | | | |
| Total | 11,656 | −3.2 | −10.5 | 5.6 | 2.9 | 15.5/−18.7 |
| East Europe[a] | 1,129 | −6.6 | −33.1 | −7.1 | 24.5 | −0.6/−25.3 |
| FSU | 1,274 | −13.9 | −25.7 | −6.0 | −42.5 | |
| *Hungary* | | | | | | |
| Total | 10,680 | −3.3 | 0.6 | 5.1 | 4.4 | −16.5 |
| East Europe[a] | 672 | −9.7 | −31.4 | −43.4 | 12.9 | −5.6 |
| FSU | 1,403 | −11.9 | −20.7 | −29.0 | 2.5 | |
| *Poland* | | | | | | |
| Total | 13,187 | 0.6 | 24.7 | −18.5 | −11.6 | 7.8 |
| East Europe[a] | 778 | −3.3 | −2.1 | −63.0 | −10.8 | 8.9 |
| FSU | 1,247 | −5.4 | 4.6 | −56.3 | −23.8 | |

*Notes:*
[a] Group includes Bulgaria, Czechoslovakia, Hungary, Poland and Romania.
[b] Data for 1993 given separately for the Czech Republic and Slovakia.
*Source:* Rudka and Mizsei (1995).

Table 3.13 *Export values in trade between CSFR, Hungary and Poland, 1989–93 ($ million at current prices)*

| | CSFR | | Hungary | | Poland | |
|---|---|---|---|---|---|---|
| | To Hungary | To Poland | To CSFR | To Poland | To CSFR | To Hungary |
| 1989 | 574 | 1224 | 487 | 304 | 742 | 216 |
| 1990 | 493 | 746 | 397 | 160 | 581 | 140 |
| 1991 | 488 | 784 | 221 | 210 | 689 | 110 |
| 1992 | 513 | 512 | 290 | 143 | 498 | 171 |
| 1993 | 506 | 511 | 298 | 163 | 510 | 174 |

*Source*: Rudka and Miszei (1995).

even if costs are higher. The creation of one or several areas of free trade in central Europe should therefore be a priority.

As a response to these needs, the four Visegrád countries created CEFTA; they were joined by Slovenia and by Romania in July 1997. CEFTA had an ambitious programme of eliminating all tariff and non-tariff barriers (NTBs) in industrial goods trade between the members (summer 1997). Recently agreement was reached also to include agricultural products. CEFTA could become a body with far wider interests, promoting the integration of CEFTA members with the European Union, though there is resistance to this idea from some members who feel that it might be considered as an alternative to EU integration. The real problem with CEFTA is that there is understandably a great resistance to creating a new bureaucracy and therefore the organisation does not have a permanent structure able to enforce rules. Without this, it is unlikely that even free trade can be permanently achieved, because it will be difficult to police competition and state aids, even though all the members are tied into EU rules through the Association Agreements.

CEFTA has only six members, and there is a question mark over its enlargement. Obviously it would be counter-productive to enlarge the organisation to countries which were not following a clear reform course or had radically different economic policies. Already there is a large range of variation in economic and monetary policies between the existing members. The extension of CEFTA should then happen only when the existing members are sure that new members will not weaken the resolve of the organisation to move quickly towards free trade. The organisation has said that to qualify new members will have to be members of WTO with their tariffs bound in the GATT and have Association Agreements with the Community.

Other regional FTAs have been created. The three Baltic countries, Estonia, Latvia and Lithuania, have created a Baltic FTA. Most countries in the region have concluded bilateral trade agreements with their neighbours, frequently including countries of the Former Soviet Union (FSU). There are clearly good trading opportunities for companies in the associated countries in their FSU neighbours, irrespective of the economic and political system which exists there. There should be no artificial barrier which shuts off the associated countries from the rest of Eastern Europe. The only limit is that none of the bilateral agreements should interfere with the establishment of free trade between the associated countries themselves, and between them and the Union.

The constraints on the development of regional trade are not only of a commercial policy nature. The lack of trade finance throughout Central and Eastern Europe is a major brake on trade and puts these countries at a grave disadvantage *vis-à-vis* Western Europe and the United States. In some cases, the imperfect regulatory framework is a problem. So, too, is the relative lack of information for exporters and services to exporters. These problems can be partly tackled through assistance from institutions such as the EBRD, WTO and the World Bank, as well as regional and national organisations. But their solution requires above all the political will within the countries themselves.

## The political economy of protection: the European Union

The previous section has shown that although there has been an important increase in the trade flows between the European Union and the associated countries since 1989, these flows remain, at the aggregate level, very small. Looked at on the theoretical level, it is almost inconceivable that integration should not lead to an important growth stimulus through trade for both the European Union and the associated countries. For integration to have a negative impact, the trade diversion effects would have to reach proportions which are almost impossible to imagine.

Yet there is considerable opposition in the European Union to trade opening towards Central and Eastern Europe. The literature on the political economy of protection is extensive, and explains much of the opposition to trade opening which has occurred in recent years. More importantly, it predicts where opposition is likely to come from in the future as enlargement of the European Union becomes a major political issue. Reference should be made to a collection of extremely interesting articles on this subject, edited by Riccardo Faini and Richard Portes, which explores these issues in depth.[12]

### *The economics of political economy*

Realistically, there should be no demand for protection of the EU market against imports from the associated countries, when the picture is considered at the level of the economy in general. This has been shown in the previous section in the consideration of total flows of goods, sectoral and regional flows and in terms of the visible trade balance. This has also been confirmed in a series of analyses on France, Spain and Greece, which found no reason for those three countries to worry about increasing trade with the associated countries.[13]

It is most important to realise that there is a market for protectionism. One of the most successful lobby groups for protection in Western countries, the farmers, form a relatively small group in the population and contribute an even smaller percentage to GDP. While the cost to agriculture of mounting major protection campaigns is high, this is dwarfed by the income redistribution to farmers represented by the Common Agricultural Policy (CAP). On the other hand, granting protection to agriculture is not costly for the government, as it is equal

---

[12] Faini and Portes (1995).      [13] Faini and Portes (1995).

to a very small loss of welfare for the other 95% or 97% of the population who are not farmers. Often in the associated countries the sale of protection has been very direct, and paid for through inward investment. The clearest case is that of cars, where in return for inward investment the Western car makers have been granted tariff protection – frequently the car firms have made it clear that without such protection they would not invest. Protectionism is therefore about appropriating part of national income for a particular sector or region at the cost of other participants in the economy, usually the consumer.

Most demands for protection have come from narrow industry pressure groups. Agriculture is the prime example, but looking at the requests for anti-dumping measures or safeguards leading to investigations in 1993 and 1994, one can add specific basic chemical products, the iron and steel industry and cement. Certain areas predicted by Neven (1995) as protection seekers have not been active. Textiles is one such area where, however, both the specific textiles agreement and the operation of outward processing reduces tension considerably. It is to be seen if the expiry of these agreements in 1997 will lead to renewed pressure for specific protection. It is too early to see any development of protectionist pressures in the automobile industry in the Community. As most investment in the associated countries in this industry has come from Community companies, it is probable that demands for protection will be muted and restricted to companies without major interests in the region.

Interestingly, almost all the requests for protection have indeed come from the Northern countries in the Community. This is partly of course a response to geography as these countries absorb the largest part of the imports from Central Europe. Otherwise there have been few if any demands for protection at the regional level. Perhaps the one exception might be considered to be Portugal, which has resisted attempts to liberalise more quickly in the clothing and textile areas. Portugal, however, with a very constructive approach to European integration, has rarely pushed its case to the bitter end. It does, however, illustrate Neven's analysis that an abundance of small countries will tend to raise the demand for protectionism.

### The politics of political economy

Institutionally the European Union is more open to protectionist pressures than normal Member State governments. This occurs because of the absence of a government with collective responsibility for policy decisions, because of the rules governing decisions in the Council and because of the imperfection of information flows. In a normal democratic nation state, a minister who wishes to propose a protectionist measure has to convince not only those who may suffer from it in his own area of responsibility, but also the other government ministers in cabinet. There is therefore a control on the degree of protectionism which any sector or region can obtain, because the decision will be taken as a collective decision, which at least theoretically ensures that all sectors and all regions are taken into account.

At the Community level, there is no government and no cabinet. The institution which gets closest to this is the European Commission, where the Commissioners, each with a different portfolio, meet on a weekly basis. The Commission does take some decisions in its own right where power has been delegated to it, for instance in competition policy and state-aids control. However the Commission does not decide on most really important matters but makes proposals to be decided by the Council and the Parliament. In the European Council there are only specific sectoral councils. The Council of agricultural ministers makes decisions in agriculture without reference to the Council of industry ministers or, except in times of crisis, the finance ministers. As sectoral ministers are sometimes just as much 'captured' by their sectors as are their civil servants, there is a tendency for each sectoral Council to cede to demands coming from its sector without reference to other Councils.

It may be objected at this stage that each sectoral minister comes to Brussels with a decision which has been discussed in cabinet in his home country and therefore there is a sort of consensus building which has gone on before the meeting in Brussels. This is, however, a perfectionist view of the world which is right in major questions, but not in small matters of a little additional protection here and there. The result is then that the sectoral councils tend to be far more protectionist than national governments, especially those in the large countries.

This effect is intensified by two further phenomena. The important role of small countries has been mentioned above but it is worth mentioning here from another angle. Small countries are not only more likely than large ones to raise protectionist issues, they are also often completely unaffected by protectionist measures proposed by other countries, because of the small size of their economies and the fact that many sectors may not be present. In this case trade-offs are possible where smaller countries agree to support others on one point in return for support on another. Logically, this could work in favour of promoting liberal trade regimes, but in fact horsetrading of this kind in practice almost always leads to a more protectionist outcome.

Secondly there is always a strong desire from the Presidency to avoid voting on issues but to look for consensus, even in areas where majority voting is the rule. In the context of Community solidarity this is good; it does, however, frequently lead to compromises which are not satisfactory to anyone, where the wishes of one or two states have been allowed to dominate over the desire of the majority. This also favours protectionist measures, opening the Council to special pleading.

Information flows on proposals to increase protection are usually better at the nation state than at the Community level. This is because the media is national and geared to reporting national events. It is also because in general national governments are better at disseminating proposals and information through a well established network of national NGOs and business organisations than is the case of the Community Institutions with a much younger and less well developed network. While the situation today at the Community level is far better than it was at the beginning of the campaign to complete the internal market in 1985, it is still far from perfect, with the result that matters decided in the Council of Ministers are often less subjected to public discussion than national decisions. Under these circumstances it is easier for special pleading to succeed at the Community than at the national level.

## The tools of EU commercial policy

The commercial policy of the European Union is a Community policy, applicable throughout the Union without exception; title 7 of the Treaty establishing the European Community. The essential article 113 describes the mechanisms which are used to make decisions on the common commercial policy. The Commission has the key role as the source of proposals to the Council and as negotiator on behalf of the Community in international negotiations. The Community, as an original member and signatory to the agreement establishing the WTO is of course subject to its rules. The Association Agreements, being preferential agreements, are not bound by the rules of the WTO, but are by definition assumed to give advantages over other third countries in trade relations with the Union. This is true in terms of access to the Community market in industrial products; it is not so clear in the application of commercial defence mechanisms.

The commercial defence mechanisms in the Association Agreements have been dealt with above. Of the different measures – anti-dumping, anti-subsidy and safeguards – anti-dumping has clearly been the most important in the past, though safeguards are the most dangerous in the sense that they can be imposed with little procedure and very rapidly.

This makes them a potential threat leading to reversibility of trade liberalisation. These commercial safeguards are not simply a vicious European invention. They are in certain ways less arbitrary than the American rules (for instance in anti-subsidy cases), they have always been used in a GATT compatible way and they are now backed by the new improved rules of the WTO. This does not, however, justify their liberal use against countries in the difficult process of transition and prospective candidates for accession to the Community.

The Community's anti-dumping regulation has been changed following the agreement on dumping in the Uruguay Round; these modifications are however unlikely to make significant changes to procedures.[14] The basic elements of the regulation are as follows:

- A complaint can be made to the Commission by any natural or legal person or by any Association acting on behalf of Community industry. The opening of an investigation to determine whether dumping is actually taking place is then initiated.
- A distinction is made between non-market economies and market economies. With the former the regulation allows latitude to the Commission's services to establish the normal price. However the associated countries have been treated as market economies since the signing of the Association Agreements.
- A normal value is calculated based on prices paid or payable, in the ordinary course of trade, by independent customers in the exporting country. There are rules which give some discretion in the calculation of this normal value, especially where the good is not traded in substantial quantities on the exporter's home market.
- The export price is the actual price paid or payable for the product when sold from the exporting country to the Community.
- A comparison is made between the normal price and the export price under specific rules laid down in the regulation, and the dumping margin is calculated.
- Material injury or the threat of material injury to Community industry is assessed, where both the terms 'material injury' and 'Community industry' are defined in the regulation.
- Provisional measures may be taken starting 60 days after the

[14] EC Council Regulation, 3283/94 (22 December 1994). The Community has, however, set new deadlines for itself for the different stages of an anti-dumping procedure, and is doubling the number of staff working in the anti-dumping service.

initiation of the proceedings, once a provisional affirmative determination of dumping has been made.

- When dumping has been established, either dumping duties, with a maximum level of the established dumping margin, or price undertakings from the exporter can be imposed.
- At the end of the regulation, article 21 introduces the notion of 'Community interest'. Before measures are taken, the Commission is expected to make an assessment of the impact of the measures on the whole Community (the article specifically mentions consumers). This article has rarely been seriously used.

The statistical evaluation of the scope of dumping penalties (duties or price undertakings) suggests that they are insignificant. In 1992 anti-dumping measures were in force on only 0.36% of industrial imports from the six CEE countries, ranging from 0.05% in the former Czechoslovakia (where, however, safeguards were being applied to steel products) to 1.42% in Romania.[15] Between 1990 and 1994 measures had been imposed in respect of the Central and East European countries in only 15 cases, however this was roughly the same as the number of measures against Japan.[16]

The only sort of dumping which can be considered an economic threat to the rational allocation of resources in the Community is predatory dumping.[17] This is when an exporter sets out to gain a dominant position on the Community market through dumping, with the objective of gaining monopoly rents. Such activity is clearly anti-competitive and strong action should be taken to prevent it. However predatory dumping is probably extremely rare. Patrick Messerlin and Jacques Bourgeois screened 297 cases of Community-initiated anti-dumping cases between 1980 and 1989 to determine how many of them could possibly be predatory.[18] The result of a careful analysis was that only seven cases or 2% could be considered for a closer examination for possible predatory behaviour.

It is extremely difficult to believe that predatory dumping could be practised by companies from the associated countries. Setting prices below short-run marginal cost for a sufficient period to drive out competitors and gain monopoly power would require resources that the companies of Central Europe are most unlikely to possess. They normally do not have a large enough share of the market as a base, the

[15] European Commission, *European Economy, Supplement A*, no. 7 (Brussels, July 1994).
[16] European Commission (1995e).
[17] Nagarajan (1994).       [18] OECD (1994c).

organisational capacity to maintain such a campaign over some period, the power to prevent entry or the financial resources to sustain losses.

If dumping is not predatory, it is difficult to make an economic case against it. If foreign countries wish to transfer resources to the Community, as long as there is no predatory intent, this can only benefit the Community at the expense of the exporting company. However even if the strict economic reasoning is considered to be somewhat *'weltfremd'*, it must be shown that dumping is taking place – i.e. that the 'normal value' is above the 'export price' and that this is causing 'material injury' to domestic industry. And, as seen above, the whole Community interest should be taken into account. Even under the new WTO code and the new EU Regulation, there is sufficient flexibility given to civil servants to use anti-dumping as a political instrument serving narrow interests. The hard fact is that the history of Community anti-dumping policy has seen the legal dominate over the economic and the Community interest submerged beneath the narrow interests of the special pleaders.

There are several general aspects of the way the Community uses the anti-dumping instrument which have been much criticised. The first is the degree of secrecy which exists, which makes it especially difficult for accused firms to defend themselves. Then the methods used in calculating the various elements of normal value, export price and doing the comparison between them and measuring injury are all open to criticism, especially in the case of countries classed as non-market economy countries.

One of the most serious criticisms is that the structure of the market seems to play no role in determining injury. Where firms in the Community enjoy monopoly rents, the Community price will be higher that in a competitive market. The measure of the dumping margin and the measure of injury (if determined by price under-cutting) will be greatly exaggerated. In such a case, the exporter will be working very much in the Community interest to bring more competition into the sector. In 1994, a typical case of an attempt to use anti-dumping to maintain a monopoly situation in the Community market was the complaint of an Association of cement producers against producers in the Czech Republic, Poland and Slovakia. Firms in this industrial federation were some time later fined for price fixing in the Community by the Commission. This was a clear case of the use of the anti-dumping weapon for narrow private gain against the interests of consumers in the Community.

There are, however, several specific reasons why anti-dumping is more significant for the associated countries than the statistics above would seem to show. Firstly the regular use of the threat of anti-dumping can reduce confidence and therefore investment in industries which form the basis for export growth in the early phases of transition. This has various aspects:

- It is not the conclusion of the anti-dumping enquiry but the opening of an enquiry which does the damage to the companies affected. As exports of products affected by measures usually decline by 50% in the immediate period after measures are taken, the simple opening of an investigation weakens the companies likely to be affected. In the associated countries, where there is little knowledge of the intricacies of Community anti-dumping policy, just the threat of a complaint gives commercial power to EU businesses which can damage potential competitors (and work against the Community interest!). This will reduce confidence and investment in the affected firms and hit exports.
- The same threat will tend to reduce the level of foreign investment. Both Community SMEs and third country businesses will take the threat of commercial defence instruments into account when making decisions on foreign investments. A Japanese company, for instance, looking for a manufacturing base to serve the European market, may well decide for a location inside the Community rather than one in Central Europe because of the fear of being locked out of the EU market through relatively arbitrary commercial defence instruments.

It is therefore the very existence of the anti-dumping weapon and the knowledge that the European Union is always prepared to use it which does much of the damage.

Secondly during the crucial early years of the transition process from a centrally-planned economy to a market economy, the use of anti-dumping against the associated countries has a psychological impact which affects economic policy. Through the use of anti-dumping, often in dubious circumstances (for instance, to maintain monopoly rents for EU producers within the European Union), the credibility of market reforms is put in doubt. The reversal in early open trading policies in many associated countries is partially the result of the observation that the European Union is not an open liberal trader, in agriculture through the CAP and in industrial products through contingent protection. Yet the reversal of liberal trade policies threatens to delay reform and recovery in these countries.

Thirdly the cases of suspected anti-dumping against CEE countries are concentrated in a few sectors, as suggested by Neven's analysis mentioned above. These sectors, for instance steel and basic chemicals, are potentially key export sectors for the associated countries, at least in the early years of the transition. The effective reduction of exports in these sectors (where anti-dumping has not been available, safeguards have been invoked, as in the Czech case) has led to an important hard currency loss to these countries at a crucial time in their development.

Fourthly the companies targeted by anti-dumping complaints in these countries are usually financially weak and cannot defend themselves. They also frequently have accounts and records which are considered inadequate by the dumping inquiry. Concepts are often different to those used in the European Union. The result is that the officials making the investigation often have to construct elements of the normal value artificially. This then becomes an extremely complex operation, which the accused companies find impossible to follow or to oppose.

Finally there are elements of the transition which can lead to arbitrary or simply incorrect results in the anti-dumping inquiry. High variability in exchange rates, frequent devaluations (sometimes monthly under crawling peg systems) make it difficult to keep export prices stable, which can lead to lower export prices being measured than have really been charged over a longer time frame. There are also uncertainties about what the prices of public utilities or of energy really mean, in a situation where prices are being liberalised. There is also the question of depreciation on already depreciated assets. All these uncertainties leave everything open for the anti-dumping instrument to become a protectionist instrument.[19]

Faced by such instruments, a popular topic of technical assistance has become how to avoid anti-dumping measures. An unfortunate by-product of this is of course to encourage anti-competitive behaviour in economies which are in the process of adapting to a competitive market economy with properly contested markets. The typical advice that is given enterprises in Central Europe is to avoid under-cutting West European prices. Analysis of past cases has shown that the Commission's dumping margin is biased in favour of Community producers, therefore the best hope for exporters is to concentrate on the injury criteria. As the injury margin is not a very scientific calculation and usually based on the level of price under-cutting, it is advisable for exporters to concentrate on not undercutting prices. Vandenbussche concludes, 'this means that the mere threat of antidumping measures

---

[19] A very interesting account of the problems encountered by operators in CEE countries coping with anti-dumping actions and the sometimes strange way in which normal values or export prices are calculated is given in OECD (1994b). The paper was written by Dr Ewa Kaliszuk.

can serve as a means to shelter European producers from foreign price competition but at the expense of European consumer's welfare'.[20]

The other instruments of commercial defence, anti-subsidy and safeguards do not have the same high profile as anti-dumping but they are nevertheless important. Safeguards were imposed on iron and steel imports from the Czech and Slovak Republic in 1992 and were changed into tariff quotas for the period 1993–5. The problem with safeguards is that the clauses in the Association Agreements allow safeguards to be implemented at short notice and with little justification being given. In a period of recession the present restraint might give way to their more widespread use.

There are perhaps three main criticisms of the use of the European Union's instruments of commercial defence: it has caused damage to the economies of the associated countries at a particularly important time in their transition to market economies, caused the agents in these economies to doubt the wisdom of trade liberalisation and had a negative impact on the voters in these countries in relation to government policy of seeking closer relations with the European Union.

The Essen Summit made two small moves to recognise these weaknesses, but these initiatives were watered down by the protectionist majority in the Union. The first was to promise to give the governments of the associated countries prior information on dumping cases which concern them before the opening of the investigation. The second was gradually to reduce the use of contingent protection instruments as the associated countries implement Community competition law and control state aids. It would indeed be much more sensible to push hard for the implementation of competition policy and the control of state aids in the associated countries than to use the anti-dumping instrument. If this was to become the Community's policy, it would help the transformation to a market economy and improve competitive conditions on EU markets.

Recently the Commission has taken significant steps to make commercial policy fairer but it is meeting considerable resistance from some of the more protectionist Member States and sectors.

### Liberalisation and renewed protectionism in central Europe[21]

In all the countries of Central Europe, the first phase of the transition to a market economy was marked by trade liberalisation. This was an

---

[20] Vandenbussche (1995).     [21] OECD (1993).

important element of the move to the market economy and above all, through bearing down on monopolistic production in the domestic market, contributed to the creation of contested markets and to the fight to reduce inflation during the stabilisation phase of economic reform. Poland, for instance, through its new customs law of 1989 and associated regulations completely freed trade from government monopoly and created current account convertibility of the Zloty and also reduced the average unweighted rate of customs duties to around 5% at the end of 1990 through the suspension of tariffs on 60% of duty items, probably the most liberal regime in Europe. The Czech and Slovak Republic took the same liberal course, leading to a simple average tariff of 5.9%, but in contrast to Poland it bound 97% of tariffs in the GATT. Hungary also reduced its protection in 1991, but much less radically, from 16% to 13% average tariff .

In spite of the efforts of the Finance Minister Leszek Balcerowicz to resist a hike in tariffs in 1991, the average level of Polish customs duties rose to 16% on 1 August 1991.[22] The new customs tariff contained a series of bands from 0% to 45% for most items, but rising to 120% for tobacco products and 145% for certain alcohols. Industrial goods bore in general a tariff of 20%. Romania and Bulgaria in 1992 also raised their tariffs sharply to levels roughly similar to those of Poland. Only the Czech and Slovak Republic, through the binding of its tariffs, avoided any serious increase in tariffs.

However renewed protectionism in the associated countries since 1991 has not only been reflected in tariff hikes but also in the use of less transparent NTBs. These have become an important part of the foreign trade regime of the associated countries and an important part of the disagreements between them and the European Union. National certification and quality control systems have been reinforced, frontier charges to pay for 'administrative costs', export restrictions and other measures now contribute to making the trade regimes less transparent.

The reasons for this change in attitude to trade liberalisation are of both domestic and foreign origin. The increases in 1991 were to some extent explained by the impact of subsidised EU agricultural products swamping the domestic market and the supposed need to raise tariffs before fixing them in the Association Agreements. With tariffs on the import of agricultural produce low in 1990 and 1991, the Community was able to export with export subsidies to under-cut local produce. On all the local markets in Central Europe at this time, Community produce was pushing out local produce, which was often badly packaged

---

[22] Warsaw School of Economics (1994).

and marketed. Considerable pressure built up for countervailing measures to be taken against subsidised imports. In countries with a large agricultural constituency, this pressure was hard to resist.

The general rise in tariffs, however, could also be explained by the negotiation of the Association Agreements. As was seen above, these agreements include a standstill clause, which prohibits increases in tariffs from the entry into force of the agreements. It is from these basic tariffs that the reductions listed in the agreements apply. In an attempt to increase the asymmetry of the agreements as much as possible, the governments raised tariffs before the conclusion of the negotiations.

There are, however, many reasons for recent protectionist behaviour associated with the practice and institutions of trade law in the central European countries.[23] One of the important points raised by Patrick Messerlin is that trade laws often have low legal status in the associated countries and can therefore be more easily influenced by powerful pressure groups.[24] Very often trade laws date from the period before 1989 and have simply been amended to eliminate reference to the planned economy. The gaps in the laws have been filled by government decrees or even ministerial regulations. This allows trade policy decisions to be taken at quite low levels in the bureaucracy, with totally opaque alliances between the administration and business being built up. Agency capture in these circumstances will come to be quite common; this brings the danger that uncompetitive state industries can negotiate increased protection for themselves much more easily than if trade laws had a higher standing in the hierarchy of law.

Protectionist forces find it easier to realise their goals in situations of political instability than in stable periods.[25] This is particularly true in some of the associated countries, where falls in living standards in the first years of the transition left many voters wanting to apply the brakes to reform. As unemployment has risen in all countries (except, until recently, in the Czech Republic where protectionist demands have indeed been less), the threat of closure to large state enterprises has become a potent weapon to prise out protection from often-changing governments. The general disillusionment with the reform process, combined in some cases with strong nationalistic tendencies, has added to these pressures. Such pressure is understandable but must be resisted, protection usually being offered to uncompetitive enterprises and therefore having a negative impact on resource allocation. While it is clear that attention in the transition must be paid to alleviating the social

---

[23] A very instructive series of essays on this subject is to be found in Winters (1995).
[24] Messerlin (1995), pp. 40–63.        [25] Csaba (1995), pp. 64–88.

consequences of change, and that this indeed in some cases may warrant measures to make change more gradual in specific circumstances, using trade restrictions is rarely the best way. In confused political situations, however, these pressures can be much more effective as politicians are prepared to pick up any cause which they think will make them popular.

As in all countries there is a strong demand for protectionism in the associated countries from both domestic and foreign firms. One of the main roles of managers under the communist system was to lobby bureaucrats for more resources, more realistic plan targets, more foreign exchange, and so on. Although this type of thinking was interrupted at the beginning of the transition, it still lives on in some minds. An interesting documented case is that of the famous Gdansk shipyard, now bankrupt.[26]

But foreign companies as well have been at the forefront of demands for protection. Most of the large Western companies have negotiated higher tariff protection with governments before agreeing to invest in their countries. This has been common in the car industry, where tariffs have been raised under direct pressure from EU companies. Imports of cars are subjected to well above average duty levels in Poland (35%), Hungary (13–18%), Romania (30%). The extremely bizarre arrangement between the European Union and Poland made in 1992, which gave a duty-free tariff quota of 25,000 cars with catalytic converters and 5,000 without, was clearly made to satisfy Western car companies which have invested in Poland. The fact that Poland excluded its car tariffs from its Uruguay Round offer was also certainly influenced by its desire to retain and attract Western car makers. Unfortunately until recently this has the effect of keeping out more efficient Asian producers. Very recently, however, with the prospect of accession, both Suzuki and Daewoo have made significant investments.

A key to preserving a 'sound' trade policy in any country, including the associated countries, is to make sure that the institutions dealing with trade policy have horizontal responsibilities and that trade policy is dealt with at the highest level on the basis of good trade laws. This means that trade policy should be made by the executive branch not by the legislature, where specific regional and sectoral interests have their (sometimes paid) representatives. Within the executive, the worst institutions are surely the sectoral ministries like industry and agriculture, where many of the officials, and indeed ministers identify with the aims and objectives expressed by the sector. Clearly horizontal agencies are better adapted for dealing with trade policy and in all cases national

[26] Johnson and Loveman (1995).

competition offices also need to be deeply involved in the making of trade policy.

One aim of the Association Agreements was to prevent protectionism, but there are at least two areas where the agreements have failed in this respect. As has been mentioned, the Association Agreements instituted a tariff standstill from the signing of the agreements; this standstill includes tariff equivalent measures and QRs. There are, however, exceptions made for the associated countries in certain situations. The countries can take protective measures if the objective is to help infant industries, sectors undergoing restructuring or facing serious difficulty, especially where major social problems are involved, as we saw above. Both Hungary and Poland have based most of their increases in tariffs on this clause in the agreements. The agreement of the Community side is not required though both countries, and especially Hungary, have tried to get EU agreement. This special safeguard clause has introduced, for a transitional period, a degree of flexibility which encourages protectionism.

Secondly, in agriculture the agreements put no real brake on increasing agricultural protectionism. As long as measures are taken in the context of the country's overall agricultural policy, they can be taken at will. This laxity is the fault of the Community, which wished to grant itself complete freedom within the CAP, and it has led to the introduction by some countries of CAP-like schemes of protection, against which interestingly the Community has protested.

While it is clear that the Association Agreements were not decisive in liberalising trade, indeed they led to tariff hikes on the associated country side, nevertheless they have had an impact in dampening the rise of protection since 1991 in spite of the above provisos.[27] They have certainly made the introduction of new measures more difficult, if only because all trade measures which are not in conformity with the agreements must be brought to the Association Council/Committee for discussion. That they have been effective is also attested to by the regional discrimination which has been characteristic of the associated countries' trade policy over recent years. Non-EU third countries have faced far higher protectionist barriers than EU countries. Indeed the associated countries have become quite active in using contingent protection measures, but almost exclusively against other associated countries or against countries of the FSU. The use of these instruments is likely to increase now that the associated countries have tied most of their tariffs in the GATT.

[27] Sapir (1995).

There is no doubt that the associate countries (possibly with the exception of the Czech Republic, the Slovak Republic and Estonia) have become more protectionist since 1991, in spite of the Association Agreements. This is a route which leads to the misallocation of resources and to slower structural change. The European Union has not been the most helpful trading partner in encouraging a more open approach towards sound trade policies. Through its trade arrangements, especially in agriculture, but also through its use of contingent protection and its use of state aid, it has given a poor example to the countries of Central Europe.

Many trade experts maintain that the associated countries would have been better served by the new GATT (1994) and GATS than the Association Agreements as far as trade is concerned. They feel that the Association Agreements have the disadvantage of discouraging trade with areas outside the Community, leading to inefficiencies and mis-allocation of resources. They also feel that the restraints on protectionist behaviour are not sufficient in the agreements. Such a severe criticism of the Association Agreements is probably unjust and politically unrea-listic, but it raises the whole question of the merits of regional trade agreements (RTAs) as opposed to the developing international regula-tion of trade problems, a subject which goes well beyond that of this book.

### Conclusion: trade policy strategy

Politically, more damage has been done to the relationship between the Union and the associated countries by petty trade disputes than by any other single event. While the setting of high minimum prices on sour cherry imports from Hungary and Poland passes without notice in the West European press, it makes the headlines in Central Europe, where it is interpreted as the real face of the Union. At the political level, too, the new generation of politicians in these countries was shocked by the apparent lack of support for the transformation of their economies which was evident in the protectionist behaviour of the Union in even the smallest detail of trade. This attitude certainly led to a loss of confidence in the Union amongst Central Europeans, but more impor-tantly it stimulated the re-birth of protectionism in the region itself. Agricultural protectionism was usually at fault, supported by some particularly bizarre positions taken by the European Union in negotia-tions. Again agency capture and root prejudice has done immense damage.

On the brink of the opening of negotiations on membership these positions seem strange. It has been shown that imports from Central Europe pose no threat to EU Member States: indeed, trade integration will be of benefit to the Union. On the side of the associated countries renewed protectionism is partly a reaction to the severe rise in unemployment which has occurred following the reforms. Reform has been particularly hard on certain groups in the population who have not been able to adapt to the new environment. Nevertheless protecting uncompetitive sectors is not likely to lead to higher growth and employment in the future.

A strategy for trade development which would at the same time advance the reform process in Central Europe and benefit the European Union would include the following elements:

- the Union and the associated countries should both announce that they will restrict the use of anti-dumping actions to cases where predatory dumping can be shown to be present, and where injury is clearly demonstrable
- the Union should clearly lay out what it means by the Essen Summit statement that it will progressively reduce its commercial defence instruments as the associated countries implement competition policy and the control of state aids and begin to take on the *acquis communautaire* in the area of the internal market
- the Union should give much more attention to the market structure in the Union and to the criterion of Community interest when dealing with anti-dumping
- safeguards should be made more difficult to implement, and should require a far more detailed justification
- competition policy should be made the key to getting rid totally of contingent protection
- the associated countries should agree not to use the specific safeguard for industrial goods unless the EU side agrees
- the associated countries should be encouraged and helped to bring forward the liberalisation agreed in CEFTA and to extend the geographical scope of the organisation; CEFTA should have a permanent secretariat with the power to enforce the agreement.

# 4 The creation of the market economy: competition, factor movements and economic cooperation in the Association Agreements

## Introduction

Following the important trade articles in the Association Agreements, those dealing with the establishment and functioning of the market economy appear much less structured and in a way less important. This is far from the truth. The paragraphs on competition policy, the control of state aids, the protection of intellectual property, on establishment, the movement of workers and capital and trade in services are some of the most important in the whole agreement, with far-reaching economic consequences. Through these articles the European Community has encouraged the associated countries to implement rules which are essential for the functioning of the market economy. At the same time, they have adopted the main elements of a business environment which is similar to that within the Union, with positive effects on investment and growth.

This chapter investigates these areas of the agreements, although it is still a little early to give a balanced account of how the articles are working in practice. This is more easily done for the competition and state-aids areas because the associated countries quickly began to implement these policies, which were considered vital for the reform of the economic system. In establishment, where the Community has been relatively liberal, the first cases of dispute are arising in the Association Committees. The Member States realised at a rather late stage that they had been more liberal in this area during the negotiations than they had supposed. The consequence is that there has been a boom in the establishment of individuals and companies from the associated countries in certain of the Member States, with naturally a small number of conflicts arising.

Several of these areas are intimately linked. Establishment and the supply of services, for instance, both depend on there being a degree of labour mobility if they are going to be of full value to both parties.

Establishment also requires the recognition of diplomas and professional qualifications and the existence of visa freedom.

### Transformation and the foundations of the market economy

The fundamental characteristics of the market economy obviously did not exist in the associated countries prior to the beginnings of reform in 1989. These fundamentals ensure that markets are contested fairly and freely in order that resources are allocated in an efficient way. These requirements involve government regulation of the framework within which the market mechanisms operate and the policing of this framework, but they also involve the government refraining from interfering with market mechanisms once these have been established. The basic tools of this framework are competition policy, anti-subsidy policy and the rules which define the operation of the national (internal) market (for instance, rules governing the operation of the banking system or rules establishing minimum standards for products).

The cornerstones of this regulation were absent in the legal base of the previous centrally-planned regimes and had to be created from scratch. This is worth restating because the old market economies take their basic rules for granted and assume that they are very easily translated and applied in other economies. This is not the case, and old thinking on occasion tends to surface automatically in the most reform-minded individuals, just as national protectionist thinking still exists in the most liberal politicians in the Union's internal market.

By definition, competition policy was unnecessary under central planning since there was no market and companies usually had to meet quantitative objectives with set allocations of resources. The control of state aids was also unnecessary because the state existed to distribute state aid: one of the main qualities of a company manager was to be able to maximise the amount of state aid obtained. Other important areas of regulation such as the protection of intellectual property were also not applied satisfactorily, the associated countries not being party to the international agreements on such matters.

The early reformers realised the importance of immediately creating competition offices to administer new competition law and of cutting state subsidies savagely (though often without a system to control state aids being put in place). The Polish government programme of October 1989 stated 'In order to set up an environment conducive to competition in the economy, an active anti-monopoly policy will be pursued. The anti-monopoly agency will be set apart from the structure of the

Ministry of Finance and will be given more extensive powers.' The anti-subsidy message also went strongly through the whole programme.

Competition and subsidy policy was seen by the reformers as having an important role in the reform in several respects. The primary objective was clearly to reduce the power of monopolies, both the old state enterprises and the possible new monopolies springing up after privatisation. Stripping away subsidies from the state sector would also tend to move market structures in the same direction. These measures would help the shift towards more competitive management systems, preparing the way for the economy to raise productivity from the extremely low levels of the pre-reform period. They would therefore bear down on inflation and reduce the government deficit, again leading to less pressure for inflationary financing.

The pressure against the implementation of competition and anti-subsidy rules in the associated countries was always strong. It was therefore very important to establish independent cartel offices which had real independent power. This was extremely difficult to achieve even in the most liberal environments immediately after the revolution. It was therefore all the more important that the Association Agreements put real pressure on governments to ensure that both the regulation and implementation of competition policy was done in a way which prepared the countries for accession.

### What the Association Agreements say

#### Competition and state aids

The inclusion of competition law and the control of state aids was an innovation in the Association Agreements and marked them off clearly from other agreements which had gone before. There were probably three main reasons for their inclusion:

- the first agreements were drafted at a period when competition policy was beginning to be seen as a crucial element in new efforts to liberalise world trade and as a substitute for traditional commercial policy instruments (although the agreements contain both)
- the Community was very afraid of competition from countries where traditionally there had been a dominance of monopoly producers and a generalisation of state aids
- the associated countries required support through agreements with the Community for their efforts to establish this regulatory framework as a cornerstone of the market economy.

The agreements follow closely the rules of the Union Treaty, reproducing articles 85, 86 and 92 of that Treaty as one article of the agreements. Article 85 forbids agreements and concerted practices between undertakings which have as their object the prevention, restriction or distortion of competition. Article 86 prevents the abuse by one or more undertakings of a dominant position in the territories of the Community or of the associated country as a whole or in a substantial part. Finally article 92 forbids any public aid which distorts or threatens to distort competition by favouring certain undertakings or the production of certain goods. On all of these articles, the agreements say that the assessment of practices contrary to these articles will be based on the criteria arising from the application of these articles within the Community: in other words, Community case law will be applied.

The associated countries agreed to introduce the rules to implement articles 85, 86 and 92 within three years and that these rules would be adopted by the Association Councils. Of course, these rules affect only trade between the Union and the associated countries. They do not prevent the associated countries from introducing different rules to deal with domestic trade or, indeed, trade with other geographical areas.

In the area of state aids, the agreements are more precise. It is stated that during the first five years of the transition period (until the end of 1999 for the three Baltic countries), state aid to the associated country will be assessed on the basis of article 92(3)(a) of the Treaty establishing the European Community. This article allows aid to promote the economic development of areas where the standard of living is abnormally low or where there is serious under-employment. This possibility is subject to certain limits, which are, however, quite generous. The highest level of aid allowed has been fixed at 75% of the net grant equivalent of initial investment or alternatively a ceiling of ECU13,000 per job created. Even operating aids may be allowed within very strict limits. With the agreement of the Association Council the benefits of article 92(3)(a) can be extended for further periods of five years (three years in the case of Estonia). As the possibility of giving regional aids is permanent and part of the Treaty creating the Community, it must be presumed likely that extensions will be granted, as long as the associated countries remain at levels of GDP per head well below the Community average.

The agreements also state that the provisions restricting the use of public aids do not apply to either agriculture or fishing and that any competition cases involving agreements between undertakings in these sectors should be dealt with according to the relevant articles 42 and 43 of the Treaty. These general competition and state aid rules do not apply to the ECSC sector, where a specific Protocol of the agreements applies. These specific rules are similar to the general articles covering state aids but instead of referring to article 92(3)(a) they lay down that state aid may be given to these sectors for the first five years of the agreement as long as the aid is given for restructuring purposes and:

- is linked to a restructuring programme which encompasses global rationalisation and reduction of capacity
- leads to the viability of the benefiting firms under normal market conditions at the end of the restructuring period
- is limited to what is absolutely necessary to ensure viability and is degressive.

Both the general state-aid articles and the specific ECSC Protocol have rules governing transparency through 'full and continuous' exchange of information. The general state-aid clause in the agreements specifies that this transparency will be ensured '*inter alia* by each side reporting annually to the other party on the total amount and the distribution of aid given and by providing, upon request, information on aid schemes, including information on particular individual cases of public aid'. In the specific area of coal and steel aids the agreement states that this information should include the amount of the aid, its intensity and purpose and a detailed restructuring plan.

In both the general state-aid articles and the specific ECSC articles, a safeguard clause permits the aggrieved party to take appropriate measures where it is considered that either the competition clauses or those relating to state aid are not being applied as laid down in the agreements. These measures are taken after consultation in the Association Council or after 30 working days following the referral of the matter for such consultation. Measures can therefore be taken unilaterally and rapidly.

As far as public undertakings or undertakings to which special powers have been granted, the agreements lay down that the Association Council will ensure that the rules established by article 90 of the Treaty establishing the Community should apply, within three years of the entry into force of the agreements (beginning of 1998 for the three Baltic countries).

### Intellectual property rights

The protection of intellectual, industrial and commercial property rights is an area which at the world level has proved very difficult to achieve. Even within the Community, problems persist. With the absence of any real enforcement of intellectual property rights in most of the associated countries before the revolution, the Member States of the Community were particularly keen to see that a start was made to reinforce such protection.

The Association agreements tackle this question from two angles. Firstly the agreements lay down that the associated countries will improve property rights in order to provide, within five years from the entry into force of the agreements (or the end of 1999 in the case of the three Baltic countries), a level of protection equivalent to that which exists in the European Community, including the enforcement of these rights. This gives, at the same time, a measurable objective to track progress in the implementation of such rights and a legal basis for governments which meet opposition to such protection to overcome this opposition.

The second track followed by the agreements is to insist that the associated countries apply to join the key international agreements on the protection of property rights within a five-year period. This is sensible, because there is a long history of agreements at international level which have led to international conventions. Apart from the Munich Convention on European Patents, these bodies are listed in an Annex to the agreement. This approach has its difficulties, in that not all the EU Member States themselves are signed up to all these agreements. This problem is solved by the curious device of stating that the associated countries shall accede to all those conventions to which the Member States have acceded or which they apply *de facto* and by stating with respect to certain international agreements that the parties 'express their attachment to observing the obligations' flowing from these agreements.

As with many other areas, the Uruguay Round agreements have had an important impact in this area. Those countries which are Members of the WTO – the Czech Republic, Hungary, Poland, Romania, Slovenia, Bulgaria and Slovakia – are parties to the GATT Agreement on Trade-related aspects of Intellectual Property Rights (TRIPs).[1] This agreement binds these countries into introducing advance protection of intellectual property and ensuring thorough enforcement.

### *Public procurement*

Public procurement rules are not laid down in the agreements. The two sides simply agree that the opening up of awards procedures on a non-discriminatory basis is a desirable objective. However, the agreements do give associated country companies and Community companies established in the respective associated country national treatment in the contract awards procedures from the entry into force of the agreements. Other Community companies will be granted the same

---

[1] The three Baltic States have applied for membership.

treatment from the end of the transitional period, and the associated countries promise to attempt to advance this date. In the agreements with the Baltic countries certain changes were made to the standard clauses in the earlier agreements. Firstly, the difference is drawn between companies and subsidiaries on the one hand and branches and agencies on the other; in these agreements, the latter do not enjoy the rights to national treatment for public procurement purposes in the associated countries until the end of the transition period. Secondly, Estonia granted immediate national treatment to Community companies from the entry into force of the agreement.

### Movement of capital and current payments

The main objectives of the Association Agreement in the area of capital movement are to ensure total freedom of movement on the current account, to guarantee that investors can move their invested capital and profits and to prepare the associated countries for total convertibility.

The first objective is met by declaring immediate total liberalisation on the current account on transactions between the parties. At the same time the free movement of capital on the capital account is ensured from the entry into force of the agreement for all matters related to direct investments between the parties, for companies formed on the legal base of the home country and in accordance with the terms of the agreement on establishment. The same is ensured for Community nationals establishing as self-employed persons in the associated countries under the terms of the establishment rules of the agreement either at the end of the first transition stage (the early agreements) or at the entry into force of the agreement (Lithuania). In addition, a standstill is included in terms of foreign exchange restrictions between the parties from the entry into force of the agreement for the European Community and from the end of the first stage in the case of the associated countries.[2]

In order to bring the associated countries nearer to the legal framework of the Community, the agreements also foresee that further measures should be taken in the first stage of the agreement permitting the creation of the necessary conditions for the further gradual application of Community rules on the free movement of capital. During the second stage, the agreement states that the Association Council will examine ways of enabling Community rules on the movement of capital to be applied in full.

It is worth noting that in this area the progress made in many countries of the region has been remarkable and far more rapid than

---

[2] This is not the case for the three Baltic agreements, or for that with Slovenia.

assumed in 1991. This is reflected both in the movement to complete liberalisation in the sense of the provisions of article VIII of the Articles of Agreement of the IMF in the case, for instance, of the Czech Republic and in the considerably more liberal articles of the Association Agreements with the three Baltic States.[3] With Estonia and Latvia having totally liberalised capital movements, the agreements simply point to the need over time to apply in detail the Community rules on the movement of capital. In the case of Lithuania, while there is not full liberalisation, nevertheless portfolio investment-induced movements of capital are totally liberalised. The rules of the OECD on capital movements are also applied by the three new CEE members – the Czech Republic, Hungary and Poland.

Safeguard clauses are included in the agreements. The early agreements allow the associated country to introduce exchange restrictions where these are imposed on the country as a condition for the granting of credits and where these controls are permitted by the IMF. The associated country and the Community are also allowed to introduce restrictions, including restrictions on imports where this is absolutely necessary for balance of payments reasons. These restrictions must not restrict freedom of transfers related to inward investment.

### *The importance of competition policy and state-aid control for the transition process*

The economic arguments for competition policy and the control of state aids are well documented.[4] These arguments suggest that the implementation of competition policy leads to improvements in allocative, technical and 'X'-efficiency. Allocative efficiency means that there is no way in which resources can be reallocated between factors of production which will lead to an increase in welfare. Technical efficiency exists when the factors of production are used in a way which minimises production costs. 'X'-efficiency refers mainly to managerial efficiency which comes from improvements in managerial techniques, very often because of competitive pressures. Both allocative and technical efficiency can exist at the same time as 'X'-inefficiency. Competitive markets in general stimulate all three economic mechanisms.

While the optimisation of economic performance requires markets to be contested, there is considerable discussion in the European Union and in the other main industrial economies on how to implement competition policy. There are those who believe that competition is

---

[3] Hungary and Poland are also moving rapidly to complete convertibility.
[4] For instance Boner and Krueger (1993).

good *per se* and others who believe that the aims of industrial policy can in some cases justify not taking action against companies which actually or potentially threaten competition. In the associated countries these discussions are even more complex, because the process of economic reform towards the market economy is not complete. Many in these countries maintain that adopting a strong competition policy and controlling state aids will lead to the demise of many local companies which, if exposed to full competition, will not survive.

### Freedom of entry

Most specialists would agree that the most important element that characterises contested markets is *freedom of entry* into the relevant market.[5] Indeed, it is very difficult to show market dominance in anti-trust markets if there is freedom of entry into the market. Where entry into the market is easy, any attempt at collusion in order to use market power will be destabilised by new entrants under-cutting the prices charged by the colluding firms. There are many economic barriers to free entry which exist in any economy. The existence of very large sunk costs which are required to start up production or the existence of economies of scale to the extent that an entering firm has to immediately gain a large market share both naturally make entry more difficult. Regulation also may make entry more difficult. This includes licensing laws, as with New York taxi-cabs; quotas, as with EU milk quotas; certification, as with new drugs; but also trade policy regulation, including quotas and tariffs and other similar measures.

In the associated countries such barriers to entry also exist, but there are additional problems which are particular to the transition from central planning to the market economy. If one looks at the figures for the creation of new businesses in the associated countries since the reforms began, they show an explosion of enterprise creation.[6] It would therefore appear that entry is relatively easy. However, a closer look at the statistics suggests that the great majority of the new firms are very small and concentrated in certain sectors, notably in services. In many industrial sectors, the degree of concentration is often still very high and entry is difficult because of the dominant position held by the former state monopoly producer or its private sector counterpart. Fingleton *et al.* (1996) report that for the Czech Republic the four-firm concentration ratios for sectors have indeed fallen considerably since 1989, to reach levels similar to those in the United States; the difference is that in

---

[5] Exit costs are, of course, also of great importance for competition, especially where there are large sunk costs involved.

[6] See, for instance, Johnson and Loveman (1995).

the Czech Republic, there is little difference between the market share of the largest firm and the four largest, suggesting remaining strong dominance for the major producer.[7]

Entry is also restricted by the inadequacies of the financial system in the associated countries. Data shows that most investment by new entrants is financed by the owner's own sources of finance (family savings) and also that most development capital is financed through retained profits. The inadequacies of the banking system and capital markets restrict the ability of firms to enter new markets and small firms to grow to challenge the market position of larger and perhaps dominant competitors.

Entry may also be restricted by the continuation of the collusive habits of the previous system, when companies cooperated without any notions of competition. Where such relationships still exist, it may be more difficult for a new entrant to break into a system which resembles a completely vertically integrated industry.

### Market structure

In terms of *market structure* a legacy of the past monopolistic or oligopolistic structure still remains in most of the associated countries in spite of a concerted attack through the break-up of state monopolies, state trading companies and through the efforts of competition authorities and, to a lesser extent, privatisation agencies. The fact that state or private oligopolies and monopolies still exist, with all the possible elements of collusive behaviour or abuse of dominant position and the presumed existence of entry barriers, suggests that competition policy needs to be especially vigilant. The process of breaking-up these market structures is sometimes complicated by political support for monopoly, often with the argument that it is essential for the country to have a strong national 'champion'. At best such arguments are usually economic and business nonsense, at worst they cover up political interests in business which are unhealthy for the country's economy. There are of course always arguments between the advantages of competitive markets and the existence of scale economies. In the associated countries, it is in most cases better to err on the competition side of the argument.

### Market power

The fundamental concept of *market power* – the ability to vary price without losing sales – is essential to the implementation of competition

---

[7] Fingleton *et al.* (1996).

policy. Market power is exercised in an anti-trust market, which is defined as a set of sellers and buyers who make up all the competitive forces acting on the price of products in the market.[8] The anti-trust market has two components: the product market and the geographic market. The former is a group of products whose short-run price is dependent on competition from within the group. The latter is the geographic region where competition occurs – for instance, in the market for steel or cement, transport costs essentially limit the geographical scope of competition. The ability to exercise market power implies either monopoly or the ability to coordinate amongst firms within the market. As such coordination is easier between fewer rather than more firms, concentration indices are good indicators of at least potential market power. Market power is also more easily wielded in markets for standardised products where the possibility of product differentiation is less than in markets with goods differentiated by quality, design and other non-price features. The exercise of market power is also more common in stagnant markets than in fast-growing ones.

In the associated countries, the exercise of market power is linked to market structure and to the existence of old networks of cooperation between firms, as discussed above. The much less well developed private and public information networks also make the exercise of market power somewhat easier than in regions where information flows more easily and there is greater transparency. But the exercise of market power is also affected by the degree of import penetration, itself dependent on the degree of protection offered by government against foreign competition. In Central Europe, such protection has frequently been demanded by foreign investors, as a price for investing.

### Market dominance

Much of the law on competition refers to the existence, and especially to the abuse, of *market dominance*. While most competition law refers to the abuse of dominant position, the very existence of dominance is regarded by some as a potential threat of predatory practice. While the existence of highly vertically integrated enterprises, as well as horizontal state monopolies, in the associated countries led to real dominance and potential abuse, economic reforms and the economic crises which have affected Central Europe have tended to break up at least the vertically organised businesses into their component parts.

The associated countries have made enormous progress in moving

---

[8] See Boner and Krueger (1993).

their economies towards the market economy. Indeed it seems strange to think that in countries like the Czech Republic or Hungary the economies were other than market economies. However in no country has the reform run its course to produce economic and enterprise structures which are as diversified as those in the European Community or the United States. There are also still some natural tendencies to protect national companies over foreign entrants, even when this leads to the exercise of market power. While the creation of new business has been very rapid, there are still sectors characterised by the dominant position of one or a few firms. And in some countries, some of the old enterprise networks of cooperation still operate to the detriment of competition. In these circumstances, it is important that the associated countries redouble their efforts to promote contested markets and control the exercise of market power. This is perhaps more important for the promotion of economic efficiency and economic growth than it is for these countries' integration into the European Union.

### Progress with competition policy in the associated countries

All the associated countries have made considerable progress in the introduction of competition law.[9] They have all satisfied the European Commission in carrying out their obligations under the Association Agreements to introduce Community competition rules as far as trade between the two parties is concerned. The Fingleton *et al.* study of competition law in the Visegrád countries suggests that as far as the adoption of competition law is concerned, progress has been impressive. While there remain some weak areas in some countries, this is no worse than the anomalies in competition law in the Union.

More important than passing laws and regulations is, however, the creation of institutions to implement the law. The associated countries all have anti-monopoly offices (AMOs), created since 1989 and charged in general with implementing competition law. Fingleton *et al.* in their study analyse the structure and responsibility of the AMO in the four Visegrád countries. Three of the four Visegrád countries have Offices which are independent; in the case of the fourth, the Czech Republic, the Office is in fact an independent Ministry of Economic Competition. The Offices are headed by a President (or in the Czech case by a Minister), but they have a different status in each country. The Czech Minister is appointed for the period of the electoral cycle and can be replaced by the Prime Minister; in fact, the same Minister has been in

---

[9] Reference should be made to Fingleton *et al.* (1996).

charge throughout the life of the Republic. At the other end of the scale, the Chairman of the AMO in Slovakia is a civil servant appointed by the Government and with no fixed term of office. Here, there have been five heads of the AMO in three years! In Hungary, the position of the AMO President is very secure in that he or she can be removed only by a plenary session of Parliament. Finally, in Poland, the President is a civil servant who can be sacked by the government at any time. But here, the first President resigned and the second is still in office. In each country, the head of the AMO is either part of the government or is invited by right to Cabinet meetings. The staffing of the Offices is considered by Fingleton *et al.* to be adequate.

The AMOs' core responsibility is in all cases the implementation of the competition laws where, except in Hungary, they have the power to break up firms or force them to divest certain activities. In addition, these responsibilities include in all cases the drafting of changes to competition law but also the verification of all draft laws which are produced by the government. The Office also has a variety of other responsibilities which vary from case to case: in Hungary, for instance, it is responsible for consumer protection, as is the new Office for Competition and Consumer Protection in Poland; in the Czech Republic, the Office deals with public procurement.

The powers of the Offices also vary, with the Polish and Slovak having on paper considerably more powers than the Czech and Hungarian Offices. All Offices can collect data and evidence and access unpublished national sources in their investigations, though they cannot access government files. They can also all prohibit anti-competitive behaviour and impose exemplary fines. But whereas the Polish Office can alter market structure, enforce its decisions and impose penalties for non-compliance, the Hungarian Office can do none of these. But the value of these powers depends on whether they are used, which itself depends on the political support which the Offices enjoy. The Hungarian Office appears to enjoy the highest level of support, which probably reflects its weaker powers. Rarely have very high fines been used in any of the countries, and little use has been made of the power to alter market structure.

The scope of competition policy in the countries varies somewhat. Fingleton *et al.* look at scope in relation to the private sector, the state sector and privatisation. In general it is in the private sector that competition rules bite the hardest. The main exception is in the agricultural area, where only Poland seems to seriously investigate infringements of competition rules. This is unfortunately one of the vices transferred from the European Union, where agricultural markets also fall outside the competition rules. Apart from aberrations such as the exclusion of foreign firms from Hungarian competition rules, the implementation of competition rules in the private sector appears to be adequate. It is in the state sector where implementation is perhaps more difficult. Many state-run industries are subject to special rules which take them outside the scope of action of the AMOs. Even where the scope of competition law does reach to the state sector, as in the treatment of public utilities in Poland, implementation is weak. Nevertheless a number of cases have been brought against state monopolies and in several cases violations of the law have been established. AMOs have been more active in the area of privatisation. In Poland, the Office has been able to force the break up of firms prior to privatisation on many occasions and the Czech Republic and Slovak Offices have also been very active in the field.

The conclusion of Fingleton *et al.* is that competition policy still has weaknesses in the four countries investigated. They list three principal weaknesses: the Offices have little influence on trade policy or industrial policy decisions, they are less tough on the state-owned sector than on the private sector and they are subjected to some extent to political pressure. These three criticisms can be levelled at Union competition policy as well; experience over the last three years has produced a series of cases where trade and industrial policy objectives were advanced before competition, where large state-owned companies were given massive state aid and where severe political pressure was brought to bear on the European Commission. The spectacular success of the introduction of competition policy in such a short time in the associated countries should be measured against the 30 years that it took the Union to really establish serious policy in this area. There are certainly weaknesses, and these need to be addressed, but the standards required by the Union need to be those really applied in the Union, not those theoretically applied.

### The impact of EU competition and state-aid rules on the economies of the associated countries

There is no dispute that the introduction of competition rules and the control of state aid in the associated countries has been a very important part of the move to the market economy, and has underpinned the economic growth which is now being experienced. There is also no dispute that the adoption of Treaty of Rome competition rules as far as trade within the Union is concerned is vital to accession. However, there is a suspicion that in this area, as in others, the Union is trying to apply purist rules to the associated countries which are not applied in the Union itself.[10]

There are two sets of considerations. Are the rules as applied through the Association Agreements fair and even-handed? And is it reasonable to expect the associated countries to adopt fully EU competition rules and rules on state aids before there is a commitment from the Union on accession? Perhaps the most serious criticism of the position of the European Union is that it is forcing the associated countries into adopting its own competition and state-aid rules without any guarantee of trade access to Union markets and without any guarantee on accession. In the EEA agreement, commercial policy instruments, anti-dumping and safeguards are no longer available to the Union because competition policy and state-aids rules are applied. The Union briefly mentioned this possibility for the associated countries at the Essen European Council, but no action was taken. No other applicant was ever forced to take on the Union's laws before accession.

In various areas there is a feeling that the Union is expecting the associated countries to use competition policy or the control of state aids in ways which they have never been applied in the Union. For instance, there is some pressure on these countries to take over Community rules not only as far as trade with the Union is concerned but also for their internal competition rules. This is not the case in the European Union, where different national rules apply. In the Union, exceptions have been made to the application of competition rules in certain Member States, when apparently more important objectives were at stake. Holmes mentions the case of Greece, which was given special provisions in the liberalisation of the telecommunications sector because of the need to maintain monopoly profits to finance investment. There seems to be little willingness on the part of the Union authorities to make special exemptions for special situations. This is probably good news for the associated countries, but it shows a certain theoretical bias in their dealings with the Union. A major danger is that these rules will be used to benefit EU firms to the detriment of local or non-EU firms. Given the degree to which competition and state-aids policies have become politicised, it is to be expected that wherever these rules can be used against Japanese or South Korean investments they will be. Similar one-sidedness is seen in the treatment of parallel imports, which are permitted in the Union but which can be excluded in franchising

---

[10] An interesting consideration of this point is found in Peter Holmes, 'Competition integration and business interests: levelling or tilting the playing field?', conference paper at the Conference on Competition Rules and Relations between the European Union and East-Central Europe, Prague (March 1995).

agreements between EU companies and producers in the associated countries.

The impact of Union competition policy and state-aids control on the economies of the associated countries could be quite negative in scaring off non-EU investors and putting local companies at a disadvantage. These problems would not really be considered as serious, however, if there were a credible commitment of the Union to rapid accession. Indeed, if this were the case the associated countries would have probably agreed to handing over authority to Brussels in various areas already. Giving up sovereignty now, knowing that accession will happen in 2002–3 would be thought of as a good arrangement by most countries.

Competition and state-aids rules are good for the economies of the associated countries, and maintaining pressure on the associated countries to properly implement these rules is important. It is, however, to be hoped that Brussels has constantly before its eyes the difficulty which it faced and still faces with the application of these rules. A daily reading of the *Handelsblatt* or the *Financial Times* suffices to convince the reader that the Union is far from a perfect region as far as these policies are concerned.

### The movement of workers, establishment and the supply of services

The movement of people between the associated countries and the European Community has been both one of the most difficult issues and technically one of the most complicated. Politically these subjects are difficult because the European Union and its Member States have become extremely sensitive to migration and employment issues. Since the fall of the Berlin Wall stories of millions of people moving from 'the East' to look for the better life in Western Europe have been commonplace. Even when these millions did not materialise, the trauma of the asylum crisis in Germany and migration from other parts of the world have led to considerably more restrictive policies being applied by Member State governments to movements of people across frontiers. This cautious attitude has frequently been reinforced by worries about mounting crime, some of it clearly accounted for by the development of organised crime in Eastern Europe; the enormous rise in car theft and the proportion of stolen cars not being traced is just one element of this problem.

On top of the general attitude to movements of people, problems in the labour market have reinforced the cautious attitude taken by

Member State governments. With social and labour market policies leading to a considerable rise in the natural rate of unemployment in Western Europe, and with cyclical unemployment also contributing, overall unemployment levels have been historically high since the end of the 1980s.[11] There is a fear therefore that more workers will be displaced by migrants from the associated countries coming into the Community and working for wages considerably lower than those paid to domestic workers. Although the experience of previous accessions, and some simple economics, may contradict this assertion, nevertheless political pressures have been such that the Association Agreements are very restrictive in all areas which treat the movement of workers.

The three items dealt with in this section are all linked through the labour market, even if they appear to be very different subjects. Rules on the movement of labour deal with the general problems of labour migration. The establishment rules determine under which circumstances companies and nationals can establish undertakings and engage in operations on the territory of the other party; establishment usually means that there will be at least a limited movement of labour across the frontier. The supply of services is a very wide area, but as far as the associated countries are concerned it applies at present above all to construction and transport services. The supply of both of these is intimately related to the movement of workers.

### What the Association Agreements say

#### Movement of workers
The agreements provide no improvement in the possibilities for the movement of labour over the situation existing before the agreements, though they do aim at getting close to national treatment for workers from the other party who are already legally working in the country.

The agreements lay down that for workers from the associated country who are legally employed in the Community there should be no discrimination on the basis of nationality compared to nationals in the areas of working conditions, remuneration and dismissal. In addition, the spouse and children of the worker can also have access to the labour market while he or she is employed. These rules do not apply to workers doing seasonal work or who enter on the basis of strictly regulated bilateral agreements with individual Member States (for instance German '*Werkverträge*'). The associated country also agrees to introduce similar arrangements for workers from the Community.

---

[11] The average rate of unemployment in the Community in the period 1990–5 was of the order of 10% of the civilian labour force.

The agreements lay down for legally employed workers from the associated country that benefits accumulated in the Member States of the Community should be cumulated for the purpose of pensions and annuities in respect of old age, invalidity and death, as well as for medical care. Any such benefits (excluding non-contributory benefits) should be transferable according to the laws of the Member State concerned. The agreements also state that family allowances should be paid for the Members of the worker's family. The detailed rules for realising these advantages are to be laid down by the Association Council, and these rules must not in any way reduce the advantages for workers from the other party that already exist at Community or Member State level.

The agreements suggest that bilateral arrangements on the movement of workers between the associated country and a Member State should be maintained or, if possible, improved, and that other Member States should consider introducing similar arrangements. This applies mainly to the German *Werkverträge* scheme. According to the agreements the Association Council should consider granting rights to professional training to these and all other workers legally employed from the associated country. There is a vague promise that the Association Council will examine further ways of improving the movement of workers in the second stage of the agreements or, in the case of the Baltic countries, after the end of 1999. Finally a promise is given to provide technical assistance to the associated country to help establish a 'suitable social security system'.

All of this adds up to no flexibility on the part of the Member States but a keen interest to make sure that there is no discrimination against workers from the associated countries legally resident in the Community. There has if anything been a hardening of attitude amongst the Member States between the negotiation of the first Association Agreements and the later Baltic Agreements.

### Establishment

This extremely important chapter of the agreements lays down under which conditions companies and nationals of one party can establish themselves and operate on the territory of the other party.

The essential concepts of the rules on establishment are relatively clearly set out. The agreements are built around the concept of national treatment, the ultimate objective being that each party grants the same treatment to companies and nationals of the other party as granted to its own nationals.

The chapter makes distinctions between:
- companies, subsidiaries and branches
- establishment and operations
- and between nationals who are effectively establishing as self-employed persons and those really just looking for employment.

As far as associated country companies are concerned, the situation is clear. Associated country companies, subsidiaries and branches, receive national treatment or MFN treatment in the right of establishment and of operation on the territory of the Member States of the Community from the entry into force of the agreement, whichever is the most favourable.

For Community companies, treatment varies between agreements. In the case of Hungary, for instance, Community companies, with the exception of those in financial services and certain excluded sectors, receive national treatment in establishment and operations only at the end of the first stage of the transitional period. Financial services companies and those dealing in state-owned assets under privatisation only receive this treatment at the end of the transitional period – that is, after ten years from the entry into force of the agreement. Certain sectors in Hungary are completely excluded from the agreement on establishment: these are primary agriculture, forestry and fishing (but not processing of primary products), ownership, sale or long-term lease of real property, land and natural resources, legal services and betting and gaming.

Each agreement, except those with Estonia and Latvia, has such permanent exceptions. They universally deal with agricultural land, forests, real estate and natural resources. They sometimes include gaming, which was usually a state monopoly, and national cultural or historic sites. In the case of Romania the agreement permanently excludes legal services, in Bulgaria the ownership of real estate in certain geographic areas of the country. These exceptions, which the Community hopes will eventually be included, are justified by the associated countries through the fear that foreign residents could otherwise buy up large tracts of the country or the sectors mentioned at the prevailing low prices. In all the agreements, however, there is a clause which states that Community companies, established on the territory of the associated country, must have the right to acquire, rent and sell real property and to lease agricultural land, forests and natural resources where these are directly necessary for the conduct of the business for which they are established. Whereas therefore it is generally not possible for a Community company to buy farms and work them, it is possible for a Community company to buy the site on which its factory is situated.

Once again, the three new Central European OECD Members had to liberalise their regulations on land purchase further.

The Community also has one permanent exclusion from the national treatment on establishment, though this is not included in the agreements with the Visegrád countries. This consists of the acquisition of real-estate in certain frontier regions and refers notably to the exception made in the Maastricht Treaty which allows Denmark alone to maintain a restriction on the purchase of certain real-estate in the internal market.

The temporary exclusions are also very diverse, ranging from the production of vodka and postal services in Lithuania, to defence industries and steel in the Czech Republic and Slovakia, high-voltage power lines and pipeline transport in Poland to the ownership of port infrastructure in Latvia. These exclusions are more numerous than the permanent exclusions, and depend on certain particular circumstances which exist in the different associated countries.

The Hungarian agreement is the most restrictive in that although Community company operations are granted national treatment from the entry into force of the agreement, establishment is basically not permitted until the end of the first stage of the transition period and the temporary exceptions are not lifted until the end of the transition period. In the other early agreements national treatment is given to Community companies' establishment and operations from the entry into force, with the exception of the excepted sectors. Most of the excepted sectors are protected for the full transitional period, though in the case of Poland some sectors are liberalised at the end of the first stage.

In terms of nationals rather than companies the agreements are very different, depending on whether they are early or late agreements, for the Member States of the Community have become far more restrictive over time. The early agreements, those with Hungary, Poland, the Czech Republic, Slovakia, Romania and Bulgaria, granted nationals of the associated countries immediate national treatment as far as both establishment and operations in the Community were concerned. In the case of the three Baltic countries, however, the Community was prepared to allow only establishment and operations of nationals of those countries from the end of 1999, even though Estonia has agreed to totally liberalise establishment for Community nationals from the entry into force of the agreement. In the case of Estonia, therefore, the famous asymmetry of the Association Agreements has been reversed to the advantage of the Community! This growing restrictiveness relates to the experience of certain Member States following the entry into force of the early agreements. The Member States have also become worried by the possible misuse of the right of establishment by nationals simply seeking paid employment.

The associated countries, however, have always treated the establishment and operation of Community nationals parallel to that of Community companies. The only exceptions are Latvia and Lithuania, which decided, unlike Estonia, against creating asymmetry in favour of the Community and have taken the same regime for liberalisation as the Community.

The financial services sector is treated in this chapter apart from other sectors, owing to the need for adequate prudential rules for financial institutions. An identical Annex in each agreement defines financial services, insurance, banking and other financial services. In most cases, the associated countries did not offer immediate national treatment to this sector but only at the end of the transitional period.[12] While the Member States offer immediate liberalisation, it is clearly stated in the agreements that

in respect of financial services, notwithstanding any other provisions of this Agreement, a Party shall not be prevented from taking measures for prudential reasons, including for the protection of investors, depositors, policy holders or persons to whom a fiduciary duty is owed by a financial service supplier, or to ensure the integrity and stability of the financial system. Such measures shall not be used as a means of avoiding the Party's obligations under the Agreement.[13]

It would therefore not be possible for a financial institution from one party establishing on the territory of the other party to avoid the prudential rules of that party. The agreement even allows in the financial services sector some deviation from national treatment, where this is justified by prudential reasons. This is the case particularly where branches of financial service companies are established in the other party but without the incorporation of the company in that party's territory.

In general terms, each party can regulate the establishment and operation of the other party's companies on its territory as long as the principle of national treatment is maintained. This does not apply to branches of the foreign company, which can be regulated separately as long as this difference in treatment does not go beyond what is strictly necessary for legal or technical reasons.

The chapter on establishment also deals with the question of the employment of nationals of one party when its companies establish and operate on the territory of the other party. The agreements state that

---

[12] Romania will give national treatment to the banking sector at the end of the first stage.

[13] Taken from the agreement with Latvia but, in slightly changed form, present in all the agreements.

a 'Community company' or a [for example] 'Latvian company' established in the territory of Latvia or the Community respectively shall be entitled to employ, or have employed by one of its subsidiaries or branches, in accordance with the legislation in force in the host country of establishment, in the territory of Latvia and the Community respectively, employees who are nationals of Community Member States and Latvia respectively, provided that such employees are key personnel as defined in paragraph 2 of this Article, and that they are employed exclusively by companies, subsidiaries or branches. The residence and work permits of such employees shall only cover the period of such employment.

The agreements define key personnel as

persons working in a senior position with an organisation, who primarily direct the management of the establishment, receiving general supervision or direction principally from the board of directors or stockholders of the business or their equivalent, including directing the establishment of a department or sub-division of the establishment, supervising and controlling the work of other supervisory, professional or managerial employees or having the authority personally to recruit and dismiss or recommend recruiting, dismissing or other personnel actions.

Key personnel also include

persons working within an organisation who possess uncommon knowledge essential to the establishment's service, research equipment, techniques or management. The assessment of such knowledge may reflect, apart from knowledge specific to the establishment, a high level of qualification referring to a type of work or trade requiring specific technical knowledge, including membership of an accredited profession.

To be classed as 'key personnel', employees must have been employed by the company concerned for at least a year preceding the move to the territory of the other partner.

These clauses are more or less common to all the agreements. In the case of the latest generation of agreements, those with the Baltic States and Slovenia, the concept of the 'intra-corporate transferee' was invented to define these key personnel more narrowly. This shows the considerable increase in nervousness which has arisen in Member States since the first agreements with the Visegrád states. In the general provisions of this title, an article also underlines that nothing contained in the title shall prevent the parties applying their laws and regulations regarding entry and stay, work, labour conditions and establishment of natural persons and supply of services, as long as these do not nullify or impair the benefits accruing from the Association Agreement.

As far as the regulated professions are concerned, the agreements promise that the Association Council will examine what steps are necessary to be taken to provide for the mutual recognition of qualifications on both sides.

The final part of the chapter on establishment is a unilateral safeguard clause for the associated country similar to that in the trade chapter of the agreement. The associated country can derogate from the rules on establishment where industries are undergoing restructuring, are facing serious difficulties (notably social difficulties), are suffering a drastic reduction in market share, or are infant industries. The use of such a safeguard is limited to the transition period (with some variations between countries), must be reasonable and necessary and must not discriminate against Community businesses already established in the country. Though the Association Council must be consulted and normally the measures should not be put into effect until one month after notification of the measures to the Association Council, in fact the Council can be informed *ex post* where there is a 'threat of irreparable damage'. After the transition period (or the appropriate limits in the different agreements), such measures can be introduced only with the agreement of the Association Council.

As is normal, the provisions on establishment may be derogated from on grounds of public health, public security or public policy. The same is true where the activities are connected with the exercise of official authority.

These articles on establishment are liberal in the sense of allowing national treatment immediately for the companies and, at least in the older agreements, for nationals of the associated countries. This liberalisation is however constrained by the very restrictive articles on the movement of labour.


### The supply of services

The chapter on the supply of services concentrates on transport services, which are excluded from the articles on establishment. For the supply of services in general, there is only a global statement that the parties will undertake steps to progressively allow the supply of services to the other party. The passage from the establishment chapter on key personnel is repeated. In the early agreements it was stated that the Association Council would take the measures necessary to implement the gradual liberalisation of trade in services. The increased prudence of the Community side is shown by the fact that in the Baltic agreements it is stated that the Association Council will take such measures at the latest eight years after the entry into force of the agreement.

The transport articles regulate the unrestricted access to markets in international maritime transport and the national treatment of each other's ships in access to ports and infrastructure. They refer to future agreements still to be negotiated in land, inland waterway and possibly air transport between the parties and establish a standstill in protectionist measures until these negotiations have finished. Finally in the Baltic agreements it is proposed to negotiate an inter-modal agreement on transit through each other's territory before the end of 1999.

### Experience with implementation

As mentioned above, it is too early to make any balanced judgement on the application of these parts of the Association Agreements. The main outlines of the problems can, however, be discerned.

### The problems are geographically concentrated

Establishment and the mobility of labour are questions which affect the countries close to central Europe – mainly Germany, Austria and to a lesser extent the Nordic countries. Most experience has obviously been gathered in Germany, where by far the largest number of associated country citizens and companies have established themselves. It is also the country which has the most migrant workers from Central Europe. There are now so many Polish firms in Germany that there is a flourishing German Association of Polish Enterprises.

In general, the whole process of establishment, organised through the Chambers of Commerce, has proceeded smoothly, with few apparent problems. The most difficult problems were those encountered with certain liberal professions, where doctors and dentists from Central Europe were able to establish themselves if their diplomas were accepted, while there was a general prohibition of establishment for German doctors because of an over-supply situation. There have been technical problems in the interpretation of the agreements, but they appear to be relatively minor.

Germany is also the main destination for workers moving from Central Europe to the Union. Germany had, until mid-1997, the most generous national scheme with its *Werkverträge*, although this system caused problems with German trades unions who claimed that the migrant workers worked for lower wages than the German official rates (which must be true otherwise presumably German unemployed workers would be hired). The scheme was stopped by the German government after the European Commission protested that it gave advantages to German over non-German companies. In spite of the concentration of cases in one Member State, however, Germany has been the most tolerant of hosts in general, with application of most of these rules having gone smoothly.

*These areas are not the competence of the Union but have not been transposed into national legislation*
An important problem is that the Association Agreements are directly applied in these matters by the Member States and there is no national law on which to base decisions. Local officials are in charge of establishment and frequently have only vague notions of the Association Agreements and no real guide to their interpretation. In these circumstances, misunderstandings are bound to arise. A typical case was the refusal to allow a student to establish as a self-employed artist in Berlin because she was not 'exclusively self-employed' as required by the Association Agreement. This case was eventually settled in the student's favour.

*It is not clear to some Member States that the Association Agreement takes precedence over national or local laws*
There are numerous national or local laws in the area of labour mobility, self-employment and establishment which are over-ridden by the Association Agreements. Local officials often do not know this, or do not want to know it. A typical case is that of the Polish airline LOT in Austria, where a key member of staff was refused the right to move to the LOT office in Vienna because there was an overall limit of the number of foreigners working in Austria and this quota was exhausted. This is clearly contrary to the articles of the Association Agreement.

*Administrative procedures are used to prevent the use of the Association Agreement articles in these areas*
The possibilities of using administrative procedures to delay the use of these articles are enormous. In Greece, for instance, examples of delays being used to prevent the spouses of legally employed persons from the associated countries receiving work permits have been recorded, but this occurs also in other Member States.

*The recognition of professional qualifications by one Member State may not allow the holder to move to another*
Citizens of the associated countries who practise the liberal professions can obviously do so only if their professional qualifications are recognised. Given the progress in this area which has been made in the Union's internal market, it must be assumed that if one Member State recognises professional qualifications the others will automatically do so. This has been refused, however, by the French government, which

decided that even though Germany recognised the qualifications of a professional from the associated countries, France would not.

There are no doubt many other types of problems which will arise in these areas, but in general the rules on establishment seem to be working well, while the expectation of liberalisation in the other areas was never very high in the associated countries.

### Economic and cultural cooperation

The titles on economic and cultural cooperation in the Association Agreements are simply long wish-lists for future cooperation between the two parties. They are not the result of thorough analysis of needs. They are not even the result of tough negotiation, the negotiation of these articles occupying only a very small part of the total negotiating time. In fact, it is likely that these articles will remain unused and unloved for reasons of resource limitation and substance. The reasons concern both the lack of staff to manage such cooperation and the fact that many of the areas cited in these articles are already being addressed within PHARE or in other assistance programmes, or in the context of normal contacts between officials.

# 5  Financial assistance to Central and Eastern Europe

## Introduction

In the early 1990s, at the very beginnings of reform, assistance was often seen by the donor countries as the most important element of policy. The establishment of the G24 coordination process in 1989 by the 24 major donors directed the world's attention to this aspect of policy. The creation of the EBRD specifically to serve the region, and the development of lending to the region by the World Bank (IBRD) and the EIB mobilised significant resources. The agreement by the European Community in 1989 to create a grant programme, later to be known as PHARE, and the establishment of several significant bilateral aid programmes, notably in the United States, Germany, the United Kingdom and France led to modest amounts of grant funds also being made available. Politicians from all the donor countries emphasised repeatedly the importance of the funding which the G24 was making available to support the establishment of democracy and the market economy in the countries of the region.

Seven years later, it is interesting to draw conclusions on the success of G24 assistance. Overall the conclusion must be that assistance has been marginal to the transition process, with the early balance of payments or stability loans and later loans or equity participations in the private sector playing a much more important role than grant assistance. Indeed some authors consider grant assistance to have had a perverse impact on reform, encouraging bureaucracy and discouraging enterprise and the taking over of responsibilities by government.[1] On the other hand, it is possible to point to many initiatives which have been very important for reform in the associated countries, which would have been difficult to implement without grant funding. Whether overall grant funding has been efficient in terms of its contribution to the reform policies of the countries is nevertheless doubtful.

---

[1] De Crombrugghe, Minton-Beddoes and Sachs (1996).

Today, many donors are beginning to run down their funding to Central Europe, considering the greater part of the reform to have been achieved. For the European Union, however, the funding of accession preparations and of the physical integration of the Continent through infrastructure developments remains a significant financial contribution to reform and integration in the region.

## The global assistance effort: the G24 process

### The G24 process

The origins of the G24 process were outlined in chapter 1. The 24 donor countries are full Members, and the International Financial Institutions, the EIB, EBRD, OECD and EFTA also attend the meetings.[2] The Secretariat is provided by the European Commission. The objectives of the G24 were initially linked to the coordination of the assistance effort, but progressively the process became more political.

G24 coordination, in the sense of a system which works through transparency, frequent *ex ante* coordination between the major donors and joint medium-term programming of assistance, never really worked. Coordination has occurred in individual countries or on specific projects, but always outside the G24 framework and always between the major donors. In the case of the G24 there were the usual bureaucratic jealousies between countries added to those between international organisations. There have been some shining exceptions to this rule, notably that of Sweden, where assistance was seen as a national duty rather than a politicians' plaything. Assistance has also been used to buy strategic positions for donors' companies or other interests, which also reduces the capacity to cooperate.

An overall judgement of the coordination effort in the G24 has to conclude that there has been remarkably little coordination of assistance between the major donors, even between Member States of the European Union. However G24 political coordination was important at the beginning of the transition. In-country coordination by G24 has tended to be the most effective part of the coordination effort, while certain specific parts of the G24 work have proved very worthwhile, notably macro-financial cooperation.

With 15 of the G24 countries now inside the European Union, with a decline in US assistance to the region and little interest from any other

[2] The 24 were the EU-15, the United States, Canada, Australia, Turkey, New Zealand, Switzerland, Japan, Norway and Iceland.

country except Japan (only really in the macro-financial area), the G24 process is virtually dead.

### Overall funding

Some conclusions can be drawn here on the scale and scope of this effort on the basis of the G24 scoreboard (appendix tables 5A.1 and 5A.2). The tables show that a total of ECU86 billion was donated to the CEE countries in the six years 1990–5 of which 29.4% was in grant form. However the tables make it clear that quite a substantial proportion of this grant assistance was given in the context of debt restructuring. Debt reorganisation assistance amounts to ECU13.2 billion (this debt reorganisation is concentrated on one country, Poland, which has received ECU12.8 billion). Grant finance in debt reorganisation makes up ECU8.2 billion or 32% of total grant assistance. Debt restructuring is clearly assistance, but it is not new money which the governments of the region can use to support reform. In the case of Central Europe it is particularly ironic that a considerable proportion of the grant financing of reform is going to pay the debts which were incurred by communist governments in Poland trying to spend their way into their consumers' hearts and to keep democracy at bay.

Deducting debt restructuring from the grant element of assistance brings its percentage in total assistance down to 20%. If in addition emergency assistance, either as food aid or other emergency aid (ECU4.8 billion) is subtracted, then the real grant percentage is reduced to a mere 15.6%. Again, emergency aid is clearly grant assistance. However roughly 60% of this aid has been given to help the victims of the war in Yugoslavia, most of the rest was concentrated in a short period at the beginning of the transformation. A small part of grant aid was also a misuse of the term 'aid'.[3]

It would appear therefore that the real grant element of assistance has been around 15% of the G24 assistance figure, but it is also dubious to accept the overall figure of ECU86.2 billion at face value. This figure includes ECU17.6 billion of official export credits, 20.4% of total assistance. Export credits are important in order to stimulate trade, they are not however 'assistance' in the strict meaning of the term. If export credits are subtracted, the overall level of assistance is reduced to

---

[3] One 'donor' country supplied surplus fruit to a small country in Central Europe. The fruit had to be sold on the local market by the authorities of the 'beneficiary country' the receipts were paid into a specific account, which could only be used to buy products from the 'donor' country. In this way, the 'donor' obtained free marketing of surplus produce and added to its exports by forcing the 'beneficiary' to buy industrial products in that country.

ECU68 billion, and if emergency aid and debt restructuring are also subtracted, the total level of assistance is reduced to ECU50 billion.

On the donor's side, multilateral agencies (for this purpose including the European Union and EBRD) account for 40% of total assistance. These agencies have the advantage of not providing strictly tied assistance (EU aid is tied but procurement can be made in the Member States and the 'PHARE countries'). The largest bilateral donors are Germany and the United States, though in both cases official export credits figure highly in the total. The United States has provided the highest grant component of all bilateral donors, but with a large amount of debt restructuring. Germany and France follow, but with an even higher percentage of debt restructuring. The largest pure grant donor has been the European Union, mainly through its PHARE programme, hence its importance. In total, the European Union and its Member States have provided slightly over ECU46 billion or 53% of the total G24 assistance, the non-European G24 ECU18.8 billion or roughly 22% and the International Financial Organisations (including the EBRD) ECU21.4 billion or 25%.

On the recipient's side, Poland has received 35% of total assistance if debt reorganisation is included, but this falls to 26% if debt reorganisation is totally excluded. Hungary has received 14.7% of total assistance and the Czech and Slovak Republics 12.9%. These four countries have received 63% of total assistance (58% with debt forgiveness excluded). Romania has received relatively somewhat less, 9.5%, and Bulgaria 4.6%. Together, the three Baltic countries have received ECU3.4 billion or 5%. Finally, Albania has received slightly under 2%. The donor countries' 'giving pattern' is determined by many factors including geography. The Nordic countries have been major donors in the Baltic countries, while Italy has been by far the largest bilateral donor to Albania. Germany has concentrated its assistance on the 'Visegrád' countries, though it is also the largest bilateral donor to Romania.

Provisional figures for G24 assistance in 1996 suggest that an additional ECU11.5 billion was made available in that year, bringing total assistance for the period 1990–6 to ECU98 billion.

The real value of this assistance has also been criticised strongly on grounds other than its volume. Much of the grant assistance provided has gone towards purchasing technical assistance. With most bilateral assistance being tied aid, this has meant that the aid was spent on consultants in the donor country. As the amount of finance available was large in relation to the supply of high-quality consulting, some of this technical assistance was of low quality and a small proportion a downright waste of money.

Early on in the transformation process, there were many calls for a new 'Marshall Plan' (European Recovery Programme or ERP) for Central and Eastern Europe. The appeals were repeated in 1997, the fiftieth anniversary of the Marshall Fund. There have been several attempts to show that the assistance provided to Central and Eastern Europe has been of a different nature to that provided to Western Europe under the Marshall Plan.[4] The clearest difference between the two assistance efforts is that whereas the Marshall Plan was dealing with a situation where market economies had been devastated by war, in Central and Eastern Europe there was economic destruction, but on the basis of a planned economy rather than a market economy. The Marshall Plan also only had one donor and therefore coordination on the donors' side was not necessary; the G24 assistance effort comprised 24 countries and the international financial organisations as donors. Most of the Marshall Fund finance, which in volume terms was also bigger than the G24 effort, was provided as grants (roughly 80% against 15%) and therefore did not add to the debt problems of the recipient countries. It is not clear, however, that grants are always more valuable than loans in economic assistance.

Marshall Plan assistance provided, over a three-year period from 1948 to 1951, roughly $13 billion to the destroyed economies of Western Europe; in the fairly meaningless conversion to current dollars this is somewhat in excess of the finance made available over the seven years 1990–6 by the G24. In terms of percentages of GDP, ERP assistance was a very significant transfer for all countries except Belgium–Luxembourg and Sweden.[5] In 1949, the Netherlands, for instance, received between 16 and 23% of its GNP from ERP, France between 10 and 11.5%, Italy around 9% and the United Kingdom and Germany around 5% depending on which exchange rates are used. For the Netherlands this was roughly four times its annual growth rate. Compared to this scale of transfer, G24 assistance has been rather modest.

De Long and Eichengreen (1993) argue that even large amounts of grant finance under the Marshall Fund were not sufficient to accelerate the growth process in Western Europe in a very marked way.[6] They argue that it was the fact that the Marshall Fund forced the economies of Western Europe to take the market economy course and to open up their markets to trade which was the most important aspect. In other words the importance of the Marshall Plan was more in the strong

---

[4] For instance, Eichengreen and Uzan (1992).
[5] Milward (1984).        [6] De Long and Eichengreen (1993).

conditionality imposed on the aid than in the aid itself. Generally speaking in the G24 exercise there has been little discussion of specific conditionality. This is perhaps for three reasons: the aid has been very limited in quantity, there have been many donors and conditionality has been imposed by the IMF.

The balance of the aid effort for Central Europe is certainly less rosy than the donors pretend, but sometimes better than some of the over-hasty judgements from governments in the region. It is clearly not through aid, however, that the CEE countries will succeed in their reforms and achieve accession to the European Union. Such success will come through trade and investment and through appropriate macro-economic policies.

### EU assistance

The European Union has provided, as might be expected from a neighbour, more than half of the total assistance to Central Europe. It is even more important if grant finance is considered, where the European Union is the most important donor. It is therefore vital that EU assistance is efficient and effective.

#### What the Association Agreements say

Financial cooperation is a standard element in the Association Agreements. The Community, which by 1991 had passed through various budgetary crises, was not prepared 'for technical budgetary reasons' to agree to financial Protocols in the Association Agreements but only to chapters on 'financial cooperation'. In the event, this may have been better for both parties.

The agreements foresee three main sources of Community assistance: PHARE grants, EIB loans and, in appropriate circumstances, financing to support medium-term stabilisation and economic restructuring efforts, including balance of payments support. All of these types of assistance have been called on, though the latter medium-term lending has turned out to be predominantly relatively short-term balance of payments financing through the G24 complementary financing facilities.

The agreements state that assistance will be given either as grants from PHARE or as loans from the EIB. The agreement with Hungary made in 1991, for instance, specifies that 'grants will be made available . . . within . . . Phare on a multi-annual basis'. In the earlier agreements, the Community had already agreed to a multi-annual basis of financing for PHARE, although it had never implemented this. It was only after the decisions at the Essen and Cannes European Councils that this really became possible.

The agreements also deal with part of the programming cycle of PHARE, namely the indicative programme. It is strange to find this one part of the cycle in an agreement but in clearly stating that the indicative programme has to be agreed between the two sides, it firmly anchors the rights of the associated country to be equally involved in key decisions.

The article concerning loans determines the conditions for the granting of loans to support moves towards currency convertibility, medium-term stabilisation and structural adjustment including balance of payments loans. The restrictions in this article reflect the caution of the Member States. It subordinates the granting of all loans to the prior existence of an agreement with the IMF and stipulates that loans will be granted only within the context of the G24 to avoid the Community carrying the burden alone. The words 'temporary financial assistance' might also be thought to be incompatible with the stated objective of supporting 'medium-term stabilisation and structural adjustment', and in fact the Member States of the Union have agreed only to short-term balance of payments finance.

Other articles in the agreements lay down certain conditions for Community assistance and notably progress with market reforms and restructuring, as well as the financial situation of the country, and insist on the necessity of coordination of Community aid with that from the IFIs, the Member States and the G24.

### The PHARE programme

The PHARE programme began in January 1990 with an annual financing volume of ECU300 million for the provision of grants to Poland and Hungary. In mid-1997, it serves 13 countries and has a medium-term financial envelope 'guaranteeing' ECU6.7 million for five years.[7] It supports not only associated countries but all the reforming economies of Central and Eastern Europe and will be extended to the successor states of Yugoslavia as they fulfil the Community's criteria for the PHARE programme.[8]

The PHARE programme has a unique legal base, Regulation 3906/89

---

[7] There is no real budget guarantee given, only a political pledge. This became immediately obvious when soon after the 'guarantee' was given, ECU600 million was deducted to help the Bosnian reconstruction effort.

[8] The PHARE programme covers Estonia, Latvia, Lithuania, Poland, Czech Republic, Slovak Republic, Slovenia, Hungary, Romania, Bulgaria, Albania, Croatia (blocked at present), Macedonia and Bosnia-Herzegovina.

of 18 December 1989. The PHARE Regulation lays down the objectives of the programme and the fundamental rules by which it operates. The original objective was to assist the CEE countries (at first, only Poland and Hungary) to meet the financial requirements of the economic and social reform with which they were faced. The demand-driven nature of the programme is also indicated in the Regulation. This has meant that the governments of the PHARE beneficiary countries have had a much stronger control over the use of PHARE funds than was the case with US or other bilateral assistance.

The Copenhagen Summit in June 1993 added the so-called 'Copenhagen' facility, which for the first time allowed PHARE to become involved in major infrastructure development (up to 15% of the programme). Notable is the fact that at the European Council where the Community agreed on the common objective of accession for the associated countries, the Community also took the first step towards using PHARE assistance as structural assistance.

At Essen, further major progress was made in directing the assistance effort. The Essen strategy to prepare the associated countries for accession to the European Union, which is clearly a medium-term strategy, required a medium-term commitment to financial assistance. The Essen Summit agreed that at least the 1995 level of budgetary funding (ECU1.1 billion) should be made available until the end of the current financial guideline (1999), with additional funding agreed in 1995. In the context of the necessity of improving infrastructure in the region prior to accession, Essen also decided that up to 25% of the PHARE programme could now be used for the 'Copenhagen facility'. At Essen, it also became perfectly clear that PHARE had now a second objective beyond that identified by the PHARE Regulation, namely the financing of the process of integration with the European Union.

*The volume of PHARE assistance and its distribution over time and space*[9]

By the end of 1996, PHARE had committed a total of ECU6.6 billion. The European Council meeting in Cannes in June 1995 agreed that ECU6.7 billion should be allocated to spending on Central and Eastern Europe between 1995 and 1999. PHARE commitments can be expected to increase from the current level of just below ECU1.2 billion in 1995 to approximately ECU1.5 billion in 1999. The Essen European Council decision on a multi-annual financial envelope for PHARE, to accompany the multi-annual strategy for accession, and the setting of a

[9] For further details, see European Commission (1995b, 1996a).

Table 5.1 *PHARE assistance to beneficiary countries, 1990–6 (ECU million)*

|  | 1990 | 1991 | 1992 | 1993 | 1994 | 1995 | 1996 | Total | % |
|---|---|---|---|---|---|---|---|---|---|
| Albania | 0 | 10 | 110 | 75 | 49 | 88 | 53 | 385 | 5.8 |
| Bulgaria | 24.5 | 106.5 | 87.5 | 90 | 85 | 83 | 62.5 | 539 | 8.1 |
| Czechoslovakia | 34 | 99 | 100 | 0 | 0 | 0 | 0 | 233 | 3.5 |
| Czech Rep. | 0 | 0 | 0 | 60 | 60 | 110 | 54 | 284 | 4.3 |
| Slovak Rep. | 0 | 0 | 0 | 40 | 40 | 46 | 4.5 | 131 | 2.0 |
| Estonia | 0 | 0 | 10 | 12 | 22.5 | 24 | 61.8 | 130 | 2.0 |
| Hungary | 89.8 | 115 | 101.5 | 100 | 85 | 92 | 101 | 684 | 10.3 |
| Latvia | 0 | 0 | 15 | 18 | 29.5 | 32.5 | 37 | 132 | 2.0 |
| Lithuania | 0 | 0 | 20 | 25 | 39 | 42 | 53 | 179 | 2.7 |
| Poland | 180.8 | 197 | 200 | 225 | 208.8 | 174 | 203 | 1389 | 20.9 |
| Romania | 15.5 | 134.3 | 152 | 139.9 | 100 | 66 | 118.4 | 726 | 10.9 |
| Slovenia | 0 | 0 | 9 | 11 | 24 | 25 | 22 | 91 | 1.4 |
| Multi-country/other | 150.5 | 111.8 | 207.3 | 212 | 230.5 | 372.2 | 452.7 | 1734 | 26.1 |
| Total | 495.1 | 773.6 | 1012.3 | 1007.9 | 973.3 | 1154.7 | 1222.9 | 6636 | 100 |

*Source*: European Commission.

figure at Cannes in June 1995 has made it possible for the first time to undertake multi-annual programming. The distribution of PHARE funds by beneficiary country in table 5.1 shows that Poland, with approximately 21% of total assistance, has been the most important recipient, but with approximately 35% of the population of the region it is clear that population size is a major but not the sole criterion. In general, the smaller countries have tended to receive proportionately more than the larger countries; and countries where disbursement has proved difficult have tended to receive a proportionately smaller allocation.

In terms of the sectoral distribution of commitments, shown in table 5.2, up to 1995 the largest amount of PHARE financing had been spent in the area of private sector development. This reflects the importance given to private sector development in the PHARE regulation as well as the perceived needs of the PHARE countries. Infrastructure spending, with 22.1% of the total, reflects the large shift towards investment which was carried out in 1993–6. Starting from nothing in 1990, infrastructure spending made up one-third of total spending in 1994 and 40% in 1995. Education, health, training and research is the next largest sectoral allocation, reflecting the size of the TEMPUS programme which supports educational cooperation between the CEE countries and the European Union, with an annual financial volume of around ECU100 million. Agricultural reform and environment and nuclear

Table 5.2 *Sectoral distribution of PHARE assistance, 1990–6 (ECUmillion)*

|  | 1990 | 1991 | 1992 | 1993 | 1994 | 1995 | 1996 | Total | % |
|---|---|---|---|---|---|---|---|---|---|
| Agriculture | 136 | 89 | 80 | 78.5 | 17 | 40.6 | 27.9 | 469 | 7.1 |
| Education/health/ training | 36.8 | 140 | 151.5 | 188.6 | 182.9 | 149.1 | 126.4 | 974 | 14.7 |
| Environment/nuc. safety | 102.5 | 100 | 87.3 | 34.1 | 77.5 | 82 | 55.5 | 538.9 | 8.1 |
| Humanitarian/ food aid | 101.7 | 71.4 | 119.7 | 44.9 | 30 | 25 | 125 | 517.7 | 7.8 |
| Infrastructure | 7.3 | 50 | 88.8 | 114.9 | 326.4 | 457.2 | 424.4 | 1469 | 22.1 |
| Private sector dev. | 71 | 220.5 | 237.2 | 255.5 | 149.4 | 179.7 | 107.1 | 1219.2 | 18.4 |
| Approx. of legislation | 0 | 0 | 0 | 0 | 0 | 2 | 33.5 | 35.5 | 0.5 |
| Public administration ref. | 10 | 26.5 | 25.2 | 65.7 | 81.9 | 26.6 | 125.2 | 361.1 | 5.4 |
| Social/employment | 3 | 35.5 | 48.2 | 15 | 28.5 | 47.3 | 17.7 | 195.2 | 2.9 |
| Civil society | 0 | 0 | 9 | 10 | 16.2 | 10.5 | 23.7 | 69.4 | 1.0 |
| Integrated regional dev. | 0 | 0 | 20.8 | 10 | 4 | 47 | 79 | 160.8 | 2.4 |
| Other | 26.9 | 40.8 | 150.1 | 184.2 | 59.1 | 87.7 | 77.5 | 626.3 | 9.4 |
| Total | 495.2 | 773.7 | 1017.8 | 1001.4 | 972.9 | 1154.7 | 1222.9 | 6636.1 | 100 |

*Source*: European Commission.

safety were among the early priority areas for the programme, both having been allocated between 7% and 8% of the total programme. Much smaller proportions of assistance have gone to the reform of the public administration and to the social and employment policy areas, though these have become clear priorities in the recent past. PHARE is an important part of the EU's budget. If essential spending on the Structural Funds, agriculture and administration of the Union's institutions are excluded, it equals 10.4% of the remaining resources (it is only 1.4% of the total operational budget of the European Union). Such a large amount of finance is of obvious significance to the budgetary authority and especially to the European Parliament, whose main area of real power is the Community budget. If, however, PHARE is related to the total public sector spending in the Community or to Community GDP, it is of no significance. It is worth remembering that the Member States have reduced their grant spending to the Central European countries in favour of joint spending through PHARE, so that PHARE represents the overwhelming share of total EU grant finance to the region. As a proportion of EU GNP, PHARE is just 0.02%. With total net government outlays in the European Union at around 50% of GNP, this means that PHARE represents 0.04% of total government resources.

Looked at in relation to its significance for the beneficiary countries, PHARE finance is also relatively small. In Hungary, for instance, general government outlays in 1995 were around ECU18 billion, with a PHARE allocation of ECU100 million; PHARE resources are equal to around 0.5% of the total national budget. Looked at in terms of assistance per head of the population of the Central European region, the PHARE allocation works out at almost exactly ECU10 per head per year.

It is also interesting to compare the level of PHARE funding with that of the EU Structural Funds. Total spending on structural actions will rise according to the conclusions of the Edinburgh European Council to an annual ECU30 billion in 1999 at constant 1992 prices. If spending on the most disadvantaged regions is considered (objective 1) then this alone will reach almost ECU22 billion at 1992 prices by 1999 (including the Cohesion Fund). With a population of around 88 million in these regions, this works out at a *per capita* transfer in that one year of ECU250 at 1992 prices.

PHARE resources are therefore very limited resources in terms of almost any order of magnitude one likes to take as a basis. At the same time they are a non-negligible part of discretionary resources in the Community budget and for European parliamentarians they have a high opportunity cost.

*New directions of the PHARE programme*
The PHARE programme objectives change over time, sometimes in line with the changing needs of the PHARE countries. Three relatively recent changes are worth emphasising.

Firstly support for the accession of the associated countries to the Union has become a major objective of the programme since the Essen Summit in 1994, though the approximation of laws has been supported in sectoral programmes since the beginning of the programme.

However, with the majority of the financing from PHARE remaining in the area of the financing of transition, it is important that the programmes which are undertaken provide the sort of assistance which the countries need at the particular point in the transformation process which they have reached. In the early phases of transition there was a concentration on the provision of know-how or technical assistance, as well as some emergency help where required. As the transition has progressed, the requirement for technical assistance has declined relatively but the need for assistance with investment, especially in areas such as the building of infrastructure or in the cleaning up of the environment, has become far more important. This move in emphasis towards investment in PHARE, the second major development, is likely to continue. Much of the investment will be co-financing with other main donors such as World Bank, the EBRD or EIB and normally local co-financing will be required in all investment. The Commission's stated objective in 1997 was that 70% of the PHARE programme should be devoted to investment spending.

It is not conventional to use large parts of a grant assistance programme for such investment financing, but PHARE is gradually moving towards a Structural Fund, the objective of which is to stimulate economic development in these countries. While this may be resisted, it has its precursor in funds made available to Portugal prior to accession, and in the case of the associated countries it would appear to be a normal reaction to the perspective of accession only a few years away.

The third major change in the programme is the emphasis which is now given to supporting cross-border cooperation. This is both the result of the introduction by the European Parliament of the large cross-border programme in the 1993 budget, partly the result of the new importance given by both Essen and the Pact for Stability to regional cooperation and partly a response to the simple needs of economic development in a region where cross-border movement is becoming more and more frequent. In 1995 the cross-border cooperation programme provided almost ECU170 million in addition to around ECU30 million for the new frontier crossing improvement programme. The 1997 budget for the cross-border programme foresees expenditure of ECU280 million. It is to be assumed that spending in this area of activity will continue to expand in the future, as the needs of accession increase.

### The major problems of PHARE[10]

The PHARE programme still faces the following problems on the EU side:

- PHARE procedures are cumbersome and slow
- the relationship between delegations and Brussels and between different parts of the Brussels structure leads to inefficiency and waste
- too few resources are put into managing the programme in relation to its size

[10] For more on evaluation of the PHARE programme, see Mayhew (1996b).

- practically no conditionality is imposed
- there is growing political control over programme detail.

One of the ways which might improve efficiency would be to give most responsibility for implementation to the Commission delegations in the countries. The problems that can occur, because the roles of the delegations and the Brussels PHARE administration are not always clearly determined and because there are sometimes bureaucratic jealousies, are obvious. The relationship between host countries and the Commission delegations has not always been good, which has slowed implementation. However, the inefficiencies which occur because of the multitude of controls effected by Brussels and the delegation should be reduced by decentralising the system further.

A more fundamental problem is that of conditionality – or, rather, the lack of conditionality. The low level of financing means that PHARE alone cannot seriously affect overall progress with macroeconomic reform. The Union should find ways to increase its possibilities of reinforcing reform in the countries of the region. This can only be done by combining PHARE with the other more important areas of leverage which the Union has, notably in the context of the preparation of accession or in the granting of balance of payments assistance.

The final problem listed on the donor side is that of increasing political influence on the programme. PHARE started off as a largely demand-driven programme; today it is much less so, thanks largely to increasing political control of the programme. The problem really comes when decisions are made which change the objectives of the programme, or when changes are made abruptly which complicate the programming cycle or when changes are made to benefit political interests of a particular politically active person or group. Recently all of these have occurred.

On the beneficiary country side, the main problems remain:

- the frequent changes of government or of personnel cause major interruptions in the programme
- the lack of political consensus on how best to use the resources leads to a lack of prioritisation and a dispersion of aid
- PHARE assistance is small and is in the form of grants; this means that it is not given the same importance as, for instance, large World Bank loans, which have to be serviced.

The frequent changes in government and personnel in the different ministries or offices is quite typical for the transition period as a stable system of political parties is developing. It does, nevertheless, lead to considerable problems for the running of programmes. On the one hand, policies tend to change abruptly. For instance, the early privatisation enthusiasm generally gave way to a much more cautious approach by later governments. Early PHARE privatisation programmes therefore became extremely difficult to manage, and very slow to disburse. On the other hand, the officials or ministers dealing with PHARE change quite regularly, often causing lack of institutional memory which affects the running of programmes. These problems were especially difficult at the beginning of the transition when instability in some countries was greater than it is now.

A major problem in the beneficiary countries has been the lack of political consensus on the prioritisation of PHARE resources. The political influence here has been present since the beginning and matches to some extent that in the Union. While PHARE resources are not large, they nevertheless represent free budgetary resources for each Ministry which controls PHARE programmes. Ministers therefore fight for control of this finance, leading often to the division of PHARE into small and often badly prepared projects.

PHARE has never been given the same importance by the recipient countries as resources coming from the Bretton Woods institutions or even other bilateral donors. Grant money needs less control from the beneficiary country than loans, because it does not represent a future charge on the budget. As it is also relatively small, the Finance Minister is usually not interested by PHARE. Usually grant money is dealt with not by the Finance Ministry but by a specific aid coordinator. It is therefore rarely coordinated with either national budgetary expenditure or with other foreign loan sources. This means that the efficiency to be obtained by integrating grant assistance with national expenditure programmes or with foreign loans is lost.

There are certainly many other problems which exist and which need to be solved if PHARE is to have an important impact on the transition and the process of integration into the European Union. However, no assistance programme has ever been perfect and PHARE is far from the worst.

### 'Agenda 2000' and PHARE reform

The latest Commission proposals for both the reform of PHARE and its integration into the accession process are made in two documents published in mid-1997: 'New policy guidelines for the PHARE Programme in the framework of pre-accession assistance' (European Commission, 1997c) and 'Agenda 2000', volume 2 (European Commission, 1997a).[11]

---

[11] EU Commission (1997a, 1997c).

The first document is a political statement of objectives and it will be sensible to wait for an interpretative operational paper and the results of discussions in the Council and the Parliament. The objective is to turn PHARE into a more useful tool for promoting the accession of the associated countries. This will involve on the one hand prioritising far more severely and concentrating PHARE finance on investment and institution building and on the other making the management of PHARE more efficient. The new guidelines suggest that there should be an indicative breakdown in the distribution of PHARE funds between investment (70%) and institution building (30%). Both areas should be geared towards preparing accession.

Infrastructure investment would therefore be used, but not exclusively, for Trans-European Networks (TENs) and other networks which are important in the context of accession, as well as for environmental infrastructure and investment in human capital. It is to be hoped that this investment will not squeeze out private investment in the region just as capital markets are developing well. Considerable emphasis is put on PHARE funds being combined with loans from the IFIs and the EIB.

Institution building includes the whole preparation of government and relevant institutions for accession. The paper talks about 'public services', but no doubt this will include private and public institution building (the institutions involved in the new approach to harmonisation are usually in the private sector). Four areas are underlined – the approximation of laws, regional policy institutions, third-pillar institutions and the further opening of Community programmes to the associated countries.

The core of reforming PHARE management is to move from a 'demand-driven' programme to an 'accession-driven' one. It is a little unclear what is really meant here. 'Agenda 2000' suggests that rather than the associated countries determining their priorities for use of PHARE resources, these will be determined by the Union side, in the context of 'accession partnerships'. Accession partnerships will replace the existing programming tools. They will be multi-annual programmes and will be essentially based on the needs of each country revealed by the Commission's opinion on their Membership applications. Conditionality will be applied in the sense that progress will be analysed at the end of each year's partnership agreement and the following year's partnership will depend on progress made. As far as is possible, all sources of Union grant assistance will be programmed under these instruments.

Together with the proposed limitation on very small programmes (normally in future projects should have a volume of at least ECU2–3 million), it is hoped that the accession partnerships will considerably shorten programming cycles and lead to a more rapid disbursement of funds. Commitments should not be valid for more than two years after the signing of the financing agreement.

Overall there is much to be said for these proposals of the Commission on PHARE reform. The positive elements of these ideas include reinforced conditionality and the emphasis laid on investment, as long as this is not used in a way that distorts capital markets. Whether the operational papers, when they appear, will show a major change in the programming of PHARE is perhaps less sure, given the complexities involved. And the limitation of the validity of programmes to two years will also prove very difficult in some areas, with the risk that finance could be wasted on rapidly thought-up schemes. Perhaps the most dangerous part of the proposals is the lack of clarity on the question of more or less decentralisation of PHARE. While delegation of implementation for certain projects to certain countries is proposed, the overall tenor of the proposals is that there should be more control from the centre. The opinions should play a greater role in determining programmes than the perception of need in the beneficiary country. This could be a very dangerous move from 'demand-driven' to dictates from the centre, with all the increased waste that that would involve. Each country will have a different way of preparing for accession, with different sequencing appropriate to that country; imposition of different sequencing from Brussels might be counter-productive. But even here it is to be hoped that the operational papers will clarify this question in a satisfactory way.

'Agenda 2000' also proposes that the associated countries should receive additional pre-accession assistance from the year 2000 in the form of ECU500 million for agricultural structures and ECU1 billion for pre-accession Structural Funds. This additional assistance will be provided essentially for improving market structures and food quality on the one hand and infrastructure on the other. The scale of this pre-accession assistance is modest, leading to a doubling of existing PHARE assistance from the year 2000. This will take the level of total grant funding from the Union (including PHARE) to around 0.5% of the associated countries' GDP. Most estimates assume that these countries will need to devote at least 6% of their annual GDP to the additional investment costs caused by the need to adjust to the EU *acquis*.

*Policy recommendations*
There are two ways to go in the search for improvements to the implementation of Community aid; the first is to take the present system

and improve it, the second is to try a totally different system. The proposals of 'Agenda 2000' appear to fall somewhere in between.

Certain important elements should be considered before deciding for the one or the other solution:

- We are dealing with European countries which may be Members of the Union by 2002 or 2003. Yet the PHARE system was set up in the traditional way development assistance has always been run in Africa and elsewhere and the financial regulation governing assistance to third countries applies equally to Africa and South America as it does to the Czech Republic.

- Secondly the aid should be used for preparing the associated countries for accession. This is the theme of 'Agenda 2000'; this means carrying out programmes to help them adapt their legislation and introduce necessary institutions. But above all it means helping them as well as possible to create the economic and physical infrastructure necessary to allow them to grow strongly and to physically integrate with the Union. In this sense, PHARE assistance should be seen as helping these countries to change and adapt their structures, in other words, as a Structural Fund. The notion of pre-accession Structural Funds will give considerable political offence to some Member States, but in reality this is what PHARE should become.

- Thirdly it is important to find a way of protecting the PHARE programme from day-to-day political influence, which means that the programme diverges more and more from the terms of the PHARE regulation and loses its impact on the course of the transition. On the other hand, there should be stronger conditionality, so that a government which clearly turns its back on reform can be deprived of PHARE assistance, something which only occurs today when a country shows aggression against its neighbours (e.g. ex-Yugoslavia).

- Finally a way needs to be found to use the few resources available to the management of the programme, as efficiently as possible.

If the current system of PHARE programming and implementation is to be retained, the improvements which can be made are probably relatively small considering the constraints imposed by the financial regulation. The essential point of decentralising more authority in programming and implementation to the beneficiary country should be followed up, and progress should be possible even within existing rules. Passing more authority to the delegations and avoiding multiple controls between Brussels and the delegations is a distant second best to giving control to the PHARE countries.

The other extreme would be to treat PHARE resources as balance of payments loans are treated. This would mean that the funds allotted to each country would be applied for by the PHARE country for a specific purpose, such as infrastructure development or industrial restructuring. The assistance would be paid in tranches, each tranche having clear conditionality attached to it. The authorities of the country would be responsible for determining the use of the finance in consultation with the Commission. The release of a second tranche of money would depend on the conditions for continued assistance being met and a satisfactory account being given for the use of the first tranche. Some elements of this system appear to be found in the idea of accession partnerships.

While the last possibility is in many ways the most transparent and most efficient system of transferring assistance, it is unlikely to be adopted. It would also represent an important blow to many who benefit from the PHARE programme, notably the consultants, supported by their Member States, and those who wish to derive some political advantage from influencing the way the funds are distributed.

A final possibility would be to move to a situation equivalent to the Structural Funds inside the Community. The system of assistance described by the Regulation (EEC) no. 2081/93 on the tasks of the Structural Funds would be a considerable improvement over the current way in which PHARE is implemented. The objectives of regional development fund support (ERDF) are listed as follows:

- productive investment
- creation or modernisation of infrastructure
- to exploit the potential for internally generated development of the regions concerned
- investment in the field of education and health.

Several advantages would result. Firstly the beneficiary country would effectively be in control of its own programme, though in partnership with the Commission. Secondly the beneficiary country would have to co-fund projects, which would ensure that they really take ownership of the projects and that they are coordinated with national budgetary objectives. Thirdly the possibility of budgetary carry-overs would improve the effectiveness of multi-annual programming. Finally such a system would considerably reduce the need for human resources in Brussels or in the delegations and by putting much more responsibility on the beneficiary countries' services would also lead to improvements in public administration.

The Structural Funds approach is at the same time politically the most appropriate, while increasing the efficiency of the programme. To make this change would probably require a new PHARE Regulation and the approval of the Council and the European Parliament. It would be a major step, but one worth taking for the sake of efficiency, effectiveness and good relations with future Members of the Union.

### Community loans

The Association Agreements state that

the Community shall, in case of special need, taking into account the availability of all financial resources, on request of [Estonia] and in coordination with international financial institutions, in the context of the G24, examine the possibility of granting temporary financial assistance
  - to support measures with the aim of maintaining the convertibility of the [Estonian] currency;
  - to support medium-term stabilisation and structural adjustment efforts, including balance of payments assistance;
This financial assistance is subject to [Estonia's] presentation of IMF supported programmes in the context of the G24, as appropriate, for convertibility and/or for restructuring its economy, to the Community's acceptance thereof, to [Estonia's] continued adherence to these programmes and, as an ultimate objective, to rapid transition to reliance on finance from private sources.

In practice, out of this wide definition of the objective of Community loans has come a practice which limits them to temporary and complementary balance of payments loans.

### The principles of Community loans to Central Europe

While the first loan to Hungary was made solely by the Community, there was a strong feeling in the Community that 'burden sharing' should be more emphasised. It was therefore decided that, also in the context of better coordination of assistance, the Community would provide assistance in the context of the G24 process. In this way it was hoped that other donors would join the Community in meeting the burden of lending.

In 1991, the G24 agreed the principles under which this activity should proceed. Firstly it was agreed that the loans should only be made in *'exceptional circumstances'* and on a *'case-by-case basis'*, and that the financing should be discontinued when other reliable sources of official financing or of private capital were available. Secondly, the loans had to be *'complementary'* to other preferred sources, notably the IMF and the World Bank; they would be made available only after the Bretton Woods institutions had demonstrated the existence of a financing gap after all other sources had been taken into consideration. Finally there was to be strong macroeconomic *conditionality* attached to the loans, this conditionality being closely related to the IMF performance criteria established for the country.

The way in which this system operated was of considerable benefit to the associated countries and to other countries in the region at a crucial period in their transition. The IMF and the World Bank calculated the financing gap for each country which existed after loans from these IFIs were taken into consideration. This financing gap was then put to the G24 via the Commission, which then attempted to close it through G24 contributions. It became almost a tradition that the Community itself would contribute 50% of the financing requirement, the other 50% being spread across the G24. However as the United States always refused to contribute significantly to these G24 efforts, the burden fell essentially on the Member States of the Community and Japan. The result was that the Community and its Member States together contributed the vast bulk of the loans. Altogether over the period 1991–4 nearly 82% of the identified cumulative financing gaps had been covered by G24 lending, a remarkably good performance.

Certain Community Member States were not at all in favour of this process, believing that the Community had almost blackmailed itself into becoming the main source of loan finance for the transition. In 1993 therefore, ECOFIN (the Council of Economics and Finance Ministers) discussed the Community's macro-financial assistance and drew up a new code of conduct. They reaffirmed the three G24 principles of exceptionality, complementarity and conditionality. They added however certain political pre-conditions. These were that the countries receiving assistance should be geographically proximate and that they should be democracies with full respect for human rights and the rule of law. And the ministers referred back to the passages in the Association Agreements as the guiding rules to this activity. This was a generally favourable conclusion on this activity and quietened some of the critics. However, by 1993 the zenith of the balance of payments finance had already passed, as the needs of the countries became less 'exceptional' and the IMF was better able to cope with the financing difficulties itself. The recent crisis experienced by Bulgaria as well as the problems of some of the countries of former Yugoslavia have led to a reawakening of complementary Community financing.

### The experience of Community loans to Central Europe

Macro-financial support was extended outside the Community to Central and Eastern Europe in 1990 in response to the critical payments situations in several countries. Finance was important to underpin the stabilisation programmes run by governments in the region and especially to support the move to current account convertibility. With available finance from the IMF and the World Bank being insufficient to cover these needs, especially as the economies were rocked by the loss of the COMECON market, and with no access to private capital flows, Community financing became extremely important.

The first loan was made available to Hungary in February 1990. This balance of payments loan, made exclusively by the Community outside the G24 framework, amounted to ECU870 million. This was followed by a further 12 classic G24 operations and two 'balance of payments grants' to Albania. The total amount of Community loans made up to the end of 1994 was ECU2,755 million, together with EU105 million in grants to Albania.[12] Of this, ECU2,070 million had already been disbursed by the end of 1994 (table 5.3). Loans are generally divided into tranches, with specific conditions linked to each tranche and the disbursement of the second tranche depending on the respect of conditions attached to the first. Non-respect of the conditions has led to delays in disbursement on several occasions. This affected, for instance, disbursement of the 1992 loan to Bulgaria and the 1994 loan to Romania. The latter had not been disbursed by mid-1995 owing to slippage in Romania's exchange rate policy.

The degree of coordination and cooperation with the IMF and the World Bank in this area of financing is extremely high. The loans are never made without prior agreement between the IMF and the country concerned and the conditions attached to the loans are set in agreement with the IMF. They are definitely not a way to finance getting around IMF conditionality, in fact they reinforce it.

*The future of macro-financial assistance*

In the preparation of the Essen Summit in the second half of 1994, the Commission proposed to the Council that the loan instrument which until then had been exclusively used as a short-term balance of payments instrument, should be developed into a medium-term structural pre-accession loan instrument. Indeed the Association Agreement cited above specifically mentions loans to 'support medium-term stabilisation and structural adjustment efforts'.

This proposal had some logic on its side. At Essen, the Community proposed a medium-term strategy to prepare the associated countries

---

[12] The Community considered that Albania was too poor to repay any loans given to it. It was therefore decided to give two grants totalling ECU105 million, where the finance was taken from the PHARE grant programme.

Table 5.3 *Community macro-financial assistance to Central Europe,*
*1990–4 (ECU million)*

| Country | Maximum authorised | Date of decision | Amount disbursed |
|---|---|---|---|
| Hungary | 870 | 22.2.90 | 610 |
| Czech/Slovak | 375 | 25.2.91 | 375 |
| Hungary | 180 | 24.6.91 | 180 |
| Bulgaria | 290 | 24.6.91 | 290 |
| Romania | 375 | 22.7.91 | 375 |
| Albania | 70 | 28.9.92 | 70 |
| Estonia | 40 | 23.11.92 | 20 |
| Latvia | 80 | 23.11.92 | 40 |
| Lithuania | 100 | 23.11.92 | 50 |
| Romania | 80 | 27.11.92 | 80 |
| Bulgaria | 110 | 19.10.92 | 70 |
| Romania | 125 | 20.6.94 | 0 |
| Albania | 35 | 28.11.94 | 15 |
| Slovakia | 130 | 22.12.94 | 0 |
| Total | 2,860 | | 2,175 |

*Source*: European Commission.

for membership. The PHARE grant programme was transformed into a medium-term pre-accession programme, which was also permitted to fund a much higher volume of investment-related activities. The EIB was also given a new higher ceiling to make project-related investments in these countries. These additional financial facilities are required to support the major investment effort which the countries will need to make in a short time to prepare for accession. But both PHARE and EIB finance slow-disbursing projects. Macro-financial assistance, if approved by the Council, would disburse much more quickly and without bureaucratic delay and put substantial finance at the disposal of governments faced with rapid modernisation needs.

Of course, structural loans would slightly change the framework of Community macro-financial lending. Balance of payment loans have a maturity of five to seven years; structural loans would have somewhat longer maturities. There would be no financing gap to be closed by the loan, but the loan would go to support a medium-term development strategy approved by the Community and consistent with the macroeconomic framework agreed with the IMF. But the other conditions for macro-financial assistance, agreed by the Council, would also be respected.

While the logic of providing structural lending to rapidly reforming associated countries preparing for accession appears to be strong, the proposal was rejected by finance ministers. The main reason appears to be that there are other sources of such lending, notably the World Bank. However, the specific challenges of accession and the need for non-project specific finance means that this proposal will certainly be kept on the table for future consideration.

### EIB financing

The EIB was allowed to begin lending to projects in Poland and Hungary in October 1989 up to a level of ECU1 billion set in February 1990 by the Council. This level of lending was subsequently increased by ECU700 million to include Czechoslovakia, Romania and Bulgaria. Then in February 1993, this lending limit was raised by a further ECU200 million to permit lending to the three Baltic countries to begin. The lending limit was raised by ECU3 billion for the period 1994–6 and finally an additional ECU3.5 billion was agreed for financing for the period from 1997 to 2000. In addition, the EIB has agreed to make a substantial pre-accession support facility available from its own resources.

EIB loans are made available at very competitive rates owing to the Bank's high credit rating, due in no small part to the fact that its loans are guaranteed 100% through the budget of the Community. The loans are all project-based loans. They are made mainly in the productive or infrastructure areas: the Bank is prohibited from lending to certain social sectors. The Bank rarely goes beyond lending 50% of the value of the investment, the remainder coming from domestic sources in the country or other international sources of finance. The Bank makes individual large loans to governments or project promoters. In the case of small loans, for instance to SMEs, with a total investment cost of less than ECU25 million, the Bank provides global loans to financial intermediaries for on-lending to final borrowers.

Between 1992 and 1996, the EIB lent ECU4,280 million to the countries of Central Europe. Of the 1994–6 loans, roughly 58% were for communications infrastructure projects (including telecommunications), 26% for energy projects, 2% for water management while 14% were made available as global loans. In terms of country distribution, Poland with 27% of all loans, the Czech Republic with 25% and Hungary with 15% received the vast bulk of the funds.

The EIB attempts to use its lending to further the objectives of Community policy, where this is also in the interests of the borrower. Much of the finance for transport, for instance, has been lent for building trans-European networks. In 1996 the Bank lent ECU200 million to upgrade the Warsaw–Ostrava–Vienna railway line, ECU95 million for upgrading the M3 motorway in Hungary and ECU70 million for road rehabilitation in European corridors in Romania. It should be expected that lending in the future will be to some extent concentrated on such major axes of European importance. This is a questionable policy from the point of view of the CEE countries, which could probably obtain a higher return on investment in other parts of the road or rail network. For the Community naturally improvements in these transit roads to Russia, the Ukraine, Greece and Turkey are very welcome.

### Further development of EIB lending

EIB lending was very important to the associated countries, which at the beginning of the reform process did not necessarily have easy access to private sources of capital, and even then only at several points over LIBOR. Today many of the associated countries have relatively easy access to international capital markets but they still find the EIB an interesting source of capital for long-term development.

Two proposals might improve the EIB's performance further. The first would be to reduce the level of Community guarantee on the loans to Central Europe from the current 100% to 75%. Unlike normal banks or, indeed, unlike the World Bank, the EIB takes no risk in lending to Central Europe because all the loans are guaranteed by the Community. Yet practically none of the Bank's borrowers ever default and, apart from the former Yugoslavia, there has never been a default in Central and Eastern Europe. The consequence of these high guarantee levels is that it is the level of the guarantee fund in the Community budget which is the limiting factor on EIB lending rather than the availability of capital or of good projects to finance. A reduction in the level of the guarantee would a priori allow the EIB to increase the level of its lending. This proposal has already been made by the Commission, but with no success as yet.

The second proposal has to a certain extent already been realised. It is to coordinate better the various Community financial instruments, EIB loans, PHARE grants and, in the future, structural adjustment loans. With PHARE providing more finance for investment, it is natural that the EIB should co-finance investment projects, which it leads, with PHARE supporting with grants. With non-project structural loan finance available as well, the Community could provide considerably more valuable financial assistance to the transformation and to the objective of accession than it does now.

## Conclusion

The old clichés 'trade not aid' or 'trade and aid' are usually found in discussions on assistance programmes. There are no firm answers to the question of the importance of assistance in supporting the transition and accession. It is certainly true that open trade regimes, wise stabilisation policies, growth-oriented macroeconomic policies and appropriate microeconomic policies are far more important than assistance. But we are not in an 'either or world'. The transformation, especially of physical infrastructure, will take longer if assistance is not available, as will the preparation of accession. And time in Central Europe is a most valuable commodity. If through the appropriate investment of foreign assistance, successful transformation can be advanced by several years, popular support for the sometimes socially difficult but necessary changes may hold up long enough to allow these countries to complete the transition to democratic market economies. In this sense aid can be crucial.

What is certainly true is that without these other fundamental policy changes assistance is a waste of resources. This is why the chapter pleads for more conditionality in the provision of assistance. Conditionality does not have to be one-sided; it would be preferable in Central Europe to set up a regular mutual surveillance exercise, similar to that established under stage 2 of the Maastricht monetary union construction, where conditionality was verified by both sides and where early corrective measures could be jointly decided.

Finally, it is important that the relatively small amount of aid which is available should be used as efficiently as possible. It should certainly not be used in a way to crowd out private capital flows, and it should be made available in the simplest and most direct way possible. Undoubtedly it is time to move towards providing a Structural Fund for the associated countries, giving these countries essentially control over the assistance and preparing them for accession.

## Appendix: G24 assistance tables

Table 5A.1  *G24 assistance, by donor and type of assistance, cumulated,*
*1990–5 (ECU million)*

| | Total assistance | Debt reorg. | Off. export credit | Emergency/ food aid | Total *less* (2)+(3)+(4) | Of which grants |
|---|---|---|---|---|---|---|
| | (1) | (2) | (3) | (4) | (5) | (6) |
| Austria | 3,422 | 146 | 1,884 | 16 | 1,376 | 814 |
| Belgium | 271 | 8 | 166 | 1 | 96 | 89 |
| Denmark | 1,093 | | 236 | 29 | 828 | 753 |
| Finland | 721 | 156 | 54 | 62 | 449 | 232 |
| France | 6,162 | 2,314 | 3,005 | 9 | 834 | 2,290 |
| Germany | 14,646 | 5,204 | 5,091 | 104 | 4,247 | 3,769 |
| Greece | 87 | | 21 | 54 | 12 | 66 |
| Ireland | 3 | | | 1 | 2 | 2 |
| Italy | 1,543 | | 686 | 396 | 461 | 605 |
| Lux. | 30 | | 19 | 4 | 7 | 10 |
| Neth. | 1,268 | 280 | 504 | 90 | 394 | 696 |
| Portugal | 4 | | 2 | | 2 | 0 |
| Spain | 1,040 | 37 | 966 | 78 | −41 | 7 |
| Sweden | 1,487 | 546 | 293 | 89 | 559 | 405 |
| UK | 836 | 628 | | 5 | 203 | 159 |
| EU bilateral | 32,613 | 9,320 | 12,926 | 939 | 9,428 | 9,899 |
| EU progs | 9,632 | | | 1,867 | 7,765 | 6,870 |
| EIB | 3,645 | | | | 3,645 | |
| CECA | 200 | | | | 200 | |
| EU total | 46,090 | 9,320 | 12,926 | 2,806 | 21,038 | 16,769 |
| USA | 9,757 | 2,047 | 3,026 | 1,644 | 3,040 | 5,637 |
| G24 | 64,870 | 13,164 | 17,553 | 4,761 | 29,392 | 25,373 |
| EBRD | 3,455 | | | | 3,455 | |
| IBRD | 8,396 | | | | 8,396 | |
| IMF | 9,512 | | | | 9,512 | |
| Total | 86,234 | 13,164 | 17,553 | 4,761 | 50,756 | 25,373 |
| % | 100 | 15.27 | 20.36 | 5.52 | 56.86 | 29.42 |
| Grant compon. | 25,373 | 8,161 | | 3,744 | 13,468 | |

*Source*: European Commission.

Table 5A.2 *Assistance, by beneficiary, cumulated, 1990–5 (ECU million)*

| | Total | Debt reorg. | Off. export credit | Emer- gency/ food aid | Total *less* (2)+(3) +(4) | Grants as % of total | As % of (1) | As % of (5) |
|---|---|---|---|---|---|---|---|---|
| | (1) | (2) | (3) | (4) | (5) | (6) | (7) | (8) |
| Albania | 1,585 | 4 | 105 | 381 | 1,099 | 936 | 1.8 | 2.2 |
| Bulgaria | 3,981 | 253 | 317 | 143 | 3,268 | 911 | 4.6 | 6.4 |
| Czech Rep. | 3,289 | | 975 | | 2,314 | 355 | 3.8 | 4.6 |
| Czechoslovakia | 6,353 | | 2,739 | 24 | 3,590 | 496 | 7.4 | 7.1 |
| Estonia | 917 | | 105 | 81 | 731 | 345 | 1.1 | 1.4 |
| Hungary | 12,651 | 64 | 3,140 | 115 | 9,332 | 1,084 | 14.7 | 18.4 |
| Latvia | 1,051 | | 141 | 86 | 824 | 286 | 1.2 | 1.6 |
| Lithuania | 1,445 | | 196 | 128 | 1,121 | 435 | 1.7 | 2.2 |
| FYROM | 590 | 10 | 75 | 94 | 411 | 186 | 0.7 | 0.8 |
| Poland | 30,394 | 12,798 | 3,864 | 498 | 13,234 | 11,540 | 35.3 | 26.1 |
| Romania | 8,191 | | 2,537 | 537 | 5,117 | 1,204 | 9.5 | 10.1 |
| Slovak Rep. | 1,439 | | 467 | | 972 | 225 | 1.7 | 1.9 |
| Slovenia | 870 | | 301 | 50 | 519 | 125 | 1.0 | 1.0 |
| Ex-Yugoslavia | 4,780 | 35 | 1,036 | 2,357 | 1,352 | 2,250 | 5.5 | 2.7 |
| Unspecified | 8,697 | | 1,555 | 267 | 6,875 | 4,996 | 10.1 | 13.5 |
| Total | 86,234 | 13,164 | 17,553 | 4,761 | 50,759 | 25,373 | 100 | 100 |

*Source*: European Commission.

*Part III*

# Making enlargement a reality

# 6    Going beyond the Europe Agreements: the European Union's pre-accession strategy

The Europe Agreements provide the basis for the European Union's relationship with the associated countries. However, as has been seen in preceding chapters these agreements were not sufficient to take the associated countries to accession.

Since the beginning of 1993 the Union has taken several major political steps to open the way towards greater integration and accession; these include the policy packages of the European Councils in Copenhagen in June 1993, Essen in December 1994, Madrid in December 1995 and Amsterdam in June 1997, as well as the Commission's Opinions on the applications for membership and its policy papers on the budget, the Structural Funds and agriculture presented as 'Agenda 2000' in July 1997.[1] The Luxembourg European Council will take the key decisions on the opening of negotiations with the associated countries in December 1997.

These steps as important political landmarks were dealt with in chapter 1. The objective of this chapter is to analyse the detailed, mainly economic, components which helped to steer the relationship between these countries and the European Union from association to accession.

## The Copenhagen Council: the common objective of accession

The Copenhagen European Council meeting in June 1993 took the historically important step of agreeing that

the associated countries in Central and Eastern Europe that so desire shall become members of the European Union. Accession will take place as soon as an associated country is able to assume the obligations of membership by satisfying the economic and political conditions required.

The conditions imposed by the Union for accession were very general:

---

[1] EU Commission (1997a).

- the stability of institutions guaranteeing democracy, the rule of law, human rights and respect for and protection of minorities
- the existence of a functioning market economy
- the capacity to cope with competitive pressures and market forces within the Union
- the ability to take on the obligations of membership, including adherence to the aims of political, economic and monetary union.

In addition the Council underlined that accession would depend on the capacity of the Union to take on new members while maintaining the momentum of European integration.

The Copenhagen criteria for accession remain the only clear statement made by the Union on the character of the test which will be used for deciding which of the applicants can join:

- The first criterion concerning democracy, the rule of law, human rights and minorities is not surprising, given the Union's consistent position over many years and the fact that this criterion has found its way into the new Amsterdam Treaty as amended article F. Certain of the current applicants for accession have caused the Union worries over recent years, especially on the treatment of minorities, and the clear statement in the Copenhagen criteria has exerted some pressure for reform.

- The second criterion, the existence of a functioning market economy, is clearly not an absolute and measurable condition; in the Union itself the 'market' is developed to varying degrees. It is as much a qualitative as a quantitative condition. Certain elements must clearly be in place: the dominance of the private sector in output, price liberalisation, competition policy and some restriction on state aids, some degree of capital movement liberalisation, and so on. But the qualitative characteristics of an open market economy are just as important: does government policy aim towards developing contested markets and to reduce subsidy, does it support national champions to the detriment of inward investment? Three of the applicant countries, the Czech Republic, Hungary and Poland, had by 1997 received the ultimate recognition as market economies, membership of the OECD.

- The third Copenhagen criterion, the capacity to cope with competitive pressures, is strange. If markets are flexible and adjustment is rapid, competitive pressures from the Union should not be a problem. However given that adjustment has been slow in some countries and in certain sectors, opening the economies at accession to competition within the internal market is likely to cause sometimes difficult adjustment problems, even if they are transitional. It is extremely difficult to see how the Union could make such a criterion operational, though the judgements in the Commission opinions on the extent of structural problems still persisting in the associated countries is probably as near as the Union can come.

- The fourth criterion refers to the ability of the applicants to adopt and implement Community laws, regulation and policies. It is undoubtedly the most discriminant criterion – the problems involved are discussed later in this book. It is interesting that while adopting the *acquis* is a condition for membership, the Union is using it as a condition for the opening of negotiations. Adherence to the aims of political, economic and monetary union is hardly likely to figure highly in the decisions on opening negotiations.

While the common goal of accession was clearly the most important step forward taken at Copenhagen, other important decisions supporting accession were also made. The decision to create a multilateral structured relationship responded to two necessities. The first was the need to bring the associated countries into discussions of problems affecting them directly or affecting future accession. It was also felt that only by much better cooperation between ministers could the close working relationships be achieved which would be required to solve future problems on the way to accession. The other need was to reduce the importance of bilateral political dialogue, instituted in the Association Agreements, but which, as the number of associated countries grew, had become almost impossible to carry out for lack of available ministerial time. To avoid devaluing the political dialogue through low-level representation on the Union side, it was clearly considered better to propose a high-level but multilateral political dialogue (see chapter 2).

The Copenhagen European Council came after a great deal of bad feeling had arisen amongst the parties on relatively trivial trade disputes, usually in the agricultural area. The Community felt that it was necessary to demonstrate goodwill by proposing unilateral trade concessions of a horizontal nature. These concessions were not significant in terms of the volume of extra imports which were allowed or the changes in tariffs, but they were significant as an indication that the Community could still bring itself to make unilateral concessions, recognising that the relationship with the associated countries was a special one. Finally the Commission was invited to 'effect a study of the feasibility and impact of the cumulation of rules of origin for products from the associated countries of Central and Eastern Europe and the EFTA countries and, in the light of the findings, to submit to it appropriate proposals'.

The Copenhagen trade package went beyond the Association Agreements, but only by a relatively small margin. Nevertheless politically this was an important breakthrough in an area where most observers had maintained before Copenhagen that nothing was possible.

Copenhagen also reinforced the commitment to accession by asking the Commission to come forward with proposals to open up Community programmes to the associated countries and to set up a new Task Force on the approximation of laws. The former proved to be more complex than at first imagined and the second was never activated as other solutions to the problems were chosen by the Council meeting in Essen 18 months later.

The final significant part of the Copenhagen package of measures concerned the assistance programme PHARE. It was agreed that up to 15% of the programme could be used for infrastructure development subject to certain constraints, which have been analysed above. This new departure also fitted in closely with the process of preparing the accession of the associated countries. This decision marked a decisive move in the Community's assistance programme in the direction of supporting investment spending.

The Copenhagen European Council may go down in history as a decisive step in the integration of Western and Central Europe. From this point on, enlargement obtained a sort of inevitability without a timetable. It is an interesting comment on the European Union that while there was little discussion or dispute on the common objective of accession, the minor trade concessions proved very difficult to negotiate.

It was clear to many people that further steps would have to be taken to follow on from Copenhagen and to push the integration process well beyond the Association Agreements. The follow-up to the Copenhagen measures took the form of a strategy for preparing the associated countries for accession, agreed at Essen 18 months later.

## The Essen Council: the pre-accession strategy

The European Union proposed a strategy for the accession of the associated countries to the Union at the Essen European Council in December 1994 under the German Presidency.

There were several reasons for the Union to prepare such a proposal.

Perhaps the most important was to bring the whole politically charged debate down to the working level. The ultimate decision on accession is always a political decision. However the political decision was unlikely to be taken if the hard practical work of the detailed preparation for accession to the internal market of the Union had not been accomplished. For this reason it was important to accelerate the preparation of accession in both the associated countries and in the Union.

The core of the Essen strategy is summarised in the Essen documents themselves:

The goal of the strategy . . . is to provide a route plan for the associated countries as they prepare for accession. The essential element of the strategy is their progressive preparation for integration into the internal market of the European Union, through the phased adoption of the Union's internal market *acquis*. This strategy will be supported by the implementation of policies to promote integration through the development of infrastructure, cooperation in the framework of the trans-European networks, the promotion of intra-regional cooperation, environmental cooperation, as well as the Common Foreign and Security Policy, cooperation in the areas of judicial and home affairs, and in culture, education and training. This integration will be supported by the Union's PHARE programme which will develop on an indicative basis into an enhanced medium-term financial instrument with improved possibilities to promote infrastructure development and intra-regional co-operation. It is recognised that the Community *acquis* and Community policies will themselves continue to develop.

Politically the strategy will be realised through the development of a structured relationship between the associated countries and the Union. This will promote an atmosphere of mutual confidence and allow for the consideration of issues of common interest in a specially created framework.[2]

The Essen pre-accession strategy then had six main building blocks. Central is the preparation of the associated countries to join the internal market of the Union; around this core there is the promotion of economic integration of the associated countries with the Union, cooperation between the associated countries themselves, cooperation in a series of areas incorporating all three pillars of the Maastricht Treaty and the development of assistance to these countries. This essentially economic strategy is supported politically by an extensive multilateral political dialogue.

### Preparing entry into the internal market

The basis on which the European Union is built is its internal market; it is hardly conceivable that the other elements of the Union could operate if the functioning of the internal market was to be seriously threatened.

[2] European Council (1994)

It is for this reason that the relaunch of the European Community began in 1985 with the completion of the internal market as its centrepiece and that few other policies really attracted any attention until this key element was put in place through the '1992' programme. The internal market is therefore the natural place to begin a strategy to prepare the associated countries for accession to the Union.

The Essen strategy recognised three key areas for action: competition policy, the control of state aids and the *acquis communautaire* relating to the internal market.

### Competition policy

Competition policy was considered from the start of the association process as a vital component of the new relationship with Central Europe. The key consideration in the Essen strategy was not the creation of the legal basis for the introduction of the equivalent of articles 85, 86 and 90 of the Treaty establishing the EEC; the associated countries had already introduced the necessary legislation and rules of operation, as the Essen conclusions recognise. The emphasis was now put on the implementation of these rules in the associated countries. Essen promised that the Union would set up a competition policy training programme to help with the difficult task of training officials who would be charged in their own countries with this implementation.

### The control of state aids

The control of state aids as provided for in the Treaty of Rome, article 92, is the second element of the internal market strategy. Progress in controlling state aids is a relatively recent phenomenon in the Union itself; even today Member States are still frequently tempted to give substantial state aid to 'national champion' firms for electoral or other reasons in spite of the clear economic arguments about the efficiency of such operations. Nevertheless the associated countries must introduce such systems to limit subsidies in order to keep control over public finances, avoid waste of valuable state resources, and provide a defence against the pleading of poor management in large state enterprises or in some cases newly privatised enterprises as well as to integrate into the European internal market.

In this area of state aids, however, the situation is not straightforward. On the side of the associated countries there is frequently a lack of understanding of the breadth of measures which are included in the definition of 'state aids'; for instance, tax breaks given to certain groups of enterprises. On the side of the Union, however, it must be realised that not all state aids are given in Central Europe in order to distort competition. As was the case in the New Länder of Germany after reunification, many state aids are given in order to help move the economy towards a market-based system. As it is not in the interest of either the associated countries or the European Union to slow down this transformation process, an aid regime for the associated countries needs to take this problem into account.

On this point, the Essen strategy clearly indicates:

- that 'the Commission [in whose area of competence the control of state aids and competition lie] will assist the associated countries to draw up and thereafter update an inventory of state aids, established on the same basis as in the Union'
- that 'the Commission is requested to make an annual report on these inventories'
- that 'the Commission will give guidance on the compatibility of aid designed to combat the specific problems of the associated countries as they undergo reform'; this clearly refers to a specific regime for associated countries.

This extensive list of actions puts considerable burdens on the Commission to provide help to the associated countries in this area. The relative lack of expertise in the area means that whatever assistance can be spared by the Member States and by the Commission will be extremely valuable, but progress in implementing rigorous controls on state aids may take somewhat longer than expected, especially considering that the associated countries are coming out of an economic system where the use of state aids was all-embracing.

### Adoption by the associated countries of the internal market acquis –the White Paper

The adoption of the internal market *acquis* is the important third element of the internal market strategy. The adoption of the *acquis* in the internal market area has been an extremely long process even within the Union; certain of the Directives have not yet been transposed into national legislation and implementation has in some areas been slow. The work which the associated countries will have to do to adopt and implement the same legislation is far greater in that they are starting from a lower base of market economy legislation. In the associated countries each piece of legislation adopted does not mean a marginal change to existing legislation but is usually a major policy choice.

The Essen strategy proposed that the European Commission should write a White Paper on the internal market in order to guide the associated countries in their preparation for accession. As one of the main parts of the strategy for preparing to integrate the associated countries into the Union, the White Paper has a considerable importance, and is dealt with in detail in chapter 8 of this book.

This core strategy of assisting the associated countries to prepare for entry into the Union's internal market must not be allowed to slow their economic growth. The unwritten rule that rapid economic growth is the most important criterion for accession must be kept in mind. Taking on Union competition rules, reducing state aids further, taking over Community law on companies, accounting, banking and insurance and moving towards European and international product norms will have, in general, a positive medium-term effect on growth. It is very important however that the associated countries look carefully at those areas of Community policy and law which will have the effect of restricting growth potential.

### Promoting economic integration

Much of the remainder of the Essen strategy was devoted to the promotion of economic integration: the creation of a physically integrated region, trade and commercial policy and the cumulation of rules of origin.

The creation of a physically integrated region concentrated on programmes for frontier crossing improvement financed by the PHARE programme, and improving large-scale infrastructure through support for Trans-European Networks (TENs) in Central and Eastern Europe. It was decided to increase to 25% the amount of the PHARE programme which could be used for infrastructure investment.

Essen has little to say on further trade liberalisation and practically nothing on agriculture. On commercial policy instruments, the Essen strategy promises three things:

- that 'the Commission in the exercise of its responsibilities for anti-dumping and safeguard measures and in the framework of the individual Europe Agreements, will offer information to any associated country before the initiation of proceedings'
- that preference would be given to price undertakings rather than duties in cases where dumping is proved
- that 'as satisfactory implementation of competition policy and control of state aids together with the application of those parts of Community law linked to the internal market are achieved, providing a guarantee against unfair competition comparable to that existing inside the internal market, so the Union should be ready to consider refraining from using commercial defence instruments for industrial products'.

In fact none of these decisions radically improved the situation of the associated countries; the first has been applied but has not had much real impact, the second is dangerous in that it attempts to create European-wide price fixing, the third has been disregarded.

It is unfortunate that the Essen strategy made little progress in these important areas of trade relations. However on the cumulation of rules of origin, it did lay down a strategy, which appeared disappointing at the time, but which was later realised in part with great determination (see chapter 3). In fact the Union has established a Pan-European origin area, with the result that from 1 July 1997 the cumulation of rules of origin throughout Western and Central Europe has been achieved.

Globally, then, the Essen strategy, while recognising that trade is vital to the economic reform process and to the integration of the associated countries into the Community, did not signal any real advance in the three major problem areas – agriculture, trade in services and contingent protection.

*Cooperation between the associated countries themselves*

The Member States put great emphasis on the promotion of regional cooperation within Central Europe itself. They considered this to be a guarantee that the acceding countries would be also able to work together inside the Union.

The instruments displayed at Essen were of two overlapping types: on the one hand the Pact for Stability, already mentioned, which tackled essentially political and security aspects, and on the other a series of initiatives in the PHARE programme to strengthen regional economic cooperation.

The work to produce the Stability Pact consisted of intensive consultations and negotiations, with two round tables bringing together the Baltic countries and Poland in the one case and Bulgaria, Hungary, Poland, Romania, Slovakia, the Czech Republic and Slovenia in the other. The result is an impressive number of bilateral agreements, a few of which were negotiated during the preparation of the Pact and were assisted by its existence. This was particularly the case of the first agreement between Hungary and Slovakia signed in March 1995. The Hungarian–Romanian Treaty, eventually signed in September 1996, can also claim to have its genesis in the Stability Pact.

Three PHARE initiatives were proposed in Essen. The first concerned the promotion of trade within the region. The second proposed the expansion of the programme which deals with promoting cross-border activities with EU Member States to include the borders between the associated countries and those with the newly independent states of the FSU (NIS). The third element was the programme for the improvement of border crossings, mentioned above.

### Cooperation in the three pillars of Maastricht

The Essen proposals also dealt with cooperation at the level of the Community in education and training and in environment policy, as well as in the two other 'pillars' of the Maastricht Treaty, the CSFP and justice and home affairs.

On cooperation in education, little was achieved. On the environment, which is, by the nature of the problems, more clearly a Community area of competence, the proposals were more concrete. They also resulted from discussions at an enlarged Environment Council meeting held in the context of the structured relationship and had therefore the prior consideration and approval of the line ministers. The Community proposed to use the PHARE programme to provide assistance to reach the objectives agreed in this meeting. It also proposed that the countries be closely associated with the new European Environmental Agency and that there should be increased mutual exchange of information, especially in the context of taking on the Community *acquis* at or before accession.

On cooperation in the CSFP field, the Essen Council proposed nothing beyond what had already been approved in the context of the structured relationship.

In the very important area of justice and home affairs, Essen picked up the results of the meeting of Ministers of Justice and Home Affairs held in Berlin in September 1994. Closer cooperation in the areas of preventing the drug trade, illegal trade in nuclear materials, illegal immigration networks and the trade in stolen vehicles was suggested.

### Improving the effectiveness of assistance

At Essen, the Union also reviewed the PHARE assistance programme in the light of the strategy for accession. This strategy logically implied several major changes: the clear affirmation that the objectives of PHARE were now enlarged to include preparation for accession; the confirmation that PHARE was a medium-term programme which would be funded over the whole life of the Union's financial perspective; that PHARE finance would be dealt with on the Structural Funds model giving implementation to the beneficiary countries; and that PHARE funding could be increasingly used for investment purposes. The Essen Council clearly stated the dual objectives of the programme:

to 'help the associated countries to absorb the *acquis communautaire*' and to 'complete market reforms and the medium-term restructuring of their economies and societies so as to create the conditions required for future membership'.

No real progress on moving to a Structural Funds model of implementing aid was made after opposition within the Commission, in the European Parliament and in the Council.

Finally, Essen agreed to a further increase in the 'Copenhagen' facility from 15% of the total programme to 25%. This facility is used for the co-financing of infrastructure developments with the International Financial Institutions (IFIs), the EIB and the authorities of the beneficiary countries.

On assistance, the Essen summit therefore brought real progress and opened the way, partially at least, to a more efficient use of a slightly enlarged assistance fund. On the other hand it did little to move PHARE from a traditional development assistance programme to a pre-accession fund suitable for future members of the Union.

### The multilateral structured relationship

This essentially economic strategy to prepare for accession was accompanied by a political structure, the multilateral structured dialogue.

The objectives of the structured relationship are clearly set out in the conclusions to the Essen Council. They are: to 'encourage mutual trust and . . . provide a framework for addressing topics of common interest' and that 'the associated countries can play a positive role in discussions on matters of common interest'. In fact, the promotion of close relationships between ministers and civil servants of both the Union and the associated countries is an important part of the process of growing together on the way to accession. Problems can then be solved on the telephone, which without this close relationship might turn into major clashes.

Essen confirmed the central importance of the structured dialogue and gave concrete indications to its organisation and content. In any year, the two presidencies of the Union would fix a calendar of meetings with the associated countries, linked to regular Council meetings, at the beginning of the year. In principle, such meetings should take place with the following regularity:

- an annual meeting of heads of state and government on the margins of a European Council meeting
- semi-annual meetings of justice and/or home affairs ministers and of foreign ministers
- annual meetings of ministers of culture and education, finance

and economics, agriculture, transport, telecommunications, research and environment.

These meetings were to be prepared by COREPER, the Committee of EU Member State ambassadors, to ensure horizontal coordination.

These decisions on the structured dialogue must be assessed as going very far towards the wishes of the associated countries and being a very important part of the strategy for accession. Of course, the value of the structured relationship depends very much on how it takes place in practice. So far, experience has been mixed but there are signs that the structured relationship can be made to work.

### The Cannes European Council: the White Paper on the Internal Market

The Cannes European Council meeting in June 1995 brought just two decisions affecting Central Europe. The first was the final settlement of the medium-term budget allocation which had been held up by a squabble over the sharing out of resources between this region and the Mediterranean.

The second decision was to approve the White Paper on preparing the associated countries for their entry into the internal market of the Union, which was announced in the Essen pre-accession strategy.[3] The objective of the paper was not to establish new criteria for accession nor to be a sort of binding and policed programme for the approximation of laws. Building on the recent experience of the Member States of the Union and of the European Commission, the White Paper simply set out to guide the associated countries in their preparation for accession (see chapter 8).[4]

The White Paper is seen to be one of the major vehicles for advancing the strategy of accession. It will rank as such only if it is accepted for what it is, technical assistance. There is obviously a considerable danger that in a few years time it will be used by the opponents of enlargement as a vehicle to prevent enlargement – in other words, it will be used as a very sophisticated list of criteria for opposing accession. It should always be remembered that the adoption of the *acquis*, including the internal market *acquis*, will form part of the accession negotiations. Normally at that stage the associated countries would be able to negotiate transition periods in order to adapt to some of these measures which require considerable investment and structural change. The economic challenges which the associated countries have to face are so immense that the Union should not be tempted to try to avoid being as generous to

---

[3] European Council, *Conclusions of the Presidency* (Essen, December 1994).
[4] European Commission (1995d).

these countries as it was with Portugal and Spain by forcing them to adopt expensive change now rather than after accession. It is therefore very important that the technical assistance nature of the White Paper is continuously emphasised.

### The Madrid European Council: the Member States take over the reins

The preparation of the Madrid European Council meeting in December 1995 gave little sign that it would lead to any new initiative in the relationship between the associated countries and the Union. Three papers were submitted by the Commission; one extremely good paper on agriculture which will be extensively referred to in chapter 9 on agriculture, one paper on the effects of enlargement on the policies of the European Union and a progress report on the implementation of the Essen pre-accession strategy. The two latter papers contained no proposals of any importance.

For the first time the Madrid European Council produced conclusions which drove the whole process of accession preparation forward, again without major proposals from the Commission. The Council was now clearly in the driving seat as far as both proposals for policy development and decisions on policy were concerned. And in the Council, it was Germany which was pushing ahead with what it saw as one of the most important planks of its European policy, enlargement.

The Madrid European Council took the following key decisions:

- It asked the Commission to

    expedite preparation of its opinions on the applications [for membership] made so that they can be forwarded to the Council as soon as possible after the conclusion of the Inter-Governmental Conference, and to embark upon preparation of a composite paper on enlargement. This procedure will ensure that the applicant countries are treated on an equal basis.

- it asked the Commission

    to undertake a detailed analysis of the union's financing system in order to submit, immediately after the conclusion of the IGC, a communication on the future financial framework of the Union as from 31 December 1999, having regard to the prospect of enlargement.

- it stated that after the end of the IGC and in the light of its outcome and of the Commission opinions and reports, the Council will take the necessary decisions for launching the accession negotiations. The European Council expressed the hope that the preliminary stage of the negotiations would coincide with the start of negotiations with Malta and Cyprus.

These decisions were the result of German pressure to accelerate the preparation for enlargement. The German idea was in addition to privilege the three neighbouring countries Poland, the Czech Republic and Hungary, which in its eyes should become members before the other associated countries. This latter idea was resisted by some of the other Member States, which have their own 'client' countries in the region (Finland–Estonia or France–Romania, for instance). However, the insistence of Germany led to what amounted to a promise to open negotiations in 1998, and to start preparing the Commission Opinions immediately.

The statement on the date for the opening of negotiations is the nearest the Union had come to agreeing a timetable for accession. It still did not create total credibility, but that was probably impossible. It did give all the associated countries a date to aim for in their preparations for accession. Again, it would seem that they had the German government to thank for this advance.

The third element of the Madrid statement was obviously necessary, not only because of enlargement but because the Union needs a new financial basis for its operation after 1999.

The Madrid European Council marked an important advance on the road to accession. The Union was still not committed to accession, and certainly not to accession for all the applicants. Nevertheless, the summit took the essential next steps in the process and with each step the commitment of the Union becomes greater and the risk of it pulling back less.

It is important that the European Commission continues to play a high profile in the enlargement process. The history of European integration has shown that the Commission has usually been the motor of new policies and has been able to convince a sometimes doubting Council of the wisdom of its proposals. As is discussed in chapter 12, this role can be faulted from the viewpoint of the democratic deficit, but it is a fact of Community life. Left to themselves, the Council members are unlikely to muster the necessary consensus to promote the policy changes necessary to make enlargement a success. It is vital for the process of enlargement that the European Commission continues to play the role of initiator of policy development in this area.

### 'Agenda 2000' and the Commission's Opinions on membership applications

The Madrid Council's request for the Commission to prepare its Opinions ('*avis*' in French) on the applications for membership of the associated countries and to look at the impact of enlargement on the policies of the Union launched the next concrete step on the road to accession.

### The Commission Opinions

Article O of the Union Treaty establishes that the Commission is consulted in the context of an application for accession. Although the opinion of the Commission is not anchored anywhere in law, it is regarded as a normal part of accession proceedings.[5] The Commission began its work in early 1996 and published its findings on all the applicants in mid-July 1997.

Commission Opinions on applications for membership are technical assessments of the applicant country's capacity to be members. The Opinions are an aid to the Council in deciding whether to open negotiations with the country in question. They are taken into consideration by the Council but they are not necessarily decisive. The Commission's negative Opinion on Greek membership was ignored by the Council and in the cases of Spain and Portugal and the EFTA applications, there was never any doubt that the Council would open negotiations.

The opinions on the ten applications from the associated countries are however liable to be more influential, simply because there is no unanimity in the Council on their accession. Some Member States are probably against enlargement, others are for some sort of partial membership while yet others support only a sub-set of the ten applicants. In these circumstances the Commission Opinions will be used by the different camps in the Council to support their various points of view.

The ten Opinions delivered by the Commission in July 1997 all have a similar structure. The review of the suitability of the country to negotiate for entry to the Union is assessed on political and economic criteria and on their ability to assume the obligations of membership and their administrative capacity to apply the *acquis* – in other words, on the Copenhagen criteria. The greatest detail is reserved for the ability to

---

[5] In fact, the Commission is consulted but does not have to give a written Opinion to the Council; alternatively it can give several Opinions at different times. In the case of Malta and Cyprus, for instance, it has already given one Opinion but could give another before the negotiations take place. It has, however, become accepted practice that the Commission gives an Opinion before negotiations start on the problems which should be addressed in the negotiations. The Commission also normally gives a final Opinion after the conclusion of the negotiations.

assume the obligations of membership (the ability to adopt and implement the *acquis*), where each Directorate General in the Commission
contributed its own analysis. These analyses, which in general are
accepted as reasonably accurate and objective, will be important, not
only in guiding the associated countries to tackle certain identified
weaknesses, but also in helping to form the accession partnerships,
through which assistance in the coming years will be channelled to these
countries.

The Commission's analysis led it to recommend that the Union
should open negotiations with five countries in Central and Eastern
Europe – the Czech Republic, Estonia, Hungary, Poland and Slovenia.
While it was universally expected that for political, as well as technical,
reasons the Commission would support negotiations with the Czech
Republic, Hungary and Poland, the decisions on Estonia and Slovenia
gave interesting pointers to the Commission's intentions. While Estonia
and Slovenia on technical economic grounds compare quite well with
the other three Visegrád countries, both are situated in politically
complex regions. The choice of Estonia is a pointer to the eventual
membership of the other Baltic countries, perhaps in the future in the
face of Russian opposition. That of Slovenia points to the possibility of
stable countries in the ex-Yugoslav Republic becoming members.

The Commission rejected Slovakia only on political grounds (treatment of minorities, democratic practice) but made it clear that when
these problems were resolved, Slovakia could expect to join the five
negotiating associated countries. Latvia, Lithuania, Romania and Bulgaria were all rejected on economic criteria, but again the Commission
makes it clear that they can all join the negotiations when basic
weaknesses have been tackled.

It is the Council, however, not the Commission which will decide
with which countries to negotiate at the Luxembourg European Council
in December 1997; however the dynamics in the Council mean that the
Commission's proposal on which countries should be chosen for
negotiations is likely to be approved because any move away from it will
make a decision very difficult. Negotiations are likely to start in Spring
1998, but no one knows how long they will last. Some Member States
may want them to last longer than the two years which most people are
suggesting. If agreement cannot be reached on reforms to the CAP,
structural policies or the budget, or if EMU is delayed, the negotiations
could last much longer than two years. Negotiations with the individual
countries will be organised separately, but the Council will try to keep
them roughly at the same pace. However if they prove difficult with one
country, accession may not be simultaneous.

### *'Agenda 2000' and the reform of Union policies*

While the opinions on the applicant states clearly point to the work which the associated countries will have to do before accession, 'Agenda 2000' underlines above all the changes which the Union will have to make in its policies. It deals essentially with the changes which will be necessary in the CAP, in the Structural Funds and in the financial perspective of the Union from 2000 to 2006.

The Commission proposes the following key assumptions for the reform of Union policies to accommodate the challenge of enlargement:

- The Community budget should not exceed the own-resources ceiling of 1.27% of Community GDP in the period to 2006.
- Expenditure on the Structural Funds should not exceed 0.46% of Community GDP over the same period. A reform of the Structural Funds must be carried out leading to greater prioritisation and a transition period for the entry of the new Member States into the system. Transfers will be capped at 4% of a recipient country's GDP.
- Reform of the CAP must continue, with a progressive change from price support to direct income support.
- Reform of the Community institutions must be accelerated.
- 'Agenda 2000' is based on the assumption that Monetary Union starts on time, and that the Amsterdam Treaty is signed and ratified.

It is important to note that these are only proposals of the Commission. The Council must decide on these policy changes. It is probable that the key reforms will not be finally decided until 1999, the latest possible date for the approval of the next financial period (2000–6), for the WTO negotiations and for the enlargement negotiations. The detail of these proposed policy changes will be dealt with in the following chapters.

It is important to note, however, that all of these policy changes are necessary with or without enlargement. The CAP will have to be reformed before the next WTO trade round and before the adoption of the new financial framework. The Structural Funds already cover a far too large part of the population of the Community and need concentration and prioritisation, with or without enlargement. Reform of the Community institutions is necessary again irrespective of enlargement.

In many ways, 'Agenda 2000' also represents a possible negotiating position of the Union in accession negotiations on points of essential interest to both sides. On the three main financing issues – CAP, Structural Funds and the budget – it spells out how the new Member

States will be dealt with before and after accession. Again it will be for the Council to decide negotiation and in these areas, as indicated above, agreement may be possible only in 1999.

## Conclusion

The Copenhagen and Essen European Councils, together with the follow-up given by the Cannes Summit in June 1995, the Paris meeting on the Stability Pact, the decisions of the Madrid summit and 'Agenda 2000', have certainly gone well beyond the Association Agreements. To some extent, they had the effect of creating the expectation of accession in the medium term. This feeling of irreversibility has been reflected in speeches by leading politicians on both sides, and most prominently by Chancellor Kohl in July 1995 and President Chirac in September 1996 in Warsaw.

But very few situations in politics are irreversible. There remain severe problems in the way of accession. These problems lie on both sides and include the reform of agricultural policy, changes in the Structural Funds and the budgetary implications which these might have, progress with implementing the *acquis communautaire* and the restructuring of the administration in Central Europe. 'Agenda 2000' has made proposals in all these areas. These questions will be tackled in the following chapters.

# 7    The costs and benefits of enlargement

## Enlargement: ending post-war divisions

Before considering the 'objective' costs and benefits of enlargement of
the Union to include the CEE countries, the historical arguments are
worth considering. Most of the countries of Central Europe have
suffered throughout history by being sandwiched between expansionist
powers in Russia and Prussia or Germany. The three partitions of
Poland in the eighteenth and nineteenth centuries are just examples of
this situation.

Today, the situation is different. Germany is a model federal democracy anchored in the European Union while the Soviet Union has
disintegrated, leaving a reforming Russia as its largest successor state.
But the successes of the last five years or even the last 50 years cannot
wipe out centuries of insecurity and persecution. The repeated requests
of the associated countries, including those now run by 'post-communist' governments, to join NATO and the European Union reflect the
worry of once again finding themselves 'free' but 'un-anchored' in a
rapidly changing Europe. All governments in the region feel the need to
be bound into NATO and the European Union for security reasons as
well as the more obvious economic and political reasons.

On the EU side, there is a strong determination not to put at risk the
real advances that have been made in integrating Western Europe and
creating a stable area where war has become totally improbable. This
integration is not superficial; it relies today on a considerable body of
legislation and legal precedence and has led to a deep interpenetration
of the national economies of the Union. In other words, the Union is
not a club which can be joined without first undertaking fundamental
changes in economy and in law. This was true for advanced market
economies such as Austria and Sweden, and will also be true for the
enlargement to the East. Deep-rooted change has also started in
Western Europe as progress with European integration has been made.
The regionalisation of Belgium, for instance, can be understood only in

179

the context of ever-deepening European integration. Enlargement is likely therefore to be opposed by countries or regions which feel it will weaken the level of integration in the Union.

The CEE countries which wish to join the Union must put an important effort into continuing economic reform and the preparation for accession. A country which does nothing and expects simply a political decision on accession should normally not expect to be taken into the Union. And all the new members must be prepared, after some years of transition, to take over the same responsibilities as the existing members.

However, a refusal to enlarge the Union, as well as turning our backs on history, might put the future existence of the Union itself at risk. If enlargement to those countries, which have carefully prepared their economies and citizens for accession, does not take place, then these countries are liable to descend – politically and then economically – into chaos as one of the main props of their foreign policies is removed. Chaos developing on the Eastern border of the Union would be destabilising to the future development of the Union, and would probably lead to its disintegration.

It is inconceivable that the Union should invent a new division of Europe by keeping the associated countries of Central Europe at bay through a reinforcement of 'Fortress Europe'. It would not only be unhistorical, it would also be in vain. Only 'iron curtains' can separate perfectly and experience shows that even they rust away. On the other hand, the associated countries have to recognise the great achievements of the Union and be prepared to work for accession. For both parties, the enlargement of the Union to Central Europe, and the development of peaceful constructive relations with Russia and the Ukraine, will bring large 'objective' benefits, which clearly outweigh the costs.

## The problems of enlargement

Enlargement of the European Community has never been taken lightly, has always been well prepared and has always caused considerable problems. The problems have usually been resolved before accession has taken place and have normally been resolved without major changes in the policies or the institutions of the Community or of the way in which the Community performs its business.

The next enlargement to include the countries of Central Europe (and Cyprus) will be of a very different nature. The associated countries have a combined population of 28% and a combined area of about one-third of the existing EU-15 (see table 7.1). In these terms alone, the next enlargement, if it is to include all the associated countries, will be on a very major scale. It is important to note that the ten countries include only one large state in the usual meaning of that term in the Union – Poland, which has almost the same population as Spain. Romania, with its 23 million falls between the 'large' EU Member States and the 'small' ones. All the other potential Member States in Central Europe are small states with 10 million people or less. Physically the countries have borders with states which are truly East European or Balkan, and their accession will therefore lead the European Union to having frontiers with states which are totally different to the predominantly 'West European' Member States of the current Union. These neighbours will include Russia (which, of course, already has a common frontier with the Community in Finland), Belarus, the Ukraine, Moldova, Croatia, Serbia, Macedonia and Turkey (already with a common border with Greece). The geography of the next enlargement brings profound changes to the nature of the European Community.

The associated countries are poor countries in terms of *per capita* GDP. The total GDP at market prices and current exchange rates of all the ten associated countries was estimated at ECU234 billion for 1995, approximately that of Belgium.[1] This amounts to only 4% of the GDP of the European Union, or roughly one-ninth of the GDP *per capita*. If GDP is measured in purchasing power standards (PPS), the situation improves but still the contrast remains stark. The average level of GDP *per capita* measured using PPS is still a little less than one-third of the average EU level. The country with the highest *per capita* GDP, Slovenia, lies some way behind the poorest Community country, Greece.

There is also a greater dispersion of income across the associated countries than within the existing European Union. If Luxembourg is ignored (for reasons of size and economic structure), the relationship between the highest and lowest income countries in the Union (ratio of GDP *per capita* at PPS in 1995) is 1.8, whereas for the associated countries the same ratio is 3.2. The associated countries are therefore not only in income terms poorer on average than the poorest of the existing Member States, there are also large variations between them. It

---

[1] It should be noted that the measures of GDP at market prices and current exchange rates, and especially of these measures at PPS, are subject to large margins of error. Apart from the problem of data availability and quality in all the associated countries, the figures may be distorted by differences in the size of the informal (black) economy and the ways in which this part of the economy is estimated for statistical purposes.

is erroneous to think of the associated countries as a uniform bloc; GDP *per capita* simply underlines this point.

Whereas in the existing Union the large countries are all at or above the average level of GDP *per capita*, the two largest associated countries are probably at or well below the average level amongst the ten countries. Poland, with 36% of the total population of the region, had a GDP *per capita* figure at PPS of ECU5,320 in 1995, around the average for the region, whilst Romania, with 22% of the population, had only ECU4,060 *per capita*, or just 36% of the level of Greece. Of course these considerations based entirely on GDP *per capita* (PPS) represent only part of the economic health of the associated countries. Other factors such as the level of indebtedness (low in the case of Romania but high in Hungary, for instance), the structure of the economy and the entrepreneurial spirit of the people are also of vital importance for their future and that of an enlarged Community.

One characteristic of the structure of the economies of the associated countries can be seen in a very simple way by comparing the contribution of agriculture to GDP and the numbers employed in agriculture as a percentage of the labour force (table 7.1). On average, the importance of agriculture measured in terms of its contribution to GDP in the associated countries is over three times that in the European Union. In terms of employment the contrast is even greater, with the proportion of the workforce employed in agriculture between four and five times higher.[2] Several of the associated countries still have over a fifth of the labour force in agriculture, including the two largest states, Poland and Romania.

In the associated countries, however, industry is also a greater contributor to GDP than in the European Union. Although agriculture is still so important to some of these states, they are almost all industrial countries. Industry was seen by the communist governments before 1989 as the real source of wealth and power and was therefore developed – and often over-developed – after the Second World War. The missing part of the economy, compared to the economies of the Union, is the service sector. Prior to the reforms, many services were provided to workers through their state-owned enterprises (SOEs) and these services were counted as industrial rather than service output. But there was also no scope in the communist economies for the development of private services.

---

[2] Again, these statistics should be considered approximate. The employment in agriculture figures for the associated countries may well be somewhat inflated, because of the former system of including certain service workers in rural areas in the agricultural workforce.

Table 7.1 Basic data on the ten associated countries

| | Bulgaria | Czech R | Estonia | Hungary | Latvia | Lithuania | Poland | Romania | Slovakia | Slovenia | AC10 | EU? |
|---|---|---|---|---|---|---|---|---|---|---|---|---|
| Area (million ha.) | 11.1 | 7.9 | 4.5 | 9.3 | 6.5 | 6.5 | 31.3 | 23.8 | 4.9 | 2.0 | 107.7 | 323.4 |
| Population (million) | 8.4 | 10.3 | 1.5 | 10.3 | 2.7 | 3.7 | 38.6 | 22.7 | 5.3 | 2.0 | | 369.7 |
| GDP (ECU billion)[a] | 9.9 | 36.1 | 2.8 | 33.4 | 3.4 | 3.5 | 90.2 | 27.3 | 13.3 | 14.2 | 234 | 6442 |
| GDP/*cap* (ECU, PPP)[a] | 4210 | 9410 | 3920 | 6310 | 3160 | 4130 | 5320 | 4060 | 7120 | 10110 | 5530 | 17260 |
| GDP 1996 as % of GDP1989 | 68 | 89 | 69 | 86 | 52 | 42 | 104 | 88 | 90 | 96 | – | – |
| Agriculture as % of GDP[c] | 11 | 5.1 | 6.4 | 6.4[b] | 9.1 | 11.4 | 6.6[b] | 19.1 | 5.2 | 4.3 | 7.0 | 2.4 |
| Agriculture as % of lab. force[a] | 23.2 | 6.3 | 13.1 | 8.0 | 18.5 | 23.8 | 26.9 | 34.4 | 9.7 | 7.1 | 22.5 | 5.3 |
| Industry as % of GDP[c] | 32 | 33.8 | 18.9 | 23.9[b] | 27.8 | 28.3 | 28.9[b] | 36.0 | 26.3 | 27.2 | – | 22.3 |
| Private sector in GDP %[b] | 40 | 65 | 49 | 60 | 58 | 55 | 56 | 35 | 58 | 33 | – | – |
| Unemployment (% lab force) | 12.5 | 3.5 | 5.6 | 10.5 | 7.2 | 7.0 | 13.6 | 7.8 | 11.1 | 13.9 | – | 10.7 |

Notes:
[a] EUROSTAT 1995 data.
[b] 1995.
[c] 1996 (estimate).
Sources: EBRD (1997), Transition Report data for 1996 except where stated.

Not only do the associated countries show greater differences between themselves in some economic respects than the existing Member States of the Community, they are also very different from the point of view of their cultures and civilisation. In fact what might be called the 'Huntington fault line' of civilisation passes through the middle of the associated countries.[3] Huntington refers to William Wallace's notion that the most significant dividing line in Europe is that of the Eastern boundary of Western Christianity in the year 1500. This may seem a far-fetched notion, especially as this line also divides up the existing European Community. It does, however, serve to highlight that there are significant differences of culture between the associated countries. Even between the three Baltic countries, from the Nordic Protestant Estonia to the Central European Catholic Lithuania, there are major differences in the way problems are approached, in the style of negotiation and in general attitudes of the population. In contemplating these differences, however, it is important to keep in mind the major contrasts in culture within the existing Union, which do not appear to prevent the Member States from working well together.

The associated countries also contain minorities which come from very different cultural backgrounds than the majority. Romania is a case in point with a large Hungarian minority, which has a very different cultural, religious and linguistic character. In Bulgaria, there is a Turkish minority and in the three Baltic States there are sizeable Russian minorities, which again are different culturally from the majority populations of those countries. It is true that there are sizeable minorities with totally different cultural backgrounds in the existing Member States of the Union; however most of these minorities have grown up through migration very recently and might be expected over time, perhaps a very long time, to assimilate with the majority communities. Often, however, in Central Europe, minority problems have been caused by the arbitrary shifting of frontiers, which have simply put an ethnic group established over centuries in a particular region under the political control of a different ethnic group.

Many other fundamental differences amongst the associated countries and between them and the Union's Member States could be pointed out. None of this changes the overwhelming advantages to be drawn from enlargement of the Union to these states. Writing in the 1930s an author would have drawn just as diverse a picture when comparing France and Germany, as has been drawn in the previous paragraphs, yet today these two countries appear to be very closely related. A consistent

---

[3] Huntington (1993).

effort at cooperation between peoples can render history less determinate than suggested by Huntington. What, however, these differences do point to is that the next enlargement of the Community will be very different to the last two enlargements, to the EFTA countries and to Spain and Portugal.

## The costs and benefits of enlargement

The work which has been done on the costs and benefits of enlargement has almost always shown that the accession of the associated countries will bring net benefits both to the existing Union and to the acceding countries.[4] However not all Member States and not all associated countries will gain to the same degree and certain individuals and groups in all countries will consider themselves disadvantaged by the process. Enlargement will be affected by both the overall balance of advantage but also by the activities of those groups which gain or lose in the process. It is therefore important to look at the detail of the calculations of costs and benefits.

### *Benefits of enlargement for the European Union*

The benefits of enlargement are often perceived by politicians in the European Union as exclusively accruing to the associated countries. But the benefits are not unidirectional. Indeed, an argument can be made that enlargement is necessary for the future survival of the Union.

The discussion of the costs and benefits of accession is obviously affected by whether the current Union is considered as an exclusive club reserved for the existing members or whether it is an open association of all democratic European countries. The first interpretation, which seems to be held by some current Member States, eliminates by definition some of the advantages of accession of new members or increases the cost to existing club members. Any accession brings a dilution of voting rights in the Council, for instance. An accession of on average poorer agricultural countries leads, on current policies, to an increase in the demand for resources in the Union, which is met either by an increase in the size of the budget or by a reduction in the transfers paid to existing Member States. A change which forces structural change on a Member State will be interpreted as a disadvantage by the economic agents in that country if the Union is regarded as a club. But a judgement should be made not on these individual 'costs' but on the

---

4 Baldwin, Francois and Portes (1997), pp.125–76. This article gives an overview of the work done in the field as well as original calculations of costs and benefits.

basis of a thorough economic analysis of the costs and benefits of enlargement.[5]

### Political and security benefits

The political benefits of accession will be significant, leading to an increase in the power and prestige of the Union in international arenas and in international negotiations. While it is true that the addition to the Union is more in terms of population than in GDP or share of world trade, nevertheless successful enlargement will enhance the Union's influence with the other world trading and political blocs.

At a more concrete level, accession will help the final rapprochement between Germany and Poland and Germany and the Czech Republic and should lead to improvements in relations also in Southern Europe between Greece and Bulgaria and Italy and Slovenia. After Spain and Portugal joined the Community the relations between these two Member States improved considerably and similar results can be expected of the new accession. The 'Aussöhnung' between Germany and Poland, where considerable progress has already been made, is as essential a part of European reconciliation as that between Germany and France. This process will be much easier within the Union than outside it.

The security of the European Community was always provided by NATO and the 'Iron Curtain'. This might seem a precarious security constellation but for many West Europeans and even for some West Germans, the fall of the Berlin Wall is considered to represent a serious loss of security.

After the democratic revolutions of 1989–90, Central and Eastern Europe has been opened up to many different forces. Tensions which were kept under control, such as those nationalist and racist tensions in the former Yugoslavia, have become open conflicts, whilst crime and terrorism have been able to flourish as the control of the Communist Party and of the army has declined. Europe at the end of the 1990s is a freer and more democratic continent than ten years ago, but it is living with the dangers of nationalism and social disintegration, which were not to be seen at that time. For the fruits of the victory of democracy to be enjoyed, security must be increased.

It is difficult to imagine that the existing Community would be left unaffected by political and economic disintegration in the associated countries. But if accession does not take place, or at least if there is no credible progress made, disintegration could occur. This might be the

---

[5] See Baldwin, Francois and Portes (1997).

result of the following scenario. The associated countries, which have already undertaken painful economic systemic change, are now developing strategies for accession which involve further costs for many sectors of the population as legal and institutional change takes place. As it becomes clear that accession will either not take place or only after a long period of time (say 20 or more years, which in the present situation is as good as never), the governments will be forced to admit that the prize at the end of the long path of sacrifice is no longer available. The search for other political anchors will begin but will fail because the only other alternative is a newly developing Russian sphere of influence, which will not be acceptable for the voters. With rejection from the West and rejection of the East, the political situation will deteriorate as politicians find it impossible to find an alternative to the policy of integration with the Community. Reform will become progressively difficult and the economy will increasingly become prey to the old established nationalist–communist forces. Economic performance will decline, and foreign investors will stay away. With political paralysis and economic disintegration, instability will become the rule and large numbers of the more aware citizens will attempt to leave to look for a new life in the West.

In the medium term, the accession of the associated countries would guarantee stability in Central Europe during a period which is liable to be marked by a relatively unstable political situation in Russia and the Ukraine, as these two countries struggle with reform. Such stability would add greatly to the security of the current members of the European Union and especially to those on the Eastern borders of the Union: the Nordic countries, Germany, Austria, Italy and Greece. With the reunification of Germany being followed by a long period of growing-together of the two parts of the country, it is important that the New Bundesländer are not confronted with problems across the borders in Poland or the Czech Republic. The accession of the associated countries would guarantee the development of normal political and economic relations with Germany. The need for such a reconciliation is especially clear in the New Bundesländer, which were cut off from the process of internationalisation which other parts of the European Union underwent between the Second World War and 1989.

The value of increased security for the existing European Union from enlargement cannot be over-stated. It should not lead, of course, to the import of unresolved ethnic or other conflicts. Already the power of the Union to bring opposed elements together to discuss mutual problems was shown by the work of the Stability Pact. Undoubtedly more such work needs to be undertaken by the Union before enlargement.

The cost to the Union of the associated countries not being allowed to join might be extremely high, in that it would put great strains on the Union's internal stability. The countries bordering Central Europe would be quite naturally pulled in the direction of maintaining stability in that region, while the Southern Member States would be less affected. Eventually the forces pulling the Union apart could come to dominate as the Eastern Member States decided that peace and stability in Central Europe was more important than the relationship with the Mediterranean. Accession would internalise many of the problems, making them easier to deal with.

### Economic benefits of accession

The economic benefits of accession to the existing European Union come essentially from three sources. Firstly the 106 million consumers who live in the associated countries and the thousands of enterprises established there are an important market for existing Community producers. Secondly, the associated countries are a potentially important production location for Community companies wishing to expand to lower-cost locations. Thirdly the entry of the associated countries will bring more competition into markets in the existing Community, leading to a break-up of market rigidities and in the longer term a stronger European economy.

### The benefits of an enlarged single market

The benefits from the enlargement of the single market to include the associated countries can be considered in terms of both market expansion and market integration.

The ten associated countries have a population of 106 million or 29% of the population of the current EU-15. These consumers represent a potential additional market for Community producers which is likely to grow substantially in coming years. It is true that the GDP *per capita* of these millions is probably only around 11% of that of the current Union if measured at current exchange rates, and perhaps around 30% if measured in PPS. Nevertheless if economic growth continues into the medium term at around double that of the Community, this market will grow quickly in importance.

The trade statistics and certain company reports already show an important positive impact coming from trade with the associated countries. The trade figures which were used in chapter 3 show the increase in trade which has taken place since 1989. The estimates of potential trade also discussed in that chapter suggest that there is scope for further increases over the coming years. West European companies like ABB or the Dutch bank ING are already earning considerable income from serving the rapidly developing markets in Central and Eastern Europe.

The market opening benefits of enlargement can be criticised in that they are really an argument for free trade, which itself is possible without enlargement. This is, of course, to some extent true but it ignores an important point. On the one hand it is only when the associated countries are inside the Union that all economic agents can be sure that there will be no backsliding in terms of trade opening and that they will be able to count on the persistence of a business environment which is similar to that in the Community. Only then will the associated countries be protected from the use of Union commercial defence mechanisms against them, and it is only then that they can be sure that intellectual property rights will be properly defended and other areas of business law applied as in the Union. Accession is vital for the future stability of these markets as has been seen above. The advantages which Community businesses have at the moment cannot therefore be guaranteed for the medium term if accession fails.

Central and Eastern Europe is providing a market for Community producers of both investment and consumer goods. Exports of consumer goods have grown fast over the past five years, in spite of their generally high price in relation to average earnings. Quality, presentation and marketing have all helped Western goods to gain a major share in many markets. As domestic producers and foreign investors improve the quality of locally produced consumer goods, so imported consumer goods will feel considerably more competition. However, the same is not true for investment goods where, if the reforms and economic development continue, high levels of EU exports to the region can be expected over the medium term as businesses re-tool. Again, such trade will be made more secure when these countries are members of the Community. The provision of services, financial or otherwise to the associated countries is likely to be an important growth sector in the near term and here again the Community has a clear competitive advantage over domestic service industries. But in this area it is even more important that the countries accede to the Community in the near term, because the regulations governing the establishment and the operation of service industries, particularly the financial services, are usually more complex and more easily exploited for protectionist purposes than those applying to trade in goods.

It is always more difficult to be sector-specific in assessing the benefits of integration than it is when one is looking at the costs. The benefits are likely to be spread widely across the whole of the economy, though it is possible, for instance, to identify the investment goods sector or financial services as being clear winners, because these are areas where there is a systemic weakness in the transition countries themselves. The opportunities are there, however, for entrepreneurial companies in all sectors, but these opportunities will be more easily exploited if the accession of the associated countries is a near-term certainty.

Finally it should also be remembered that market expansion not only works on the 'export' side but that access to competitive imports from the countries of Central Europe is also important to large numbers of enterprises in the Union.

Many of the advantages which accrued to the European Community through the programme to complete the internal market in the middle of the 1980s will also accrue to an enlarged Europe after the accession to the internal market of the associated countries.

The advantages listed in the Cecchini Report (1988) were in three groups related to the elimination of trade barriers; physical frontiers, technical barriers and fiscal barriers.[6] The quantitative estimates of benefits made in the Cecchini Report have been criticised heavily, but the mechanisms through which the benefits arise have not been seriously attacked. In the context of Central Europe, given that the trade flows are considerably smaller, the benefits will also be on a smaller scale.

The elimination of physical frontiers and of the various services associated with the processing of goods across frontiers is an important advantage of accession. The current arrangements at the external frontiers of the Union lead to major costs for business, especially for small business. This is the case for instance with sub-contracting along the frontier where just-in-time (JIT) methods are not compatible with the present unpredictability of frontier clearance.

The other advantages claimed by the Cecchini Report in the area of technical barriers to trade and fiscal barriers will also, of course, apply to this accession. The problems experienced by Union producers conforming to standards, quality control procedures, certification and other such matters will be sharply reduced on accession. Perhaps the most important benefit will simply be the elimination of relatively arbitrary acts of the administrations in Central Europe which disrupt trade in order to appease one or other domestic economic interest group.

As in the internal market of the Community, accession will allow existing Community producers to rationalise the way in which they service the new markets in Central Europe. This may lead, of course, to a lower propensity to locate production in those countries as the markets

---

[6] Cecchini (1988).

can be serviced from existing sites in the old Community. On the other hand, many producers may decide to locate in Central Europe to benefit from cost advantages to supply local markets.

*The benefits of increased direct investment*
There is a considerable amount of disquiet amongst trade unions and politicians in several Member States of the Union about the 'delocalisation' of employment to Central Europe. The Belgian government commissioned a major study on the subject, the general findings of which were that there was no real danger to Belgian employment, and a similar finding was established for Bavaria and for Germany as a whole.[7]

EU direct investment in the associated countries picked up in 1996 as the economy recovered from the recession of the early 1990s and as accession to the Union became more of a probability. This trend is likely to be particularly marked in those Member States which have the highest unit costs in the Union and which are geographically closest to Central Europe. It might be expected therefore that enterprises in Germany, Austria and to a lesser extent the Nordic countries and the Benelux would be attracted by the new production locations. The most recent published data on foreign direct investment (FDI) shows that there has indeed been an increase in FDI from the Union; this is notably the case for Germany where German enterprises have expanded into the associated countries and in some cases shifted production sites, the cost structure of which was particularly dependent on labour costs. As economies in the associated countries have recovered and as labour costs expressed in a common currency have risen strongly in Germany in recent years, and notably since 1994, many German companies have looked for additional or alternative sites outside Germany. This has been reflected in a significant increase in overall outward direct investment, some of which has gone to Central Europe. In table 7.2, the overall figure for flows to the other Member States of the Union is included to put these flows in perspective. The first years of reform were weak years for FDI outflows from Germany to Central Europe because of the effort to build up the former DDR and the relatively high level of uncertainty in the associated countries. Since then, however, outward flows to the region have increased sharply and 1995 showed a rise of over 50% in relation to outward direct investment in 1994. Flows to Central Europe are still, however, only small compared with those to other EU Member States; nevertheless, those to the Visegrád countries were around one-third of flows to the other EU Member States in 1996.

[7] Bernard, *et al.* (1994). Deutsches Institut für Wirtschaftsforschung (1996).

Table 7.2 *German FDI in the associated countries, 1993–6 (DM million)*

|      | Czechoslovakia | Hungary | Poland | EU-12  |
|------|----------------|---------|--------|--------|
| 1993 | –              | 916     | 438    | 17,363 |
| 1994 | 1,174          | 949     | 419    | 12,732 |
| 1995 | 1,122          | 1,585   | 818    | 25,396 |
| 1996 | 1,072          | 919     | 1,945  | 12,611 |

*Source*: Bundesbank, *Statistisches Beiheft zum Monatsbericht*, 3 (June 1997).

Accession to the Union is likely to increase these flows further as the degree of political risk attached to such investments falls and investment decisions are taken on the basis of normal commercial considerations. It may seem strange to count the possibility of Union enterprises locating in Central Europe as a positive impact of enlargement but from the point of view of the economic wellbeing of existing Union enterprises, it should be seen as such.

Many of the enterprises which have invested in Central Europe have done so in order to serve the growing markets of the region.[8] This was the case of ABB, for instance, which has had a long history of investment and cooperation with Poland and whose investment in the region has clearly had the aim of dominating the Central European market. The investments made even by some of the car firms appear to be mainly aimed, at least in the first instance, in serving local markets. But it is equally clear that some investments in the associated countries have coincided with the closing of production sites in the Union.

For these latter enterprises, operating in the associated countries offers them the possibility of substantially cutting costs in order to compete more effectively with other companies. In those cases where labour costs are an important part of the total costs, especially when the labour supplied is not at a high skill level, a location in Central Europe is often not an alternative to keeping a plant open in the Union but an alternative to locating in South East Asia or Latin America or closing the firm down altogether. That there is a possibility of building up a production location in the associated countries for such firms is a way of guaranteeing the future existence of the firm and a future stream of profits, some of which will flow back into the old Union. The only way in which companies which have cost problems can be protected is by shutting the Union off from overseas competition, which is unthinkable, or by making factor markets in the Union more flexible, which will take time.

[8] Lankes and Venables (1996), pp. 331–48.

With the creation of a large European economic zone which includes almost the whole of Western and Central Europe and which hopefully has free trade and constructive economic relations with Russia and the Ukraine, the opportunities for EU businesses to invest and expand in markets in the other countries of the zone would be considerable. Accession is another stage in this development.

*Economic renewal as a consequence of enlargement*
An even more difficult argument concerning the economic benefits from enlargement is that it will lead to an increase in flexibility in factor markets leading to increased productivity and rising standards of living over the longer term.

The European Union is characterised by major inflexibilities in its economic system, which have led to high unemployment levels and low medium-term growth in productive potential. There have been a large number of studies of these effects, especially in the labour market. The objective of such studies has usually been to explain the far lower rates of unemployment in the United States and the fact that unemployment rates rise from cycle to cycle in the Union.

Many Member States have started to try to redress these problems. In 1995, the French government started to reform the social security system, the German government tackled the restrictions on shop opening hours, and the privatisation of state companies has progressed. In September 1996, the German Bundestag agreed a series of measures designed to cut costs, though these measures were later 'defeated' in the process of collective bargaining. The changes which are being made are difficult to achieve in a relatively stable situation because they lead to certain groups in society, which are receiving significant rents, losing them and others having to increase efficiency considerably. At the end of 1997 reforms appear to have stalled. While change is always difficult, it is easier to achieve when an outside shock hits the system. Major fuel economy efforts were undertaken only after the first oil shock and reinforced after the second. Reforms in many countries in the 1980s were undertaken only after the countries had technically become bankrupt. So also in the European Union the necessary reforms to the economic system will happen only when it is affected by a major shock. Enlargement will be such a shock. At the policy level, many Community policies such as the CAP will have to be reconsidered and the Structural Funds will have to be reformed. In the economy, many existing structures will be challenged and enterprises will be faced with new risks and opportunities. Some of the changes brought by enlargement may be uncomfortable but they can lead in the longer term to a considerable gain in efficiency and flexibility in the European economy, with renewed scope for entrepreneurial activity.

### Measuring the benefits

The most serious calculations to date of the costs and benefits for the existing Member States of the Union from enlargement have been made by Baldwin, Francois and Portes (1997).[9] Using a general equilibrium model they estimate the gains and losses from enlargement.

The gains for the Union with relation to GDP are obviously far smaller than for the associated countries; nevertheless there are net gains for the Union, not losses. The authors estimate the total net gain at ECU11.2 billion with reference to the no-enlargement base case. The distribution of the gains between Member States reflects their size and the structure of their economies (those countries with industries which will supply the markets in Central and Eastern Europe with investment goods will gain most). The result of the calculation shows that Germany, France and the United Kingdom will together have more than two-thirds of the total gains, Germany alone having 34%. Interestingly however, although the gains for the other Member States are smaller, only one, Portugal, actually loses through enlargement – and this loss is so small as to be barely measurable.

These calculations, however, are the result of econometric simulations and do not reflect the more obvious gains or losses through the impact of enlargement on Union policies, notably the CAP and the Structural Funds. These questions are dealt with in some detail in the chapters which follow.

### Benefits of enlargement for the associated countries

The associated countries' relative weak security and economic situation and the need for a strong anchor for the market economy and democracy make the benefits of accession for them perhaps more obvious and better rehearsed than those for the EU Member States.

### The political and security benefits of membership

The political benefits of membership consist essentially of being part of the organisation which is making the key decisions affecting the West and Central parts of the European Continent and which has the political and economic weight to enter international negotiations as one of the three powerful world trade blocs.

---

[9] Baldwin, Francois and Portes (1997), pp.148–9.

The discussions which took place at the EU's Inter-Governmental Conference (1996–7) touched on matters which intimately concerned the Central Europeans; yet the associated countries did not take part, having been refused observer status and were merely offered a debriefing every two months by the Council Presidency. The Union finds it difficult to deal with countries which are neither members nor really third countries. This is not astonishing in a Community with such a high degree of integration where everything affects everything else. But the IGC discussed matters of absolutely crucial importance to the associated countries: foreign policy of the Union, the future of European common defence and 'third-pillar' matters (justice and home affairs). Accession is the only way in which the associated countries can fully participate in the key decisions affecting policy on the European Continent.

A similar argument holds true for participation in international negotiations or in international organisations, where the Member States frequently act together as the European Union, representing over 350 million people, the largest trading power in the world and with an important share in world GDP. The power of the Union was seen in the Uruguay Round negotiations, where many of the Union positions were taken over in the final texts. For the associated countries, membership of such a bloc brings many advantages, which probably outweigh the loss of sovereignty, which in today's integrated world is worth little.

The security benefits of accession for the associated countries are often considered to be more important than the economic benefits, although in reality the two go together. The Union does not, of course, provide any sort of security guarantee to its members, but it is considered inconceivable today that a Member State would be attacked without a major response from the other members. This security aspect of membership may be weakened in the future as the Union expands, but at present is a great attraction for the countries in Central Europe.

This would, of course, be a less significant advantage of membership if it was certain that NATO membership was going to be extended to the whole region. However, the first expansion of NATO is likely to include only the Czech Republic, Hungary and Poland. It is unlikely that it will be extended quickly to the Baltic States or to South Eastern Europe.

For all these reasons, which are different from one associated country to another, the importance of accession for security reasons has become more important for them all. The great worry in most of the associated countries is that Russia will remain unstable. This could lead to particularly difficult situations arising in the three Baltic countries, formerly part of the Soviet Union. Accession to the Community is clearly an imperfect security policy for the Baltic countries but it is the only one available. The same is, however, true in a somewhat less acute way for the other associated countries.

### The economic benefits of accession for the associated countries [10]

The economic benefits of accession for the associated countries are to be seen both in terms of access to markets and, at least to some extent, the adoption of the market economy regulations of the European Union.

For industrial goods, as mentioned above, it might be asserted that free trade, which the associated countries now enjoy with the Community, can hardly be improved on through accession. Indeed in some ways the alternative to accession, that of remaining outside the restrictive regulation of the Community while enjoying free access to markets, might seem attractive. However, this argument has two major drawbacks: free trade is always reversible and the interests of the associated countries go far beyond the industrial sector.

As was shown in chapter 3, the importance of the Community market for the associated countries is unlikely to be diminished, indeed trade development between these two partners still has some growth potential. In the same chapter, however, the reversibility of trade liberalisation and the dangers arising from the relatively weak association agreement constraints on protectionist measures were also discussed. Because of the different importance of these trade flows to the two partners and of the concentrated nature of the trade on a few sectors, it is conceivable that the Union would take measures in a crisis to protect certain sectors, which would pose serious economic problems for the associated countries while carrying no real risk of retaliation for the Union. The only way for the associated countries to be relatively certain to keep open their markets in the West in times of economic recession is to become members of the Union.

More generally, accession will provide the stimulus to a far greater integration of the economies of the associated countries with those of the Community Member States. Only when accession takes place, providing the guarantee of a similar business and legal environment throughout the whole Union, will business really consider that investment risk significantly diminishes. The integration of Spain and Portugal in the mid-1980s had a major impact on investment by

[10] Baldwin (1994). This book gives an excellent account of the economics of integration for the associated countries.

Community companies in those countries. At an earlier period, the accession of the United Kingdom, and perhaps even more so Ireland, had a fundamental impact on the integration of those economies with the Continent. There is no reason to think that this would be different for the accession of the associated countries. Indeed, given the level of costs in these countries, it should be expected that the impact of accession might be stronger than in previous accessions.

The real advantage in terms of markets for their industrial goods lies therefore in the certainty provided by accession, which will positively influence both domestic and foreign investment. In the other parts of the economy, accession will bring real advantages in market penetration. In agriculture, accession will bring an end to the very restrictive rules on market access established by the association agreements (unless a partial accession is contemplated, see below). Undoubtedly integration into the Community's CAP will also bring many problems with it, but market access will improve. In the service area, where the associated countries' strength is restricted to one or two very specific sectors (construction, transport, restoration of architectural heritage, for instance), accession may be less advantageous than expected if the Community negotiates a long transition for the free movement of workers. Some improvement in access will, however, almost certainly result from the accession negotiations.

Apart from these direct benefits from accession, the associated countries will also gain through joining a Community where the regulations and practices of the market economy are firmly entrenched. Even though in some areas long transition periods may be negotiated, the adoption of the *acquis communautaire* will firmly anchor the associated countries to the market economies of Western Europe. This will help governments in the region to resist the sectoral pleading of interest groups for protection and to 'sell' certain unpleasant changes to the voters, which might be more difficult if accession were not at the end of the road. It will, of course, also increase the confidence of foreign investors, especially those from the Community, who will have the possibility of appeal in certain cases of dispute beyond the courts of the associated countries to those of the Union.

Here, too, it can be objected that either this process of adapting regulation and institutions of the associated countries to those of the Community can be achieved without accession or, going one step further, that the essence of the market economy is already in place and accession will simply mean that damaging over-regulation will be introduced. Neither of these arguments is convincing. Without the prize of accession, it would appear difficult for the governments of the region both to resist the demands of the electorate for a pause in the reform process and to protect the reforms from the interests of strong vested interests in the economy. As for the second argument, while there has been an enormous effort made to establish the principles of the market economy, there are still many areas of work, especially on the institutions of the market economy, where there remains much to reform. In some countries further privatisation must be undertaken, while elsewhere the firm control of government subsidies has to be made effective. Accession will help governments to continue the reforms. The point of over-regulation is very valid, but should not be tackled by slowing the preparation for accession, but rather by preparing to negotiate limited transition periods in a few crucial areas and supporting the deregulatory forces within the Community.

The most important economic advantage for the associated countries to be expected from accession is therefore that both through improved and more secure market access and the establishment of a business and legal environment similar to that in the Community itself, investment – both domestic and foreign – will grow more rapidly. Foreign investment is important not just for its impact on the stock of capital and therefore the future production potential of the economy, but also because it brings modern techniques of management and transfers technology.

### Measuring the benefits

Baldwin, Francois and Portes (1997) estimate the real income change as a percentage change from the base case of their study to be 1.5% for the seven associated countries, not including the three Baltic states. This growth in income is derived from these countries' entry into the internal market and by taking account of tariff changes.

However, it is the decline in the risk premium on investments in the associated countries which these authors consider to be the most important source of gains. They estimate that as members of the Union the risk premium will decline to that roughly present in the cohesion countries of the present Union. As interest rates fall with the risk, so investment and the capital stock expands beyond what they would be if the countries were not members of the European Union. The authors see a similar boom in investment in the associated countries after membership as was observed in Spain and Portugal. Including this effect, the authors conclude that the real income change for the seven associated countries would rise to ECU30 billion (in 1992 prices) with respect to the base case, a rise of 18.8%.

This estimate has been contested as being too optimistic by some authors, but it is useful in pointing out the significance of the rise in inward direct investment and domestic investment which should take place once these countries are full members of the European Union.[11]

### Conclusion

Enlargement is a win-win situation: all parties will gain in general. However chapter 14 in this book deals with the political economy of enlargement and points to the groups or individuals in society who may oppose enlargement because they feel themselves to be potential losers. As usual, the opponents of enlargement will be more effective lobbyists than the groups who will gain from the process. A clear political course will be required to satisfy all those involved.

[11] See the discussion by Dani Rodrik in Baldwin, Francois and Portes (1997), pp. 170–3.

# 8 Preparing for accession: problems for the associated countries

## Introduction

While the net advantages of membership of the European Union for the associated countries, outlined in chapter 7, are evident, major problems will occur in their preparation for accession. The balance of advantage is just that – a balance between positive and negative impacts of accession to the Union. And, as in the Union itself, there will be groups of losers in the process who will oppose accession. There will also be practical problems such as the capacity of the administration to make preparations for accession at a speed commensurate with politicians' ambitions. In addition, the transition process has not advanced smoothly in all areas and an acceleration of this process is necessary. Finally, there is a question mark over the compatibility of the two processes of integration and transformation.

This chapter analyses these questions, attempts to identify the problems and to indicate ways in which they may be dealt with.

## The political economy of accession in Central and Eastern Europe

The changes required to prepare for accession follow on from the difficult years of economic, political and social transition in the associated countries. It has frequently been pointed out that the majority of those who forced through the systemic changes in 1989–90 – the intellectuals, teachers and organised labour – lost out in the first two or three years of the reform, whilst those who gained, the new entrepreneurs and the nomenclatura entrepreneurs, were relatively few in number. The losers included the new unemployed, the old, those whose skills became irrelevant and state sector employees in general. Today in most of these countries there is a feeling that the medium-term losers are now in a minority, but the memory of the hardships of the first years of transition remain.

Accession brings new change when many would prefer stability. An analysis of the political economy of accession suggests that those most affected will be:

- state-owned sectors of the economy, which have not restructured adequately, because they have continued to be protected in some way from competition
- enterprises, private and public which, through their inability or unwillingness to invest in new technologies, will fall victim to increased domestic and foreign competition
- enterprises which are dependent for their existence purely on the low relative level of wages and salaries, and which cannot adjust as these rise after accession
- enterprises which, through accession, will be required to invest large amounts over a short period of time to bring their standards (for instance, environmental and social protection) up to EU levels
- enterprises which operate on the basis of domestic legal rules (or behind tariff barriers) which will be swept away through the process of approximation of domestic law to that of the European Union
- those employed in the above enterprises who find it difficult or impossible to retrain
- political elites and civil servants whose power is curtailed by accession – those in agricultural policy and operations, in commercial and competition policy, for instance; politically, some groups of politicians in Parliament or indeed in government may well oppose accession because of a perceived loss of power.

In contrast to the political economy of enlargement in the European Union, opposition to accession from organised labour should not be a major problem, as accession should increase the return to labour in real terms. There will obviously be protests from workers in those industries which suffer from a loss of protection. Such protests could be important in areas like the steel industry and shipbuilding, but if the pace of job creation related to high economic growth rates can be maintained, the impact even here should be limited.

Depending on the solution found for agriculture and the implementation of the CAP in the new Member States, there may be a negative reaction from peasant agriculture. However, with the prospect of somewhat higher prices for agricultural products and open markets in Western Europe, even this potential source of opposition has been muted in most associated states.

While many businesses will be affected by accession, in general terms the flow of new capital into these countries and the further opening of markets will probably lead to higher growth rates in the economy and more opportunities for dynamic entrepreneurs to prosper. A relative decline in the return to capital after accession is therefore unlikely to spark off major protests here.

The most dangerous resistance to accession is liable to come from the public sector, and especially from the civil service and from parts of the political class. It should be remembered that one of the most potent forces in the rejection of the union between the Länder of Brandenburg and Berlin in Spring 1996 was the opposition from officials in the two State governments fearful of losing their influence, and perhaps their jobs. The same phenomenon can be expected in the associated countries. Opposition will also occur at the political level, and may be very potent. The liberalisation of the economy in certain areas will cause loss of influence for specific political groupings in the country. This may affect agricultural parties, for instance, or parties deriving much of their support from state industry and its workers. More generally the re-awakening of a national spirit after decades of being trodden on by Moscow has given scope to parties strongly supporting national independence and against integration with another power bloc. Such parties have moderately strong support in several of the associated countries and have reached government, in coalition, in some of them. This movement may become stronger, especially if economic conditions become more difficult.

In spite of this potential opposition to accession, there is still a good majority in most countries in favour. This support is shown by the Eurobarometer polls.[1] The question posed was: 'if there were a referendum tomorrow on the question of European Union membership, would you personally vote for or against membership?' Those in favour of membership varied from 80% in Romania down to 29% in Estonia. Overall, 61% of those questioned in the associated countries answered 'yes', 7% 'no', with 15% 'undecided'. There was not a single country where there was a majority against membership. If there was a real referendum closer to accession, when many of the disadvantages of membership are known, these majorities would certainly be far lower, but they would still be majorities in favour. The reasons are complex and not always convincing. One very important reason is that people believe that membership of the Union will make them richer and guarantee a better future to their children. This reason will still be valid

[1] European Commission (1997b), pp. 34–5.

at the time of accession referenda, if they are held. Other reasons such as security issues or political issues will also play a role in maintaining a majority for accession.

## Transition and integration

The most important objective of any accession strategy must be the same as that of any economic strategy in the associated countries: the highest level of economic growth combined with macroeconomic stability. It would, however, be an important problem for the associated countries if policies adopted as part of the preparation for accession led to slower economic growth. The question is: is there a risk that the policies of transition and integration conflict?

### Economic transformation

The enormous task of transforming whole economies and societies from centrally-planned dictatorships to market economy democracies has been achieved with different degrees of success in all the associated countries. While today there is much criticism of detail, the achievements have been remarkable overall. Indeed if one compares the capacity of these economies and societies to undertake massive structural change with the incapacity of the Union's economies to tackle minor changes (the 40-year discussion over shop-opening hours in Germany or the problems to achieve modest liberalisation of labour markets in certain countries), the criticism from the Union is put into a different perspective.

The achievements in the area of the democratic process proved to be somewhat less difficult and certainly less controversial than economic and social reforms. In all the associated countries free and fair elections have been held, in most of them on several occasions, and there have been quite normal changes of government. The party system is still evolving as different parties gain and lose their support, leading to shifts in alliances and to government crises. But these are the natural constituents of democratic control, and occur in mature democracies as well. Only Slovakia failed to meet the criteria in these areas set by the Commission in its 'Opinions'.

It is in the economic area that the main challenges for reform lie, and it is true that much remains to be achieved. The progress here too, however, has been remarkable. To make a judgement on the success of the economic transformation, it is necessary to consider the starting position of each of the associated countries. It is impossible to make general statements on which reform programme was the most successful, or on the question of whether a 'shock therapy' is better than a more gradual reform, without looking closely at both the macroeconomic aggregates at the end of the 1980s and the political and social climate in which the reforms were being undertaken. There was little real alternative to the Polish reform programme of Finance Minister Balcerowicz, given the economic situation which the first Solidarity Government inherited.[2] A policy which attempted to reform more slowly would have achieved only a small part of the progress made in the Polish economy and would not have released that country's entrepreneurial spirit. This does not mean that the same policy was appropriate for Hungary, where reform had been taking place for over 20 years before 1989 or for Romania, the economy of which had been distorted by the extremely autarkic regime of Ceaucescu.

Table 8.1 shows macroeconomic data for 1992 and 1996/7 taken from the EBRD *Transition report* (1997).[3] Although not the beginning of transformation, 1992 data still shows major differences between the associated countries. In Poland, 1992 was the first year of positive growth since 1989, while many of the countries were still recording major declines. The three Baltic countries had inflation rates of around 1,000% and little unemployment. Bulgaria and the Slovak Republic had exceptionally large general government deficits. In 1989, the differences were still large between the Visegrád countries: Hungarian inflation in 1989 was a high 18.9%, the Polish figure was an astronomical 640% while in Czechoslovakia it was around 1.5%. However the Visegrád countries and Bulgaria and Romania had national economies which were structurally separate to that of the Soviet Union. This was not the case for the three Baltic countries, which were part of the Soviet Union, and therefore had a much more difficult task of structural adjustment. Slovenia was to some extent between these extremes, being part of former Yugoslavia, but with a high degree of regional independence.

As far as the achievements at the macroeconomic level are concerned, there is a relatively clear pattern of initial recession as the liberalisation of prices made some capacity redundant, as consumers reduced their purchases as prices rose, and as the negative impact from the loss of trade with the CMEA countries became obvious. This phase (which may be over-stated by the statistics) was followed in most countries by a strong and sustained recovery based on investment growth, returning consumer confidence and export growth. While it proved possible to reduce inflation from very high levels using relatively standard stabilisa-

[2] Balcerowicz (1995).    [3] EBRD (1997).

Table 8.1 *Macroeconomic data for the associated countries, 1992 and 1996*

| | GNP$/cap | | GNP$ (PPP)/cap | GDP average annual growth | | Consumer price % change[a] | | Unemployment rate | | Govt. deficit % GDP | |
|---|---|---|---|---|---|---|---|---|---|---|---|
| | 1992 | 1996 | 1996 | 1990-3 | 1993-7 | 1992 | 1997 | 1992 | 1996 | 1992 | 1997 |
| Bulgaria | 1012 | 1038 | 4190 | −7.2 | −3.3 | 82 | 1049 | 15.6 | 12.5 | −5.2 | −6.3 |
| Czech Rep. | 2903 | 5340 | 9770[d] | −4.8 | 3.4 | 11.1 | 9.5 | 2.6 | 3.5 | - | −1.0 |
| Estonia | 1105 | 3000 | 4431 | −10.0 | 3.3 | 1076 | 11 | 5.0[c] | 5.6 | −0.3 | −1.5 |
| Hungary | 3617 | 4357 | 6410[d] | −5.3 | 2.1 | 23 | 18.0 | 12.3 | 10[d] | −5.5 | −5.0 |
| Latvia | 525 | 2010 | 3484 | −20.9 | 1.5 | 951 | 8 | 2.3 | 7.2 | −0.8 | −0.9 |
| Lithuania | 515 | 2700 | 4766 | −25.8 | 3.0 | 1021 | 9 | 1.3 | 7.0 | 0.8 | −2.8 |
| Poland | 2197 | 3459 | 5400[d] | −0.03 | 5.9 | 43 | 16 | 13.6 | 13.6 | −6.6 | −4.0[b] |
| Romania | 859 | 1437 | 4591 | −6.9 | 3.4 | 210 | 145 | 6.2 | 7.8 | −4.6 | −4.5 |
| Slovak Rep. | 2216 | 3596[e] | 7970 | −8.3 | 5.8 | 10.1 | 6.5 | 12.2[c] | 11.1 | −7.0[c] | −3.5 |
| Slovenia | 6261 | 9058 | 10594[d] | −4.0 | 4.1 | 201 | 9.0 | 11.5 | 13.8 | 0.2 | −1.0 |

*Notes:*
[a] Annual average.
[b] state budget balance.
[c] 1993.
[d] 1995.
[e] 1997.

*Source:* EBRD (1997).

tion policies, it has proved more difficult to reduce it from 20% down to levels nearer those prevailing in Western Europe. The government deficit has been reduced in most countries very sharply, mainly through the reduction of subsidies to the economy (Hungary in 1992–4 and Bulgaria and Romania are to some extent exceptions) and is now generally at levels below those in the Union's Member States. Unemployment has risen sharply as very large productivity gains have been achieved; unemployment is, however, levelling off in most countries with a tendency for net job creation to exceed the growth in the labour force.

It is, however, in structural reform where both some of the best performances but also some of the most difficult problems for the future lie. Price liberalisation has been achieved almost totally in these economies. Some controls remain in the energy sector, especially in prices to domestic consumers and in the housing sector, for social reasons. Price controls are not obviously the best way to cope with social problems and these remaining controls need to be removed, although this will cause important political problems and will need to be combined with social measures for certain parts of the population. Privatisation in the economy has progressed at very different paces in the associated countries, though all of them now have a substantial share of the economy in the private sector (Czech Republic 70%, Bulgaria 50%). As time moves on, privatisation gets more difficult in some countries than at the beginning of the transition; Balcerowicz (1995) refers to the initial years of the transformation as a period in which reformers have to achieve a maximum of reform, after which the normal political process tends to hamper progress.[4] Further progress with privatisation in those countries where it has become slow is important not only for the vitality of the economy in the future, but also as a sign to the European Union that market economies are really being created (one of the Copenhagen criteria for accession!). Liberalisation of trade, one of the principal pillars of the reform programmes, has tended to be reversed somewhat in some countries; again this is bad for the economy and bad for accession preparations.

In spite of the overall positive development of the economies of the associated countries, all of them remain at a low level of output *per capita* with low capital endowments. As one of the main (unwritten) criteria for membership of the Community is likely to be that the applicants can show that they are in an accelerated process of economic

---

[4] Balcerowicz (1995).

catch-up, it is vital that economic growth remains high, which itself will facilitate further structural reform.

In this context, the question of whether the processes of transition and integration are mutually supportive or whether there are certain aspects of the preparation for accession which will tend to slow down economic growth is important.

### Regulation, integration and transition[5]

It is true that much of the dynamism that the CEE economies have shown in the last three or four years has been due to the expansion of a very entrepreneurial private sector, working in an environment with relatively less regulation than in the economies of much of Western Europe. It is certainly not the case that there is very little regulation in the associated countries. In some areas of economic activity, including the labour market, certain countries have more restrictive regulation than do some of the Union's Member States. Nevertheless, overall, the level of regulation affecting business is less onerous.

Integration with the European Union leading to accession will increase the level of regulation of business considerably, whatever the outcome of the accession negotiations. The basic position of the Community on accession issues has always been that the acceding country must take over all the *acquis communautaire* at the time of accession. This is repeated in the 'Agenda 2000' document. In negotiation this position has always given way to agreement on certain transition arrangements and indeed to amendments to certain policies (the addition of a new class of disadvantaged region in the Structural Funds on the accession of the EFTA countries in 1995, for instance). However, these exceptions to the *acquis* have always been relatively limited. In the case of the accession of the associated countries, it is certain that the Community will have to be prepared to grant more exceptions, more transition periods and to contemplate more policy changes than in previous accessions.

The benefits of enlargement to the European Union are so important that this process should not be endangered by an inability of the Union to rise above a technocratic and legalistic view of the associated countries' capacity to meet the *acquis communautaire*.

---

[5] Orłowski and Mayhew (1997).

*The White Paper on the Internal Market*

The Commission's White Paper on the preparation of the associated countries for integration into the internal market of the Union tackles three questions:

- Firstly it lists the *internal market acquis* which is essential in the early stages of preparing for accession. This is not an exhaustive list; eventually all the *acquis* will have to be taken over by the associated countries. It was, however, thought to be counter-productive to suggest to the associated countries that they take over already some of the more costly process-related measures.
- Secondly it suggests the *sequencing* of these measures. Some of the measures are absolutely essential to the operation of not only the internal market but also of any market economy – for instance, measures on company law or on accounting practice. But even in these areas it makes sense to implement certain directives before others. For this reason, the White Paper lists first-order measures (stage I) and second-order (stage II) measures. The typical stage I measures include framework directives, necessary for more detailed legislation or directives, which can be adopted at a later stage.
- Thirdly it deals with the *institutional* questions related to the implementation of the White Paper measures. It is in many senses easier to pass legislation in the Parliament than it is to implement legislation afterwards. This is not only a problem which occurs in the countries of Central Europe; in the Union, too, some internal market legislation is not being properly implemented. The associated countries, however, have special problems in that they are coming out of a system of centralised planning in which totally different institutions existed than those needed to implement market economy measures. It is for this reason that the Commission considered the institutional chapter of the White Paper as of great importance.

The heart of the White Paper is to be found in the Annex rather than in the White Paper itself, because it is here that the detail of the measures is dealt with. The Annex is also the most useful part of the paper for the associated countries. It was hoped that each country would study the list of first- and second-order measures and, taking into account the progress already made in the approximation of laws and the particularities of the country's economic reform programme and legal system, would draw up its own plans for taking on the *acquis*. The Union's White Paper would then lead to 'White Papers' in each of the associated countries. In general, this is what has happened.

Several of the associated countries have already made considerable progress towards taking on the *acquis*, as was suggested above. In the case of Poland, for instance, there already exists an extensive national White Paper that had already been prepared before that of the Union, while all new measures being proposed by government departments already have to be checked for their conformity with EU legislation in the Office of the Committee for European Integration.[6] In this case, the Union's White Paper was a useful cross-check for the Polish government in the context of its already well developed plans.

The implementation of the White Paper in the partner countries was made difficult by the relative lack of expertise in some areas within the countries and the shortage of experts in the Community. This will be a more serious problem than that of finance. The human constraint will have to be tackled with some care. The shortage of expertise suggests that as much of the work as possible should be done at the horizontal level in programmes which cover all the associated countries. This approach will, however, have a natural limitation in that the interest of the partner countries will be to have their own national White Paper programmes because each of their situations is different and because each individual country will be judged on its merits domestically and by the Union.

Under the PHARE programme, national 'White Paper' programmes were set up in each associated country. In addition a Technical Assistance Information Exchange Office (TAIEX) has been set up centrally in Brussels both to assist in the provision of technical assistance and progressively to monitor progress made; this Office began to operate in Spring 1996. Important as this initiative is, it is unlikely to be sufficient to tackle the vast problem of legal approximation.

On the side of the Union, further consideration must be given to the most efficient use of its available resources. However, more must be done to mobilise as many resources as possible from national administrations and from the Commission – after all, much of the most relevant experience resides here. However, as the Member States attempt to cut government spending it is often difficult to persuade governments to release good quality officials for anything more than a few days each year. To some extent retired officials can be more useful than serving officials because they can serve for longer periods and are therefore more reliable. However, this is still a relatively small pool of labour even when added to by available consulting companies from the private sector.

[6] Urząd Rady Ministrów, Biuro do spraw integracji Europejskiej oraz pomocy zagranicznej, *Biała Księga* (Warsaw, 1995).

To assess the enormous effort required of the associated countries to take over and implement the laws and regulations of the Union, it suffices to look at the table of contents of the Annex to the White Paper (figure 8.1). There are 23 separate chapters to the Annex, which covers 438 pages. Some of these chapters present totally new challenges for the associated countries, such as the area of mutual recognition of professional qualifications. Other areas are relatively recent innovations to their statute books, such as regulations on data protection, the protection of intellectual property or consumer protection legislation. Yet other chapters of the White Paper deal with existing areas of regulation in the associated countries, but where approximation to Community law will require very considerable adjustment to national law. Agriculture, the environment and the energy fields are typical here. Finally the new approach directives, the key to the completion of the internal market, suppose the existence and efficient operation of a whole infrastructure of bodies to carry out regulatory enforcement, market surveillance, standardisation and conformity assessment. It should be noted that the White Paper is not an exhaustive but a selective list. The actual work of legal approximation and institutional development goes beyond what is to be found in the White Paper itself.

The White Paper includes both product-related and process-related legislation as well as legislation basic for the operation of a competitive market economy. Product-related legislation determines the characteristics of products and services which are sold in the internal market and in some cases the way they are marketed. Typical for such legislation is that part of the White Paper dealing with chemicals and reproduced in figure 8.2. This legislation is specific and sectoral rather than using the new approach to technical harmonisation and standards.

Almost all of the legislation in this area regulates the contents of the product or the way it is put on the market (labelling, etc.) in order to protect the consumer. Some of the regulations refer to the way in which chemicals are prepared and the testing procedures to be used, but again the objective is to make sure that they are prepared in a way which does not lead to any dangers for the consumer.

It is very important that the associated countries approximate their legislation to product-related directives in the Union. Without such approximation and the implementation of the resulting laws, it will not be possible for the associated countries to join the internal market and enjoy the free circulation of goods and services. There is little room for compromise in these areas, and even relatively little room for negotiation. If product-related directives are not implemented, it will be necessary to maintain frontiers indefinitely between the Union and the

**Introduction**

**1 Free movement of capital**

**2 Free movement and safety of industrial products**
I     Prevention of new barriers to trade
II    The new approach directives
III   The sectoral approach directives:
    1  Type approval system for motor vehicles and their trailers
    2  Type approval of two and three wheel motor vehicles
    3  Chemical substances
    4  Foodstuffs
    5  Medicinal products for human use
    6  Medicinal products for veterinary use

**3 Competition**
I     State aids
II    Merger control
III   Restrictive agreements and abuse of dominant positions
IV   State monopolies and public undertakings

**4 Social policy and action**
I     Equal opportunities for men and women
II    Coordination of social security schemes
III   Health and safety at work
IV   Labour law and working conditions
    1  Tar content of cigarettes
    2  Labelling of tobacco products

**5 Agriculture**
I     General overview
    1  General introduction
    2  Veterinary, plant and animal nutrition legislation
    3  Agricultural markets legislation
II    Veterinary, plant health and animal nutrition legislation
    A  Veterinary legislation
      1  Trade in live animals, semen, ova and embryos
      2  Trade in animal products
      3  Control measures
      4  Marketing of animal products
      5  Measures covering more than one sector
      6  Imports from third countries of live animals and animal products
      7  Control and protection system
      8  Breeding stock and pure-bred animals
      9  Animal welfare
    B  Plant health and animal nutrition legislation
      1  Seeds and propagating material
      2  Plants or plant products
      3  Animal nutrition

17 **Civil law**

18 **Mutual recognition of professional qualifications**

19 **Intellectual property**

20 **Energy**
   I      Hydrocarbons
   II     Security of supply/stocks
   III    Price transparency
   IV     Transfer of electricity and gas through transmission grids
   V      Nuclear sector
   VI     Liberalisation of the electricity and gas markets
   VII    Hot water boilers
   VIII   Sulphur content of certain liquid fuels
   IX     Crude oil savings through the use of substitute fuel components
          in petrol

21 **Customs and excise**

22 **Indirect taxation**

23 **Consumer protection**

*Figure 8.1* Table of contents of the Commission's Internal Market White Paper
*Source*: European Commission (1995d).

**Dangerous preparations** : The Directive on dangerous preparations (mixtures of chemical substances that are dangerous to human beings and/or the environment) is intended to harmonize the following:

1 the classification of dangerous substances as a function of the level of danger that they display;
2 their labelling in order to ensure the safety of the persons handling them;
3 their packaging.

The Directive also incorporates calculation methods enabling an assessment to be made of the health hazards presented by a preparation. The greatest difficulties in implementing that directive arise with small and medium-sized businesses (SMBs). SMBs have fewer technical and financial resources for compiling the safety data sheets required by law, the content of which has been standardised at world level, although the aspects linked with the classification, labelling and packaging of pesticides, which are currently covered by Directive 78/361/EEC of 26 June 1978, could, in the long term, be covered by Directive 88/379/EEC on dangerous preparations.

**Restrictions on the marketing of dangerous preparations and substances**: Harmonization in this area relates to the action to be taken by the Member States in order that the substances set out in the Annex to the directive are only marketed under certain conditions. The Directive on marketing restrictions requires a certain level of supervision by the Member States. There is no obligation as regards the action to be taken. Member States are free to select and implement the structure which to them seems to be the most adequate. The responsibility for supervision that is incumbent upon a Member State may also be assumed by a centralized or decentralized administration or even be delegated to a competent independent body. The solutions available vary widely from one Member State to another. As a general rule those bodies carry out downstream checks on the market.

**Detergents**: European directives in this area have enabled biodegradability thresholds to be set for detergents (anionic, cationic, nonionic and ampholytic surfactants) and also analytical methods to be used in order to measure biodegradability (anionic and nonionic surfactants). The transposition of European directives at national level enables the 'foaming' effects of certain detergents to be combated. Thought is currently being given to updating all of the directives.

**Fertilizers**: Harmonization with regard to fertilizers is not mandatory, but optional. It is aimed at virtually all fertilizers, while the categories still not covered continue to be so by the national laws. It has been possible to define forms of action to apply to the composition, detonability and analytical and sampling methods designed for checks on simple ammonium-nitrate-based fertilizers and high-nitrogen-content fertilizers. Compliance with the European directives enables the 'EEC fertilizer' Label to be obtained.

## CONDITIONS NECESSARY TO OPERATE THE LEGISLATION

**Dangerous preparations:** The Directive 88/379/EEC on dangerous preparations makes specific reference to the Directive on the packaging, labelling and classification of dangerous substances (67/548/EEC) (see contribution under Environment). Indeed the following are considered to be dangerous:

- preparations of which at least one of the constituent substances is classified as being dangerous by Directive 67/548/EEC;
- preparations considered to be dangerous according to the methods referred to in the Directive on dangerous preparations.

These two conditions are cumulative and not alternative. It is thus necessary to transpose Directive 67/548/EEC – simultaneously, or indeed in advance.

As regards the implementation of said Directive 88/379/EEC, Article 12 of said Directive 88/379/EEC provides that bodies be set up in the Member States that are responsible for receiving information on health. These are bodies of the 'poison antidote centre' type.

**Restrictions on the marketing of dangerous preparations and substances**: the existence of national laws restricting or banning the marketing of certain substances, and also laws on the bodies responsible for conducting market checks in order to ensure that the Regulations are properly applied, are a desirable prerequisite.

**Detergents and fertilizers**: no specific conditions.

## KEY MEASURES

The Directives selected below constitute a comprehensive entity and represent the core of the chemical laws in force. Certain chemical products (solvents) which have been covered by separate directives, are now covered by the dangerous preparations Directive.

### CHOICE OF STAGE I MEASURES

### DESCRIPTION & JUSTIFICATION:
Owing to their repercussions on both health and the environment and on the proper functioning of the internal market, the laws on chemical products can only be implemented in several stages. They therefore constitute a block, and it is suggested that they be adopted in Stage I.

### STAGE I MEASURES

**Dangerous preparations:**

| | |
|---|---|
| Directive 88/379/EEC *OJ* L 187/14, 16.07.88 as last amended by Directive 93/18, *OJ* L 104, 29.4.93 as last supplemented by Directive 93/112 *OJ* L 314, 16.12.93 | Directive 88/379/EEC of 7 June 1988 on the approximation of the laws, regulations and administrative provisions of the Member States relating to the classification, packaging and labelling of dangerous preparations. |

**Marketing restrictions**

| | |
|---|---|
| Directive 76/769/EEC *OJ* L 262/201, 27/09/76, as last amended by Directive 94/60 *OJ* L 365, 31/12/94. | Directive 76/769/EEC of 27 July 1976 on the approximation of the laws, administrative regulations and provisions of the Member States relating to restrictions on the marketing and use of certain dangerous substances and preparations. |

**Detergents**

| | |
|---|---|
| Directive 73/404/EEC<br>*OJ* L 347/51, 17/12/73 | Directive 73/404/EEC of 22 November 1973 on the approximation of the laws of the Member States relating to detergents. This Directive deals with the ban on the use and marketing of detergents where the average biodegradability of the anionic, cationic, nonionic and ampholytic surfactants that they contain is less than 90%. |
| Directive 73/405/EEC<br>*OJ* L 347/53, 17/12/73<br>supplemented by<br>Directive 82/243/EEC<br>*OJ* L 109/1, 22/04/82 | Directive 73/405/EEC of 22 November 1973 on the approximation of the laws of the Member States relating to methods of testing the biodegradability of anionic surfactants. This Directive specifies the analytical methods to be used for anionic surfactants, and prohibits the marketing and use of a detergent if its average biodegradability is less than 80%. |
| Directive 82/242/EEC<br>*OJ* L 109/18, 22/04/82 | Directive 82/242/EEC of 31 March 1982 on the approximation of the laws of the Member States relating to methods of testing the biodegradability of non-ionic surfactants and amending Directive 73/404/EEC. This Directive deals with the ban on the marketing and use of detergents if the measured biodegradability of the nonionic surfactants that they contain is less than 80% when the analytical methods specified by the Directive are used. |

**Fertilizers**

| | |
|---|---|
| Directive 76/116/EEC<br>adopted of the<br>*OJ* L 24/21, 30/01/76<br>and last amended and<br>supplemented by Directive<br>93/69<br>*OJ* L 185, 28/7/93 | Directive 76/116/EEC of 18 December 1975 on the approximation laws of the Member States relating to fertilizers, |
| Directive 77/535/EEC<br>*OJ* L 213/1, 22/08/77<br>as last amended by<br>Directive 93/1, *OJ* L 113,<br>7/5/93 | Directive 77/535/EEC of 22/6/77 on the approximation of the laws of the Member States relating to methods of sampling and analysis for fertilizers. |

| Directive 80/876/EEC<br>*OJ* L 250/7, 23/09/80 | Directive 80/876/EEC of 15/7/80 on the approximation of the laws of the Member States relating to straight ammonium nitrate fertilizers of high nitrogen content. |
|---|---|
| Directive 87194/EEC<br>*OJ* L 38/1, 07/02/87 | Directive 97/94/EEC of 8/12/86 on the approximation of the laws of the Member States relating to procedures for the control of characteristics of, limits for and resistance to detonation of straight ammonium nitrate fertilizers of high nitrogen content. |

*Figure 8.2* Chemical products: description of the legislation
*Source:* European Commission (1995d).

associated countries. With the internal market the cornerstone of European integration today, this would mean that only an improved association rather than a real accession would be on offer.

The second group of regulations in the White Paper are those which are fundamental to the operation of a market economy and which are therefore basic to the operation of the Union's internal market. Typical here is the area of competition policy, the control of state aids, public procurement, company law, accountancy and the protection of intellectual property. Most the associated countries have introduced legislation in all of these areas as part of their reform programmes. Where this is not the case, it makes sense for the legislation to be introduced and implemented as fast as possible. Even if accession were not to take place, legislation in most of these areas would still be necessary in order for the economy to function efficiently.

One of the main questions for the associated countries is how far to go in implementing process-related directives prior to accession. Typical of this sort of regulation is the social field and, in part, environmental regulation. The Union's *acquis* in the area of labour law and working conditions regulates the way in which workers are treated by employers and the representation of employees in company decisions. These regulations in no way affect the physical characteristics of goods or the quality of goods and services marketed in the internal market. They are also not attempting to protect the consumer, nor are they fundamental to the operation of the market. The internal market can operate without such legislation, though there are political constraints, which may affect the operation of the internal market where it is felt that minimum standards are not respected. This does not mean that all the legislation is superfluous; it is justified by society's desire to protect employees in particular areas where exploitation may occur or to protect accepted norms of societal behaviour. Typical of the latter is the directive on the protection of young people at work. More contested would be the directives imposing minimum rest periods or maximum working time or those relating to the role of employees in the running of the enterprise. The associated countries, faced with the enormous task of economically 'catching-up', require as flexible markets as possible. The objectives of social policy must therefore be restricted to guaranteeing basic minimum conditions across the various fields that it treats without limiting the capacity of enterprises to compete nationally and internationally. In fact there has been much over-dramatisation of the problem of taking over the social *acquis*. In many ways the Polish labour code, for instance, is far more constraining. There should be no confusion between taking on the social *acquis* and adopting some of the over-regulated national social policy in the Member States. It is probably only the regulations on health and safety at work which will cause major problems in the associated countries.

In the environmental area, the arguments are more complex. Here the White Paper also shows considerably more reserve in suggesting which directives the associated countries should implement. White Paper measures concentrate almost entirely on product-related environmental standards, respect of which is essential if the associated countries are going to join the internal market. The directives on the lead content of petrol, the sulphur content of liquid fuels and the transport of toxic waste are typical in this area. Other areas of environment policy such as legislation referring to pollution from stationary sources, air and water pollution, nature protection and environmental impact assessment are not contained in the White Paper. However the whole *acquis* in the environment area will be the subject of the accession negotiations. The 'Agenda 2000' package already acknowledges that it will be impossible for the new Member States to implement the whole environmental *acquis* immediately on accession. This view is also supported by the World Bank Country Economic Memoranda on Poland and Slovakia.[7] The associated countries will have the possibility to negotiate transition periods for those areas of legislation which will impose major financial burdens on enterprises or on the state. It is, of course, important that in the negotiations those Member States which are less enthusiastic about

[7] World Bank (1997a, 1997b).

accession and those which are very ambitious in environmental policy observe the same prudent line as the Commission in its White Paper.[8]

The Commission made it clear that it expected the associated countries to draw up national work programmes for the implementation of these recommendations and to review, with the Commission, existing work on the approximation of legislation. The adoption of the *acquis* requires therefore an important institutional response of the associated countries and a coordination system which functions properly.

*Legal approximation in the associated countries*

In order to respond to the challenge of adopting the Community *acquis*, the associated countries have all introduced measures to ensure that legislation is progressively adapted. As far as the adoption of laws and regulations are concerned there are two clearly distinct problems: how to deal with the changes which are necessary in existing legislation, and how to deal with new legislation which is submitted to Parliament. In both cases the legal problems are considerable, partly because of the shortage of legal experts in the associated countries and partly because of the relatively restricted assistance which the Member States of the Community and the Community institutions can make available.

Hungary can be taken as an example of the systems which the more advanced associated countries have adopted to tackle these problems. In Hungary's case, the fact that it was the most advanced CEE country in terms of reform before 1989 meant that thought had been given to legal approximation in certain areas, notably trade, even before the overthrow of Communism. As one of the first three countries to negotiate an association agreement with the Community, Hungary instituted an intensive programme of legal approximation as early as 1991. The current situation is summed up in the Hungarian National Strategy for the implementation of the White Paper on the Internal Market published in December 1995.[9]

Hungary, like several of the other associated countries, has institutionalised the process of legal approximation. The first legal step was the entry into force of the Europe Agreement Act in 1994 which places an obligation on the government to inform Parliament whenever a draft law is presented within the scope of the Europe Agreement, whether the draft is compatible with Community legislation and whether it can be

---

[8] At the Environment Council meeting in September 1996, in the context of the structured dialogue, the Commission representatives apparently made it clear that they considered that the associated countries should take over the whole of the environmental *acquis* before accession.

[9] Government of the Republic of Hungary (1995).

considered as approximating Community rules. A similar obligation has been enacted by the government regarding the preparation of the governmental and ministerial legal measures. In 1995, Government Resolution 2174 laid out a work plan based on a comprehensive legal harmonisation programme for the first five-year stage of the transitional period as defined by the Europe Agreement. A second Annex to the Resolution laid down a priority three-year programme of approximation specifically in the area of internal market legislation. The National Strategy itself, agreed at the end of 1995, contains a very detailed timetable of legal approximation, which has the aim of achieving a high degree of compliance with the recommendations of the White Paper by the end of 1997.

The core part of this policy, like that in the Czech Republic and Poland, is the operation of checking procedures on new legislation or changes in existing legislation operated by government before the drafts reach the Parliament. In Poland, for instance, the legal team operating this system celebrated its first thousand opinions on draft legislation in July 1996! The second component of a strategy is a programme, with a timetable to adjust existing legislation to Community legislation. Such a programme is a mammoth operation, involving all ministries and government offices and imposing significant burdens on the administration and Parliament alike. In Hungary, this programme is computerised and the state of legal harmonisation can be accessed on CD-ROM.

The process of legal approximation poses several problems for the associated countries. The fundamental economic problems involved are briefly dealt with below, but there are also many purely technical problems. One is that Community legislation is continually evolving: new legislation is being passed and existing legislation is being amended. This unavoidable problem makes approximation a very difficult and uncertain process, with considerable waste of resources when legislation is radically amended by the European Union after corresponding legislation has been adopted in the associated countries. Fortunately the pace of new EU legislation has eased after the 'completion' of the internal market, but problems will still arise. One way of improving this situation would be for the Community to institute a much closer relationship with the associated countries, so that they receive very early warning of the Community's legislative and regulatory programme. An even better procedure would be a consultation procedure, where the associated countries were consulted about new legislation. It is, however, most unlikely that the Community would agree to such a step. Where possible, however, the associated countries should be included in established Community information exchange and notification systems, rather than having separate systems set up for them.

A second technical problem is that there is no procedure in the European Union to check laws in the associated countries to make sure that they do correspond exactly to those required by the Community *acquis*. This may well lead to serious problems in a few years' time when, closer to accession, it is discovered that the European Union requires changes in existing associated country laws to guarantee complete correspondence with EU directives. The Union could tackle this problem in the same way as with the EFTA applicants, where it verified legal conformity well before accession.

An associated problem is that the current Union *acquis* sometimes does not represent the latest developments in regulation. One area where this might be the case is in the accounting directives. To judge by the experience of several large European companies, the regulations at European level allow them to show balance sheets which have a net profit while the same balance sheets prepared according to the stricter American regulations (to which they must conform before being quoted on American stock exchanges) show a net loss. In these cases, it is obvious that the closest cooperation with the Community authorities is necessary before a judgement is made.

Finally, it is important that the Community and its Member States provide as much assistance to the associated countries as possible. Most of the effort will have to come from the Member States, because in most areas of the internal market, it is the Member States, not the Community institutions, which possess the expertise. However in one or two areas, such as the control of state aids, the Community institutions will also be called upon to provide human capital.

### Institutional change and legal approximation

While the problems of adopting the Community *acquis* are considerable, the problems of implementing the legislation are even more daunting. Implementation requires both an institutional infrastructure for implementation and an effective means of enforcement. To take the example of competition policy, three separate steps are necessary to take on the *acquis communautaire*. Legislation has to be passed by Parliament. Secondly an institution needs to be set up, which is as independent of government as possible, to take charge of competition policy, including the establishment of subsidiary implementing rules on which the legislation depends and the taking of decisions on the interpretation of the law. Finally, there must be access to legal remedy in the general courts or specialised competition courts.

The associated countries have made considerable progress in this area, in spite of the great difficulties involved. Most institutions, such as the anti-monopoly or competition offices, have had to be created since the start of reforms, as they are intimately related to the establishment of the market economy and the democratic system. It is true that some institutions, such as the Courts of Auditors or standardisation bodies, have a longer history. However, even here it has been necessary to make significant changes in operations and this process is sometimes more difficult in existing than in newly created institutions. An example would be the standardisation institutions which have a history of issuing mandatory standards, and which will find it difficult to move to the Union's tradition of setting voluntary standards.

The main problems in the institutional area would appear to be:

- the weakness of organisations in the market economy which can take on the burden of self-regulation or voluntary regulation
- the lack of experience and precedent in the new institutions which have been created since the reforms began
- the lack of trained personnel to staff the new institutions
- the question of training and retraining staff in these institutions
- the difficulty of creating the conditions under which individuals and companies can have access to the courts in these specific areas of market economy regulation.

A mature market economy has access to a huge variety of institutions which are used to regulate the economy. An example would be the standardisation authorities such as the DIN, AFNOR or the BSI; another would be the Chambers of Commerce and the Industrial Federations which exist in all countries. These latter bodies often take on the burden of self-regulation, and in some countries certain regulation is totally delegated to them by the state. The Chambers of Commerce in Germany, for instance, are responsible for questions of establishment and the registration of companies; those in France often run ports or airports. In most countries there are self-regulating institutions of actuaries, accountants, veterinarians and most other professions. Beyond these business and professional organisations, all local authorities have offices which deal specifically with the regulation of business and which perform essential duties in the internal market.

In the associated countries, business and professional organisations are in general far too weak to take on the sort of self-regulation or delegated regulation that their West European counterparts have done. This means that the government or some specific state or local institution has to deal with the problems of implementation of regulations. However, there is a double danger here. Firstly, a state organisation is unlikely to have the same degree of knowledge and experience about a business area than an organisation close to business. Secondly, a state institution is likely to implement regulation in a bureaucratic manner which impedes management. However as it is unlikely that there will be sufficient progress in the development of business and professional institutions in the short term, it will be necessary for the government to step in, at least temporarily, to establish the institutions which are required.

Most the Union's institutions work on the basis of generations of experience, with a large amount of case law on which to base new decisions. This is missing in the new institutions in the associated countries, which have very little past experience or evidence on which to base their current decisions. Again, there is little that can be done in the short term, apart from assistance from the Member States of the Union where it is appropriate. Already, however, experience is being accumulated and written up for the use and guidance of officials in the new institutions in some areas of regulation. There are already books of case law in the field of competition policy, for instance, which explain the already large number of decisions in this area.

The recruitment of trained staff and the training of staff in the institutions are major constraints. This problem is common right across all the specialised institutions which have been or are in the process of being created. This is another area where the Member States of the Union can help by inviting staff from the associated countries for training periods in their own corresponding institutions. They can also help with the systematic training of officials in the associated countries, though the constraints on the public service or the business institutions in Western Europe are such that this assistance will never be adequate. The retraining of staff in existing established institutions in the associated countries is a particular problem, as it is always difficult to change long-established habits and procedures.

Finally, the same problem of a lack of experience and training afflicts the legal systems of the associated countries, which are required today to give judgements on totally new areas of law. This may well be a very important bottleneck as more and more companies or individuals seek legal recourse against the decisions of the institutions set up to regulate the market economy. Normally lawyers and judges do not have the necessary experience and training to perform this function, and it will take some years before such specialised lawyers are available.

*Is legal approximation inimical to transformation?*
There is a considerable danger that this process of legal approximation will be seen by both sides as a straightforward legal exercise. In fact each

new law which is adopted is clearly a policy choice, which will affect the performance of the economy and society is some way. Too often, straightforward timetables are established as a function of the *acquis* on the one hand, and the availability of legal staff on the other. It is, however, conceivable that a blind legalistic approach to approximation will lead to a reduction in the flexibility of the economy, and thus create an additional constraint on the transformation process.

The associated countries need to consider the following points in approaching this process:

- Economic impact analysis should be carried out on groups of directives before the approximation process begins, in order to establish what impact changes in the law may have on the economy. Such analyses will be vital in deciding the sequencing of legislative change and will help to define the negotiating position of the country for the accession negotiations.
- Such analyses cannot really be carried out successfully without the full cooperation of the business community and other interested parties. Consultation should ideally therefore be very wide. This is particularly difficult for the associated countries because business organisations are weak. It would be wise for ad hoc committees to be established for consultation purposes, as was done in some of the EU Member States at the beginning of the internal market campaign after 1985.
- Careful sequencing is necessary in order to maintain the coherence of sectoral legislation (as clearly indicated in the Commission's White Paper) and in order to minimise the cost and disturbance of approximation to the economy. An economic consideration of the approximation process will also suggest measures which should be taken as late as possible, and perhaps in some cases after accession itself.
- The current strategy is a very dangerous one, and has never been applied to previous applications for membership. In the case of the associated countries, the European Union has, without admitting it, imposed a programme of legal approximation, without giving any guarantee of membership. This is the reason that certain observers in Central Europe caution against a too rapid approximation in areas where there are economic difficulties. The associated countries should bear in mind that it is entirely possible that their accession preparations may fail on resistance in the European Union to enlargement. In this case there are some parts of the *acquis* which they would not want to take over too soon, while there are other

parts where it makes sense almost under any conditions to take over EU legislation.

- Finally, the associated countries should try to avoid the necessity of maintaining frontiers after enlargement, as this will reduce the quality of their accession. This means that, other things being equal, they should try to approximate to all legislation which is necessary for the elimination of frontiers.

In general, it makes considerable economic sense for the associated countries to take over the major part of the Community *acquis*. This should not, however, take place through a blind legal approach, but should be the subject of considerable analysis and discussion with economic interests in the countries. The associated countries have the added problem that the European Union will also probably apply a relatively blind legal approach and will classify the associated countries by the percentage of the *acquis* they have already implemented. The European Union's real interest is to have strong economies joining the Union rather than over-regulated weaker economies.

For the associated countries, the recipe must be to take on as much of the *acquis* as they can justify economically and can manage legally in order to get EU approval, while keeping back costly and inappropriate approximation until the end of the accession process.

### Policy adjustment

In their preparation for accession, the associated countries face the particular problem of how to adjust to certain clearly or less clearly defined EU policies. The major difficulty is uncertainty:

- over the direction of Union policy: it would be senseless to adjust to policy as it is today in the Union if this policy will change radically before accession
- over the period of time which they may be granted in the accession negotiations to make the necessary adjustments to policy
- over the whole process of accession: there may well be no interest in already adjusting to Community policy in certain areas if accession is going to fail.

Given the uncertainties which still surround the accession process, the advice which has to be given to the associated countries is essentially to take over those parts of policy which make sense in the current phase of the transformation but to avoid taking over policy which is likely to damage the process of economic recovery.

The most straightforward example is that of the CAP, which is dealt with at length in chapter 9 of this book. Many of the countries still have very large agricultural sectors, and farmers need to know what medium-term policy the country is going to run in the sector. The governments are, for obvious financial reasons, loath to introduce the CAP mechanisms before they have access to Community funding. But they are also unable at present to determine what the CAP will look like at the beginning of the next century, because it is in the process of rapid change. The result is that the agricultural sector is faced with a tentative waiting policy stance of government, leading to tension in the industry and a slow rate of structural reform.

But other policies pose other problems for the associated countries. Adjustment to the Common Commercial Policy will have both financial and trade policy implications, which have not been seriously explored to date. Financially customs revenues still account for a considerable part of central government revenues in many of the associated countries: around 8% in Romania and Poland in 1995, over 10% in Hungary but only around 3% in the Czech Republic. On accession, not only will the common external tariff (CET) applied to imports be significantly lower than the existing levels of import duty but, unless the financing of the Community budget is radically altered, customs duties will be handed over to the Community. This will lead, other things being equal, to an important loss of revenue, at a time when other major strains on the budget, such as pension reform, will probably be pushing up government expenditure. Of course, other things will not be equal, and it is misleading to think of the loss of customs revenue as a straight increase in the deficit; nevertheless the loss will be significant.

Apart from the financial implications, joining the CCP will also mean taking over the trade policy of the Union, a policy which has been dictated by the needs of current members (for instance, the banana regime or the treatment of non-Community Mediterranean countries). The particular trade requirements of the Central Europeans will take some time to be reflected in the policy of the Community and this could lead to some dislocation of trade if it is not satisfactorily dealt with in the accession negotiations. If there is a continued strengthening of the WTO system and a steady move to liberalised world trade, these effects should not, however, be too dramatic.

Though Economic and Monetary Union (EMU), unlike the Common Commercial Policy, is already a policy characterised by flexibility, there will be considerable pressure put on the Central Europeans to agree to entering the Monetary Union eventually and there may well be pressure on them joining the Exchange Rate Mechanism (ERM). Preparation to join EMU, deficit reduction, inflation below 3% and exchange rate stability against the euro, may well not be advisable or even possible, considering the needs of the transition. It is unlikely that the associated countries could join EMU early in their membership of the Union, but it may well not be advisable for them to try.

Other policy areas, such as industrial policy, are unlikely to cause major problems in their present state of development, because they essentially reflect a liberal policy, based on improving the working of market mechanisms within the internal market. Individual elements of policy – for instance, in the steel sector – may cause specific problems to certain of the associated countries, but this is liable to have a limited impact. The situation will be more serious if the current rise in protectionism in the individual Member States becomes institutionalised at the Community level. This includes the renewed tendency of powerful governments within the Union to bail out major industrial or service enterprises (while frequently violently criticising the puny and fruitless attempts of the associated countries to do the same). These developments are, however, uncertain and it would be difficult for the associated countries to prepare to meet these challenges today.

Finally, there are the areas of policy which are liable to have an important 'cost push' effect in the associated countries, notably social and environmental policy.[10] These are difficult areas because they will be used by those in the Union who are against enlargement to block the process. These policies, too, are in a period of rapid change. Environmental degradation progresses at such a rate that it should be expected that environmental standards will be far higher by the time enlargement takes place than they are today, and that the concept of sustainable development far more to the fore. It makes sense for the associated countries to establish policy in this area which will lead to the meeting of Community standards over the longer term, with a cost profile which can be borne by the economies. The Community cannot expect the associated countries, however, to implement current standards by the time that accession takes place and to delay accession on environmental grounds would be unjustified. If the Community wishes to accelerate the adoption of environmental standards in Central Europe, it could propose a major clean-up programme in the context of the development of the Structural Funds for the new Member States. Given the imperative of reducing government deficits in the context of the Maastricht criteria for Monetary Union this would, however, seem unlikely.

While adjusting to the Community's environmental standards re-

---

[10] Orłowski and Mayhew (1997).

quires considerable preparation and planning by the associated countries, it has the advantage that the direction of environmental policy in general terms is clear. Social policy, like the CAP, is however in a phase of development where the very direction of policy is unclear. Much of the Community's social policy reflects ideas of the 1960s and 1970s. As the unsustainability of this policy has become progressively clear, especially in the light of the demographic development in Europe, so Member State governments are beginning to review policy. As with the adjustment to the CAP, associated country governments would be wise to be very prudent in adjusting to a policy which may well change radically by the time accession takes place.

### Accession and administrative reform

The process of preparing for accession requires an efficient administration in the associated countries. The absence of such an administration may well prove to be one of the most crucial constraints.

The main problems would appear to be:

- the lack of appreciation at government level of the administrative burden of preparing for accession to the European Union
- a generalised refusal by government to pay salaries to civil servants which are competitive to private sector salaries, with all the associated problems of attracting good staff
- the relatively weak development of appropriate management techniques for the civil service at government level
- the lack of adequate training for civil servants, both in the techniques of efficient management and in the specialised areas required by the preparation for accession
- in some countries, the difficulty of sacking inefficient civil servants due to the over-protective labour rules in the government sector.
- in some sectors the inadequate staffing levels required for the new tasks related to regulating a market economy and preparing accession.

Some of the problems which are being encountered by the associated countries in preparing for accession come from inadequate ministerial interest in and control of the civil service. This is partly due to the nature of the political revolution which has taken place. Ministers in the new democratic governments, which took over power in the associated countries, frequently had no experience in administration. They were also naturally consumed by the political necessity of reforming their economies and societies as rapidly as possible. This meant that there was generally little time spent on giving clear direction to the civil service, or to improving its efficiency. The existing civil service, which had served the previous communist regimes with totally different priorities and working methods, had to cope with new regimes. In a situation where massive training and reorganisation was necessary, resources of time and money stretched to neither. With the return of post-communist governments in some of the associated countries, ministers with considerable administrative experience have in some cases taken over. Here, however, the problem is that they sometimes do not understand well the requirements of accession to the European Union (or, indeed, of membership of the WTO or OECD).

One of the neglected but perhaps most important constraints on the development of an efficient and effective civil service is the poor level of remuneration. Though there are important differences between the situations in each of the associated countries, the private sector is paying good-quality graduates with relevant qualifications three or more times the salary which they would receive in the civil service. When the civil service does manage to recruit good people, they are frequently enticed away by the private sector once they have received basic training and have some experience of the administration. This reasoning also applies to high-quality junior ministers, whose salary package, although being more complex to calculate because of certain non-salary advantages, does not match in any way what they are paid in the private sector. This leads to a constant loss of potential future leaders and frequently leaves political dinosaurs in unrestrained control over policy.

Management techniques employed in the civil services of many of the associated countries are relatively under-developed considering the challenges which they face. The advanced management techniques which have been developed in the administrations of Western Europe in the past twenty years, including the borrowing of many management tools from the private sector, are relatively new and under-developed in most of the region. Again, this is not surprising given the multiple priorities which governments have had over the past six years, but it will make preparation for accession and the efficient management of regulation after accession more complex.

A considerable effort has been made in several countries to improve the training of civil servants, going as far as the creation of specialised institutions partially on the model of the Hautes Ecoles in France. Many donors have made training of the administration an important issue for their technical assistance programmes, partly because it is serving a real need and partly because the assistance is relatively easy to mobilise using national resources. Specific training of the civil service for the task of preparing the accession to the European Union again varies much between the different associated countries. In some countries, a relatively systematic training programme has been established, often using institutions from the European Union. An example is the annual cycle of training sessions organised by the Polish government on different aspects of Community policy with the assistance of the Maastricht European Institute of Public Administration (EIPA). Small numbers of civil servants are also invited to the Commission in Brussels and to certain national administrations in the Union for relatively short training courses. These latter are extremely important, for not only is training received in a Community environment, but valuable personal contacts are made, which may last for several years and have important multiplier effects on both sides. Nevertheless, the requirement both for general training and specific training in EU matters is so great that these efforts will have to be increased in the coming years to facilitate accession preparation.

Some of the civil servants who served in the administrations under communist governments have found the transition to the new system difficult. Others, both from the old and the new system are simply ill-adapted to the work. It is very often the case that, as in Western Europe, it is extremely difficult to sack unproductive staff in the public sector. This is in some cases dramatic, with responsibility for relatively unimportant matters having to be taken at a high level in the hierarchy because of incompetence of staff. This leads in some extreme cases to ministers controlling almost every piece of paper which leaves the Ministry.

Finally, there are simply too few civil servants in central government in some of the countries to deal adequately with the work which needs to be done. This is particularly acute in some of the smaller associated countries. The preparation of accession requires a relatively much larger amount of effort in the smaller associated countries than in the larger ones, simply because the process of legal approximation and the work required for the implementation of new legislation is similar in all the countries. Even in Poland, Hungary and the Czech Republic a scarcity of human resources is evident for the tasks involved in accession preparation; in the Baltic States and Slovenia, with populations of less than 3 million, this problem becomes acute.

Generally too little attention is paid to the problems of improving the quality and performance of the administration in the context of accession. This is a crucial problem which needs continuous attention paid too it, above all by the governments of the associated countries, but also by the sources of foreign assistance, especially those within the Community. Already there are national initiatives taken by the German government in the context of the TRANSFORM programmes, by the French and by the British Know-How Fund. At the international level, there have been certain programmes within the context of the Union's PHARE programme. The latter also sponsors the OECD SIGMA programme, which is dedicated to the improvement of the public administration in Central and Eastern Europe, but which has limited resources. For the future, it will be important that these efforts contribute more systematically to the creation of an efficient structure of civil service management and to a proper system of regular and appropriate training. While it may be true that in well established market economies in mature democracies savings can be made in the quantity of civil servants, this is certainly not the case in the associated countries. The twin processes of transformation and accession are putting an extraordinarily high burden on the civil service, and will continue to do so for several years to come.

### Commission Opinions and the preparation of negotiations

The Opinions on the membership applications of the associated countries presented by the Commission in July 1997 provide a detailed analysis of the weaknesses of the economies, administrations and institutions of these countries, viewed from the perspective of future accession. The opinions are based around the Copenhagen criteria and concentrate very much on the degree to which the applicants have already adopted the *acquis communautaire* and the areas where they need to accelerate adoption of the *acquis*. They are written from a Union point of view, and are designed to give opinions to the EU Council of Ministers. They are therefore not concerned with many of the key problems of economic management or with strategies for economic development.

The Opinions are, however, extremely valuable to the associated countries as a guide to tackling some of the areas of weakness in their preparation for accession and in their development of a negotiating position with the Union. As the Union will certainly view improvements in these areas as a sign that the associated countries are progressing towards accession, it is in the interests of the countries to use the Opinions as an important, but not exclusive, source of input for their future reform programmes.

The accuracy of the Opinions has already been contested by some of the applicant countries which were not selected by the Commission for negotiations, the hope being that the Council will overturn the Commission's Opinion and open negotiations with more or all countries. Now, however, for those countries which will be selected by the Council for negotiations, emphasis has to be put on the preparation of these negotiations.

The tasks which have to be accomplished in these preparations are formidable:

- a full analysis of the EU *acquis* and its impact on the economies and societies of the applicant country must be made
- areas of policy where the adoption of the *acquis* or of a particular policy will cause important costs, financial or other, must be identified
- policy objectives and priorities must be established for negotiating these particular areas
- alternative strategies need to be designed to ensure that at least a second-best result is achieved
- negotiating teams must be established in each ministry, in which the members have the capacity to negotiate in a Community language
- institutional changes must be decided upon, such as the reinforcement of missions in Brussels or of embassies in certain of the Member States
- training programmes for all those involved must be intensified
- budgetary calculations of the costs involved in institutional change and other areas linked to enlargement must be made.

As an illustration of these preparations, the Polish situation can serve as an example (figure 8.3).

### Accession, sovereignty, expectations and the political system

Politically, some of the most difficult problems may come from the need to give up sovereignty in certain areas on accession. Having only so recently regained sovereignty from the break-up of the Soviet Union, the Warsaw Pact and the CMEA, the associated countries will be loath to cede it again to Brussels. Today, this is not yet perceived as a major problem, because politicians are not thinking that far ahead and because many of them know that they will be personally unaffected by a loss of sovereignty that is likely to occur between five and ten years in the future.

Already, however, certain signs are evident. A recovery in nationalistic political parties has occurred in several of the associated countries. Even

Preparation for accession started with the establishment of the Office for European Integration in the Council of Ministers in early 1991. Legal approximation has progressed adequately, regular training for civil servants in European Union matters has been carried out for several years and a considerable body of expertise has been built up. Nevertheless given the needs of economic, political and social reform since 1989, European integration did not receive adequate attention until relatively recently.

Institutionally preparation for the negotiations was marked by the creation of a strong coordination ministry (the Committee for European Integration) presided over by a powerful group of Ministers including the Prime Minister, Foreign Minister and the Finance Minister. This new Ministry was created from the previous Office for European Integration through its integration into the heart of government and through its reinforcement in staff. Within each line ministry, cells for European integration, which were created several years ago, have become negotiation teams, responsible for analysing the *acquis* in their area and costing the impact of the most important directives. The Committee for European Integration is at the centre of the network of European integration units in the line ministries.

A national strategy for integration was presented to Parliament in early 1997. This strategy analysed the main areas where adjustment of policy in Poland would be required, including changes in institutions. It was followed by an action programme based on the strategy with a timetable for implementation. A thorough analysis of the *acquis* has subsequently been carried out by the line ministries, leading to a 1,000-page analytical paper, which investigates the options open to Polish negotiators in those areas of the negotiations which will create problems for the economy or the society in Poland and identifies critical national priorities. The analysis was carried out in the same sectoral breakdown chosen for the negotiations with the EFTA countries.

At the same time, groups representing business, the unions and other non-governmental groups have been created in order to discuss these questions with the responsible ministries in the same sectoral breakdown.

The identification of a negotiating strategy will be extremely difficult in spite of this preparation. The number of areas where adopting EU policies and regulation will cause serious problems is very wide.

While this organisational structure is adequate for the current stage of preparation, it will be vital to increase the training available to the negotiating teams in the ministries. For certain key officials training in English is necessary. For others, technical training in key areas of the *acquis* is still required. Above all, the number of officials in the different technical areas needs to be increased.

*Figure 8.3* Polish preparations for negotiations

in the mainstream democratic parties there is an increasingly strong nationalistic sentiment (as indeed there seems to be in Western Europe as well). The dangers of handing over policy in such sensitive areas as agriculture or trade, not to mention certain aspects of foreign policy or monetary policy may well be an important potential political weapon in the hands of certain politicians in these countries in the future. As accession approaches and as these forces become stronger, it will require government resolve and astute public relations campaigns to keep the preparation for accession on course.

These forces could become stronger if there is a turndown in the economy associated with an increase in unemployment. They will also become stronger if the European Union is seen to be exploiting its position as powerful neighbour. Action by the European Union which is perceived in these countries as being unfair or against their interests will be used by these groups as further evidence that it would be inappropriate to give up national control of policies. This is one reason why the Union should try to avoid petty trade disputes such as those over sour cherries or garden gnomes or protectionist anti-dumping and safeguard measures.

Expectations of accession are still very high amongst the populations of the associated countries, who generally consider membership a guarantee of prosperity and peace. They are probably right to hold these expectations in the long term. Unfortunately they will not be realised in the short term and certainly not before accession. With such exaggerated expectations the scope for disappointment, and then rejection of accession, is obviously great. The governments will have to take action soon which is aimed at cooling these expectations without affecting the overall popularity of accession.

Certain economic interests will also progressively move into opposition to enlargement, reflecting the loss of power or income that they will suffer as a result of accession. This will be the case of powerful interests in SOEs, which on accession will be exposed to competition and progressive privatisation. With the links between SOEs and the political parties still strong in several of these countries, this is a real danger. Progress with privatisation and with the regulation of state monopolies would go some way to reducing this risk, but the only real solution is a complete break in the privileged access of managers of SOEs to government.

Furthermore the adoption of the CAP by the new Member States may well prove popular with farmers but it is unlikely to attract consumers. One major impact of the CAP, at least in an unreformed state, will be to increase food prices. As food purchases remain a much larger part of the average household budget than in Western Europe, such increases will be extremely unpopular. This potential source of inflation, bearing directly on the consumer, could well form part of the ammunition of those parties opposed to accession.

The problems of loss of sovereignty, exaggerated expectations, price hikes and losses of privileges for certain important groups in the economy will all be reflected in the political parties in the run-up to accession. It is practically certain that one significant party at least in each country will adopt a negative attitude to accession in order to attract the disillusioned section of the electorate. The challenge for present governments is to minimise the force of these negative elements in order to maintain a strong push for accession.

## Conclusion

While it is certainly true that the most important problems to be solved in the preparation of accession are on the side of the European Union, nevertheless the challenges to the associated countries are very significant. This chapter has identified a certain number of these problems but as accession approaches others will no doubt come to be as important. It is too early to be sure that all ten countries will be able to satisfactorily tackle these problems in the appropriate time span. The stakes for the Union in the question of enlargement are, however, so high that it would be wise for it to provide as much assistance as possible, and to be extremely flexible when setting the absolute criteria for membership in the accession negotiations.

# 9    Agriculture

## Why is agriculture a problem for the European Union?

It may appear strange that the problems which the accession of the associated countries may cause for an industry which contributes only 2.5% of GDP and only 5.7% to total employment in the European Union should be considered crucial to the realisation of enlargement. But agriculture has never been regarded in Europe, either in West or East, as simply another sector of the economy. Agriculture is different and, probably unfortunately, has been totally separated from the rest of the economy by European policy-makers.

### General support for agricultural policy

Agriculture has always had an important place in the social fabric of Western Europe and particularly so in some continental European countries. In 1950, agriculture still provided 30% of total employment in the 12 Member States of the Community (excluding the recent enlargement) and contributed 12% to GDP.[1] Even in 1970 agriculture still employed 13% of the labour force. The relative decline of agriculture, particularly in what were partly peasant societies, has happened so rapidly that generations of voters still have to adapt to the changes. Rural agricultural society, dominated by the family farm, is still regarded as something of an ideal by urban dwellers. For a majority of the population some level of subsidy is certainly supported in order not to lose these values.

Agriculture not only represents a value in society but also produces services, other than food production, for which the public is willing to pay. The most obvious of these services are the protection of the environment, maintenance of the natural landscape and rural tourism, and there are no doubt others. Even in those Member States where

[1] Molle (1994), p. 247.

agriculture enjoys the least popular support, these services are recognised. In the United Kingdom, for instance, there is little opposition to the payment of subsidies for hill farmers or crofters, both of whom are regarded as vital for maintaining important natural habitats. And in countries where agriculture enjoys higher public support, such as Germany, there would be little public discussion of subsidies for farmers in important natural or cultural landscapes such as the Black Forest or the Alpine Foreland.

It would therefore be wrong to confuse the sometimes ferocious criticism of the CAP with a lack of support for farming and the farming community. Criticism of the CAP is usually directed at the inefficiencies of its support mechanisms, not at the principle of support for agriculture.

Within the European Community, the CAP also has a special place in the history of European integration. Seen as a deal between the interests of German industry and French farming at the origins of the Community in the 1950s and as a successful system to ensure adequate food supplies at a time of shortage, the CAP has always been considered to be the main common Community policy. Detractors of the CAP, however serious their criticism, have often been treated as opponents of the whole process of political and economic integration in Europe. While this special situation of agricultural policy has been eroded as surpluses soared and the budgetary consequences became apparent, it is still true that the CAP is seen as something as a totem for European integration.

### The strength of the agricultural lobby

As a clearly defined sector, enjoying this high level of public support, it was possible for the agricultural industry to establish extremely powerful lobbying organisations with a low ratio of costs to benefits. As subsidies increased, it became worthwhile for the farming community to invest some of these rents into lobbying to ensure that long-term subsidisation was maintained. The result was the development in the 1970s and 1980s of the most powerful lobbying machine in the European Community.

The effectiveness of this lobby can be seen from the growth in budgetary support for agriculture in the Community budget. Total agricultural spending declined in relative terms as new policies were introduced through the 1970s and 1980s and, of course, notably after the introduction of the Structural Funds and their doubling in the period 1985–92. In absolute terms, however, budgetary support for agriculture rose from ECU2 billion in 1970, to ECU11.6 billion in 1980 and ECU31.6 billion in 1990.[2] Even the most timid reforms were opposed successfully by this lobby and it was only in dramatic over-supply situations (for instance, in the milk market of the early 1980s) or in financial crises that small reforms were possible.

While the power of the agricultural lobby is somewhat diminished in the mid-1990s, it should not be under-estimated; politicians facing elections will listen to the lobby's arguments today just as they have done in the past. And some of the arguments which will be brought will be justified. The CAP will probably undergo either new reform or an acceleration of the existing 'McSharry' reforms in order to accommo-date enlargement only a few years after farmers were told by politicians that these latter reforms were the last this decade. Such changes in policy make investment decisions particularly difficult, and cause losses for operators. The arguments about further CAP reform will have to be put very carefully to the farming industry, if the power of their lobby is not to derail the enlargement process. The reform proposals put forward in the Commission's 'Agenda 2000' documents were, for instance, attacked by some farm ministers even before publication.[3]

### The situation of Community agriculture

The high level of support through the price mechanism combined with the incredible complexity and opacity of the CAP have condemned European farmers to operate in circumstances similar to those suffered by CEE industry under central planning: distorted price systems, high levels of subsidy and managed foreign trade. The minimal threat of competition from Central Europe posed by slightly increased conces-sions has already led to defensive reactions from the industry and from politicians representing it. After the very small additional concessions in agriculture made at the Copenhagen European Council, the German Agriculture Minister speaking at the 'Grüne Woche' in Berlin in January 1994 could say that

through the decisions of the Copenhagen Summit in June last year, these concessions on market entry [i.e. those in the Association Agreements] have been advanced by six months. Considering the actual situation on our agricultural markets, the German view is that these concessions represent the absolute upper limit of our negotiating margin.[4]

---

[2] Molle (1994). These figures are five year averages around the reference date. The 1990 figure is the average spending in 1991–3.

[3] European Commission (1997a).

[4] Speech given by Minister Borchert, German Minister of Agriculture, at the East–West Forum of the International 'Grüne Woche' (Berlin, 15 January 1994).

The concentration of subsidy on price support, understandable perhaps at a time when it was important to raise output, produced the famous 'mountains' and 'lakes' of products in the 1980s. The extremely high intervention prices led to an enormous increase in productivity and in production in Community agriculture. The farming practices which developed were fully adjusted to this high level of support and were different from practices which would have developed if no subsidy had been paid or if subsidisation had concentrated on farmers' incomes rather than price support. Price subsidies went mainly to large efficient farms in the more prosperous parts of Northern Europe and did not favour the small family farms, which were always stated to be the objective of support. In fact, agricultural income in real terms fell sharply over the period 1972–92, and even when expressed as income per person employed it barely increased over these 20 years.

As the cost of the CAP rose to take 60% of the Community budget, measures had to be taken to curb agricultural expenditure. A reform of the policy was also forced on the Community through the negotiation of the Uruguay Round, with agricultural products included for the first time in the GATT. The 'McSharry reforms' which were decided in 1992 see a progressive reduction in price support and an increase in direct payments to farmers to compensate them, including payments dependent on land being taken out of production. These reforms were hard fought by the agricultural lobby and have led to considerable uncertainty in the industry. Much effort was made by politicians to convince farmers that these reforms were all that was needed in policy terms until 2004, when the next WTO Round, which should start in 1999, is expected to end. A combination of policies to reduce stocks of products and favourable developments in world food markets have led to a situation today where agricultural incomes in general have recovered, and with lower stocks the short-term future looks more positive.[5] Because of past policies, however, Community agriculture has found the adjustment required by the McSharry reforms difficult. A requirement to reform further in order to permit enlargement will no doubt cause real difficulty to an industry which has been badly served by policy-makers over many years.

### Agriculture and the Community Budget

Agriculture is also of considerable importance to the European Union because of its impact on the budget. In 1995 46.8% of the total

---

[5] The BSE crisis has, however, led to major shocks in the beef market.

Community budget of ECU76.5 billion. was spent on the CAP. This percentage has been reduced from over 73% in 1985 when however the total budget was only ECU28 billion Agricultural spending has therefore continued to rise strongly in real terms throughout this period, reaching ECU37 billion in 1995.

Pressure on the Community to reduce the level of agricultural spending has been intense. The financial guideline, the maximum level of permitted commitments for Community spending up to 1999, allows for very little increase in agricultural spending beyond current 1996 levels. Net contributors to the budgetary resources will look upon any increase in budgetary expenditure on agriculture negatively, even though it is the net contributors to the budget who benefit most from agricultural spending. The need to meet the Maastricht criteria for monetary union has led these countries to look very hard at all public spending, and especially at transfers to the Community. Any increase in agricultural spending resulting from enlargement will be regarded as 'unwelcome' at this time.

## The problem of agriculture in the associated countries[6]

### *The significance of agriculture in Central Europe*

Agriculture is not only a major problem for the European Union. In the associated countries agriculture plays a far greater role in the economy and society than in the Union. Under central planning, agriculture in most of the countries of the region was collectivised. The chief exception was Poland, where a substantial private agricultural sector survived, though under the control of centralised economic planning. Because of the concentration on manufacturing industry throughout the communist world, agriculture suffered from low investment and low productivity. The industry supported a large agricultural population, with an extremely high level of under-employment. Rural areas were also generally badly treated in terms of investment in public infrastructure and public services. Communist society was essentially an urban society, even though a large proportion of the population lived in rural areas. As a consequence, priority of supplies in these shortage economies was given to the capital city, followed by the larger towns or by certain privileged groups in society (such as coal miners or scientists). Rural populations always came at the end of the list.

---

[6] The reader is referred to an excellent series of short monographs on each of the associated countries' agriculture published by the Directorate General for Agriculture at the European Commission in July 1995. European Commission (1995a).

To a certain extent, the reformers after 1989 treated agriculture as a sort of buffer in the economy. As state-owned manufacturing industry bore the brunt of reforms, agriculture was given little prominence though privatisation was pursued in most countries. It was clearly not in the interest of the reformers to raise productivity and diminish employment in agriculture just as manufacturing industry was releasing labour. In some countries agricultural employment actually rose during the first years of reform, underlining this buffer function. In Romania, for instance, agricultural employment rose from 28% of the employed population in 1990 to 39% in 1994, although this was partly but not wholly a statistical impact of raising the retirement age in Romania. In Bulgaria, too, the share of agricultural employment rose over the period, while in Poland agricultural employment has remained almost constant as a share of the total. The result is that agriculture remains of major importance as an employer of labour and source of GDP.

Table 7.1 (p. 183) shows the significance of agriculture in production and in total employment. It is really only in the Czech Republic that agriculture resembles the situation in the Community, with employment as both a percentage of total employment and a contribution to GDP at around 5%. In the ten associated countries employment in agriculture comfortably exceeds that in the Community (9.5 million against 8.2 million). Employment at this level can obviously not be sustained over the long term and it therefore hangs over the labour market as a major threat for the future.

The agricultural area in the associated countries will also be a very large addition to the existing area in the Community. Whereas only about 43% of the total land area of the Union is devoted to agriculture, this reaches 56% in the associated countries. With a higher proportion of the total agricultural area in arable cultivation, the associated countries will add some 55% to the total arable land area of the Union (see table 9.1). Agriculture from all points of view is of far greater importance to the economies of the associated countries than is the case in the Union, and agricultural policy cannot be considered marginal to economic development and reform or to political life. Such is the importance of agriculture in several of the associated countries that it can play a very major role in politics and have an important impact on the transformation process. Poland has had a Prime Minister from the peasants' party.

However, agriculture should also be making a larger real contribution to GDP. This would benefit economic growth in general but also would improve conditions of life for the employed in some of the more depressed parts of the region. The necessary reform will, however, have

Table 9.1 *Agricultural and arable areas in the associated countries, 1993*

| | Agricultural area | | Arable area | |
|---|---|---|---|---|
| | million ha. | % total | million ha. | % agr. area |
| Poland | 18.6 | 59 | 14.3 | 77 |
| Hungary | 6.1 | 66 | 4.7 | 77 |
| Czech Rep. | 4.3 | 54 | 3.2 | 74 |
| Slovak Rep. | 2.4 | 49 | 1.5 | 63 |
| Slovenia | 0.9 | 43 | 0.2 | 28 |
| Romania | 14.7 | 62 | 9.3 | 63 |
| Bulgaria | 6.2 | 55 | 4.0 | 65 |
| Lithuania | 3.5 | 54 | 2.3 | 66 |
| Latvia | 2.5 | 39 | 1.7 | 68 |
| Estonia | 1.4 | 31 | 1.0 | 71 |
| CEC-10 | 60.6 | 56 | 42.3 | 70 |
| EU-15 | 138.1 | 43 | 77.1 | 56 |
| CEC/EU | 44% | | 55% | |

*Source*: European Commission (1995a).

to consider the negative impact on employment in the countryside and design measures to encourage private sector non-agricultural employment creation. For this to happen, domestic policy towards the industry must be extremely well designed, but this will depend to a large extent on the course of CAP reform and the prospects for accession.

### Structural problems in Central European agriculture

Central European agriculture suffers from major structural problems. Some of these problems result from the decades of central planning and collectivisation, others from the changes which have taken place since 1989. As a result of these problems, output in agriculture has fallen in most of the associated countries since 1989.

Table 9.2 shows that apart from Romania and Slovenia, all the other associated countries had a lower real gross agricultural output in 1996 than in 1989. By 1996 there were signs in almost all countries that production was stabilising, but in the major agricultural producing countries this is happening at a low level compared to the pre-reform period.

The reasons for this decline vary from country to country but some, resulting from the impact of the transformation process or of certain external factors, are common to all. A certain part of the decline can also be attributed to natural factors. For certain countries the drought

Table 9.2 *Real gross agricultural output, 1989–96*

| | Total GAO (1989=100) | | | | | Crops | | | | | Livestock | | | | |
|---|---|---|---|---|---|---|---|---|---|---|---|---|---|---|---|
| | 1990 | 1993 | 1994 | 1995 | 1996 | 1990 | 1993 | 1994 | 1995 | 1996 | 1990 | 1993 | 1994 | 1995 | 1996 |
| Poland | 94.5 | 84.5 | 78.6 | 88.8 | 89.1 | 95.1 | 88.7 | 74.1 | 86.0 | | 94.2 | 78.8 | 81.6 | 88.1 | |
| Hungary | 95.3 | 64.7 | 65.6 | 66.1 | 69.4 | 90.7 | 63.3 | 69.6 | 68.8 | | 99.8 | 66.6 | 60.0 | 61.9 | |
| Czech Rep. | 97.7 | 76.4 | 72.2 | 75.2 | 74.1 | 99.3 | 83.7 | 78.7 | 82.5 | | 96.6 | 71.4 | 67.6 | 70.2 | |
| Slovak Rep. | 92.8 | 68.4 | 74.8 | 76.2 | 79.3 | 88.4 | 76.0 | 90.6 | 92.3 | 97.5 | 96.2 | 66.5 | 66.5 | 67.9 | 69.4 |
| Slovenia | 104 | 98.0 | 109 | 111 | 111 | 109 | 95.1 | 114 | 114 | 112 | 98.4 | 94.5 | 93.7 | 97.1 | 99.0 |
| Romania | 97.1 | 95.7 | 95.9 | 100 | 102 | 92.8 | 96.8 | 97 | 102 | 104 | 102 | 92.1 | 92.1 | 94.9 | 96.5 |
| Bulgaria | 94.0 | 67.5 | 72.1 | 83.2 | 72.3 | 92.6 | 74 | 89.5 | 108 | 75.8 | 95.4 | 64.1 | 59.3 | 66.3 | 64.6 |
| Lithuania | 91.1 | 61.1 | 47.4 | 52.0 | 60.0 | 82.2 | 73.7 | 51.5 | 67.8 | 88.8 | 95.6 | 59.1 | 53.4 | 52.6 | 52.6 |
| Latvia | 89.8 | 56.9 | 45.3 | 48.7 | 52.3 | 80.7 | 75.3 | 57.2 | 67.7 | 79.6 | 94.5 | 48.6 | 39.8 | 39.9 | 39.4 |
| Estonia | 86.9 | 62.7 | 56.4 | 55.7 | 53.7 | 75.3 | 76.1 | 66.0 | 69.5 | 68.4 | 92.0 | 54.1 | 47 | 44.2 | 41.8 |

*Source*: OECD (1997).

Table 9.3 *Expenditure on food as proportion of household income, 1995 (%)*

| | | | |
|---|---|---|---|
| Poland | 28 | Romania | 66 |
| Hungary | 23 | Bulgaria | 40 |
| Czech Rep. | 32 | Lithuania | 58 |
| Slovak Rep. | 37 | Latvia | 44 |
| Slovenia | 23 | Estonia | 32 |
| European Union | 22 | | |

*Source*: OECD (1997).

conditions of 1992 and 1993 were largely to blame; this was especially the case for the Baltic countries, Poland and Hungary.

Domestic demand factors were also important. With severe output declines accompanied by declining real wages and rising unemployment, the demand for agricultural output fell. Families in the region were already spending a large part of their income on food and, as real incomes fell, they further restricted their consumption (see table 9.3). Food prices rose more rapidly in many countries as pre-reform price subsidies were stripped away and as price liberalisation enabled food processors and food importers to raise prices. While these price and income effects depressed domestic demand, farm-gate prices first stagnated and then began to fall in real terms as demand fell away.

Foreign demand also began to fall sharply in 1990 and 1991 as the CMEA system began to break down and the traditional food exports from Central to Eastern Europe declined. Well established patterns of agricultural trade were suddenly disrupted, leading to the need to find new markets. Unlike producers of industrial goods who found relatively open markets in Western Europe, this was not true for agricultural products. The Community and the EFTA countries were not prepared to absorb large flows of imports coming from Central Europe. Worse still for farmers was the fact that as the reforming economies battled with inflation, they understandably reduced external protection to a minimum, leaving their domestic markets open for imports to compete with often still monopolised domestic production. The European Union, with its subsidised exports, managed to take a part of the high value added sector of food consumption in the associated countries away from domestic producers.[7]

With domestic and foreign demand falling away, farmers were caught in the scissors of falling prices and rising costs. Inputs into agriculture were no longer subsidised; fuel prices rose sharply, as did fertiliser and

[7] OECD (1997).

machinery prices. Profitability in farming slumped. Without guaranteed prices, there was no escape through higher production levels, which would have simply made the situation worse. Instead, production was cut back sharply. On the basis of a normal calculation of profit and loss, many of the farms in Central Europe were operating at considerable loss in the early 1990s. Today profitability appears to be recovering in some countries, partly as a result of the general economic recovery and partly because of the agricultural policies which governments put in place after 1992.

The problems for agriculture are also due in many countries to the problems caused by ownership change following privatisation. Apart from Poland and Slovenia, which had retained private individual ownership in agriculture, all the other countries had collectivised agriculture in the form either of cooperatives or of state farms.

The degree of state control prior to the transformation can be seen in table 9.4. The table distinguishes between countries where the land was held primarily through farmers' cooperatives and those like Bulgaria and the Baltic countries, where farming was organised around large state farms. The countries have adopted varying systems to achieve privatisation. In some cases, such as Estonia (and, indeed, in East Germany), restitution has been given precedence over compensation. Here legal complexities of restoring land to previous owners will take many more years, leading to considerable uncertainty and delays in developing a land market. The same approach has been adopted in Bulgaria, where progress is equally slow, leaving much of the land in state-controlled farms. In Romania, on the other hand, there has been an effort to keep existing agricultural enterprises alive but privatised, either by creating state-controlled commercial companies out of the old state farms, which will later be privatised, or turning the old cooperatives into farmers' associations, where the land is held by a group of farmers.

The disputes over exactly how the reforms should be designed, together with the physical and legal complexity of carrying out the reforms, has caused considerable dislocation in agriculture and explains part of the fall in output discussed previously. The current ownership situation can be seen in table 9.4. Latvia, Poland and Slovenia all have more than three-quarters of agricultural land in private ownership. At the other end of the scale, the slow pace of privatisation in Bulgaria and Slovakia is evident.

In terms of agricultural structure, privatisation appears to have produced small and often fragmented holdings. Table 9.4 shows that, with the exception of the Czech Republic where private farms on

Table 9.4 *Farm structure in the associated countries, 1989–95*

| | Share in total agricultural area (%) | | | | | |
|---|---|---|---|---|---|---|
| | Cooperatives | | State farms | | Private farms | |
| | Pre-1989 | Current | Pre-1989 | Current | Pre-1989 | Current |
| Poland | 4 | 4 | 19 | 18 | 77 | 78 |
| Hungary | 80 | 55 | 14 | 7 | 6 | 38 |
| Czech Rep. | 61 | 48 | 38 | 3 | 1 | 49 |
| Slovak Rep. | 68 | 63 | 26 | 16 | 6 | 13 |
| Slovenia | | | 8 | 7 | 92 | 93 |
| Romania | 61 | 35 | 14 | 14 | 25 | 51 |
| Bulgaria | | 41 | 90 | 40 | 10 | 19 |
| Lithuania | | 35 | 91 | 1 | 9 | 64 |
| Latvia | | 17 | 96 | 2 | 4 | 81 |
| Estonia | | 33 | 96 | | 4 | 67 |

| | Average size (ha) | | | | | |
|---|---|---|---|---|---|---|
| | Cooperatives | | State farms | | Private farms | |
| | Pre-1989 | Current | Pre-1989 | Current | Pre-1989 | Current |
| Poland | 335 | 400 | 3,140 | 2,000 | 6.6 | 6.7 |
| Hungary | 4,179 | 1,702 | 7,138 | 1,976 | 0.3 | 1.9 |
| Czech Rep. | 2,561 | 1,430 | 6,261 | 498 | 4.0 | 16.0 |
| Slovak Rep. | 2,654 | 1,665 | 5,162 | 2,455 | 0.3 | 1.0 |
| Slovenia | | | 470 | 303 | 3.2 | 4.1 |
| Romania | 2,374 | 170 | 5,001 | 2,002 | 1.5 | 1.8 |
| Bulgaria | | 750 | 13,000 | 1,100 | 0.4 | 0.6 |
| Lithuania | | 450 | 2,773 | 124 | 0.5 | 2.6 |
| Latvia | | 706 | 3,000 | 547 | 0.5 | 5.8 |
| Estonia | | 567 | 3,500 | | 0.5 | 2.1 |

*Source*: European Commission (1995a).

average have 16 hectares of land, the average size of private holdings is around 5 hectares, with some countries well below this. Cooperatives, on the other hand, though having been reduced in size through the privatisation process, still on average have several hundred hectares and in Hungary and the Czech Republic and Slovakia well over a thousand hectares. In some countries, the old state farms pose an important problem in that they have not yet been privatised, to some extent have been neglected by the government, and often have inferior management.

The agricultural industry, and indeed rural areas in general, were starved of investment in the pre-transition period, as noted above. After 1989, the lack of demand and the structural problems due to the privatisation process have also negatively affected investment in agriculture. There is little possibility for self-financing, foreign investment is not forthcoming because in general land-ownership for foreigners is not permitted and capital cannot be raised on the capital markets because of problems of security for loans and low rates of return compared to other sectors in the economy. The state has also given low priority to the improvement of rural infrastructure. Low private and public investment will pose great difficulty for the future development of a competitive agriculture.

While the present situation of agriculture in the associated countries is difficult, nevertheless there has been more attention paid to the industry by government over the last two or three years, and there are some signs that the situation is improving.[8] The problem for the remainder of the economy, however, is that as agriculture improves so productivity will rise faster than output and many of those employed in agriculture today (almost 10 million) will need to find other jobs in other sectors.

### The state of the food industry in the associated countries

The problems for agriculture are compounded by the difficulties in the downstream sectors. The food industry in the associated countries has generally not progressed as well as many other industrial sectors. Firms are often still in state control, producing to a quality below what is expected by consumers and with poor marketing and packaging. The formerly dominant Polish firm Hortex is a good example of the problems which have been encountered. As something of a national institution, the government was loath to privatise the company, which would certainly have meant breaking it up into separate profit-centre companies and stopping essentially unprofitable activities. It took far too long for the state to accept the inevitable, by which time Hortex had lost much of its market.

The inefficiencies of the food industry and the relatively low level of foreign investment has opened the way for EU imports to gain a significant part of the high-value food market. As economic growth continues and incomes rise, a considerable growth in the demand for quality food can be expected. Without improvement in the domestic food industry, much of this increased demand may be met from the Union's industry at the cost of agriculture in the associated countries.

[8] As demand in Eastern Europe began to recover from 1992 onwards, EU export subsidies also prevented the associated countries from regaining their traditional markets in Eastern Europe, as governments in the region could not afford to provide large export subsidies.

*Conclusion*

The situation of agriculture in the associated countries is unsatisfactory. It will certainly be some time before it can generally make an impact on the markets of the existing Union Member States, though in individual products this may occur sooner rather than later. In the run-up to accession, it is important that these structural deficiencies be tackled, so that the associated countries can deliver to Western markets and in order to avoid the region being swamped with products from the highly competitive (and subsidised) Community food industry. It is important that the level of protection still offered to the domestic industry through tariff barriers should be reduced progressively over the years leading to accession, to force domestic producers to adjust to foreign competition.

## What the Association Agreements say

As indicated in chapter 3, the Association Agreements are not generous to the associated countries in agriculture. The agreements abolish the QRs on agricultural imports into the Community which were introduced in 1983. The associated countries also agree to abolish certain QRs over the transition period.

The main concessions which were given to the associated countries consist of reductions in levies within tariff quotas or of customs duties. In the case of Poland, for instance, a 50% levy reduction was agreed for a five-year tariff quota of duck meat amounting to 1,300 tons in the fifth year. Other very small tariff quotas for geese, salted pork, potato starch, sausages and preserved meats were opened with the same levy reduction. Duty reductions were also given on a series of products not subject to specific regimes in the CAP. These products included, however, soft fruits, on which minimum prices were imposed on imports – the infamous sour cherries so jealously protected by the Germans or raspberries by the British. For other products, the percentage of the levy or duty reduction increased over a three-year period to reach 60% in the third year but always only applied to a minute quantity. The associated countries also agreed to reduce customs duties on a series of agricultural products.

Unfortunately, these small concessions were somewhat less significant quantitatively than they appeared because they did not correspond to the potential trade pattern of post-1989 Central Europe. The structure of tariff quotas was set up in the context of trade patterns which were established in the pre-transformation period under a system of central planning and quotas designed for trade with communist countries. In 1991, when the first Association Agreements were negotiated it was difficult to adopt any other system. However privatised agriculture after 1989 was interested in exporting different products to the Community, but was restricted from doing so by extremely tight quotas.

The concessions in those products subject to minimum import prices also led to major breakdowns in relations between the associated countries and the Community. The sour cherry case has led each year to major marketing problems for Hungarian and Polish producers, who have effectively been prevented from exporting to the Community as high minimum prices were set each summer to protect domestic producers, mainly in Germany. The proof that these prices were being used as a simple protectionist tool, rather than a way of taking care of sudden import surges, was shown by the fact that the request from Member States to establish price minima was frequently made well ahead of the harvest, when the cherries were still green on the trees!

Even these minute concessions were, however, subject to a specific safeguard clause, which allows either party to take 'the measures it deems necessary' if serious disturbance is caused to domestic markets.

A further article, insisted on by the Community, states that

without prejudice to the concessions granted pursuant to Article 20, the provisions of paragraph 1 of this Article shall not restrict in any way the pursuance of the respective agricultural policies of [Lithuania] and the Community or the taking of any measures under such policies.

In fact this article allows the Community or the associated country to introduce any measure to restrict trade within the context of its agricultural policy. Although there is an article which foresees further negotiations on concessions, the whole agricultural chapter is rendered of little value by the safeguard clause and the agricultural policy opt-out.

Negotiations on market access for agricultural products from the associated countries, as well as on subjects like veterinary and phytosanitary controls, have figured prominently in the discussions at Association Committee meetings. The Community has always taken an extremely hard line on agriculture, sometimes adopting positions which are difficult to justify. Attempts by the associated countries to raise duties on agricultural imports from the Community on the basis of the article allowing changes in agricultural policy were met for some time with the argument that the associated country in question did not have an agricultural policy (like the CAP), but only a series of measures and therefore this clause, invented for the benefit of the Community, could not be used. Requests to shift the composition of exports within an overall quota between the different components of that quota have often been contested bitterly by the Community side, even though the overall quotas themselves are very restrictive. A large part of one Association Committee meeting with Hungary was reported as having been taken up by discussion on a request by the Hungarian side to be able to supply rather more chicken-breasts and rather fewer chickens-legs in a very small overall chicken quota. At the end of the discussion on the Community side, one member state is reported to have declined to vote considering that this move would seriously undermine the CAP!

Veterinary and phyto-sanitary problems have also been frequently raised. In 1993, the Community took measures against live animal imports from all the associated countries, after an outbreak of foot and mouth disease in Italy had been traced back to imports from Croatia. This action created outrage amongst the associated countries, whose level of veterinary control was in some cases higher than that in some Member States of the Community and who resented being treated as part of an 'East European bloc'. This incident, considered by many in Central Europe to be yet another protectionist move, led eventually to a considerable improvement in cooperation and understanding between the technicians on both sides and a considerable reduction in trade problems. Cooperation in these areas is already contributing to the preparation of accession.

There have been negotiations between the Member States of the Union, on the basis of proposals from the Commission, on further concessions since the Association Agreements were signed. The first unilateral concessions were made at the Copenhagen European Council. More significant, but still small, concessions have been agreed in the context of the Protocol adjusting the agricultural (and textile) trade articles in the Association Agreements following the conclusion of the Uruguay Round and the enlargement of the Union to the EFTA countries. This Protocol increases some agricultural quotas by 10%.

The agricultural articles in the Association Agreements were not supportive of economic reform in the associated countries, and they contributed greatly to a sense of disillusionment with the market economy. It seemed somewhat paradoxical that Community political leaders were forever preaching market reform in Central Europe while at the same time closing Community markets for farm products. As Community trade surpluses in agricultural and food products with the associated countries developed, this was interpreted as the result of a cynical managed-economy game at the expense of the reforming countries.

## Agricultural policy in the associated countries

Agricultural policy in the associated countries since the reforms started has gone through two very distinct phases and has been characterised by a high level of uncertainty. Today, the development of policy is complicated by uncertainty about accession, uncertainty about the reform of the CAP and the need to implement the Uruguay Round agreements

Most countries, as was seen above, inherited an agricultural system characterised by state-controlled farming and centralised planning, with careful regulation of foreign trade. The first steps taken in general by the reformers were to liberalise foreign trade, dramatically reduce border protection for agricultural and food products, liberalise prices and eliminate subsidies to agriculture directly or via food subsidies. In addition to these measures to liberalise trade, agriculture was often given far less attention than industry in the early years of the reform. Not all countries followed this path. In Romania, for instance, considerable support for agriculture was maintained, prices were not immediately liberalised and priority was given to maintaining the supply of food to urban areas. This partly explains why the decline in output in Romania has been so small.

The results of these liberal policies in agriculture were positive for macroeconomic stability. They were, however, very difficult for agriculture, which was faced with upward cost pressures and, because of the non-contested state of the downstream markets, downward output price pressures. The terms of trade for agriculture with respect to both input prices and retail prices declined dramatically between 1990 and 1993.[9] In the extreme case of Bulgaria, the terms of trade with respect to inputs fell to 44% of the 1990 level, and with respect to retail prices to 46%. As imports, especially subsidised imports, also began to take an ever-greater part of domestic sales, countries were forced to change policies towards a more protectionist stance. The second phase, starting after 1991, was therefore a move to design a new supportive approach to agriculture.

The Visegrád countries, the first to negotiate Association Agreements and to aim at membership of the Union, looked to the CAP of the Community as an example to follow. Such a development was in general resisted by liberal reformers who wanted to avoid the errors committed in the Union. Pressure from the farming industry, the lack of openness shown by the Community and the argument that the countries had to adopt the CAP at some time forced governments to introduce CAP-like

[9] See figures quoted in Buckwell et al. (1994).

policies. Budgetary pressures fortunately meant that these policies could only provide a shadow of the support which is given in the European Union.

As in the European Union, price support policies were introduced. In Hungary, for instance, price support was given from 1993 to a series of products at the farm gate. An intervention agency was established, the Office for Agricultural Market Regime, which was in charge of intervention, but so far relatively small quantities have had to be bought in because of the high prevailing market prices. Guaranteed prices are generally low and in 1996 were well below world prices for wheat and maize. For all crops intervention prices were below those paid in the European Union. The situation in Romania and Bulgaria is, however, completely different. In Romania, prices were still controlled in 1996 for crops under the supervision of the Ministry of Agriculture and Food and therefore the system had only slightly changed from the pre-reform days, while in Bulgaria, although some minimum prices were applied in past harvests, there appears to be no systematic price policy.

As for border measures, again the Visegrád countries used a mixture of tariffs, variable levies and import licensing. Poland, for instance, increased tariffs from 10.4% to 17.7% in early 1991, and again to 26.6% in August 1991. In July 1993, the tariff schedule was reorganised to prepare the way for the GATT agreement, giving an average tariff on agricultural and food crops of 21%. Variable levies were also introduced in 1994 to protect domestic production against subsidised imports. These were collected from the importers at the border and used to finance the Agency for the Restructuring and Modernisation of Agriculture, but were later abolished in the context of the Uruguay Round Settlement. Again, the border measures taken in Romania and Bulgaria would appear to be far more opaque than those in the Visegrád countries.

Export subsidies have been used, especially in Hungary and somewhat less so in Poland, although the possibility of giving export subsidies exists. Export subsidies are clearly less of a financial problem for these countries where farm-gate prices are sometimes even below world market prices.

Finally, many countries have provided input and investment aid to farming, given the difficulty of the farm sector to raise capital from banks. In the Czech Republic, for instance, investment assistance is given by the Support and Guarantee Fund for Farmers and Forestry (SGFFF). The SGFFF provides guarantees for short-term bank loans, financing running costs but above all for medium-and long-term loans for investment in buildings, machinery and equipment. Some degree of

Table 9.5 *Intervention prices in the European Union and the Visegrád Countries, 1994*

| | Wheat | | Beef | | Milk* | |
|---|---|---|---|---|---|---|
| | ECU/t | %EU | ECU/t | %EU | ECU/t | %EU |
| Poland | 89 | 69 | 1,110 | 30 | 87 | 28 |
| Hungary | 66 | 51 | 1,609 | 44 | 201 | 65 |
| Czech Rep. | 87 | 67 | 1,566 | 43 | 171 | 55 |
| Slovak Rep. | 92 | 71 | 1,546 | 42 | 179 | 58 |
| EU | 129 | | 3,680 | | 310 | |

*Note:*
* EU target price, fixed/minimum producer price in Visegrád-4.
*Source:* EU Commission (1995a).

subsidisation is possible on the loan interest. Similar schemes exist in the other countries.

The result of all these measures has left agricultural support in the associated countries considerably below that in the European Union. In terms of net percentage producer subsidy equivalent, the figure for Poland (one of the higher levels of protection in the region) was 28% of the value of production in 1996, whereas that for the European Union was 43%. In price terms, these differences can be seen in the different levels of intervention and market prices in the two regions (see tables 9.5 and 9.6).

The comparison between intervention prices shows that in the four Visegrád countries these are well below the EU intervention prices. The intervention prices in Poland in 1994 were only 30% of those for beef in the European Union and 28% of those for milk. In the context of farm-gate prices shown in table 9.6, with the exception of Slovenia and for pork in Poland, all farm-gate prices in the associated countries were well below those in the European Union. To some extent, these low prices in the associated countries are added to by inefficient downstream processing with high margins, which raises prices at the wholesale and retail levels. It should be noted, however, that prices in certain of the associated countries rose rapidly over the period 1995–7, due to both the real appreciation of the national currencies against the ECU and to a higher level of support given to agricultural product prices.

The overall conclusions which must be drawn from a consideration of agricultural policy developments in the associated countries are:

- that policy development since 1989, at least in the Visegrád countries, has gone through two distinct phases: the first with

Table 9.6 *Associated country, EU and world commodity prices, 1994*

| | Wheat | | | Maize | | | Milk | | Beef | | Pork | | Poultry | |
|---|---|---|---|---|---|---|---|---|---|---|---|---|---|---|
| | (1) ECU/t | (2) %EU | (3) %wld | (1) ECU/t | (2) %EU | (3) %wld | (1) ECU/t | (2) %EU | (1) ECU/t | (2) %EU | (1) ECU/t | (2) %EU | (1) ECU/t | (2) %EU |
| Poland | 98 | 73 | 104 | 72 | 52 | 97 | 103 | 33 | 1,240 | 40 | 1,320 | 103 | 1,179 | 88 |
| Hung. | 75 | 56 | 80 | 100 | 72 | 135 | 220 | 70 | 1,630 | 52 | 1,260 | 98 | 1,038 | 77 |
| Czech Rep. | 88 | 66 | 94 | 93 | 67 | 126 | 172 | 54 | 1,850 | 59 | 1,200 | 94 | 910 | 68 |
| Slovak Rep. | 84 | 63 | 89 | 123 | 89 | 166 | 164 | 52 | 1,580 | 50 | 1,130 | 88 | 987 | 74 |
| Sloven. | 175 | 131 | 186 | 75 | 54 | 101 | 292 | 92 | 2,510 | 80 | 1,710 | 134 | 1,090 | 81 |
| Rom. | 81 | 60 | 86 | 71 | 51 | 96 | 179 | 57 | | | | | | |
| Bulg. | 54 | 40 | 57 | | | | 114 | 36 | 750 | 24 | 680 | 53 | 590 | 44 |
| Lith. | 60 | 45 | 64 | | | | 66 | 21 | 680 | 22 | 1,040 | 81 | | |
| Latvia | 121 | 90 | 129 | | | | 83 | 26 | 560 | 18 | 980 | 77 | | |
| Estonia | 75 | 56 | 80 | | | | 83 | 26 | 360 | 12 | 550 | 43 | | |
| EU | 134 | | 143 | 138 | | 186 | 316 | | 3,130 | | 1,280 | | 1,340 | |
| World | 94 | 70 | | 74 | 54 | | | | | | | | | |

*Note:* Wheat, maize and milk prices are farm-gate prices. World maize and wheat prices are constructed farm-gate prices based on fob export prices. EU beef and pork prices are wholesale prices. Associated country meat prices are farm-gate prices.

*Source:* European Commission (1995a).

very low protection, the second, since 1992, with growing protection and agricultural support
- the overall level of protection has been severely constrained by budgetary problems and therefore the absolute value of protection has not been high
- the Visegrád countries have tried to use a CAP-type agricultural policy, while Bulgaria and Romania have taken very different routes; Estonia until recently really had no policy and little protection
- all the associated countries have been waiting to see how the CAP is reformed and whether accession becomes more probable before finally deciding on the policy design; this has tended to cause some disturbance in agriculture.

### Agricultural policy and the Uruguay Round

Since the negotiation of the Association Agreements, the conclusion of the agricultural agreement in the GATT Uruguay Round has changed the way in which agricultural protection is organised. These changes affect the CAP as well as the policy of the associated countries.[10] They are also an important factor to be taken into consideration in the preparation for accession.

The GATT agreements covered four main areas:
- trade arrangements with third countries
- domestic support arrangements
- the protection of designations of origin (part of the TRIPS Agreement)
- veterinary and phyto-sanitary arrangements as they affect trade.

The important parts of these agreements for the integration of the associated countries into the CAP are the first two on trade and domestic support.

The trade arrangements are centred on four main points:
- tariffication
- market access arrangements
- the export subsidy system
- safeguards.

The key change in the arrangements is tariffication. This simply means that all variable charges (levies, etc.) and all non-tariff restrictions (QRs,

---

[10] At the time of writing seven of the associated countries – Czech Republic, Bulgaria, Slovenia, Hungary, Poland, Romania and Slovakia – are members of the WTO. The other associated countries are in various stages of becoming members.

licences, voluntary export restrictons (VERs)) must be replaced by stable, degressive tariffs. This change has rendered obsolete the system of variable levies in the CAP and any similar systems adopted by the associated countries. These variable systems have been replaced by bound tariffs. The tariff bindings (the maximum allowed tariffs) have in general been set at very high levels, far above the tariffs actually applied.

Table 9.7 gives only a simplistic view of the new tariffs in 1995 and 2000; in fact, it shows the maximum tariffs on imports outside quotas which are set in the context of the agreement on market access. In the agreement on market access each country has established a market access quota for 1995 which across all products increases substantially over the six years to 2000 and to which a reduced tariff rate is applied. Imports outside this quota are subject to the maximum tariff rate unless the country decides to apply a lower rate.

The countries also agreed to reduce expenditure on export subsidies and their volume over the implementation period up to 2001. The Union, for instance, is required to reduce expenditure by 36% on the basis of average expenditure between 1986 and 1990 and to reduce its volume of subsidised exports by 21%. Buckwell considers that cereals, beef and cheese may well pose problems in this context.[11] The expenditure reductions appeared not to pose a problem given the high 1995 price level, but subsequent price declines have put even this part of the agreement in doubt. However, the volume commitment assumes that production stays under control and declines substantially below pre-McSharry reform levels. Given that there has been hardly any reduction in output since the start of the reforms in spite of set-aside and price reductions, the outlook for respecting the GATT volume export subsidy conditions does not look good.

The GATT agricultural agreement also lays down rules on the aggregate level of support for agriculture (the so-called 'Aggregate Measure of Support' or AMS). This aggregate measure is also related to the base years 1986–8. Although neither this measure nor the reduction of export subsidies is inflation-adjusted, it appears that the Community will have no difficulty in meeting the objective of remaining well within the maximum support level of ECU60 billion in 2001.

The five GATT members amongst the associated countries have also made similar offers in the Uruguay Round. Two questions are of relevance: are the GATT offers consistent with accession, and how does this agreement affect the Association Agreements and trade in agricultural products between these countries and the European Union?

---

[11] Buckwell et al. (1994), pp. 13–15.

The first question, whether the GATT offers are compatible with accession supposes that when the countries join the European Union, the WTO will simply add the commitments of the five countries to those of the European Union. In this case, there is a clear risk that the aggregate offers might be exceeded.

The limit to the AMSs, where the current European Union has some slack, would however only be added to marginally by the accession of the five countries. Romania has a zero AMS and those of Hungary, the Czech Republic and Slovakia are determined in local currencies which will probably continue depreciating in nominal terms against the ECU over the years up to 2001. Buckwell presents an estimation that the overall AMS of the Union and the five associated countries could decline from ECU65.9 billion to ECU54.6 billion in 2001. With a strong recovery in Central European agriculture and alignment in these countries to EU levels of support, it is quite conceivable that the overall AMS limit could be breached.

The constraint imposed by the GATT agreement is even clearer in export subsidies. Whereas the problem of high inflation (or depreciating currencies) may be taken into consideration by the WTO as far as AMS is concerned, this is not foreseen in the agreement on export subsidies. The Union itself may well have a problem respecting its agreement in this area, but if the only very small and depreciating maximum levels of subsidy of the associated countries are added to that of the EU, it looks impossible for the overall limit to be respected. In 1994, Hungary, the Czech and Slovak Republics, Poland and the European Union were all exceeding their commitments on quantities of subsidised exports for several products.

While today's high world prices have reduced the acuteness of the problem, it is sure to return. With support levels rising to those of the European Union, the supply response from the associated countries could lead to them far outstripping the quantity commitments which they have made.

As far as market access provisions are concerned, it is far more difficult to say what the impact of the aggregation is likely to be because of the complexity of having to integrate a very large number of individual product tariffs. If overall the level of EU tariff bindings is higher than that of the associated countries and the result of accession is that these latter tariffs rise, third countries will demand compensation in one way or another.

In order to respect GATT commitments it will be necessary for further reforms to be undertaken in the CAP irrespective of enlargement. In addition to these problems, a new round of negotiations aimed at further liberalising trade will start in 1999. Many of these problems could be tackled if Union prices were moved nearer to world prices and if agricultural support took other forms than price support.

The Community and the five associated countries struggled with the second question, concerning the adjustment of the Association Agreements to the Uruguay Round changes, from the end of 1994 until early 1997. This question was linked with that of adjusting the Association Agreements to take account of the accession to the Union of Austria, Finland and Sweden. A third element to the negotiation package, that of granting increases in unilateral concessions to the associated countries, was added by the Commission.

Normally the adjustment to the agreements to take account of the Uruguay Round should be a technical adjustment. The major problem here was that the tariff bindings in the GATT have been made in general at extremely high levels (see table 9.7). The Community insisted on large preferential margins, which not all the associated countries were keen to accord.

The impact of EFTA enlargement could be accommodated reasonably easily, in that in general the preferential access which the associated countries had in the markets of the three new members or vice versa can be added to the existing preferential tariffs and quotas in the Association Agreements. However, the new Member States had some quotas open for the associated countries which did not exist at all in the EU-12, and in this case the 12 old Member States were not enthusiastic about opening new Community quotas which had not existed before enlargement. On autonomous new concessions for the associated countries, the European Council adopted a negotiating mandate which gave only extremely limited room for such concessions. In the end quotas were increased by a small margin, reaching 10% in some products.

## Trade in agricultural products

Traditionally, the Central European countries had a positive trade balance in total agrifood trade. Geographically, this was made up of exports to the Soviet Union and to Western Europe. The bulk of the exports were contributed by Poland, Hungary and Bulgaria. This trade pattern was radically altered in 1989. The reasons were fourfold: the breakdown of trade with the Soviet Union in 1990–1, the difficulties caused by the reforms themselves and by the neglect of agriculture in policy-making, the competition from well packaged, well marketed and subsidised EU imports and finally the drought in some countries.

Table 9.7 *Associated country tariff bindings relative to the European Union*

| | Crop products | | | | | | | | |
|---|---|---|---|---|---|---|---|---|---|
| | I 1995 | II 1995 | 2000 | I 1995 | II 1995 | 2000 | I 1995 | II 1995 | 2000 |
| | Wheat | | | White Sugar | | | Potato | | |
| EU | 100 | 100 | 100 | 100 | 100 | 100 | 100 | 100 | 100 |
| Poland | 173 | 174 | 148 | 101 | 101 | 103 | 1,112 | 1,112 | 1,113 |
| Hungary | 60 | 60 | 59 | 39 | 39 | 49 | 300 | 300 | 385 |
| Czech Rep. | 31 | 31 | 39 | 34 | 34 | 43 | 917 | 917 | 870 |
| Slovak Rep. | | 31 | 39 | | 34 | 43 | | 917 | 870 |
| Slovenia | 36 | 132 | 143 | | 87 | 91 | | 390 | 391 |
| Romania | | 377 | 489 | | 99 | 134 | | 1,172 | 1,635 |

| | Meat | | | | | | | | |
|---|---|---|---|---|---|---|---|---|---|
| | I 1995 | II 1995 | 2000 | I 1995 | II 1995 | 2000 | I 1995 | II 1995 | 2000 |
| | Beef | | | Pork | | | Poultry | | |
| EU | 100 | 100 | 100 | 100 | 100 | 100 | 100 | 100 | 100 |
| Poland | 169 | 169 | 169 | 140 | 140 | 162 | 268 | 268 | 292 |
| Hungary | 59 | 59 | 70 | 73 | 73 | 111 | 136 | 137 | 150 |
| Czech Rep. | 23 | 23 | 33 | 55 | 55 | 82 | 125 | 124 | 165 |
| Slovak | | 23 | 33 | | 55 | 82 | | 124 | 165 |
| Slovenia | 28 | 73 | 81 | | 72 | 89 | | 98 | 119 |
| Romania | | 176 | 257 | | 452 | 740 | 200 | 366 | 468 |

| | Dairy products | | | | | | | | |
|---|---|---|---|---|---|---|---|---|---|
| | I 1995 | II 1995 | 2000 | I 1995 | II 1995 | 2000 | I 1995 | II 1995 | 2000 |
| | Butter | | | Milk-Powder | | | Cheese | | |
| EU | 100 | 100 | 100 | 100 | 100 | 100 | 100 | 100 | 100 |
| Poland | 91 | 89 | 83 | 177 | 177 | 159 | 162 | 162 | 216 |
| Hungary | 89 | 89 | 83 | 177 | 177 | 159 | 162 | 162 | 216 |
| Czech Rep. | 47 | 47 | 55 | 49 | 49 | 58 | 7 | 7 | 11 |
| Slovak Rep. | | 47 | 55 | | 49 | 58 | | 7 | 11 |
| Slovenia | | 84 | 103 | | 91 | 95 | | 101 | 128 |
| Romania | | 146 | 179 | | 284 | 404 | | 205 | 381 |

*Notes*:
I = Rates applied in 1995.
II = GATT tariff binding *ad valorem* equivalent – maximum bound rates.
*Source*: European Commission (1995a).

Trade with the FSU and between the associated countries themselves began to recover in 1994, after the disastrous situation in the four previous years, and this trend has continued up to the present. Gradually, most of the countries are tackling at least some of the problems in agriculture caused by the reform and the uncertain owner-ship patterns, so that there is a strong hope that the industry will recover slowly in the coming years. It is really in trade with the European Community that there has been a dramatic deterioration (see table 9.8). The problem for the associated countries is the rapid increase in imports from the European Union which has occurred in every country constantly year for year since 1990. The background to this increase must lie in a combination of the extreme professionalism of the Union's food industry, with its high-quality products and good marketing and the export subsidies which are given by the Union, together with the lack of restructuring in some of the food industry in Central Europe. Tangermann and Josling in their analysis (1994) show that the impact either of the CAP or of export subsidies should not be over-rated in this explanation.[12] It would appear that the income elasticity of demand for EU products in the associated countries is quite large. This is not to say that export subsidies play no role, but it does show that for agriculture the development of quality downstream industries is most important.

On the export side the performance of the associated countries has been mixed. Overall exports from the associated countries held up relatively well with some annual variations over the whole period, but they ended in 1996 at about the same level as in 1992.[13] But normally, with the enormous switch of trade to the West, one would have expected that agricultural exports to the Union would have expanded consider-ably and probably much in line with overall exports. The fact that this did not happen suggests that the Union market has not really been opened for some of the key products produced in Central Europe. This is surely not only the result of protectionist measures in the Union – quality, marketing, available supply will all have played a role. Overall exports from the associated countries rose sharply in 1994, especially in Poland and Hungary, though their exports to the European Union only rose marginally. It would appear that the associated countries are finding new markets outside Western Europe, which may mean that the Union market is relatively more closed to them. This would be supported by the fact that the main products exported to the Commun-

[12] Tangermann and Josling (1994).
[13] Bulgaria has suffered a major slump in exports due to the loss of the Soviet market.

Table 9.8 Trade in food and agricultural produce between the European Union and the associated countries, 1989–96 (ECU million)

| | Exports to EU-15 | | | | | | Imports from EU-15 | | | | | | Net trade | | | | | |
|---|---|---|---|---|---|---|---|---|---|---|---|---|---|---|---|---|---|---|
| | 1989 | 1992 | 1993 | 1994 | 1995 | 1996 | 1989 | 1992 | 1993 | 1994 | 1995 | 1996 | 1989 | 1992 | 1993 | 1994 | 1995 | 1996 |
| Poland | 979 | 1,032 | 896 | 869 | 1,004 | 973 | 826 | 1,037 | 1,196 | 1,100 | 1,261 | 1,498 | 153 | −5 | −300 | −231 | −256 | −524 |
| Hungary | 910 | 1,005 | 865 | 799 | 940 | 997 | 151 | 299 | 439 | 436 | 440 | 377 | 759 | 706 | 426 | 362 | 500 | 620 |
| Czech Rep.* | 267 | 326 | 271 | 256 | 289 | 275 | 191 | 486 | 483 | 573 | 794 | 880 | 76 | −160 | −211 | −317 | −504 | −605 |
| Slovak Rep. | | | 52 | 48 | 61 | 63 | | | 131 | 129 | 206 | 223 | | | −79 | −81 | −145 | −160 |
| Slovenia | | 118 | 96 | 71 | 63 | 68 | | 139 | 235 | 274 | 379 | 381 | | −21 | −139 | −203 | −316 | −313 |
| Romania | 120 | 91 | 97 | 104 | 127 | 134 | 84 | 352 | 342 | 181 | 289 | 306 | 36 | −262 | −245 | −76 | −162 | −172 |
| Bulgaria | 160 | 214 | 198 | 199 | 232 | 220 | 112 | 142 | 239 | 229 | 239 | 155 | 48 | 72 | −41 | −30 | −7 | −66 |
| Lithuania | | 33 | 62 | 34 | 52 | 66 | | 127 | 167 | 179 | 170 | 216 | | −94 | −105 | −145 | −119 | −151 |
| Latvia | | 17 | 56 | 10 | 15 | 19 | | 82 | 97 | 132 | 201 | 221 | | −64 | −42 | −122 | −185 | −202 |
| Estonia | | 22 | 10 | 18 | 28 | 38 | | 85 | 126 | 86 | 184 | 226 | | −63 | −94 | −68 | −156 | −188 |
| AC-10 | | 2,858 | 2,626 | 2,408 | 2,811 | 2,853 | | 2,749 | 3,456 | 3,319 | 4,163 | 4,483 | | 109 | −830 | −911 | −1,350 | −1,761 |

Note:
* 1989–92 = Czech and Slovak Republic.
Source: EUROSTAT.

ity are live animals and meat and fruit and vegetables, both of which enjoy a very restrictive import system in the Union.

Somewhat strange in these circumstances is the fact that the associated countries have not been able to fill all the import quotas open to them in the Union. In a Commission report, submitted in June 1995, it was established that many of the quotas were less than half filled by exports from the associated countries. In the case of Romania, for instance, for the reference quota periods only one quota was filled, that for sheep and goats, two other quotas were filled to 72% and 64% (beef and strawberries) but almost all other quotas were less than 25% filled and indeed the majority were not used at all. Bulgaria was only slightly better in its use of quotas than Romania. In Poland, the quota uptake was much better, especially in dairy produce, live bovines and certain fruits and vegetables, but nevertheless there were many quotas still unfilled. In Hungary the situation was more akin to that in Poland.

The explanation for the non-filling of quotas given by the Commission includes all the reasons cited above for the poor performance of post-reform agriculture in Central Europe. It also however raises certain explanations specific to the way the quotas were established and the way in which they are managed. Firstly, the quotas were opened by reference to historical trade flows which are no longer relevant – the prime example is the unfilled buckwheat quota in Poland. The concessions granted should be revised to take account of the new supply situation. But strangely enough for many products where a tariff quota has not been filled, imports outside the quota (i.e. at the full tariff rate) have exceeded the quota. This is the case, for instance, with fruit and vegetables in Hungary. Here, more information is needed by exporters and producers on the use of the quota. But the method of managing the quota where quarterly quotas are opened throughout the year obviously makes it impossible to fill the annual quota with a seasonal crop.

Trade in agricultural products since the reform has been clearly in favour of the European Community as Central and Eastern Europe has developed into a significant market for Community producers. While the CAP through its protection of the domestic market and aggressive subsidisation of exports will have played some part in this result, the main explanation should probably be sought in the weakness of the food industry in Central Europe, as consumers demand higher quality and better presented food products.

## Scenarios for the accession of the associated countries to the CAP[14]

Agriculture poses a problem for the future of the European Union not just because of the prospect of accession. The compatibility of maintaining support to agriculture while helping it to restructure with reducing its share of the Community budget and respecting the GATT agreements is already extremely difficult and requires medium-term strategic policy planning which goes beyond projecting the status quo into the future. Accession comes on top of these difficult considerations as an additional challenge.

Policy options must be considered both for reform of the CAP and also for the agricultural policies of the associated countries. The preparation of this accession cannot be a one-sided adjustment in agricultural policy as with previous accessions, partly because agriculture is so important a part of the economies of the associated countries, but also because the world has moved on to a situation where agriculture has been taken into world trade negotiations. Neither side is any longer free to do what it wants to in agricultural policy.

The conclusions of this policy debate must be acted on quickly on both sides, as agriculture will need time to adjust to the new situation. For farmers in the existing Community, the de-linking of subsidies from price has already caused considerable problems, which will take time to solve. Producing not to maximise subsidies received but to meet the needs of the market is an important challenge for small farmers, for which the CAP has not prepared them. In the associated countries, the adjustment problems will be far greater, with large numbers of workers leaving the land. Policy-makers in these countries must be able to determine their agricultural policy stance for the period prior to accession as soon as possible.

### The future of the CAP: the impact of the status quo

The 1992 reforms of the CAP were the first comprehensive attempt at reform and were forced on the Community by the need to get an agricultural agreement in the context of the GATT negotiations.[15] The

---

[14] This section is based essentially on two of the reports requested of four well known agricultural economists and presented to the European Commission at the end of 1994 (Buckwell *et al.* and Tangermann and Josling) as well as the Commission report to the Madrid European Council (December 1995).

[15] For an assessment of these reforms and an 'economic' discussion of agricultural reform in the twenty-first century, see: European Commission, *European Economy*, 4–5 (1994).

cereals intervention price was to be reduced by about one-third in three steps to 1995–6. No further price support was to be given for oilseeds and protein crops. There was to be a 15% reduction in the intervention price for beef and the ceiling for the intervention buying of beef was to be reduced from 750,000 tons to 350,000 tons by 1997. These cuts in price subsidies were to be compensated, either through direct area payments based on historical base areas or direct headage payments. Accompanying measures included an agri–environment package.

The success of this package is not in doubt. The current high world prices which make export subsidies unnecessary and which have boosted farm incomes should not obscure the fact that cereals production in the European Union has become far more competitive on world markets since the reform and that stocks of foodstuffs have been massively reduced. However, the capacity of the reforms to deal with the medium-term problems of over-production and budgetary squeeze is in doubt. The forecasts which have been made by the Commission recently do suggest that several major products may well be in considerable surplus again in the medium term. Table 9.9 shows estimates of production, domestic consumption and the resulting supply balances for a series of products in the present Union and the associated countries for the period up to 2010. This table shows the general decline which has taken place in surpluses over the period 1989–94 in the main products – cereals, milk and beef. In the case of cereals, the decline in production which has taken place since the introduction of the McSharry reforms has been less than many experts had predicted. This is partly the result of the 'quotarisation' of the CAP, compensation payments being related to the area under cereals which are at least partly lost if alternative crops are produced. Declines in production can then come about only through set-aside or more extensive methods of cultivation, but not through substitution following price falls. The prevailing high world prices made it easy to dispose of the cereals crop in 1995 and 1996, but the estimates for the future show a sustained recovery of output, even taking into account set-aside, and only a small increase in domestic demand, leading to a substantial rise in surpluses for disposal outside the Community up to 2010. Similar developments are foreseen in milk and beef.

These forecasts, together with the constraints imposed by the GATT agreement, suggest that a continuation and extension of the McSharry reforms will be necessary even without enlargement. This is especially so because it is expected that the pressure on the Community to liberalise agricultural trade further will increase in the run up to the next WTO negotiations starting in 1999. Even without the pressure from world

Table 9.9 *Commodity supply balances in the European Union and the associated countries, 1989–2010*

| | | Production (million t) | | | | | | Domestic use (million t) | | | | | Balance (million t) | | | | | |
|---|---|---|---|---|---|---|---|---|---|---|---|---|---|---|---|---|---|---|
| | | 1989 | 1994 | 2000 | 2000[a] | 2005 | 2010 | 1989 | 1994 | 2000 | 2005 | 2010 | 1989 | 1994 | 2000 | 2000[a] | 2005 | 2010 |
| Cereals | CEC | 88.3 | 74.0 | 85.7 | 80.1 | 89.6 | 96.7 | 91.0 | 72.7 | 79.6 | 82.4 | 85.7 | −2.8 | 1.3 | 6.1 | 0.52 | 7.2 | 11.0 |
| | EU | 188.5 | 171.3 | 187.5 | | 202.0 | 217.6 | 159.3 | 154.5 | 157.5 | 160.4 | 163.2 | 29.2 | 16.8 | 30.0 | | 41.5 | 54.4 |
| Oilseeds | CEC | 4.5 | 3.6 | 5.1 | 4.6 | 4.9 | 5.4 | 3.9 | 3.3 | 4.2 | 4.2 | 4.2 | 0.54 | 0.23 | 0.84 | 0.36 | 0.66 | 1.1 |
| | EU | 11.6 | 12.5 | 12.4 | | 12.5 | 12.7 | 22.8 | 24.2 | 27.0 | 28.5 | 29.8 | −11.2 | −11.7 | −14.5 | | −16.0 | −17.1 |
| Sugar | CEC | 4.0 | 2.7 | 3.3 | | 3.5 | 3.5 | 4.2 | 3.4 | 4.1 | 3.9 | 3.8 | −0.2 | −0.7 | −0.8 | | −0.44 | −0.35 |
| | EU | 15.9 | 15.4 | 15.4 | | 15.4 | 15.4 | 13.6 | 12.7 | 12.6 | 12.6 | 12.6 | 2.3 | 2.7 | 2.8 | | 2.8 | 2.8 |
| Milk | CEC | 38.9 | 26.0 | 30.6 | | 32.1 | 32.1 | 34.5 | 25.6 | 28.9 | 29.5 | 30.3 | 4.4 | 0.43 | 1.7 | | 2.6 | 1.8 |
| | EU | 127.0 | 120.0 | 119.4 | | 119.4 | 119.4 | 119.0 | 114.0 | 112.6 | 110.8 | 108.7 | 8.0 | 6.0 | 6.8 | | 8.6 | 10.7 |
| Beef | CEC | 2.0 | 1.4 | 1.7 | | 2.0 | 2.0 | 1.7 | 1.4 | 1.6 | 1.4 | 1.5 | 0.24 | 0 | 0.11 | | 0.60 | 0.50 |
| | EU | 8.3 | 7.9 | 8.3 | | 8.3 | 8.3 | 8.1 | 7.7 | 8.2 | 8.1 | 8.1 | 0.16 | 0.13 | 0.15 | | 0.15 | 0.20 |
| Pork | CEC | 5.5 | 4.0 | 4.6 | | 4.8 | 5.2 | 5.1 | 4.1 | 4.6 | 4.8 | 5.1 | 0.40 | −0.07 | −0.04 | | −0 | 0.09 |
| | EU | 15.2 | 16.0 | 16.6 | | 17.0 | 17.5 | 14.7 | 15.0 | 16.1 | 16.5 | 17.0 | 0.56 | 1.0 | 0.50 | | 0.50 | 0.50 |
| Poultry | CEC | 1.8 | 1.3 | 1.7 | | 1.8 | 2.0 | 1.4 | 1.3 | 1.5 | 1.7 | 1.8 | 0.33 | 0.03 | 0.18 | | 0.19 | 0.21 |
| | EU | 6.5 | 7.4 | 8.2 | | 8.7 | 9.2 | 6.2 | 6.9 | 7.9 | 8.4 | 8.9 | 0.24 | 0.50 | 0.30 | | 0.30 | 0.30 |

*Note:*
[a] 15% set-aside applied.
*Source:* European Commission (1995a).

trade liberalisation, further pressure will come from within the Community because of the budgetary impacts of agricultural policy. If the CAP remains as it is without further reform, the forecasts of product balances in table 9.9 will lead to an explosion in agricultural spending at a time when budgetary rigour is felt to be more important than ever in the light of the Maastricht monetary union criteria. A 'solution' to the Community budget constraint might be to re-nationalise agricultural spending, but it is unlikely that there will be much support for shifting the budgetary burden from the Community budget to national budgets at this time, for the same fiscal restraint reasons. In the future, agriculture must be treated as an integral part of the economy, not as a sector outside it. This does not mean that all subsidy should be stripped away, but it does mean that the value of providing subsidy to agriculture should be properly compared to the use of the subsidy elsewhere in the economy.

The CAP will also continue to be pressured by those who want agriculture to be more environmentally sensitive or to respect different standards of animal protection or food hygiene. These influences will also impact on the design of agricultural policy.

The CAP has become an extremely complex and opaque system. It was designed 40 years ago for a largely Northern European agriculture amongst six countries. It has been modified hundreds of times to take account of changes within and outside the Community and is now no longer comprehensible. Even without accession, a simplification of the CAP will be necessary.

### Scenarios for accession[16]

Accession complicates matters somewhat further. It makes additional reform of the CAP vital and has implications for agricultural policy in the associated countries. In investigating scenarios for accession, policy options for both parties need to be explored.

#### Policy options for the CAP

Three options are explored by Tangermann and Josling (1994): minimal changes to the CAP, continuation of CAP reform improving coverage and adjusting instruments and finally a complete reform of the system.

- Minimal changes in the CAP was usually the Community's previous response to major challenges. Many politicians would prefer this option, because it would create less political damage. It would, however, lead to enormous political damage in the

---

[16] Anderson and Tyers (1995).

medium term (when some of today's leading politicians are in retirement) and would essentially exclude the integration of the associated countries into the CAP.

The main arguments against this strategy are that it will make the respect of the GATT agreement ever more difficult for the Community and will do nothing to prepare European agriculture to become competitive on world markets, so that it has less to fear from the next WTO round. Tangermann argues that making agriculture more efficient is important because at the moment the industry contributes practically nothing to value added and is therefore wasting economic resources.

The budgetary impact of doing nothing would be very negative. With accession of the associated countries at an unchanged CAP level, the budgetary implications of agricultural accession would be so negative that it would be impossible for the associated countries to enter the CAP. Tangermann and Josling estimate that the total additional cost of accession for the first six associated countries could well be ECU20 billion; other estimations on the basis of unchanged policy suggest that the cost could be higher

- *A continuation and extension of CAP reform* would mean changes in two further areas. Tangermann and Josling suggest that the aborted reform of the dairy sector in 1992 should now be realised, with price cuts balanced by compensation for farmers. Other 'unreformed' products could also be included in the reform – notably sugar, wine and fruit and vegetables. A second step would be to 'dequotarise' the reform of the cereals sector by separating the right to compensation payments from a continuation of cultivation which, as explained above, has led to a lower than hoped for reduction in production.

- *A more complete reform of the CAP* would aim to produce a competitive agriculture in world markets. This option is clearly the one preferred by Tangermann and Josling. Cereals prices would be reduced to roughly the medium-term world price levels and compensation payments would be disconnected from the need to continue cultivating the land. Set-aside could then be abandoned and export subsidies would be reduced or perhaps eliminated. Dairy product prices would also be reduced to near world prices over a series of years, and gradually the distorting quota system would be replaced as non-quota took the place of quota milk. Tangermann and Josling maintain that these changes could still be presented as a continuation of the

McSharry reform and not a new departure, though this might be doubted. Such a complete price reform and move to direct income payments for farmers could lead to a re-nationalisation of much expenditure, as the level of income subsidies decided at national rather than Community level would seem to be in line with the principle of subsidiarity.

One of the key elements of CAP reform must be to get away from the state-centralised planning elements of the policy and move back towards market elements. Quotas, set-asides and herd reduction schemes are the result of bureaucratic control and lead to a misallocation of resources. CAP reform must move away from central planning before the formerly central-planned economies of Central Europe accede to the Community.

The political problem of reform was posed by the extremely professional and thorough report of the Commission to the Madrid European Council at the end of 1995. This report underlines the need to continue reform of the CAP and uses the same three scenarios as Tangermann and Josling. The report, however, rejects a total reform which would cause major disruption to the industry and cost a very large amount, as farmers would receive massive compensation payments to counteract the move to world prices. Instead, the report opts for

a resolute continuation of the 1992 reform approach which would lead to a clearer distinction between market policy and income support and would not only be less distorting from an economic point of view, increase market orientation of the sector and help to make it more competitive, but would also tend to facilitate future integration of the CECs.

It is obvious that the reform course chosen must be politically sustainable. This analysis was confirmed in mid-1997 in the Commission's 'Agenda 2000' package.

### 'Agenda 2000'

In its July 1997 report 'Agenda 2000', the Commission proposes continued reform of the CAP, reducing floor prices for most products and switching subsidy to direct income subsidies in the form of compensation payments or environmental measures. It is, however, not proposed to pay compensation payments to farmers in the new Member States. This is the reason that the new budgetary estimate for the annual enlargement cost to the CAP falls from the ECU12 billion proposed in the Madrid European Council document to ECU3.9 billion in 'Agenda 2000'.

The essential reforms to the CAP proposed in 'Agenda 2000' are:

- a reduction in intervention prices for cereals, beef and milk
- a payment in relation to the crop area (direct income subsidy)
- no compulsory set-aside but voluntary set-aside gets specific crop-area payments
- specific subsidies for cattle in compensation for lower intervention prices (headage payments)
- ceilings to be established for farms receiving direct income subsidies
- reinforced rural development policy.

The objective of this reform is to reach a market situation where surpluses are not built up, exports can take place on the world market at world market prices, the incomes of farmers (in the existing Union) are protected and, through rural development, employment in the countryside is maintained. All of this should be achieved respecting the existing guideline, which forces agricultural spending down as a percentage of the total Union budget.

The cost of these measures is estimated to be:

- direct compensation payments: ECU7,700 million
- new rural development measures and existing accompanying measures: ECU1,900–2,100 million
- pre-accession aid: ECU500 million
- expenditure on accession countries in 2006: ECU 3,900 million.

Against these additional costs, savings on CAP reform by 2006 of ECU 3,700 million should be realised.

'Agenda 2000' re-states that this reform is necessary to make European agriculture competitive at the world level, to prepare for the next GATT Round, and to remain within the legal limit of the Union budget. It is not, however, obvious that the reduction in prices will avoid the build-up of stocks over the medium term. If forecasts for strong international demand and high prices over the medium term prove correct, the situation will remain under control. If competition on world markets increases, or demand dips, given the limitations on export subsidies, there could still be over-production.

The package will probably be opposed by farmers' organisations in the existing Union and by certain governments. It is therefore important that the reform is made less painful by transforming price support into direct income subsidies. There will, however, be more room for individual Member States to support their own farmers with national resources (differential ceilings on direct payments, payments for agri–environmental measures).

For the associated countries, their farmers will benefit basically only from a small amount of pre-accession aid after the year 2000 and after accession from the various market organisations and from the enhanced accompanying measures. For all the associated countries, the total expenditure would be ECU500 million per year pre-accession aid, ECU1.1–1.3 billion in market organisation (price guarantees) and ECU2.5 billion for accompanying measures.

The associated countries will be faced with a situation where their own farmers are receiving no direct income payments (except agri–environmental ones) while farmers in the old Union will be receiving considerable direct subsidy. While there is a logic behind this situation, it will be difficult to explain to farmers in the associated countries why they are being discriminated against in the common market. In budgetary terms, the associated countries will also be financing the compensation payments for old-Union farmers, although they were not responsible for the policies that led to these payments having to be made.

'Agenda 2000' speaks of the need for transition periods for agriculture at enlargement. For the associated countries, the question is whether or not this means that frontiers will have to remain after enlargement until the end of the transition period.

### Policy options for the associated countries

Tangermann and Josling also develop three policy options for the associated countries. These are based on the speed of alignment of prices to those of the CAP.

- Rapid price alignment to the CAP would undoubtedly be popular amongst farmers in Central Europe. This popularity might be short-lived in some groups, where input prices rose faster than product prices (for instance, in pork or poultry), but in general an increase in farm incomes through increased subsidy would be welcomed. This option would, however, raise serious problems for the future of agriculture and for the transformation process itself.

  Rapid alignment to CAP prices would lead to considerably higher prices for most products. Higher subsidies would slow down the rate of structural change and productivity increase in the associated countries and lead to the worst excesses of a bureaucratically run extension of the CAP. This would at some stage in the future have to be corrected by painful policy reverses.

  The impact of such policy on the budgets of the associated countries would also be immense, for at least for the first years until accession the burden caused would be borne nationally. Given the serious budgetary problems for most of the associated countries, many of which still have to tackle the problems of disinflation on the one side and future social security and pensions charges on the other, any serious rise in agricultural funding would create major dangers to stabilisation and the transformation process.

Finally such a problem would put a strain on household budgets, which are still characterised by high relative spending on food. The impact of higher food prices would squeeze out spending on other consumer products, leading to reductions in demand in other sectors; popular reaction would be presumably very negative. Such a price rise would also be unlikely to help the restructuring of the domestic food industry, which appears so necessary.

This policy of rapid alignment would also risk going in the opposite direction to the trend in the CAP itself, where as was seen above, prices are likely to trend downwards towards world prices rather than upwards.

- *Gradual price alignments to those of the CAP* would lead to prices in the associated countries rising to reach those of the CAP at about the same time as accession is realised, say around the year 2000. This has an attraction in that it is a policy which would put less pressure on the associated country budgets than rapid adjustment, but would nevertheless prepare agriculture in these countries for joining the CAP.

The main problems associated with this approach are not different from those mentioned above in connection with the rapid adjustment scenario, their scale is simply reduced somewhat. It would still pose a problem to the financial stability of households and state finances and to the respect of GATT agreements.

Tangermann and Josling have carried out simulations on such a policy for the Visegrád countries alone, assuming adjustment takes place as a straight-line adjustment from 1994 to 2000. Even assuming some downward movement in real price levels in the CAP, the model suggests that a gradual alignment policy would lead to substantial surpluses of cereals, sugar, beef, pork and butter. Until enlargement these surpluses would have to be financed by the Visegrád countries themselves. Tangermann and Josling calculate that the annual cost simply of market policies could reach ECU9 billion by the year 2000, to which might be added investment aids, social aids and other structural policies. For Poland alone, it is estimated that spending could be of the order of ECU5 billion per annum, some 60 times the level of agricultural spending in 1993. This would mean an intolerable burden on state and household finances.

This scenario would also not overcome the problems of respecting the GATT commitments of the associated countries. Tangermann and Josling consider that all or several of the Visegrád countries could fail on the tariff bindings, the aggregate measurement of support and almost certainly on export subsidies.

- *The maintenance of a low level of support for agriculture until accession* would seem to be the only viable strategy for agricultural policy in the associated countries today. This does not mean that some changes to rectify anomalies should not be undertaken, but in general support for agriculture has already risen considerably and in some cases to the limit of the affordable. To go further would be to give wrong signals.

Such a policy would leave agriculture in a situation where it must continue to struggle to become more efficient and to compete on world markets. It would help the domestic food industry by maintaining competitive prices for raw materials, which would also attract more foreign investment. And it would keep the associated countries' options open to adapt to the changes in the CAP. Agriculture should, however, undoubtedly be helped through non-price policies. Structural measures to improve agricultural structures, rural infrastructure and rural development need to be undertaken. Quality improvements can be achieved with more investment and more training and this needs to be supported by the state at least in the early phases of the transition. Such structural measures could be supported by the European Union as well as by national governments.

*Policy options for the transition period after accession*

It is not possible to consider these different scenarios which lead to accession without considering the possibilities of a post-accession transition period for the associated countries. Almost every accession has been accompanied by special conditions applying over a transitional period until full integration takes place. Portugal, for instance, was given a total transition period of ten years to complete the adjustment to EC prices and Greece was given seven years to open its markets fully to Community competition.

In the case of the associated countries, the transition arrangements may vary from quasi-exclusion of agriculture from the Accession Agreement with the associated countries, through very long transitional arrangements for price alignment, rapid price alignment to a strictly managed internal market with quota arrangements for everything.

The first and the last of these options should be excluded as being against the interests of agriculture and against the basic principles of the Community. To negotiate with the associated countries to exclude agriculture from the Accession Treaties would mean keeping permanent frontiers between Member States and would prevent the associated countries gaining better access to EU markets. Such a system could be implemented only through restrictions on imports or prohibitive tariffs. To integrate the associated countries completely into the agricultural internal market but to manage the market totally through quotas and other tools of centralised planning would lead to a massive misallocation of resources, would leave the enlarged Union with an uncompetitive agriculture and would require an enormous bureaucratic infrastructure to run it.

A very long transition period over which prices are progressively approximated has the advantage of forcing gradual change which might be politically easier to arrange than abrupt measures and would not exclude the associated countries from the CAP. It would, however, not avoid the necessity of keeping borders operating for the whole period of the transition between the old and the new Member States. The long transition approach would, however, be necessary if by the time of accession the CAP had not been reformed and the difference in prices between the two parties remained large.

The most advantageous transition would be a very quick one which would lead in a very short time to common prices and an elimination of frontiers between the old and the new Member States. This would be possible if the CAP had been thoroughly reformed by accession and if the associated countries had managed to keep their price support at or below today's levels.

### Agriculture and the impact of accession on the budget

The assessment of the cost of accession in terms of agricultural spending has been the subject of many studies, which come to a whole range of very different assessments.[17] Most of the estimates ignore the impact of

---

[17] This section follows closely the analysis of Tangermann and Josling (1994).

the Uruguay Round, some of them assuming further CAP reform, some not.

The highest estimate is that by Anderson and Tyers, which calculated a total annual increase of ECU37.6 billion for the four Visegrád countries alone.[18] This study, however, ignores the constraints imposed on agriculture by the Uruguay Round, especially in terms of export subsidies. Estimates given by the UK Ministry of Agriculture and Food estimate the cost for all the associated countries' agriculture in the CAP at between ECU7.5 billion and ECU22.5 billion The range of costs demonstrates the difficulty of this calculation – or, perhaps better, the difficulty of establishing the assumptions necessary to complete the estimates. One of the crucial assumptions which must be made is whether the farmers in Central Europe will be in receipt of compensation payments in the same way as those in the old Union, even though the former will not have suffered price reductions, if prices in the associated countries have been held down prior to enlargement.

The Commission's paper to the Madrid European Council provided a lower central assumption prior to the publication of 'Agenda 2000' (see table 9.10). This calculation suggested that, besides the annual cost of the CAP of some ECU42 billion for the existing 15 Member States, the additional cost of the accession of the associated countries would be of the order of ECU12 billion per year after a period of transition. The assumptions behind this estimate were not at all clear from the text of the paper. 'Agenda 2000' has reduced this estimate to below ECU4 billion annually. It must be seen whether this very low estimate survives the accession negotiations.

### Pre-accession measures to promote agricultural development and integration

The conclusion of the above consideration of scenarios for accession must suggest that the optimum policy consists of further reform of the CAP bringing support prices nearer to world market prices with compensation through direct transfers, and low price support in the associated countries. However, many steps can already be taken to ease the pain of change involved in this integration process.

By far the most important measure which the European Union could take would be to accelerate the policy discussion on further reform of the CAP, whether this is presented as a continuation of the McSharry proposals or not. The sooner the future of the CAP becomes clear, the

---

[18] See Buckwell et al. (1994), pp. 57–9.

Table 9.10 *EAGGF guarantee expenditure on the ten associated countries after accession, 2000–10*

| Million ECU | 2000 | 2005 | 2010 |
|---|---|---|---|
| Market organisations | | | |
| Arable crops | 5,785 | 6,164 | 6,348 |
| Sugar | 45 | −81 | −46 |
| Milk | 552 | 789 | 726 |
| Beef | 846 | 2,113 | 1,877 |
| Pork | 21 | 22 | 41 |
| Poultry | 6 | 36 | 40 |
| All market organisations | 8,446 | 10,272 | 10,220 |
| of which 1992 reform payments: | | | |
| Arable | 5,789 | 5,864 | 5,864 |
| Beef | 808 | 806 | 793 |
| Accompanying measures | 500 | 1,500 | 2,000 |
| Total | 8,946 | 11,772 | 12,220 |

*Source*: European Commission (1995).

more rapidly the associated countries can adjust their policies. While. however, the Commission has made a good start with 'Agenda 2000', it is likely that the process of convincing the Member States and the farming interests will take rather a long time. In the interval, other very practical steps can be taken.

The practical support which can be given to farming in the associated countries concerns three main areas: market opening and other trade measures in the European Union, technical assistance to CEE agriculture to ease and accelerate the integration process and structural assistance to improve the agricultural and rural infrastructure.

Trade opening for agricultural products has certainly been one of the areas where the Member States of the European Union have been least liberal with respect to the associated countries. Even at the end of 1996, the Member States found it impossible to agree to more than a very marginal improvement in market access. Such a protectionist position is very hard to justify in a situation where the European Community has a large positive trade balance with the associated countries. Tangermann and Josling estimate that the quantities allowed under the preferential quotas are so small that even if all the quotas were filled this would not reduce farm revenues in the Community by more than 0.3%. Clearly, fairly major concessions can be made without reaching a disastrous position in Community agriculture.

This message was stated clearly by the European Commission in its paper for the Madrid European Council, which made a series of proposals on trade opening. These proposals included the following:

- bound tariff levels for imports into the European Union should be introduced immediately for trade with the associated countries, thus anticipating the GATT tariff reductions
- tariff quotas should be considerably increased beyond the 25% increase over five years decided by the Council
- the reduction of in-tariff quota rates to 20% of the MFN rate could be applied to all quotas
- the entry price for fruit and vegetables should not be applied within existing quotas
- the associated countries should be allowed to trade unused quota amongst themselves.

To these proposals could be added others concerning the management of the quota system which would cost EU farmers nothing but which would improve the situation for the associated countries. At the moment, the quota system leads to windfall gains for EU importers, with none of the quota rents going to the associated countries. In fact, trade takes place at the MFN tariff and it is only later that importers receive rebates if the imports were included in preferential tariff quotas. This system could be changed if information on the use of the quotas was made available to the associated countries, and if the system was changed so that only the preferential tariff rate was charged on imports within the tariff quota. This could also be achieved by passing over the management of the quotas to the associated countries themselves.

A further area of improvement in the pre-accession market access situation could be achieved through modifications in the Community's regime of export subsidies. Early in the reforms, the large quantities of subsidised Community products, pushing out domestic production throughout the region, was one of the factors which led to increases in the exceptionally low agricultural tariffs which prevailed at that time. But while intuitively this appears wrong to the general public, it ignores the fact that export subsidies are straight transfers of resources from the Community to the associated countries. If such transfers do not seriously disrupt domestic agriculture, it would seem unnecessary to take action. Of course, in some instances export subsidies have significantly affected domestic markets: in 1993, subsidies paid on apple exports ruined the domestic market in the Czech Republic until the subsidies were removed. In any case in a market totally distorted by subsidies the removal of export aids by one exporter probably leads simply to his replacement by a subsidised competitor.

Tangermann and Josling raise these questions, pointing out that it is more important for the Community to eliminate subsidies to the traditional markets of the associated countries in the East. It is difficult for the associated countries to compete with Community products on the Russian and Ukrainian markets because they cannot meet the level of Community subsidy. However, here the Community has shown no interest, presumably because it feels that to reduce export subsidies on these markets would leave them open for US or other exporters of agricultural produce. Perhaps the best solution on export subsidies would be for the Community and the associated countries jointly to monitor markets and to selectively withdraw export subsidies where there is a risk of market disturbance.

Technical assistance continues to be needed by agriculture and the food industry in the associated countries, in order to help them transform to a true market economy and to integrate with the CAP. Help is required at all levels, and in all areas. At the policy level, assistance is required to design policy leading to integration with the CAP over a short period and to establish negotiating positions for the applicant states. Help is needed to create the service and financial infrastructure for agriculture which exists in the Union but rarely in Central Europe. Technical aid is required to ensure that veterinary and phyto-sanitary arrangements are the same as those that apply in the Union. And the food industry needs assistance to improve quality throughout all stages of production, management and marketing. This list is almost inexhaustible. The main problem is not the demand for technical assistance, but the capacity of the economic actors and administrations in the Union and the other Western countries to supply appropriate skills. The difficulty of providing technical assistance could be eased if foreign investment in agriculture and the food industry was encouraged, as this would lead quite naturally to transfers of technology and managerial and marketing skills which are at the moment lacking.

Finally structural measures need to be taken to help the development of agriculture. Most of the measures required here need to be taken by the associated countries themselves. Laws and regulations need to be changed to allow corporate ownership and foreign investment, privatisation needs to be completed, land registration needs to be speeded up and the legal framework for the development of a land market advanced. In the financial area, better access to capital and the problem of security on loans needs attention. Assistance is required to develop rural infrastructure and alternative employment opportunities in rural areas outside farming.

'Agenda 2000' proposes a modest pre-accession structural programme for agriculture starting in the year 2000 and amounting to

ECU500 million for all ten associated countries. Unfortunately, it does not include proposals for immediate trade liberalisation measures.

### The politics of agricultural reform

Whether the changes proposed here can be implemented will depend on the development of the politics of agricultural reform in the Community and in the associated countries.

In the associated countries, the essential problem is whether governments can remain firm on keeping support for agriculture at or below today's level, and how well they manage the process of agricultural restructuring. The first problem should not be too difficult, partly because the fiscal difficulties are recognised at the voters' level as a major constraint on policy, but also because the urban populations already spend a large part of their budget on food and would not be happy to see this share raised. Managing the process of restructuring in the countryside might be more difficult. Agriculture will be releasing surplus labour, especially if the profitability of agriculture is not increased through subsidy. This will occur at the same time that state-owned companies are still releasing labour as they restructure. The only solution is for the private sector to expand in both urban and rural areas. This would plead for further general measures to improve the business environment, together with specific measures to stimulate non-agricultural employment in rural areas. But while rural development is seen as the answer to the decline of agriculture, it is still not clear how it can be effectively implemented.

In the Union, the political problems will be more difficult. Germany has played the key role in pushing for enlargement since the Essen and Madrid European Councils. However, on agriculture, Germany is a most conservative and protectionist Member State.

The Commission, however, clearly supports the view that further reform is necessary. This statement appears strange when, in agriculture, the Commission has traditionally been seen as a typical case of agency capture. Any attempt by liberals in the Commission to restrict agricultural protectionism was put down by the power of the agricultural lobby. The Commission's track record on enlargement until recently seemed fully to reflect this position. The conflicts between the traditionally more liberal external relations department and the agricultural department have been well publicised – these conflicts exist in all Member State administrations as well. As the role of the Commission is crucial, it is worth looking briefly at the changes in Commission policy over the past three years.

The position taken by the Commission in the negotiation of the Association Agreements was never generous, although it must be said that the position of the Member States was even less so; and it is the Member States which determine the final negotiating position of the Community. The extremely marginal concessions made at the Copenhagen Summit were also a sign of a very restrictive position. At the Essen Summit, where the Commission tried to make a major breakthrough in relations with Central Europe, opposition was so great that none of the proposals for improvements in market access, better management of quotas or the reduction of export subsidies even managed to get into the Commission papers sent to the Council in July 1994. This basically negative position was reflected in a study commissioned by the agricultural services on the relations between the Community and the associated countries in agriculture.[19] The Nallet and van Stolk study appeared to propose a system of price supports in these countries which would be adjusted to eliminate trade between the existing Member States and the associated countries, except in times of market disturbance.

Important changes were, however, happening in the agricultural services even while these hard positions were still being taken in negotiations. The implications of the GATT agreement for the CAP were not lost on civil servants, and this suggested that policy reform would have to continue well beyond 1995–6. Gradually, the mood of the leadership in the Commission appears to have changed from one of defensiveness to one of looking for viable solutions to current and future problems. At the end of 1994, four studies were commissioned to investigate alternative strategies for the accession of the associated countries in the agricultural field.[20] These studies, by well reputed academic agricultural economists, had an important impact on thinking inside and outside the Commission. Many of their suggestions have now been taken up by the agricultural services.

The extremely serious and professional position taken in the Commission's paper to the Madrid European Council, suggested the Commission's determination to push forward its ideas for sustained but not radical reform in the CAP in order to prepare the accession of the associated countries and to assist the development of a healthier agricultural industry in Europe. The Madrid paper appeared to be a new departure, which gave hope that agriculture would be less of a

---

[19]  Nallet and van Stolk (1994).
[20]  Tangermann and Josling (1994); Buckwell et al. (1994); Tarditi, Senior-Nello and Marsh (1994); Mahe (1994).

problem for accession than many had thought in the past. 'Agenda 2000' confirmed this analysis.

The real problem will lie in convincing doubtful Member States that reform is good for agriculture. Analysis suggests that those countries with an efficient and dynamic agriculture will be less difficult to convince than countries which have a low productivity industry and a generally defensive agricultural policy. France, the Netherlands and Denmark, for instance, may well be more easily convinced than Germany. French attitudes to agricultural policy appear to have been changing as governments realise the potential of the dynamic agricultural industry in France to exploit the possibilities in Central European agriculture. At election times, the votes of small farmers in France tend to count rather more highly than at times between elections, but opinion in France appears to have moved in the right direction.

The stumbling block is liable to be Germany, a country which would stand to gain more from reform than any other. Germany was not keen to have a CAP when the European Economic Community was conceived. It grew, however, to love a policy which was a real common policy and guaranteed German farmers high prices for their output, protecting them from the restructuring which would otherwise have had to be undertaken. This stability in agriculture was, however, bought at a high price to the German taxpayer who was subsidising not only the German farmer but also the extremely rich large-scale farms of southern England and northern France. Absurd as this situation is, it was never possible to change German policy because of the delicate political balance inside coalition governments.

From a German point of view, reform as suggested in this chapter would lead to a reduction in Community agricultural expenditure in relation to the level of expenditure for an unreformed CAP and therefore lower transfers from a budgetarily strapped German government. As subsidy moves towards direct income support and away from price support, so the argument for subsidiarity in agricultural spending grows: direct income aids are more efficiently paid by national budgets than the Community budget. This would lead to Germany being able to reduce its contributions to the Community budget and at the same time raise the total subsidy level going to its farmers. The degree to which the agricultural budget was re-nationalised would need to be carefully considered, for the CAP should remain a common policy of the Union. Above all such reforms would facilitate the accession of the associated countries, one of the stated priorities of German policy. The arguments for policy reform are overwhelming for Germany. Whether there will be a change of policy, however, will depend on the German political and budgetary situation. What is clear is that if there is a reorientation of policy in Germany, the chances of the reforms outlined here taking place will be considerably enhanced.

## Conclusion

The problems of agriculture are considered to be some of the most difficult to overcome on the road towards the accession of the associated countries. This chapter suggests that if there is a willingness to reform the CAP and some discipline in terms of agricultural protection in the associated countries, the result of the accession process may be a more dynamic and more competitive agriculture in an enlarged Community. Thus the problem may turn out to be an opportunity rather than a cost.

# 10    Redistribution and the Structural Funds

### Redistribution and accession

Redistribution of income at the EU level does not take place through the normal mechanisms of a progressive taxation system and a large social security budget. In the Community there are no automatic stabilisers which switch on when the economy begins to weaken. There is not even a system, as in Germany, of regional budgetary transfers from stronger states to weaker ones. At the Community level, regional redistribution mechanisms take the form of funds for structural development purposes, the use of which is decided jointly between the beneficiary country and the European Union. These funds are also guaranteed only for the period of the financial guideline of the Community, that is at present up to 1999.[1] The traditional budgetary redistribution mechanisms operate at the level of the Member States and concern only redistribution within the Member State.

On accession, the associated countries would have the right to receive transfers from the Structural Funds. Logically such a transfer would either raise the level of finance needed for the Structural Funds or would lead to other present recipients of funds losing benefit. For this reason, the participation of the associated countries in the Structural Funds and the associated financing requirements are considered to be a problem for the accession process. There is little real regional policy dimension to the discussion which has taken place so far. The arguments have been restricted largely to budgetary problems and the rights of current recipients of funds. 'Agenda 2000' does, however, raise the problem of concentration of funds within the existing as well as the enlarged Union.

---

[1] The European Commission's 'Agenda 2000' document (European Commission, 1997a) suggests that the Structural Funds should continue in the 2000–6 financing period at the same percentage of GDP as in the previous period (0.47%). No parties realistically expect an end to transfers in 1999.

## The Community's Structural Funds

The Community's Structural Funds have a long history, going back to the beginning of the Community. They have become of real budgetary relevance, however, only since the middle of the 1980s. It was the decision to double the size of the Structural Funds which was taken in parallel with the decision to launch the '1992 programme' for the completion of the internal market of the Community which led to the first significant increase in budgetary resources devoted to this purpose. This increase in financing was decided as a result of pressure from the peripheral states of the Union to enable them to develop their infrastructure as a counterbalance to the expected attraction of the central regions of the Community when a unified common market was created. A further boost to the level of redistribution was given with the negotiation of a Cohesion Fund in the context of Maastricht Agreement. This fund, which began in 1993 (though officially commencing in Spring 1994) is restricted to the four poorest countries in the Community – Greece, Ireland, Portugal and Spain. It was seen partially in the context of the planned EMU, and was supposed to assist these countries in accelerating their economic convergence with the rest of the Community.

The three Structural Funds – the Regional Development Fund, the Social Fund and the Agricultural Guidance Fund, which had operated more or less independently of each other up to 1988 – were reformed in that year. Five main 'objectives' were established for the new coordinated Structural Funds, which in fact turned out to be six and to which a seventh was added at the recent enlargement of the Community. These objectives are:

- *Objective 1*: the development of the economically backward regions of the Community. These regions are defined as having a regional GDP *per capita* less than 75% of the average for the Community, though through political pressure, some regions with well above this limit have been included. The Objective 1 regions will absorb approximately 74% of the total Structural Funds commitments in the period 1994–9 (including the Cohesion Fund). The regions contain roughly a quarter of the population of the Community.
- *Objective 2*: this objective is the restructuring of regions of industrial decline. The criterion for participation is a high level of unemployment and a significant decline in industrial employment. Roughly 6% of the total financing will go to these regions, which have a population equal to around 17%

of the total Community population, in the current financial period.

- *Objective 3*: the fight against long-term unemployment and youth unemployment and the reintegration of excluded workers into the labour market.
- *Objective 4*: the adaptation of the workforce to industrial change and new technologies. Objectives 3 and 4, the old Social Fund, are not regionalised, cover the whole of the Community and absorb only around 11% of the available funds.
- *Objective 5A*: seeks the acceleration of structural change in agriculture in the context of the reform of the CAP as well as structural change in the fishing industry. This objective absorbs 4% of the total funds.
- *Objective 5B*: is to develop rural areas and assist in their structural adjustment. This objective uses around 5% of the funds. These two agricultural objectives can in theory apply anywhere in the Community, but are of course largely restricted to rural areas with poor agricultural structures and – in the case of Objective 5B – high rural unemployment or poverty.
- *Objective 6*: this is a newly invented objective which assists peripheral northern areas with a density of population of less than 8 per square kilometre. Its share of the total funds will remain small.

In fact, the three funds still operate largely independently, a tribute to resistance to change. The service within the Commission responsible for the coordination of the Structural Funds was scrapped in the early 1990s. In addition to these major objectives, there are also a series of Community Initiatives which cover in principle the whole Community and which attempt to promote themes leading to greater cohesion. These include programmes to promote development and trans-frontier cooperation in the frontier zones of the Community, to support Community networking amongst public and private institutions and operators or to promote rural development at the grass-roots' level.

The Cohesion Fund, which is now administered by the Directorate General for Regional Development in the European Commission, supports projects exclusively in the environment or transport infrastructure fields in the four poorest countries of the Community. In order not to put too much of a strain on the public finances of these countries, the level of co-financing required of the Member States is only of the order of 15%, in contrast to the much higher levels in the Structural Funds proper.

The programming of the Structural Funds (excluding Objective 5A and 6 and the Cohesion Fund) essentially has three phases. In the first instance, the beneficiary countries draw up development plans which, apart from the usual background information about the situation of the respective regions, identify (at least for Objective 1) the financial envelope to be given to each of the main problem areas to be tackled. On the basis of this background programme, Community Support Frameworks (CSF) are drawn up between the Member State concerned and the Commission; the initiative very much remaining with the Member State. The CSF indicate for each main area of action the financial envelopes which are available. The CSF, which are multi-annual (five-year) frameworks, are then translated into operational programmes which determine in detail how the finance is to be used.

The finance available for the Structural Funds will reach 35.7% of all budgetary commitments of the Union in 1999, ECU30 billion (in 1992 prices) or 0.46% of the GDP of the Union. This will have risen from 31% and ECU21 billion (1992 prices) in 1993. These transfers are of macroeconomic significance for the four cohesion countries, as shown in table 10.1.

The Structural and Cohesion Funds will transfer on average 2.9% of their GDP to the four cohesion countries in 1999. In the cases of Greece and Portugal, this will amount to around 4% of GDP. As a proportion of total investment in these economies, the Structural Funds amount to over 12% in Greece and around 8% on average. The corresponding figures for all the Objective 1 regions together is 2.1% of GDP and 4.7% of investment.

Such large transfers can enable these countries to develop their physical and social infrastructures rapidly, but they can also pose major problems if macroeconomic policy is not well managed. In the case of Greece, for instance, the effectiveness of the Structural Funds must be doubted, given the extremely lax macroeconomic policy which was followed until recently. Transfers clearly went into consumption spending, aggravating the current account balance and, with low domestic savings, squeezing out investment. At the other end of the scale Ireland, which put more of its transfers into education and training, appears to have maintained a more balanced economic policy in which the Structural Funds transfers were used to develop the physical and educational infrastructure of the country.[2] Here domestic savings rose both in the private and public sector to offset foreign transfers.[3]

---

[2] See research by Bradley et al., quoted in Besnainou (1995), pp. 215–32.
[3] Orłowski (1997).

Table 10.1 *Structural Fund commitments in Objective 1 regions*

| Objective 1 regions in: | ERDF commitments as % of GFCF | | | Structural and cohesion funds as % of GDP | | | Annual average |
|---|---|---|---|---|---|---|---|
| | 1989 | 1993 | 1999 | 1989 | 1993 | 1999 | 1994-9[a] |
| Greece | 7.3 | 11.0 | 12.6 | 2.5 | 3.3 | 4.0 | 3.67 |
| Spain | 2.6 | 4.0 | 6.6 | 1.0 | 1.5 | 2.3 | 1.74 |
| Ireland | 5.2 | 9.3 | 7.8 | 2.1 | 3.1 | 2.7 | 2.82 |
| Portugal | 5.3 | 7.0 | 8.0 | 2.7 | 3.3 | 3.8 | 3.98 |
| EUR-4 | 3.9 | 6.0 | 7.8 | 1.6 | 2.3 | 2.9 | |
| New German Länder | na | (0.9) | 1.8 | na | (0.8) | 1.7 | |
| Italy | 1.7 | 3.6 | 4.0 | 0.6 | 1.1 | 1.2 | |
| Other Member States | 2.0 | 3.3 | 2.5 | 1.0 | 1.4 | 1.1 | |
| All Obj. 1 regions | 3.0 | 5.0 | 4.7 | 1.2 | 1.8 | 2.1 | |
| EUR-12 | 0.4 | 0.6 | 0.9 | 0.1 | 0.2 | 0.3 | |

*Notes*:
[a] European Commission (1996b); as % of GDP.
ERDF = European Regional Development Fund.
GFCF = Gross fixed capital formation (investment).
na = Not available.
*Source*: European Commission (1994).

## The extension of the Structural Funds to the associated countries

The reconsideration of the Structural Funds for the period after 1999 is just beginning in most of the Member States and in the European Commission. Theoretically, these transfers could cease at that moment if it is considered that the problem of 'cohesion' no longer exists. This is an unlikely outcome for a number of reasons, not least the opposition which will come from the present recipients of Structural Funds. At the other extreme, there will be massive opposition from the net contributors to the budget of the Union to any proposal that increases the level of funding beyond that which has been agreed for 1999. The outcome of the discussion is likely to be that the transfers through the funds will be continued, but at a real level which remains roughly constant.

### Scenarios for accession

All of the associated countries when they enter the European Union on the basis of unchanged policies will receive Objective 1 status in the

Structural Funds and will logically also receive Cohesion Fund transfers. Under whatever suppositions are made on economic growth in the associated countries, they will remain at a level of GDP *per capita* well below the level of the poorest Member State of the EU-15 well beyond the year 2000 (see tables 10.2–10.4). Even assuming that the associated countries grow twice as fast as the Member States of the European Union over the period 1993–2000 and that there is an annual revaluation of their currencies against the ECU of 5% per annum (not unreasonable if the estimates of GDP measured in PPS in table 10.2 are considered), their GDP *per capita* will reach only around ECU4,500 in the year 2000. As recipients of transfers under Objective 1 of the Structural Funds, the associated countries will not receive funds under either Objectives 2 or 5, but they will receive Social Fund transfers as appropriate.[4]

As noted above the problem of the Structural Funds is, in the first instance, purely a budgetary, not a policy, problem for the Union. The Union must therefore find a solution to the question of the integration of the associated countries into the Structural Funds which is acceptable to the associated countries themselves, the existing net beneficiaries and the net contributors. Tables 10.2–10.4 attempt to unravel some of the data on this problem.

Table 10.2 shows various measures of GDP for the Union of 15 Member States, for an enlarged Union of 25 members and for each of the associated countries and the ten countries together for the current financing perspectives of the Union. The simplest measure, GDP in 1993 at current prices, shows that the total GDP of all ten associated countries was only ECU188 billion, just 3.2% of that of the present European Union. The GDP *per capita* in 1993 was approximately ECU1,785, or roughly 11.2% of that of the European Union.

There is, of course, considerable variation within the group of associated countries. Slovenia, with a GDP *per capita* at PPS in 1995 of almost ECU10,100, came nearest to reaching the level of the 'poorest' country in the Union – Greece, with ECU11,320. Slovenia, however, had around three times the annual *per capita* output level of Latvia at the other end of the scale. Latvia, with only just over ECU3,000 had the lowest level of GDP *per capita* of all the associated countries in 1995.

It is important, however, also to project these levels into the future to analyse what the situation is likely to be when the associated countries are admitted to membership. Columns (5) and (6) of table 10.2 show the GDP of the Community and of the associated countries on the

---

[4] Assuming that the same structure of the Structural Funds survives beyond the end of the financial period 1994–9, which appears unlikely.

Table 10.2 *GDP in the EU and the associated countries, 1993 and 2000*

| | Population[a] | GDP 1993 ECU billion[b] | GDP/capita 1993 ECU[c] | GDP/capita 1995/PPS[d] | GDP/2000 ECUbillion prices 2000[e] | GDP/2000 ECU/CAP prices 2000[f] |
|---|---|---|---|---|---|---|
| EU-15 | 369.7 | 5,897 | 15,879 | 17,260 | 8,621 | 23,214 |
| EU-25 | 475.2 | 6,085 | 12,750 | 14,727 | 8,947 | 18,828 |
| Cohesion | 62.7 | 568 | 9,056 | 12,833 | 830 | 13,238 |
| Bulgaria | 8.5 | 9.4 | 1,106 | 4,210 | 16.3 | 1,914 |
| Czech Rep. | 10.3 | 26.7 | 2,592 | 9,410 | 46.2 | 4,486 |
| Estonia | 1.6 | 1.5 | 938 | 3,917 | 2.6 | 1,622 |
| Hungary | 10.3 | 32.5 | 3,155 | 6,311 | 56.2 | 5,460 |
| Latvia | 2.6 | 2.2 | 846 | 3,157 | 3.8 | 1,464 |
| Lithuania | 3.8 | 2.3 | 605 | 4,128 | 4 | 1,047 |
| Poland | 38.5 | 73.4 | 1,906 | 5,318 | 127 | 3,299 |
| Romania | 22.7 | 21.8 | 960 | 4,055 | 37.7 | 1,662 |
| Slovak Rep. | 5.3 | 8.7 | 1,642 | 7,117 | 15.1 | 2,841 |
| Slovenia | 1.9 | 9.8 | 5,158 | 10,112 | 17 | 8,926 |
| Total AC10 | 105.5 | 188.3 | 1,785 | 5,530 | 325.9 | 3,089 |
| AC10 as % of EU-15 | 28.5 | 3.2 | 11.2 | 32 | 3.8 | 13.3 |

Notes:
[a] Million.
[b] 1993 GDP, at current exchange rates. (ECUbillion).
[c] 1993 GDP *per capita*, at current exchange rates (ECU).
[d] 1995 GDP *per capita*, in PPS (ECU).
[e] Estimated GDP in 2000 at current prices and unchanged exchange rates, assuming inflation in ECU countries is 3% per year from 1992 to 2000, that GDP grows in real terms at 5% per annum in the associated countries from 1992 to 2000 and in the EU by 2.5%.
[f] *Per capita* terms (ECU).
Source: EUROSTAT.

assumption that the Community's economic growth is likely to be 2.5% per annum until 2000 and that of the associated countries 5% and if inflation in the ECU countries is of the order of 3% per annum. These assumptions may be shown to be wrong with hindsight; for today, they do not look unreasonable. Although column (6) of the table shows the associated countries catching-up the Community, they will remain, on these assumptions, at only 13.3% of the GDP *per capita* at current prices of the Community in the year 2000. Nevertheless, it is likely that during this period the under-valuation of the associated countries' exchange rates will gradually be corrected. However, even without such a calcula-

Table 10.3 *Structural Funds spending in the associated countries under various assumptions*

| | I<br>Coh. 4<br>2000<br>ECUbillion<br>(1) | II<br><br><br>DDR2000<br>(2) | III<br><br>2.3%GDP<br>2000<br>(3) | IV<br>4%GDP<br>2005<br>ECUbillion<br>(4) | I<br>as% GDP<br>2000<br>ECUbillion<br>(5) | II<br><br>as% GDP<br>2000<br>(6) |
|---|---|---|---|---|---|---|
| Bulgaria | 2.46 | 1.48 | 0.37 | 1.05 | 15.11 | 9.09 |
| Czech Rep. | 2.98 | 1.79 | 1.06 | 2.98 | 6.44 | 3.88 |
| Estonia | 0.46 | 0.28 | 0.06 | 0.17 | 17.82 | 10.72 |
| Hungary | 2.98 | 1.79 | 1.29 | 3.62 | 5.29 | 3.19 |
| Latvia | 0.75 | 0.45 | 0.09 | 0.24 | 19.74 | 11.88 |
| Lithuania | 1.10 | 0.66 | 0.09 | 0.26 | 27.60 | 16.61 |
| Poland | 11.13 | 6.70 | 2.92 | 8.2 | 8.76 | 5.27 |
| Romania | 6.56 | 3.95 | 0.87 | 2.43 | 17.40 | 10.47 |
| Slovak Rep. | 1.53 | 0.92 | 0.35 | 0.97 | 10.18 | 6.13 |
| Slovenia | 0.55 | 0.33 | 0.39 | 1.1 | 3.24 | 1.95 |
| Total | 30.50 | 18.36 | 7.49 | 21.0 | 9.36 | 5.63 |

*Notes*:
All assumptions start from the premise that the associated countries receive funds as Objective 1 regions and from Objectives 3 and 4 but not from 2 or 5.
*Assumption I* = The level of transfers *per capita* in 2000 is the same level as for the four cohesion countries (ECU289).
*Assumption II* = The level of transfers *per capita* in 2000 is the same level as for the New Bundesländer (ECU174).
*Assumption III* = The level of transfers equals 2.3% of associated countries' GDP in the year 2000.
*Assumption IV* = The level of transfers equals 4% of the associated countries' GDP in the year 2005. There is a 2% revaluation of currencies against the ECU from 2000 to 2005, the associated countries grow in real terms at 5% annually, the Union at 2.5%. ECU inflation is 3% and the size of the Structural Funds remains at 0.46% of GDP until 2005. Columns (5) and (6) express assumptions I and II as a percentage of GDP in the year 2000.

Table 10.4 *Additional expenditure on Structural Funds for the associated countries under various assumptions*

| | Share of ACs in<br>2000 ECUbillion<br>(1) | % GDP of ACs<br>in 2000<br>(2) | As % of Structural<br>Funds 2000<br>(3) | AC-10 as % EU<br>budget 2000<br>(4) |
|---|---|---|---|---|
| I | 30.50 | 9.36 | 85.3 | 28.63 |
| II | 18.36 | 5.63 | 51.4 | 17.23 |
| III | 7.50 | 2.30 | 21.0 | 7.04 |
| IV* | 21.0 | 4.00 | 39.0 | 14.0 |

*Note*: * Figures refer to the situation in 2005.
*Source of data*: European Commission (1994).

tion, it remains certain that the associated countries will be priority 'Objective 1' regions if they accede to the Community at that time.

The additional cost to the budget of the European Union will depend on the system adopted by the two parties during the negotiations. As the negotiating position of the Union will undoubtedly be stronger than that of the individual associated countries, its position is liable to dominate the negotiation. Some of the possible assumptions which can be made to define this negotiating position on the Structural Funds are as follows:

- the Structural Funds system is left more or less unchanged, the associated countries receive the same level of nominal *per capita* spending in the year 2000 as the four current cohesion countries
- the system remains the same but the associated countries receive the lower level of *per capita* transfers which applies to the New Bundesländer in Germany
- the transfers to the associated countries are capped at 2.3% of their GDP, about the same level as the cohesion countries receive today
- the transfers to the associated countries equals 4% of their GDP in 2005, the ceiling for transfers proposed in the Commission's 'Agenda 2000' document.

Each of these alternative transfer patterns can be combined with three possibilities on the revenue side:

- allocations to the current net recipients do not fall and the overall increase is borne by increased budgetary contributions
- the total expenditure on the Structural Funds remains constant in terms of Union GDP and the adjustment is made by 'graduating' some existing beneficiary regions out of the Structural Funds, the assumption made in 'Agenda 2000'
- the increase in transfers to the associated countries is absorbed partly by increased contributions and partly by 'graduation'.

Table 10.3 attempts to put some rough figures on these possibilities. These calculations assume accession of all ten associated countries to the Union in the year 2000. This assumption is unrealistic, but is based on known magnitudes and provides a useful guide to the potential implications of accession.

Assumption I assumes that from the year 2000, the associated countries receive the same level of transfers as the four cohesion countries at the end of the current financial perspective.[5] This would be

---

[5] These calculations address only the Structural Funds. If the Cohesion Funds, amounting to roughly ECU3.3 billion in 1999, are continued and expanded to meet the needs of the associated countries, equivalent sums would have to be added to the above calculations.

the equivalent of a gross transfer of ECU 30 billion in the year 2000. Assuming that the level of Structural Funds spending and of the total Community budget remains constant as a proportion of Community GDP after 1999, this figure represents 85% of the EU-15 Structural Funds spending and over 28% of the total budget of the European Union. These transfers would also be a massive 9.4% of the associated countries' GDP (subject to the differential growth assumptions mentioned above). For individual countries the proportion of their GDP contributed by the Community under this assumption would vary from 3% for Slovenia to 27% for Lithuania and 17% for Romania.

This solution will not be adopted. For the Community, it would mean either that the net contributors would have to considerably increase their net payments or, if the total budgetary cost was absorbed by reductions in the number of regions in the EU-15 which are supported, that 85% of the current recipients would lose their transfers. The latter solution would mean, for instance, that Portugal would be eliminated from the transfers under Objective 1, as would most of Spain, and Greece would be on the very limit.

In the associated countries these levels of transfers would be impossible to absorb. The experience gained in the Structural Funds of the Community and in assistance programmes in Central and Eastern Europe and elsewhere have clearly shown that absorption of even quite small proportions of GDP (say, 0.5%–2%) can be extremely difficult. This is due to the often complex administrative procedures, problems of identifying bankable projects and the difficulties of providing co-financing or government guarantees. The problem of co-financing would prove an impossible hurdle if the rules of the Structural Funds were not modified. Normally the level of co-financing required from the beneficiary region is 50%. There is obviously no possibility of Romania finding 17% of its GDP as co-financing funds for the expected transfers from Brussels. Even if the co-financing requirement was reduced to 25%, this would still be impossible for many of the associated countries under Assumption 1. Such large flows of funds would also be extremely destabilising from the macroeconomic point of view, if they were spent domestically. As the latter is the very objective of Structural Funds spending, the macroeconomic effect, and especially the impact on inflation, could be very negative. The final problem with such large transfers is that they would destroy the very principles on which the market economy is based: they would work as a massive subsidy programme, squeezing out private capital flows, supporting inefficiency, raising domestic costs and holding back some of the reforms so desperately needed in the short term.

Assumption II uses the lower rate of transfer which is used for the New Bundesländer and which is around 60% of the level of the cohesion countries. Such a level obviously makes the pain of the exercise somewhat less for the existing EU-15 and creates less distortion in the associated countries. Nevertheless the level of transfers remain unabsorbable by the associated countries, at least in the short term. This assumption would also increase the budget of the Community by some ECU18 billion, equivalent to 50% of the Structural Funds spending or 17% of the Delors II package. Again it seems unlikely that the net contributors are likely to offer such a large increase in contributions, at least in the short term, while the tribulations of monetary union and related constraints on public deficits are still with them. If budgets remain unchanged with such an increase, Portugal and all those regions better off than Portugal would exit the Objective 1 status.

Assumption III changes the system of the Structural Funds in setting an upper limit on the transfers according to the GDP of the recipient country. If the limit was set at 2.3% of GDP, the current level of spending in the cohesion countries, the level of transfers falls to only ECU 7.5 billion.

Assumption IV calculates the impact of the Structural Funds transfers to the associated countries rising to 4% of GDP by 2005. If a regular real appreciation of the currencies of the associated countries of 1%–2% per year is assumed from 2000 to 2005 and if the EU GDP continues to grow at 2.5% per annum to 2005, the 4% ceiling would amount to around 39% of the total nominal Structural Funds available in 2005 (assuming that they remain a constant share of GDP), or ECU21 billion. 'Agenda 2000' proposes a ceiling on Structural Funds transfers of 4% of GDP for all beneficiary states but also assumes that the new Member States will take several years to reach this level of absorption.

### A politically acceptable scenario - 'Agenda 2000'

These calculations are extremely simplified but give a feeling for the orders of magnitude involved. It is important that a politically acceptable and economically defensible solution is found. Such a compromise would limit the transfers to the new Member States to a certain low proportion of GDP (certainly lower than 2.3% at the start) and would continue paying transfers to all the regions legitimately receiving transfers in 1996. Over a five- or ten-year period, transfers to the associated countries would rise, while more and more regions would be graduated out, starting with those regions with GDP *per capita* above the level of 75% of the Union average. This would all be constrained by an unchanged Structural Funds budget limited to the current level of 0.46% of Community GDP.

It is certainly true that several regions that still receive transfers as Objective 1 regions could be progressively dropped out of the Objective 1 category. This applies to many of the regions in France, the United Kingdom, Ireland and to parts of Spain and Italy.[6] The Structural Funds were not conceived as a permanent system of transfer, but as temporary assistance to help the backward regions catch-up with the average Community level of income (a concept of which the statistical logic is somewhat dubious). A combination of good macroeconomic policies, successful efforts to attract foreign investment and intelligent use of Structural Funds finance has led to Ireland, for instance, racing up the scale of GDP *per capita* and it is natural that the country, or at least part of it, should graduate from the Objective 1 regions. The political question is how many existing beneficiary regions would need to be graduated out, and when.

If it is assumed that the associated countries grow somewhat faster than the Union limiting their receipt of Structural Fund transfers, for instance, in the first years of membership to 2.3% of GDP would lead to a gross transfer of ECU7.5 billion. or some 31% of the total Structural Funds budget in the year 2000. If the plan is not to evict any existing beneficiaries at the beginning of the next financial period, then this amount of money would have to be found from within the budget of the next financing period.

This approach may well be more promising than this arithmetic suggests. It is unlikely that the new Member States could absorb 2.3% of their GDP in the first years of the next financing period (2000–6). It will probably take several years before such a level of absorption will be possible, if the experience of Spain and Portugal is relevant. In the first few years the absorbable transfers are much more likely to be in the range 1%–1.5% of GDP; this would mean a total transfer of between ECU4 billion and ECU7 billion, or between 11% and 20% of the total Structural Funds budget in the year 2000. With an increase in the absorptive capacity, or through changes in the system (see below), it should be possible to raise this level of transfer over the ten years following accession, in order to raise the level of infrastructure provision. With transfers concentrating on domestic spending, this should have a measurable impact on economic activity in the new Member States in the years following accession.

[6] In the case of Ireland, the whole country is dealt with as one region. It is obvious that if the Dublin region was separated out from the rest of the country, the less developed parts would remain as Objective 1 regions.

If the budget constraint is maintained, and there is no increase in structural spending above 0.46% of Community GDP, then a number of regions need to be graduated out of Objective 1 in the years following accession. Table 10.4 shows that, if it is assumed that there is a small exchange rate catching-up effect, by 2005 raising transfers to 4% of their GDP would be likely to absorb around 40% of the available budget. It is probable, however, that there will be some increase in the overall volume of the Structural Funds envelope over this period. This will occur because of economic growth in the Union (say, 2.5% in real terms per year) and through the graduating out of the richer regions amongst today's beneficiaries. Spending on the associated countries will increase, but not up to 4% of GDP, and transfers to existing beneficiaries will concentrate on the very poorest zones in the EU-15.

All the flows discussed above are gross flows, but of course the new Member States will be expected to contribute through the normal budgetary mechanism. The combination of low Structural Funds transfers in the next financial period and full contributions has led some associated countries to fear that they could be net contributors to the Union – remembering that, of course, Spain was, for some time after accession, a net contributor.[7] It might be expected that the associated countries would have a gross budgetary contribution of between ECU4 billion and ECU5 billion (approximately 1% of their combined GDP), assuming that they join in 2000. If, however, the associated countries receive considerably less than under the existing system through the Structural Funds, there must also no doubt be a transitional period in terms of contributions to the Community budget, in which the level of contributions would start from a low base and gradually increase as the associated countries become full beneficiaries of Structural Funds transfers. It is then inconceivable that any of the associated countries could become net contributors to the Union.

The conclusion of the above discussion must be that even if the Community decides that it wishes to retain redistribution via the Structural Funds mechanisms, this will cause some financial pain but it can be achieved even under the constraint of no increase in Structural Funds financing in real terms. A realistic scenario would see some small increase in funding in real terms, which would mean that the graduation of poorer regions out of Objective 1 status could be more gradual. It would mean that the new Member States would have to accept that they would not be full beneficiaries from the Structural Funds for a transition

---

[7] See, for instance, Kwiecinski (1995).

period of probably between five and ten years. This in turn would mean that the existing Member States would have to accept a transition period in own-resources transfers by the associated countries over a similar period. The total impact on expenditure under such a scenario is likely to be around ECU5 billion in the first year, rising perhaps to double that at the end of the transition period. These sums can be achieved through graduating out some regions and through the normal increases in own-resources, with no (or only a small) increase in the proportion of GDP going to the Structural Funds.

The proposals contained in the Commission's 'Agenda 2000' package follow roughly this proposal. The budgetary assumption of 'Agenda 2000' is that there will be no increase in own-resources as a percentage of GDP and the Structural Funds will also be capped at 0.46% of GDP until 2006. Adding the five Objective 1 countries, proposed by the Commission for the opening of negotiations, with between 60–70 million inhabitants to the existing Objective 1 regions will then clearly mean that some of the existing beneficiary regions will lose their rights to Structural Funds. The Commission proposes to limit Objective 1 status strictly to regions with less than 75% of average GDP *per capita* in the Union. But with the new members, this average will fall sharply. Therefore many politically sensitive regions will cease to receive aid.

The main outline of the proposals for the reform of the Structural Funds is as follows:

- there should be only three 'objectives' in order to concentrate funds on key problems
  - Objective 1 will be similar to the current Objective 1, applying only to the poorest regions which must not have more than 75% of average GDP *per capita* of the European Union
  - Objective 2 will include all other former priorities (urban or industrial decay, rural development, fishing, etc.)
  - human resources (old priorities 3 and 4)
- Objective 1 and 2 regions should only cover 35%–40% of the EU population, rather than the current 51%
- total allocation for 2000–6 will be ECU275 billion at 1997 prices: of this, ECU210 billion will be for the existing Structural Funds, ECU20 billion for the Cohesion Funds and ECU45 billion for the new Member States
- there will be transition periods for regions losing Structural Funds and for the new Member States, although how the transition will be arranged is not explained

- it is stated that by the end of the period (2006) 30% of total funding will be going to the new Member States
- receipts from the Structural Funds should be capped at 4% of a recipient country's GDP.

'Agenda 2000' leaves many questions unanswered, especially for the associated countries:

- Is there one system of Structural Funds after enlargement or is there one system for the old Member States and one for the new Member States?
- When the paper talks about strictly limiting Objective 1 areas to those with less than 75% of average Union GDP, is it talking about the whole enlarged Union or only about the EU-15?
- How will the transition periods function?
- Will the same rules apply to the Structural Funds after 2000 as now – for instance, will the co-financing ratio remain the same?

Assuming that ten new Member States join the Community on 1 January 2002, the Commission estimates that they will receive total assistance of ECU3.6 billion in the first year, rising to ECU11.6 billion in 2006.

While it is probably inescapable that there should be a transition period both for the EU-15 regions which will lose support and for the new Member States, it is vital to know that in 2006 there will only be one system applying equally to old and new Member States.

There is, however, no reason to suppose that the Community should maintain the current system of Structural Funds, particularly after the end of the current financial planning period. It is worth exploring modified systems which might apply to the CEE countries.

## Alternatives to the classic Structural Funds system

There is considerable dispute over the question of whether budgetary transfers like those of the Structural Funds really have a positive impact on the economic development of the recipient regions. Evidence from those regions which have benefited for several years within the Community is mixed. The case of Greece, and to some extent of Andalusia, point to the dangers of receiving large transfers if macroeconomic policy is not geared towards stability and if the institutional management of the funds is not strong. The negative impact of subsidy on entrepreneurship is well documented from Berlin and Northern Ireland, where entrepreneurs aimed to maximise subsidy receipts rather than market-based profits. This type of experience leads many economists, including Jeffrey

Sachs of Harvard, to advise the associated countries to negotiate entry into the Community without Structural Funds transfer.[8]

On the other hand, other examples, and notably the Republic of Ireland and Portugal, suggest that with appropriate macroeconomic policies and institutional frameworks, such transfers can be beneficial to finance infrastructure improvements, including the educational and research infrastructures. However, in both of these cases it took several years before the Structural Funds were used efficiently. In Ireland the existence of inefficient semi-state bodies which assumed control of this spending meant considerable waste in the 1970s and early 1980s. It was only with the reform of these bodies and the development of economic policies which were better adjusted to creating a stable economic environment for the private sector that the real benefits of these transfers could be reaped.

The experience of the existing Structural Funds and a consideration of the fundamental requirements of the economies of the associated countries suggest certain modifications which could be considered in planning for enlargement. As in Ireland, it will take the associated countries some time to create the institutional establishment necessary to deal efficiently with such large transfers. It would make sense, therefore, to deal with the existing resources which are transferred to these countries as pre-accession Structural Funds. The PHARE programme represents only an extremely small proportion of the regions' GDP (roughly 0.2%), but if it was turned into a real Structural Fund and dealt with in a similar fashion to the Structural Funds in the Community, this would give an important fillip to the preparation for accession. In spite of the difficulties, this step makes good economic and administrative sense, and would lead to the Structural Funds being used more efficiently when the countries join the Community.

The pre-accession Structural Funds proposed in the 'Agenda 2000' package would provide an additional ECU1 billion for structural assistance and ECU500 million for agriculture. This would bring the Union grant assistance up to about 0.4% of the region's GDP. These rather limited funds should be compared to the estimates of an additional 4%–6% of GDP required for investment and operational costs annually in environmental protection, health and safety at work and other areas to meet the needs of the *acquis*.

A major constraint on Community thinking is the conviction in many governments inside the Union that macroeconomic and institutional policies in the associated countries are not adequate to avoid inefficiency

---

[8]  De Crombrugghe, Minton-Beddoes and Sachs (1996).

in the use of financial transfers. One way to overcome this problem would be to convert the Structural Funds transfers, during the transitional phase, into a major regional Cohesion Fund, which would have the aim of developing infrastructure and tackling environmental problems throughout the CEE region. Such a programme would include the financing of the Trans-European Networks (TENs), which are clearly in the interests of the existing Community of 15 as well as the associated countries, but also of regional and local infrastructure. In order to facilitate funding, the Cohesion Fund co-financing rules, whereby the Community can finance up to 85% of projects rather than around 50% in the Structural Funds, could be adopted, to reduce pressure on national budgets. EIB lending could be incorporated into the programme, as well as lending from the World Bank and the EBRD.

To prepare such a programme would be complex and would require that as a first step the PHARE programme should be used to develop the strategy, to create the necessary institutional basis and to begin certain parts of the work itself. This would be consistent with seeing PHARE as a pre-accession Structural Fund.

This strategy would have several advantages for both parties. For the associated countries:

- it would tackle one of the problems which will soon begin to hold back economic development – namely, inadequate infrastructure and inadequate maintenance of existing infrastructure
- it would reduce the overall level of budgetary funding required for a set programme of infrastructure development
- it would give an incentive to institutional development, which will be necessary in any case at the end of the transitional period
- it would create employment, often in regions which are lagging behind or undergoing economic restructuring – with all the impacts on employment which that process may have
- by tackling one of the major bottlenecks to development, it would have the impact of reinforcing the political and economic integration of Central Europe and the European Union through physical integration.

For the Union, such a system would:

- allow the Union to be involved in a much deeper way in the use of these funds than is the case in the present Structural Funds
- help the financing of trans-European networks, which are patently in the interests of the Community even though they are often presented as being a Central European priority; such networks are of considerable economic interest to the existing Member States

- reduce the worry that such funding would be lost in inefficiency, on the Greek model
- through open tendering for work, also benefit Community enterprises.

There would be many complications in working out such a programme, not least that some sort of allocation by country would have to be agreed if such a scheme were to be accepted by the Central Europeans.

## Conclusion

The problem of financing the Structural Funds would prove a major hindrance to enlargement if the current system with the current levels of financing were simply extended to the associated countries. But such a high level of transfers would also cause insuperable problems on the associated country side. The only reasonably acceptable solution would be to phase in the full Structural Funds integration of the associated countries over a five- or ten-year period. Already in the case of the New Bundesländer variable levels of Structural Funds attributions have been used. Naturally in the case of the associated countries, this would have to be compensated for by a reduction in the gross contribution of the associated countries to the own-resources of the Union. 'Agenda 2000' addresses these questions in a constructive way. The key questions will touch on the capacity of the new members to absorb Structural Funds and the ability of the Union to overcome resistance to graduating out existing beneficiary regions.

It will be important to ensure that the available resources are used efficiently throughout the enlarged Union. Efficient utilisation is as much about appropriate macroeconomic policy as about detailed implementation. Consideration should therefore be given to the surveillance of macroeconomic policies in countries in receipt of Structural Funds transfers.

# 11  Enlargement and the Community budget

One of the commonly held fallacies is that the major problem for enlargement on the side of the European Union is the impact on the budget. The previous chapters have shown that, while there will be a budgetary impact, the budget should not be the crucial factor in the decisions.

Nevertheless all Member States today consider the budgetary implications of enlargement to be important, and many are pushing these arguments to the fore. All Member States are keen to reduce their gross transfers to the Community in order to reduce government deficits. This is particularly the case for the net contributors to the Community budget, for whom net budget transfers to Brussels may become an important internal political problem. For the net beneficiaries from the Community budget, the most important objective is to make sure that the net level of transfers does not decline as a result of enlargement.

The Commission was asked by the Madrid European Council to produce a paper for the Council which would indicate the impacts of enlargement on the budget, in the context of the preparation of the new financial perspectives for the period after 1999. This paper was presented as part of the 'Agenda 2000' package in July 1997.

## The character of the Community budget

The budget of the European Union is unlike that of any normal nation state, in both its philosophy and its structure.

The Community budget was not conceived as a redistributionary tool but as a necessary instrument to achieve the objectives of the Rome Treaty. Any distributional impacts were considered to be of secondary importance. During the early years of the Community's existence, the budget was such a small part of Community GDP that the distributional impact was considered irrelevant by the Member States.

The revenue side of the budget in the early years of the Community was composed simply of fixed percentage levies on the Member States, with Germany, France and Italy each bearing 28% of total expenditure. It was only from the beginning of 1975 that the Community moved completely to an 'own-resources' basis, where the percentage levies on Member States were replaced by customs duties, agricultural levies and a small percentage (less than 1% point to start with) of Value Added Tax (VAT) proceeds in the Member States. Even at that time, the financing of the Community did not present any major political problem.

On the expenditure side, it was not until the 1970s that the one major expenditure policy, the CAP, began to consume resources in a significant way. In 1970, the total budget of the Communities was ECU2.4 billion, of which agricultural spending made up almost 90%. There was no attempt at progressive or regional redistribution through the expenditure side; only sectoral redistribution to agriculture took place. During the 1970s, however, expenditure on agriculture grew very rapidly, so that at the end of the decade the total budget had risen to ECU17 billion and the share of agriculture had increased six times over that of 1970, though its share of the total budget had fallen to 70%. It was in the 1980s that the Community budget exploded as agricultural spending continued to grow rapidly and for the first time the Community began to expand its redistributionary policies.

Regional policy did not figure in the original Treaty, and it was only in 1975 that the ERDF was set up. Even in the period 1975–84, total expenditure amounted to only around ECU1 billion per year. However, the second great period of European integration in the second half of the 1980s was accompanied by a very large increase in the Community budget, from ECU17 billion in 1980 to just over ECU80 billion. in 1997. While agricultural spending has continued to rise, its share in the budget has declined to 50% of total expenditure in 1997. There has, however, been a rapid rise in spending on redistributive programmes, as the Community expanded to include the Mediterranean countries.

The programme for the completion of the internal market launched in 1985 was thought to pose significant problems for the peripheral countries in the Community, which would potentially lose out to the centre through the economies of scale which would accrue there following restructuring. It was agreed to double the size of the Structural Funds over the period covered by the '1992' programme. With the Maastricht Treaty and the agreement on Monetary Union, yet another redistribution fund, the Cohesion Fund, was created at the beginning of 1994, which was to finance environmental and transport investments in the poorest countries of the Union. As a result of this decade of redistributional activity, appropriations for structural operations reached ECU26.6 billion in 1997 or 32% of the total Community budget. They will continue to rise sharply to the end of the decade.

The financing of this increased expenditure was achieved through an increase in the level of VAT transfers and the introduction of a new 'own-resource' which is progressive in that it is related to the GNP of the Member States. This new resource made up 29% of total revenues, with a further 52% coming from VAT. Today the Member States contribute just under 1.3% of their collective GDP to the Union's budget. In spite, therefore, of its enormous growth in the 1980s, the budget remains a relatively minor part of public spending in the Union.

The EU budget is an annual budget, which is agreed at the second reading in the European Parliament in December of the previous year. As expenditure rose with increased structural spending in the 1980s, the Community introduced a system of medium-term budgetary planning called the 'financial guideline'. This guideline covers a five-year period and gives upper limits for certain categories of expenditure over the medium term. The current financial guideline covers the period up to and including 1999, and obviously does not include any spending on enlargement. 'Agenda 2000' has made the first budgetary assumptions for the period 2000–6.

It has always been considered 'anti-*Communautaire*' to calculate the net contributions of Member States to the budget and any talk of a '*juste retour*' has been frowned on. This reflected a philosophy that put integration before finance and which regarded discussion of who finances what to be against the whole Community approach. Today, with the battle to reduce public spending being fought in all Member States, the subject is no longer taboo, though it still requires a great deal of research to arrive at reliable figures. Fortunately the Court of Auditors attempted this task in their annual report on the 1995 budget, published at the end of 1996.[1]

Table 11.1 shows the result of using the Court of Auditors' figures to calculate net receipts and payments. These figures result from an adjustment which is very rough. The Court's figures account for budgetary payments to Member States of ECU58.2 billion. It was able to allocate ECU68.3 billion of receipts from Member States. In order to arrive at the figures for gross and net receipts contained in the table, the gross receipts were adjusted downwards to ECU58.2 billion by a constant factor across all Member States. This is obviously a rough adjustment and may give very misleading results for outlier cases like

[1] European Union Court of Auditors (1996).

Table 11.1 *Net contributions of Member States to the Community budget, 1995 (ECU million)*

|  | Gross receipts | Gross payments | Net receipts | Receipts/head (ECU) |
|---|---|---|---|---|
| Belgium | 2,369 | 2,248 | 121 | 12 |
| Denmark | 1,601 | 1,064 | 537 | 103 |
| Germany | 7,893 | 17,762 | −9,869 | −122 |
| Greece | 4,474 | 883 | 3,591 | 351 |
| Spain | 10,863 | 2,918 | 7,945 | 205 |
| France | 10,150 | 10,217 | −67 | −1 |
| Ireland | 2,552 | 706 | 1,846 | 522 |
| Italy | 5,800 | 6,011 | −211 | −4 |
| Luxembourg | 123 | 141 | −18 | −45 |
| Netherlands | 2,345 | 3,529 | −1,184 | −78 |
| Austria | 858 | 1,591 | −733 | −93 |
| Portugal | 3,246 | 784 | 2,462 | 251 |
| Finland | 723 | 803 | −80 | −16 |
| Sweden | 721 | 1,448 | −727 | −84 |
| UK | 4,531 | 8,145 | −3,614 | −63 |
| Total EU | 58,248 | 58,250 | – | – |

*Source*: European Court of Auditors (1996).

Luxembourg. For most of the Member States, however, it gives a good approximation of the real situation in 1995. National sources for net transfers to the Union also tend to support this estimate.[2] It should be noted that in individual cases these figures can vary considerably from one budgetary year to another. Comparing 1994 and 1995, however, it is only the United Kingdom which experienced a serious change – a considerable increase in its net contribution.

The total receipts *per capita* of population indicate clearly there are five net contributors to the budget – Germany, Netherlands, Austria, Sweden and the United Kingdom. Of these Germany is the largest contributor. Belgium, Finland, France and Italy are practically neither beneficiaries nor contributors. The major net beneficiaries are the 'cohesion' countries, Portugal, Ireland, Spain and Greece, but Denmark is also a net beneficiary.

It should be noted that all of these numbers are relatively small in the context of the public sector finances of the Member States. Only for Ireland, Greece and possibly Luxembourg are the net receipts an important part of total public finance receipts. On the net contributor

[2] For example, Deutsche Bundesbank, *Zahlungsbilanz nach Regionen* (Frankfurt a. M., August 1996).

side, the net transfers to the Union make up only 2% of total German public sector expenditure. Nevertheless in the context of the German budget deficit in 1995, the net transfer to the Union amounted to around 20% of the deficit.

These figures illustrate the drama of the EU budget. In absolute terms, it is a small part of the total public sector financial flows in any one year, except for one or two net recipients. Nevertheless, when net flows are compared to the national public sector deficit, which is also a small number in relation to gross flows, they are seen to be significant. The consequence is that both for the net contributors and the net beneficiaries, the EU budget is an important element in the approach of the Member States to the Union and this is a major change from the situation in the first 20 years of the Community's life.

### The budget problem

That this rather limited EU budget gives rise to problems is a result of several factors:

- as Member States strive to reduce their public sector deficits to reach the Maastricht criteria for monetary union of 3% of GDP and their stock of public sector debt to below 60% of GDP, the small EU budgetary flows become significant
- as the popularity of the European Union declines in most Member States, the EU budget question has been raised by political parties searching for additional votes; the budget has therefore become a political problem nationally
- the very rapid expansion of the budget after 1980 has alarmed the net contributors, who fear that the EU budget is becoming a tool of redistribution at the EU level, which it was not intended to be, except on a temporary basis; they also tend to consider the budgetary mechanisms as too favourable to spending
- the potential loss of EU revenues worries the 'cohesion' countries where, although not a major source of revenues, they are nevertheless significant.

The struggle to reduce public borrowing to 3% of GDP and public debt to 60% of GDP is causing major problems in all countries except Luxembourg. In most cases the deficits in autumn 1997 are only slightly in excess of 3%. However, reducing deficits one percentage point takes an enormous effort in slow-growing economies. At present, this is particularly the case in Germany, the Netherlands and France, while the accumulated stock of public debt raises particular problems in Belgium.

Yet these countries are supposed to form the core of monetary union starting in 1999 and not one of them meets both these criteria. A halving in Germany's net contribution to the EU budget would reduce transfers by ECU5,000 million, or approximately 10% of the German public sector deficit or 0.3% of German GDP. In reducing the public sector deficit from an estimated 3.9% in 1996 to 3% in 1997, a saving of this order of magnitude would be extremely helpful. The same reasoning applies to the Netherlands, where the public sector deficit was estimated at 3.5% of GDP in 1996.

At the same time as being an entry criteria for EMU, Germany has proposed that if a country exceeds a deficit of over 3% after joining, it should be financially punished. Even if this proposal for a stability pact is not adopted in a strict form, there will be great pressure on members not to exceed this limit. The reticence of the net contributors to accept any increase in the Union's budget in the longer term is therefore also comprehensible.

That the budget has become a political issue is something attributed especially to the British position. However, while it is today less of an issue in that country, it has become a political issue in Germany and the Netherlands. These countries are determined not to increase their net contributions and to demand a better 'burden-sharing'. The latter argument essentially means that they want contributions to be shared out more fairly between the richer countries, with perhaps cuts in payments to the richest of the net recipients. These arguments are already creating political problems in these richer poor countries (for instance, in Ireland) which are not keen to lose transfers.

These various pressures are leading to a situation where Member States are demanding both no-increase annual budgets up to 1999 and a limit to the financial guideline after 1999 at a constant percentage of GDP.

### Enlargement and the budget

Most Member States thus fear that the enlargement of the Union will lead to additional expenditure. This results from two simple facts:

- roughly 80% of the EU budget is spent on agriculture and the Structural Funds; the associated countries are both poor and agricultural, and will therefore benefit from both these spending areas
- as poor countries, the new Member States will not contribute significantly to budgetary resources.

The possible implications for the EU budget in the particular areas of the Structural Funds and agriculture were discussed in chapters 9 and 10. The estimates given there permit maximum and minimum estimates of the impact of enlargement on the budget, at least as far as 80% of expenditure is concerned.

The extension of the CAP to the associated countries has attracted a range of estimates of additional costs from an annual addition of ECU3.9 billion up to ECU37.6 billion. The Commission estimate provided in its paper to the Madrid European Council at the end of 1995 suggested a figure of ECU12 billion annually in 2010. These estimates depend crucially on what assumption is made about the future reform of the CAP. The lowest estimate of ECU3.9 billion produced in the 'Agenda 2000' documents may turn out to be on the low side.

As far as the Structural Funds are concerned, estimates vary from zero as a proportion of GDP to over ECU30 billion in nominal terms. The figure of ECU30 billion (even higher on some estimates) would result from a full application of the present regime to the new Member States without any reduction for existing ones. The latest ideas of the European Commission in 'Agenda 2000' appear to favour the former, under which the Structural Funds in total would stay at a constant percentage of EU GDP (0.46%) over the period of the next financial guideline at least (i.e. until 2005). In real terms expenditure would then rise at the same rate as real GDP or probably around 2% per annum. While the constant percentage of GDP scenario may be slightly ambitious as far as budgetary parsimony is concerned, it is almost certainly more realistic than a scenario which simply projects today's system unchanged into the future.

On the assumption that enlargement were to take place in the year 2000, the Commission's assumption would allow a real increase in the Structural Funds of between 10% and 15% in the period up to 2005. This would imply an increase in total budget spending in year 2005 over 1999 of between ECU3billion and ECU4.5 billion in 1992 prices or, assuming an annual average rate of inflation of 3% between 1993 and 2005, of between ECU10 billion and ECU12 billion. However this will not be the real cost of enlargement because during this five-year period certain regions in the existing Member States will be graduated out, allowing a somewhat larger flow of funds to reach the new Member States by 2005. It might be assumed that the more likely budgetary implication for the Structural Funds of enlargement to all the associated countries would be slightly higher than this, as it is unlikely that such a strict budgetary line will in reality be taken. By 2005, it is therefore likely that nominal budgetary expenditures on the

Structural Funds will have risen by ECU 10–12 billion annually above that in 1999.[3]

The third element, the contribution of the new Member States, depends crucially on whether or not these countries are treated in the same way as existing Member States. It is unrealistic to suppose that, if there is a long transition period before full benefit of the Structural Funds is drawn, the new Member States will pay full contributions to the EU budget. The normal gross contribution of the associated countries to own-resources in the year 2000 can be estimated at ECU4–5billion. This may have risen to a maximum of ECU7.5 billion in 2005. This gross contribution, even if paid in whole, will be more than offset by the increase of ECU20–25 billion in spending likely to occur because of enlargement between 1999 and 2005. This would imply that enlargement is likely to lead to an increase in the Community budget of between one-quarter and one-third between 1999 and 2005 year on year. This estimate is of the same order as that of a French study of the financial consequences of enlargement and of the recent study by Baldwin, Francois and Portes.[4]

On the other hand, accelerated growth and structural change in the associated countries will with time reduce the budgetary burden on the other Member States considerably.[5] St Aubin (1995b) calculated with a simple model that the likely additional 'cost' of enlargement to the six largest associated countries would have been of the order of 25–30% if enlargement had taken place in 1992. He then calculated that, assuming an annual average growth rate of 6% per annum in the associated countries and 2% in the Union as well as some structural change (fewer people in agriculture, for instance), this additional cost would be reduced to around 15% by 2010. This would be around the same level of budgetary increase that the existing Member States agreed to in 1990 for the four cohesion countries.

Such rough calculations are important because governments should know whether enlargement is going to lead to a budget increase of 30% or 300%. However, the real answer to the question of how much enlargement will cost the existing Member States is far more complex than these back of the envelope calculations. It will depend amongst other things on:

- the economic growth rates of the existing Community and

[3] In a speech to the German Bundestag (19 June 1996), the Commissioner responsible for the Structural Funds suggested that transfers to the new Member States would reach only ECU7 billion per annum from 2000 to 2006.

[4] Delegation du Senat Français pour l'Union Européenne (1996); Baldwin, Francois and Portes (1997), pp. 125–76.

[5] Saint Aubin (1995b).

those of the new Member States between now and 2005 and the movement of real exchange rates

- changes in world agricultural supplies and prices
- the outcome of the next round of WTO negotiations
- the outcome of the continuing discussions on the future European architecture and the future financing of the Union.

It will, of course, above all depend on the extent to which Community policies are reformed and the outcome of the accession negotiations. It is for this reason that the Madrid European Council asked the Commission to produce a paper on the budgetary implications of enlargement for the new financial guideline 2000–6 and why the estimates of 'Agenda 2000' are so important.

But as the previously cited study of the French Senate points out, the budgetary cost of enlargement is only one part of the financial calculation of the effects of enlargement.[6] The result of enlargement, according to this study, is that it provides a major boost to output and therefore to taxes in the new Member States, but that it also leads to measurable output growth in the existing Community with a growth in tax revenues in excess of the likely cost to the EU budget. This result is supported by the Baldwin, Francois and Portes study.

### 'Agenda 2000' and the financial perspectives, 2000–6

In the Commission's 'Agenda 2000' proposals, the key to the financing period 2000–6 is given by the calculations for the CAP and the Structural Funds, together with the assumption that own-resources will not grow beyond 1.27% of GDP. It is assumed that spending on all other policies of the Union will grow at the same rate as nominal GDP. On these assumptions, actual spending will still be below the own-resources limit of 1.27% of GDP in 2006 (estimate is 1.22%) and as a percentage of GDP below its level today. The Commission does not recommend any change in the system used to finance the Community budget (which will not please the Germans and the Dutch) but does hint that the British 'rebate' might be put into question at the end of the period.

For the new Member States, given that the Commission proposes transition periods for both agriculture and the Structural Funds, it should be considered whether there should be a transitional period for own-resources' contributions from these new members. Nevertheless, from the figures presented by the Commission, it is clear that the new

[6] Delegation du Senat Français (1996), article by S. Cazes, B. Coquet and F. Lerais, 'Integrer les pays de l'Est à l'Union Europeenne? Une approche macroeconomique'.

members will be net beneficiaries from the Union budget on accession, and increasingly so up to 2006.

It is important to keep in mind that the budgetary cost (public and private sectors) for the associated countries of adopting the Community *acquis* will be extremely high. The World Bank suggests that the additional investment cost simply for the environmental *acquis* is likely to be up to 2% of GDP over a period of 15 years. Recent estimates in a study done for the Commission suggest that this could be on the low side.[7] The same study points to the additional operating costs in the environment area possibly being even higher in terms of share of GDP. Other areas of the *acquis* such as health and safety at work, the specific sectoral directives in areas like chemicals and the food industry and further measures in the agricultural *acquis* will require considerable investment. If the need to rapidly develop the physical infrastructure is also included, the financial strains on these economies will be very serious.

In these circumstances, it is important that the associated countries should benefit from the Community budget in a significant way. It is surely true that other factors such as following responsible macroeconomic policies and raising the domestic savings rate are more important, and that without them budgetary transfers from the Union will be wasted. However, given a responsible policy, high levels of transfer in the early years of membership would be important to fund infrastructure developments throughout the economy.

### The political economy of the EU budget

Budgetary issues will not stop enlargement, though they will be the subject of difficult negotiations between the existing Member States. Unfortunately, politicians will not necessarily want to understand that enlargement, while increasing the size of the EU budget, increases even more the capacity of the Community to support that larger expenditure. They will at times want to concentrate the minds of their partners and their voters on the simple budget cost of enlargement.

The countries inside the European Union which stand to gain most from enlargement are also generally the net contributors to the budget, while the net recipients in the cohesion countries are unlikely to be affected in a major way economically. This situation will give the cohesion countries considerable power in the discussions on enlargement to at least defend the current level of redistribution in the Union, though Ireland, given its very good macroeconomic performance over many years, will find this more difficult to achieve than the others.

[7] EDC (1997).

The five major net contributors will find the budgetary discussion difficult just because they are the main 'beneficiaries' (in a very narrow sense) from enlargement. Germany, Austria, Sweden and the Netherlands will no doubt attempt to argue that the burden-sharing in the Union is unfair and should be redistributed. This is clearly the case, and under a 'fair' system of burden-sharing Denmark and France would contribute more to the budget and Germany less. However, this argument leads smoothly over into regarding the Union budget as a redistribution mechanism, which the net contributors have never wanted to admit. The German negotiating position, in real rather than moral terms, will be very difficult and probably the best that can be hoped for by them is that their net contribution will remain constant in real terms.

The budgetary issue will also be affected by the economic situation in the Member States as accession negotiations proceed. If a recovery in economic growth reduces government deficits in the medium term, transfers to the Union budget will be easier to meet while respecting the Maastricht Monetary Union criteria. If the start of EMU was to be delayed because too few countries met the Maastricht criteria, the budgetary situation of enlargement will probably become even more difficult. If EMU were to be scrapped, there might be some relaxation of the efforts to reach these criteria, but it would be unreal to imagine that governments would not still continue to keep their public deficits under control. And a failure of EMU might create such a destabilising influence in the Union that the whole enlargement process might be put on ice.

### Conclusion

There will be numerous studies in the coming years of the impact of enlargement on the budget. All of them will have considerable margins of error because of the unknowns, such as future policy changes and world prices as well as the assumptions about the outcome of the accession negotiations. All of them will play some role in the position governments in West and Central Europe take on the enlargement issue.

But the budget is not likely to be the decisive issue in the enlargement debate that many think, for six main reasons:

- the size of the Union budget is still very limited at under 1.3% of Union GDP
- enlargement will probably take place in waves, with the first wave being restricted to the perhaps five or six countries as proposed by the Commission, leading to the full budgetary

impact of enlargement to ten countries being spread over many years

- in certain areas there are likely to be transitional periods during which transfers to the new Member States increase annually from a low base; under these circumstances, it should even be possible to hold the budget at a constant percentage of Union GDP in real terms over the period 2000–6
- those countries which have the greatest interest in enlargement will in the end probably be prepared to increase contributions somewhat to allow it to happen
- the associated countries need accession, and will probably be prepared to negotiate a short-term budgetary agreement which leads to them receiving rather less than they would otherwise get, at least for a short transitional period
- because the net gain to the Union of enlargement is far greater than the potential additional budget cost.

# 12 The future European architecture: the Amsterdam Treaty and enlargement

## Introduction

The current European Union is clearly not the same as 'Europe' or even as 'Western Europe'. The Union is a stage on the road to a political and economic system in Europe which will be very different from that which existed from the end of the Second World War until 1989. The cliché 'the new European architecture' suggests that this process of political and economic change in Europe will lead to some new and relatively stable equilibrium. This is not necessarily the case. Indeed, the likelihood that Europe will descend into an unstable and rapidly changing set of alliances and economic relationships has probably increased in the 1990s. Nevertheless, the term 'the new European architecture' is a convenient way to refer to the whole complex web of relationships between different European states, the various levels of political and economic integration on the Continent and the economic and political geography of post-1989 Europe.

Behind the vague concept of 'the new European architecture' lies the hard detail of the organisation of European integration, the way in which the Community will in future make its decisions, the representation of the Member States in the European institutions, the democratic nature of the Union, its economic development and trade policy. Many of these issues were on the agenda of the IGC which ended in June 1997. The outcome of these discussions about concrete problems concerning the powers of the Union, its efficiency and effectiveness and its democratic nature were reflected in the conclusions of the Amsterdam European Council in June 1997 and in the new Amsterdam Treaty. While the legal base of the IGC in article N of the Maastricht Treaty does not mention the enlargement of the Union, this was to be one of the main subjects of the Conference. A major question is whether the Amsterdam Treaty creates the conditions under which enlargement can take place.[1]

---

[1] European Council (1997); European Policy Centre (1997).

This chapter reviews both the general aspects of different European architectures as well as the detail of the integration of the associated countries into the Institutions and working procedures of the European Union.

## The future European architecture

Until 1989, questions of geopolitics had gone completely out of fashion in Europe. The European architecture was clear and constant: Western Europe, defended by the NATO alliance and gradually integrating economically in the European Community stood opposite and against the Soviet Empire controlled from Moscow and stretching from the Elbe to the Barents Sea and from Murmansk to the Black Sea. The scope for the expansion of either bloc was extremely limited in the shadow of the nuclear deterrent.

The changes which have taken place since 1989 have led, in the first stage at least, to the break-up of the Soviet empire and the freeing of the states of Central Europe from Soviet occupation. The result has been, of course, that the former satellite countries of Central Europe, having regained their freedom, have looked for their place in the European Union. The ten associated countries which have Agreements with the European Union and all of which have applied for membership do not, however, form the Eastern limits of Europe. Russia, the Ukraine, Belarus and Moldova are also clearly European and must be considered in any new geopolitical map of Europe.[2]

At the same time that the limits of democratic Europe were being pushed eastwards, clear differences appeared within the European Union itself over the degree of political and economic integration desired by the West European countries. Looked at in terms of political will and economic ability, a small group of countries at the heart of the European Union separated themselves out as being enthusiastic integrationists; this group is essentially made up of Germany and the Benelux countries, supported by France in many, but not in all, policy areas. Other countries appear enthusiastic about integration but find the economic discipline rather hard to accept; Italy could be included in this group. The Nordic countries, while being relatively enthusiastic about certain aspects of European integration remain sceptical about letting key decisions affecting the individual be taken in Brussels, clearly preferring their long-established direct and local democratic systems.

[2] Emerson (1996).

Finally, the United Kingdom appears today far more positive towards the European Union than in recent years, but is still mainly interested in the Internal Market and trade issues rather than political integration. Switzerland and Norway have spurned integration completely.

Both the freeing of Central and Eastern Europe and the differentiation of the Member States of the Union have allowed politicians to speculate on the new geopolitics of the Continent and the future nature of European integration.

### Architecture and geography

For many commentators, geography plays a vital role. The concepts of the centre and the periphery are understood by such commentators as geographical concepts. The proposals made by Prime Minister Balladur in France and similar ones by Minister Lamers in Germany conceive of Europe consisting of a series of concentric circles, with those countries in the innermost circle having the highest degree of integration while the outer circle containing Russia and the Ukraine, and possibly some of the countries of Central Europe, would be linked to the core essentially through FTAs or Association Agreements.

Geography certainly plays an important role in both the thinking about future possible organisation in Europe, but also in economic relations, which are usually closest between neighbours – for instance, between the Netherlands and Germany and between Spain and France. However, the concept of core and periphery is not very clear. The core to which the majority of commentators refer in the context of the European Union is that of France, Germany and the Benelux. These countries obviously have the longest tradition of cooperation in post-war Europe and the Franco-German tandem was always the motor of integration in the Union. The periphery then consists of countries such as Greece, Portugal and Ireland. Two remarks are, however, needed to qualify this judgement – firstly there are other potential cores in Europe and secondly there are other concepts of European integration which make the core weaker than it is generally thought to be and, if geography is left aside, suggest that some of the peripheral countries actually belong to the core.

That other cores are possible does not have to be proved, it is visible from the briefest view of European history. Perhaps the most obvious is a German-dominated core to which the Benelux countries, the Nordics and the CEE countries and Austria belong. Such a core of countries would have special arrangements with Russia and the Ukraine and with the former partners in the Union to the West. Such a geopolitical arrangement is certainly not desired in Central Europe and above all not in Germany, but it could slowly evolve if integration in the current Union stops or if there is a major problem on the road to enlargement of the Union.

If one lays aside pure geography, then other countries may well belong to the core in terms of policy and performance even though they geographically are on the periphery of the present Union. Ireland is perhaps a case in point. Ireland has followed a disciplined macroeconomic policy and favours a deeper integration within the Union. However, there are other perhaps equally persuasive types of integration in Europe than that followed by the core countries today, which may appeal to the populations in the core countries themselves and might change the whole concept. For instance, radical changes in the concept of democratic control in the Union might bring the Nordic countries firmly into the core.

Integration requires both a willingness and a capacity to integrate politically and economically in the Union. These two characteristics appear to be present in the core countries of the Union today. The willingness is crucial; it is based on shared values and an openness to the influence of other partners. Switzerland certainly has the capacity to integrate successfully with the Union, including in a monetary union, but the willingness to contemplate deeper integration appears, at the time of writing, to be absent. The Central Europeans appear at the moment to be willing to integrate but in some cases their capacity to do so is in doubt. But changes to the concept of integration can alter both the willingness of countries to join the core and their capacity to do so.

At the extreme, there are some commentators who point out that real integration can take place only between partners with the same values and traditions. The work of Professor Huntington has suggested for instance that Europe is split between two civilisations, which are divided fundamentally by religion, tradition and experience and are therefore unreconcilable.[3] He maintains that the line dividing the area of Western Christianity from that of Orthodox Christianity running from the Eastern border of Finland and the Baltic countries, through the Western parts of Belarus, Ukraine and Romania and swinging round to end in Bosnia is such a fundamental dividing line. Such a theory, if true, would have fundamental implications not only for enlargement but also for the current European Union, which straddles this line.

The difficulty with such geopolitical broad brush approaches is that

[3] Huntington (1993), pp. 22–49.

they are an easy way out of thinking deeply and in detail about concrete political and economic problems which face Europe today. While the Huntington thesis or the core–periphery concept may appear attractive because of their simplicity and apparent congruence with most people's understanding of recent history, they say nothing about what we should be striving for as an ideal relationship between peoples in Europe, nor do they consider the detail of continuously evolving economic and political relationships.

## Systems of European integration

Somewhat more detailed and concrete notions have been developed to discuss the different forms of integration which may evolve in the coming years, taking account of the desires of current and future members, the heterogeneity of their economic and political systems and traditions and the organisational constraints in such a multinational construction.

### United States of Europe

The further development of the ideas of the integrationist Member States would lead to a sort of *United States of Europe* sometimes referred to as a 'European Super-State'. The key characteristic of such a concept is that all Member States have to accept all the policies of the Union. With the present lack of a clear definition of the policy areas reserved for the Union and a high degree of policy activism, this would lead to an important increase in decisions taken at the centre. This is more or less the continuation of the present system of integration, which has, however, begun to create major problems as the number of members grows. It is difficult to imagine such a tight form of integration in a Community of 20–25 after enlargement. This is indeed the reason that the main supporters of a federal state in Europe are very reserved about enlargement of the Union, which they see as diluting the chance of creating a truly integrated United States of Europe. In an ideal world, there are indeed many advantages of creating a federal state in Europe: for instance, it avoids any problems with externalities which occur when not all members participate in all policies. It appears however that as a system for integrating the whole or a large part of Europe, total integration can no longer be considered in the short term, a fact clearly demonstrated by the universal acceptance that monetary union can take place only between a sub-set of members of the Union, at least in the first instance.

### Multispeed Europe

A variation on the United States of Europe model is that of a *multispeed Europe*, in which the ultimate objective remains total integration, but where individual Member States enjoy long transition periods. Again, this system already exists – for instance, in the plans for monetary union, where those countries which cannot join in 1999 can join at a later date. A multispeed Europe does not, however, satisfy the needs of an increasingly heterogeneous Union, where it is not only the speed of adjustment to common policies which is the problem, but also the fact that certain policies which appeal to one sub-set of countries are rejected by another.

### Variable geometry

The idea of the *variable geometry* models of integration which have been proposed is that levels of integration can be different in the different parts of the Community. These models encompass the core–periphery models of Lamers and Balladur. The different forms can be simple concentric circles with the highest degree of integration at the core or overlapping groups of Member States in different policy areas. While these models have the advantage of being flexible and trying to take account of different policy interests of different Member States, they suffer from certain rigidities and the fact that they clearly create groups of countries, classified by their different levels of integration. In the concentric circle model, it will be difficult for a country to move from the periphery to the core; indeed it could almost be like an accession negotiation for a non-member of the Union today.

### Flexible integration

In order to overcome these problems, a system of *flexible integration* has been put forward.[4] This system would have a series of basic core policies to which all members of the Union would have to sign up, but beyond this core, other policies would exist as a set of open partnerships to which Member States could, but would not have to, belong. Such a system, discussed in the IGC and reflected in the Amsterdam Treaty, could facilitate the accession of the associated countries in Central Europe and will therefore be discussed in more detail later.

[4] Dewatripont *et al.* (1995).

*Europe à la carte*

These different approaches to integration in Europe are important for the discussion of accession. A totally integrated United States of Europe might indeed be difficult for the associated countries to join in the short term, although this is what many of the countries aspire to. On the other hand, the associated countries will need to join the basic policies of the Union, without which they will not be considered real members of the Union and will be open to negative measures being taken against them by the inner core of Member States in emergency situations. They are, however, unlikely to be interested in a *Europe à la carte*, where each Member State freely chooses which policies it wishes to belong to without there being any real core of policies to which all members belong. This would not be considered as providing the sort of security and economic guarantees which the associated countries are looking for from the European Union.

Whatever the outcome of this discussion proves to be over the coming decade, it will not be approached in these still rather general terms. The organisational structure of the Union will grow from the result of numerous detailed negotiations, many of which started in the context of the IGC and will continue over the coming years.

## The Inter-Governmental Conference and the Amsterdam Treaty

The IGC had three areas on which it was to concentrate: the internal operation of the Union, the development of the Union's foreign and security policies and enlargement. The resulting Amsterdam Treaty reflects these areas, though in a different structure. The Treaty contains the following parts:

- freedom, security and justice
- the Union and the citizen
- the CSFP
- the Union's institutions
- flexibility
- simplification and consolidation of the Treaties.

It is immediately obvious that there is no specific treatment of enlargement, though it is mentioned in various parts of the new Treaty.

The consideration of these questions is organised around the original three-subject agenda established by the Westendorp Group which prepared the IGC.

*Internal reform*

Internal reform of the Union is certainly necessary and was considered by most participants to be the crucial area where progress had to be made if the IGC was to be called a success. The majority of the problems were related to two main themes: the democratic deficit of the Union and the efficiency and effectiveness of its institutions and its decision-making and working procedures.

*European values and the democratic deficit*

The Westendorp Group, set up to make a preliminary study of the agenda of the IGC, summarised this area as 'making Europe more relevant to its citizens'.[5] There were two related problems, both of which are important to the associated countries. One, which Westendorp referred to as 'promoting European values', concerned the basic rights of the citizen in the Union. The second dealt with the crucial point of democratic representation in the Union, and whether democracy is top-down or bottom-up.

Promoting European values consists of laying out in a formal way the rights of the citizen in the Union; in some people's view this is equivalent to establishing a bill of rights for the individual. The absolute protection of human rights and the privileging of the rights of the individual over the rights of society is fundamental to the way a society is organised and how government administrations deal with citizens. The new article F of the Amsterdam Treaty, which allows for the suspension of a Member State which transgresses in these fundamental areas, forms a real bulwark against the anti-democratic influences which occasionally still exist in some of the associated countries. The new importance given to the question of human rights could also positively affect the situation in countries in the region with unresolved minority problems.

The democratic legitimacy of the Union has clearly not been established with the citizens of the Union. This was shown most clearly by the reaction of voters in the referenda on the Maastricht Treaty, by the falling approval ratings for the Union in the regular opinion polls and by the lack of enthusiasm shown in elections to the European Parliament. The Amsterdam Treaty has done relatively little to improve this situation.

Much of the discussion around the question of the democratic deficit centred on the question of subsidiarity – that is, the level at which policy

---

[5] Westendorp (1995).

decisions should be made in the Union and the Member States. The idea of subsidiarity is used to justify both increasing centralisation of decision-making and increased decentralisation. Without some almost quantified definition it is impossible to turn the concept into a working tool. Probably a safer and more traditional approach to the question is to establish clear lists of policy areas attributed to international bodies, to the Union, the Member State and the regions.[6] Although this is no easy task, once done it does prevent encroachment by one level of government on the prerogatives of others. In such a system it must be possible to change the attributions of power, but such changes would be made difficult to achieve and only through the democratic process. This proposal, however, was rejected in the report of the Westendorp Committee, which preferred to retain article 235 of the treaty, the article which has always been used to extend the responsibilities of the Union. The Amsterdam Treaty, while containing a Protocol on subsidiarity, does not make any clear advance in this area.

*Efficiency and effectiveness of the Union and its institutions*
The main concern of those countries which are opposed to enlargement is that increasing the size of the Union beyond 15 will mean that it ceases to be an efficient decision-making body and therefore the process of European integration will stall. Some of them point out that every enlargement beyond the original six members has led to greater problems of decision-making. For some countries, such as Belgium, for which European integration is a basic necessity of life, such opposition to enlargement can be overcome only if a fundamental step towards indissoluble European union (for instance, monetary union) is taken first. For the others, it is more a question of doubting whether the Union has the capacity to reform the existing institutions adequately before the final decisions on enlargement are taken. But all Member States agree that the existing institutional set-up is inadequate to cope with the additional strains of enlargement.

Efficiency is measured by the efficiency of the Union in decision-making and in the implementation of those policies where there is Community competence. These two considerations, however, immediately open the question of the relationship between the institutions of the Union and their relative roles and powers, and the relationship between the Member States of the Union and their representation in these institutions.

---

[6] See, for instance, Dewatripont *et al.*(1995) and European Constitutional Group (1993).

*Powers of the European Council, the European Parliament and the Commission*

The power of decision in the Union rests essentially with the Council of Ministers, and the Amsterdam Treaty does nothing to change this. The powers of the European Parliament were increased through the introduction of the co-decision procedure at Maastricht and have been increased again at Amsterdam through the extension of the co-decision procedure. The division of powers is, however, an issue which is unlikely to raise many additional problems for enlargement and where the associated countries are unlikely to feel strongly in one way or another.

Far more important for the associated countries was the question of whether the European Parliament should be changed to reflect better the views of the very diverse regions in the Union or, indeed, whether a second chamber representing the regions might not be established. With enlargement, the Union will become a very much more diverse construction, where it will become more difficult for all the regions of the Union to make their opinions heard. Little progress was made here, however, although the role of the national Parliaments in Union affairs was strengthened.

While Amsterdam changes little in the role of the Commission, it does indicate that eventually each Member State will have only one Commissioner. If full enlargement took place on an unchanged basis, their number would rise to 33.

The fact that Amsterdam decided to limit the number of Commissioners to 20, and, subject to agreement on voting in the Council, to limit each country to one, suggests that it expects the next enlargement to contain no more than five countries, each with its own Commissioner. For the associated countries joining the European Union, this is an important point, for the idea of not being represented at the level of Commissioner might be difficult to accept just at a time when they are being asked to pool their new-won sovereignty.

*Efficiency in decision-making*

The ability of the EU institutions to make decisions rapidly but transparently in a democratic environment is crucial to their long-term survival. The inability of Amsterdam to agree to reform current decision-making procedures means that enlargement will be made more difficult because of the fear of a snarl-up in decision-making.

The most serious problem is that of the system of voting in the Council. Even after the modest extension of qualified majority voting decided at Amsterdam many areas still require unanimity in decision-making. This not only includes areas like the admission of new members or the conclusion of international treaties but also questions of establishment and indirect taxation, financial provisions (budgetary resources) and the nomination of the President of the Commission. As the number of members of the Union grows and as the members become more diverse, it will logically become more difficult to achieve unanimity in the Council. The obvious solution would be to extend the areas where majority voting can be applied, but Amsterdam was fairly restrictive here. However, it is not by chance that these areas have been left to unanimous decision. Three examples can be taken to illustrate the dilemma. If the Union wished to negotiate a treaty with Turkey, without unanimity there would be nothing which Greece alone could do to influence it, even though it considered its vital interests threatened. Secondly, fiscal harmonisation and the introduction of a common withholding tax could seriously weaken the Luxembourg economy but without the national veto would certainly be adopted by the other Member States. Thirdly, in a situation where the bulk of net contributions to the Community budget come from just a few Member States (Germany, the Netherlands, the United Kingdom), an extension of majority voting to issues of own-resources could mean that a qualified majority of poorer states could vote themselves increases in budgetary resources irrespective of the wishes of the net contributors unless this area remains one where unanimity is required. Such examples show the difficulty of extending qualified majority voting, but the question must be considered again in the light of enlargement.

The discussion of voting rights in the Council is usually one part of the discussion of the relative power of the large countries and the small countries in the Union. Small countries have always been over-represented in all the Institutions of the Union. This is clearly seen in the distribution of votes in the Council and seats in the European Parliament shown in table 12.1.[7] This table shows that Germany with over 80 million people has 10 votes in the Council whereas Luxembourg with 400,000 people has 2. Thus whereas in Luxembourg only 200,000 people are required for a vote in the Council, in Germany this same relationship is 1:8,100,000. In other words, in relation to Germany, each Luxembourger is 40 times over-represented. In the European Parliament, the distortion is much less, being of the order of 1:8.

However, the voting weights are only one part of the problem. With many issues agreed by qualified majority voting, the size of the qualified majority and, as importantly, the blocking minority are vital. The qualified majority is 62 votes out of the total of 87 and the blocking

---

[7] Taken in slightly amended form from Kirman and Widgrén (1995), pp. 421–60.

Table 12.1 *Projected seats and votes in the Council of Ministers and the European Parliament*

| Country | Population (million) | Votes in the Council | Population/ vote | Seats in Parliament | Population/ seat |
|---|---|---|---|---|---|
| Germany | 80.6 | 10 | 8.1 | 99 | 0.8 |
| UK | 58.0 | 10 | 5.8 | 87 | 0.7 |
| France | 57.5 | 10 | 5.8 | 87 | 0.7 |
| Italy | 56.9 | 10 | 5.7 | 87 | 0.7 |
| Spain | 39.1 | 8 | 4.9 | 64 | 0.6 |
| Neth. | 15.2 | 5 | 3.0 | 31 | 0.5 |
| Greece | 10.3 | 5 | 2.1 | 25 | 0.4 |
| Belgium | 10.1 | 5 | 2.0 | 25 | 0.4 |
| Portugal | 9.9 | 5 | 2.0 | 25 | 0.4 |
| Sweden | 8.7 | 4 | 2.2 | 22 | 0.4 |
| Austria | 7.9 | 4 | 2.0 | 21 | 0.4 |
| Denmark | 5.2 | 3 | 1.7 | 16 | 0.3 |
| Finland | 5.1 | 3 | 1.7 | 16 | 0.3 |
| Ireland | 3.6 | 3 | 1.3 | 15 | 0.2 |
| Lux. | 0.4 | 2 | 0.2 | 6 | 0.1 |
| EU-15 | 368.5 | 87 | 4.2 | 626 | 0.6 |
| Poland | 38.4 | 8 | 4.8 | 60 | 0.6 |
| Hungary | 10.3 | 5 | 2.1 | 25 | 0.4 |
| Czech Rep. | 10.0 | 5 | 2.0 | 25 | 0.4 |
| Slovakia | 5.3 | 4 | 1.3 | 18 | 0.3 |
| Slovenia | 2.0 | 3 | 0.7 | 10 | 0.2 |
| CEFTA | 66.0 | 25 | 2.7 | 138 | 0.5 |
| Romania | 22.7 | 6 | 3.8 | 44 | 0.5 |
| Bulgaria | 9.0 | 4 | 2.3 | 23 | 0.4 |
| Lithuania | 3.7 | 3 | 1.2 | 15 | 0.2 |
| Latvia | 2.6 | 3 | 0.9 | 12 | 0.2 |
| Estonia | 1.5 | 2 | 0.8 | 9 | 0.2 |
| CEEC-10 | 105.9 | 43 | 2.5 | 241 | 0.4 |

*Source*: Kirman and Widgrén (1995).

minority which can stop any measure being agreed is therefore 26. Thus countries representing a very large majority of the population of the Community can be prevented from deciding a measure by a blocking minority of a few small states. Alternatively, a measure supported by the vast majority of countries in the Union can be blocked by a coalition of only three or four countries. Examples, for instance, would be:

- a measure supported by all Member States except Luxembourg, Ireland, Finland, Austria, Sweden, Portugal and Belgium would not be agreed because these countries would be able to block the measure with 26 votes; these seven countries, however, represent only 45.7 million citizens, or 12% of the total population of the Union

- a measure supported by all countries except France, Italy and the Netherlands could not pass as these three countries have 29 votes in the Council, enough for a blocking minority.

Three other factors should also be considered which makes the decision-making situation even more complex:

- The Presidency of the Council always makes an attempt to get unanimous votes even when a qualified majority is sufficient. This is a positive element in the way the Community has operated, but which becomes, of course, harder to maintain as it grows in size. This tends to enhance the power of the individual Member State and enlarges the scope for trade-offs to operate.
- The Commission, while not having a vote in Council, very often intervenes to support the small Member States. This is not a rule but a simple observation. The logic, however, is simple. As the small Member States, at least until the most recent enlargement, tended to be the most enthusiastic about integration (Belgium, Netherlands, Luxembourg, Ireland), and not opposed to the centralisation of power in Brussels, they had similar objectives to those of the Commission.
- The existence of the national veto in certain areas and the Luxembourg compromise in areas of vital national interest gives rise to the possibility of trade-offs affecting all areas. A country can link problems which are totally independent in substance. It may agree to a proposal, in which it may have no interest, but which requires unanimity, only if its partners agree to another proposal in which it does have an interest. Member States have perfected this instrument of torture; the customs union with Turkey was agreed to by Greece only when the other 14 countries agreed to solemnly declare that they would open negotiations for membership of the Community with Cyprus six months after the end of the IGC. Such linking of questions gives enormous power to small Member States and threatens the whole decision-making process in the Union.

The enlargement to the ten associated countries obviously threatens paralysis in decision-making unless changes are agreed to in these procedures. Table 12.1 shows that if the present system of allocating votes in the Council is maintained the total number of votes will be 130, and if the blocking minority remains at roughly 30%, it will rise to 39 votes. Of the ten new Member States eight are small countries, with Romania an in-between size at 23 million. If we nevertheless count Romania in with the small countries, this gives the following interesting situations:

- there will only be six large countries in the Community of 25 states
- these six large countries will contain 70% of the population of the Community
- the ten new Member States from Central Europe will form a blocking minority and be able to block all measures in the Council
- the 'cohesion countries' (Spain, Ireland, Greece and Portugal) together with the new members will control 64 votes in the Council, almost exactly half of the votes, with 36% of the Union's population
- in those areas of policy where unanimity is still required it will be much more difficult to achieve with up to 12 new members, some of which have totally different backgrounds and political and economic systems to those of the EU-15; bearing in mind what was said above, this gives increased scope for trade-offs to block progress in the Union.

The problem of voting rights in the Council is one of the most difficult to solve in the context of enlargement, but also in the context of increasing the degree of democracy in the Union. There has always been a willingness on the part of the larger Member States to tolerate an over-representation of the smaller ones in Community institutions. This has also been the case in the staffing of the Community institutions – where, for instance, at high levels in the civil service Belgium, Luxembourg, Ireland or Portugal are over-represented compared to the United Kingdom or Germany. It would be quite difficult to show that this had negatively affected the capacity of the Union to make crucial decisions, or even that it has slowed up the pace of decision-making. There have been *causes célèbres* such as Luxembourg's opposition to a Community-wide withholding tax, but individual large countries have been just as obstructive.

Extremely worrying for the net contributors to the budget of the Union is the fact that they are already few in number and will be completely outnumbered by the arrival of more net recipients on enlargement.[8] Table 11.1 showed the approximate position of the 15

---

[8] Though some net beneficiaries today may be tomorrow's net contributors.

Member States in 1995 in terms of net budget receipts. In 1995, there were six net contributors to the budget – Germany, the Netherlands, Sweden, Finland, Austria and the United Kingdom.

One of the ideas to make voting in the Council more democratic is to effectively have two votes, one on a modified version of the present system, the other being a weighted vote according to population. In this way, a qualified majority vote would need to be also backed by a majority of the population, as expressed by the votes of the Member States weighted by their populations. An alternative would simply be to re-scale the votes in the Council, reducing but not eliminating the advantage of the small countries. Neither of these solutions would overcome the reserves of the net contributors to the Community, who will demand that own-resources continue to be decided by unanimity.

If enlargement is to take place, and to include all the associated countries, it will almost certainly be necessary to undertake some re-weighting of votes in the Council in favour of the larger countries and to extend majority voting. The fact that there was no agreement on changing the voting system in the Council at Amsterdam and that a further decision has been put off until the first new enlargement suggests several important conclusions for the enlargement process:

- limiting the Commission to 20 members, with one Commissioner per country (which is only agreed subject to an agreement on voting in the Council) suggests that the first wave of accession will include a maximum of five new countries
- this does suggest that the Union is prepared to continue with up to 20 Member States without an immediate overhaul to the institutions and decision-making process
- this enlargement assumes that there is agreement on changing the voting system in the Council
- after the first enlargement, there will have to be a further IGC to decide on the simplification of procedures before a second enlargement can be considered.

### The Common Foreign and Security Policy (CFSP) and justice and home affairs

The Maastricht Treaty divided the policy areas covered by the Union into three pillars: the first pillar covers the areas of Community competence inherited from the Rome Treaty and is mainly 'economic and commercial'; the second pillar consists of the CFSP; the third pillar concerns justice and home affairs matters. The two latter areas are essentially dealt with in an inter-governmental mode, while first-pillar matters are decided on the basis of Community decision-making involving the Commission as the initiator of measures and the Council and the Parliament as the decision-making bodies. One of the important questions on which there was no agreement is whether this pillar structure set up by Maastricht should remain, with the CFSP being clearly inter-governmental, or whether the CFSP should be treated like the Community first pillar.

Presidents Kohl and Chirac stated prior to the start of the IGC that its major goal would be to make progress in the Union's CFSP. For the associated countries, participation in a developing CFSP would be attractive as would their full participation in NATO or in a reinforced European common defence (WEU). For the Central Europeans such a development would allow them to have an important influence on policy towards their direct neighbours to the East but would also enable them to participate in the making of foreign policy of one of the major world strategic blocs.

However, practically none of these hopes was fulfilled at Amsterdam. While all IGC participants realised that the recent past has seen an embarrassing series of European fiascos in the foreign and security policy areas, with most of the world looking to the United States for leadership, they were divided on what to do about it. Even Germany and France are badly split themselves on what needs to be done to develop the CFSP. The only really significant achievements were the nomination of the Secretary General of the Council to be a sort of 'Mr CFSP', in order to give better identity to the foreign policy of the Union, and the creation of a policy planning and early warning unit in the Council to improve the strategic side of foreign policy.

In third-pillar concerns of justice and home affairs, the Amsterdam Presidency Conclusions suggest that some progress has been made, especially in integrating the Schengen Agreement into the Community sphere and the Schengen secretariat into the secretariat of the Council.

## European architecture, the Amsterdam Treaty and enlargement

There is no doubt that the questions raised in this chapter are some of the crucial ones for the success of the enlargement of the Union. Which outcomes to these discussions are necessary to clear the way for a speedy enlargement of the Union?

### The form of future European enlargement

For many of the original Member States of the Union, or even for the 12 Member States of the 1980s, it is difficult to imagine a Union of 27 members working smoothly. Some of the original members regret that there are more than six! This attitude stems from the particular nature of the process of integration and the form of cooperation which has taken place in the institutions of the Union.

The pace of integration in the Community has at times been breath-taking. This has been made possible by some changes in procedure (for instance, in the Single European Act) but above all because the Member States were sufficiently united in terms of general policy objectives and in terms of working practices. The atmosphere of cooperation at all levels in the Council, the Parliament and the Commission has been positive. The three new EFTA Member States have done nothing to change this atmosphere, although they have brought their own particular interests and practices into the Union. As an example of this cooperation, the potentially explosive language problem has never reduced the capacity of the Union to act. English and French have unofficially become the languages in which the institutions operate and the sensitive cultural questions of language have been pushed into the background in favour of progress in European integration. The fear of many is that this atmosphere of cooperation with its important impact on policy development will be lost at the next enlargement.

Apart from the style of cooperation, there is also a profound worry that the growing heterogeneity of the Union will lead to policy paralysis. It will be considerably more difficult to get agreement on new policies or changes in existing policies if there are 27 Member States than if there are 15; and even with 15, the difficulties are already obvious. Lack of agreement on policy combined with potential paralysis in the Council if the national veto is retained over a wide range of subjects would lead to gradual disintegration of the Union.

The reply to these arguments must treat them seriously, because although couched often in technical terms – the size of a qualified majority or the cooperation procedure – they go to the heart of the future development of the European Union and can build on or destroy the work of the last 40 years.

### Flexible integration and variable geometry

One political reaction to the challenge of enlargement is to wring our hands and say that the practical problems are too great, and enlargement will not take place. Another is to say that while enlargement is a political necessity, the problems are so great that the new Member States will be offered, at least in the first stage, a special class of membership which excludes them from certain policies – in other words, a sort of second-class membership. Neither of these proposals should be considered acceptable. The Union has already made so many promises and half-promises to the associated countries that to refuse enlargement now to those countries which more or less meet the Copenhagen criteria for membership would be seen in Central Europe and in other parts of the world as one of the great betrayals of history. A sort of second-class membership would be dangerous for the whole integration process in Europe, as it would be bound to eat away at the unity of the basic common policies of the Union.

A far more positive approach is to look at the different types of integration sketched out above. The heterogeneous nature of the present Union, which will increase on enlargement, suggests that in future some form of variable geometry will be necessary in order to preserve the immense achievements of the past 40 years, while permitting sub-sets of members to advance in new policy areas. A specific variation of the variable geometry theme has been proposed by a group of European economists, which they have called 'flexible integration'.[9]

The current pattern of European integration requires all Member States to sign up to all policies. Recently there have been deviations from this pattern with the UK temporary opt-out on the Social Chapter of Maastricht, the refusal of the right of establishment in certain areas of Denmark and the exclusion of certain parts of Belgium and Luxembourg from the right of EU citizens to vote in local elections and Monetary Union. The crisis in the European Union today stems partly from this inclusive nature of the integration process while there is growing divergence amongst its members, hence the need to create a more flexible process of integration. Many new policy areas are important to some Member States but not to others. Today's system of integration with tomorrow's expanded membership of the Union ensures that such new policy areas will not find agreement, with the result that sub-sets of Member States will join together in policy initiatives outside the framework of the Union. This will lead eventually to fracture. It would be far better to allow a more flexible integration within the scope of the Union, with groups of countries able to agree to develop new policies amongst themselves in open partnerships. Coun-

[9] Dewatripont *et al.* (1995).

tries which did not join the partnerships immediately could do so in the future and all Member States would be involved in drawing up the rules under which the partnerships operate. EMU is a very particular form of such a partnership, with very stringent membership criteria.

Such a flexible form of integration would allow the Union to grow with enlargement but at the same time permit those countries which wish to integrate further in certain areas to do so without being held up by the others. There are, of course, many problems with such a scheme, including the financing of open partnerships. But the crisis in the Union today is such that without some increase in flexibility, popular support will be lost entirely and integration will stall, with the danger that existing achievements will be destroyed. However, if the Union is still to operate as an economic union there must be a common basis of policies which are applied by all Member States. This common base would include internal market legislation, competition and state-aid rules, a CAP, Structural and Cohesion Funds and VAT harmonisation. All Member States would have to sign up to and apply these common policies.

There are purist integrationists who consider that every policy will need to be in the common base, because any exceptions will lead to unfair competitive advantages for those who do not take part. But they are the ones who would close off Europe from the rest of the world in a real economic 'fortress Europe'. A 'fortress Europe' is the last thing the associated countries can afford as they attempt to maintain high economic growth rates and raise productivity. A flexible integration approach would allow them to phase their integration into all Union policies over many years without being second-class members. Policies which would slow growth, as far as they are not in the common base, can be avoided in the early years of membership. Such a change in the process of integration would make enlargement easier, both for the existing Member States, who fear that enlargement will slow the pace of integration and for the associated countries, who will already have many problems in implementing the policies of the common base.

The Amsterdam Treaty includes a section on flexibility, which follows quite closely the proposals put forward above. The essential points are:

- that such open partnerships should include a majority of the Member States
- that any other Member State should be able to join at a later stage
- that such partnerships do not in any way work to the disadvantage of the non-participating states

- that any one country can veto the creation of such a partnership if it feels that its vital interests are affected.

*Enlargement and the Amsterdam Treaty*

The Amsterdam European Council and the draft Treaty of Amsterdam have disappointed most observers of the Union, and particularly those in Central and Eastern Europe. The key objectives set for the IGC have hardly been met and the changes necessary for a smooth enlargement have not been made. The Presidency Conclusions at Amsterdam were, however, very strong on enlargement. It was as if enlargement was the only matter on which the Member States could agree. The conclusions are worth quoting:

The European Council notes that, with the successful conclusion of the Intergovernmental Conference, the way is now open for launching the enlargement process in accordance with the conclusions of the Madrid European Council.

The European Council invites the Council (General Affairs) to examine in depth the Commission's opinions as well as its Agenda 2000 communication (on agricultural and structural policies and the budget in the light of enlargement) and present a comprehensive report to the European Council at its December meeting in Luxembourg.

At that meeting, the European Council, with a view to enabling the actual opening of negotiations as soon as possible after December 1997, will take the necessary decisions on the overall enlargement process including practical arrangements for the initial phase of negotiations and the reinforcement of the Union's pre-accession strategy as well as other possible means to strengthen cooperation between the EU and all applicant countries.

It is clear from this statement that in spite of not having resolved the problems which the IGC was established to solve, the Union is determined to go ahead with limited negotiations for accession, though there is still no guarantee that these negotiations will lead to accession, and if so under what conditions. It is even more clear that the failure to resolve these questions will lead to an enlargement in waves, with possibly only five countries joining the Union in the first wave. For a full enlargement, it will be necessary to tackle all the IGC questions again at the start of the next century, when they will certainly be no easier to solve than today.

# 13   Free movement of labour, migration and 'third-pillar' issues

## Introduction

This chapter deals with questions which until the Amsterdam European Council were not strictly speaking EC issues, but which nevertheless are of considerable importance in the whole enlargement/accession debate. As mentioned in chapter 12, the Maastricht Treaty consists of three so-called 'pillars'. This book is principally concerned with first-pillar issues which are dealt with as EC issues. The second pillar relates to the Union CFSP. The third pillar concerns issues in the fields of justice and home affairs and is dealt with here. The Amsterdam Treaty will pass some of these matters into the Union Treaty and out of the inter-governmental sphere.

CFSP and justice and home affairs matters are important to both the European Union and the CEE associated countries. They cover areas which are tackled typically in an international manner between nation states. Foreign policy particularly causes problems between Member States because they have different histories, traditions and objectives. The accession of the associated countries to the Union will enlarge the range of foreign policy problems. There will be important advantages to the associated countries in bringing their particular foreign policy concerns into the sphere of interest of Europe's most powerful nations; whether they will be any more enthusiastic about 'communiterisation' of foreign policy is, however, doubtful. The advantages of cooperation in the justice and home affairs areas is, however, clear to all Member States and to the associated countries. Even though progress within the Union since Maastricht has been painfully slow, this is an area where cooperation can pay big dividends.

This chapter picks out one first-pillar area – labour mobility, and the related third-pillar area of migration – for particular scrutiny. The Member States have become more restrictive in their treatment of third-country labour and of migration from outside the Union over recent years. This has also affected the citizens of associated countries, which do not in general benefit from any special regime different from the treatment of citizens of other third countries (in Germany, there have been special regimes which apply only to certain associated countries). Labour mobility and freedom of movement is likely to be a particularly painful part of the accession negotiations.

### Migration and labour mobility

In the context of accession, questions of migration and of labour mobility are treated separately. Indeed while labour mobility is a part of the core freedoms in the Union and is therefore clearly a Community matter, migration is dealt with only in the context of the third pillar of Maastricht. As was seen above in chapter 2, the freedom of movement of labour is dealt with in the Association Agreements; migration is not mentioned there. However, the Amsterdam Treaty will move the questions of immigration, asylum and the free movement of persons into the framework of the EC Treaty under a new title.

Article 8a of the Treaty states that 'every citizen of the Union shall have the right to move and reside freely within the territory of the Member States, subject to the limitations and conditions laid down in this Treaty and by the measures adopted to give it effect'. Migration is therefore something concerning citizens of third countries which until relatively recently was dealt with differently by each Member State. On the other hand, the free movement of labour is a basic right within the Community.

Outside this Community rationale, however, it does not make much sense to divide the two subjects. Of course, some movements of workers within Europe are clearly distinct from migration, where cross-frontier, seasonal or short-term labour between neighbouring countries is involved. However, the objective of most migration is economic improvement and this means that in general migrants participate in the labour market to a higher degree than nationals. Western Europe has always met its additional labour requirement in the post-war period from permanent or semi-permanent migration, usually from countries outside Europe.

Migration and the labour market have become extremely sensitive issues in Europe today. This is partly because of the feeling of '*Über-fremdung*' amongst the indigenous populations when the percentage of identifiable foreigners in the local population rises above a certain threshold. Perhaps a more important reason is that at a period where unemployment is high, both the employed and the unemployed feel that migration will make the unemployment situation even more difficult (although there is practically no empirical evidence to support this belief). It is this disquiet and how to allay it in the case of the associated countries which is important in the context of accession.

Migration issues are extremely complicated, and will not be exhaustively dealt with here. In the European context, however, it is worth pointing to the elementary difference between voluntary migration for economic, religious (Russian Jews to Israel) or other reasons and asylum. Asylum is clearly a separate issue from voluntary migration, and is usually dealt with differently in law. As the recent history of Germany shows, however, migrants often choose between the two according to which is the easier status to obtain. This meant that in the early 1990s in Germany hundreds of thousands of migrants were suddenly claiming asylum, although it was clear that most were economic migrants.

### Past migration flows in Europe [1]

Europe has traditionally been a Continent with considerable movements of population, but where the nation states have retained a degree of homogeneity of their peoples, which has not been the case in some other continents. This is partly a function of language, partly of land-owning patterns and partly of differing cultures, traditions and religions.

Until the First World War, Europe saw large flows of economic migrants leave, mainly for the Americas. Between 1901 and 1915 alone 7 million people left for overseas.[2] However, the First World War broke the stream of international migrants. International migration increased during the economic slump of the 1920s and 1930s, but never recovered to pre-war levels.

Domestically, movements in Europe have been mainly provoked by war. It is estimated that around 5 million people moved within Europe as a result of the First World War and 20 million immediately after 1945. Further large movements occurred after the 1950s as DDR citizens and ethnic Germans continued to move to the Federal Republic, as Jews left the Soviet Union and as asylum seekers from various repressive regimes came West.

Internally within Europe economic migration has been important in the past, and especially so in the recent past. Following the loss of so many men in the First World War, France and Belgium particularly invited in workers from Central and Eastern Europe to fill the gaps. Roughly 1 million workers left Poland in the 1920s and Czechoslovakia also lost around 200,000. These migrants proved very easy to integrate

[1] Economic Commission for Europe (1995).    [2] Kirk (1946).

with local populations. Whereas, however, before the First World War there had been generally free movement of labour, these post-war movements were regulated migrations: the free movement of labour was not re-established until the creation of the European Community. After the Second World War economic migration continued, but with the political division of Europe into two blocs separated by an 'iron curtain' perfected in 1961, movement from Central Europe to Western Europe became very difficult. Rather than the normal movement from areas of labour abundance in Central and Eastern Europe to areas of labour shortage in Western Europe, Western European countries chose to bring in workers from further away – workers from North Africa to France and Belgium, from its ex-colonies to the United Kingdom and from Turkey to Germany.

The attitude to economic migration in Western Europe changed radically after the end of the 1960s as labour shortage turned to rising unemployment. Strict controls on in-migration were introduced by all countries, though German controls have always been more generous than those of most other Member States of the European Union. As Western Europe has been unable to solve its unemployment problem, these anti-immigration measures have become steadily more restrictive.

Within the area of Soviet hegemony there was practically no free migration after the chaotic movements of people immediately after 1945. Migration was organised for the most part – for instance, there was a regular flow of DDR citizens to the Federal Republic, who were allowed to leave for the West against monetary payments. During the 1980s there was a steady stream of Poles who managed to escape to find work in the West, but in general movement was difficult.

The events of 1989–90 in Central and Eastern Europe sent bells of both joy and alarm ringing around the Member States of the European Union. It was feared that the end of division in Europe would lead to a significant emigration to the prosperous market economies of the West by Central and East Europeans seeking work. This resulted in a further tightening of immigration controls on the external borders of the Union.

### *Potential and actual migration after 1989*

The fear of mass immigration into the countries of the European Union, especially after the decision of the Russian government to allow its citizens to leave, led to numerous studies estimating potential flows of migrants.

The factors influencing the potential for migration are more complex than simply the wage gap which exists between East and West. They include expectations about the persistence of the wage gap into the future, comparative unemployment rates and the availability of unemployment benefits, the availability of housing, and the financial and non-financial costs of migration. The large wage gap which existed and, though narrower now, still exists between East and West is therefore not the only defining cause of migration and the costs of migration in terms of leaving one's family, friends, '*Heimat*' and culture are considerable. Some of the early estimates of migration potential were therefore exaggerated simply because too much emphasis was given to the wage-related factors and not enough to the migration-restraining factors.

Apart from these factors which tended to limit the personal decision to migrate, the EU Member States also erected particularly difficult barriers to immigration after 1989. The German system of readmission agreements with all adjoining countries on the return of migrants reaching Germany through those countries forced Poland and the Czech Republic to become restrictive on migration from further East. These countries in their turn were therefore forced to negotiate similar treaties with their neighbours. Traditional immigration countries like France and the United Kingdom also became almost closed to migrants. Nevertheless, the stream of immigrants continued, sometimes in small discrete but regular movements (for instance, Romanian immigration to Western Europe) or in great and sudden floods, like the Albanian mass movement to Italy or the great swell of refugees fleeing warring Yugoslavia.

Layard *et al.* (1992), in their review of East–West migration written early in the transition, estimated the potential flow of migrants from Central and Eastern Europe to the West at approximately 1 million per annum for several years.[3] This estimate was made assuming that no major wars or social catastrophes broke out, both of which would have boosted this number. In fact, the war in Yugoslavia did lead to the temporary migration of a large number of people from that region to Croatia and Serbia, but also to Germany and to a lesser degree other West European states. There have been large internal movements within the ex-USSR as Russians in the non-Russian republics moved back to Russia. Few of these movements have led to migration to the EU Member States, perhaps because the knowledge of the very restrictive measures taken by the EU countries has reached the potential migrants, but also because many of them were not interested in moving from one foreign country where they were rejected to another. Much of the peaceful migration in the early years after 1989 consisted of the move-

---

[3] Layard *et al.* (1992).

ment of 'ethnic' Germans back to Germany from Poland and the former Soviet Union; this ethnic movement has now slowed considerably. There was also, however, a considerable economic migration, especially from Romania to Germany and beyond and from Albania to Italy and Greece, in spite of the severe barriers erected by the EU Member States.

Overall, however, if the war-determined migration from ex-Yugoslavia is excluded, the level of migration to Western Europe has not reached the level suggested as possible by Layard *et al.* and today is considerably below the 1 million/year mark. Even in 1992, at the peak of migratory movements, if Yugoslavia is excluded, immigration from Central and Eastern Europe to the European Union reached only around 450,000, of which over 400,000 was to Germany. Since this time, immigration has been drastically reduced, due in part to the reinforced controls at the borders of the European Union and in part to the fact that economic progress in the neighbouring countries to the East has been better than had been expected by many observers.

It seems unlikely, short of another major disaster such as the war in ex-Yugoslavia, that the expected wave of immigration from Central and Eastern Europe will materialise. There would not appear to be a pent-up desire to emigrate in most of the associated countries which could be released at accession. Obviously, this will depend on the way these economies perform in the future, and whether capital moves to the sources of labour rather than the reverse. The only potential exceptions to this statement are Romania and Bulgaria, from which there has been a steady stream of emigrants to the European Union; this is presumably the reason that these two countries remain on the common EU list of countries whose nationals still need a visa to enter the European Union. But even here improved cooperation with the EU Member States, the cutting of social security payments to immigrants and improved growth prospects at home are likely to reduce these flows considerably.

### The free movement of workers

But further questions arise in respect of the associated countries:
- Is there not a large and growing stock of citizens in these countries who work legally or illegally in the European Union, and is this movement of workers not likely to grow into a flood on accession?
- Given the demographic profile of Western Europe, should the Union not be welcoming young migrants rather than turning them away?

There are indeed a large number of legal and illegal workers from the associated countries inside the European Union, although it is difficult to get statistics on the matter. There are many workers from the associated countries which do not require visas who work regularly but over short periods in the proximate EU Member States without work permits. While this seemed to create few problems in the early years after 1989, the inability of the EU countries to solve their unemployment problems has led to a much harder attitude to the employment of such labour. This has been particularly the case in Germany – the country with the highest unit labour costs in the Union – where pressure from organised labour has led to the introduction of laws which restrict the free movement of labour even within the Union, not to mention the employment of foreign workers. In many other countries the employment of illegal workers from third countries is now punishable with significant fines on employers. This development has the impact of considerably restricting the employment of workers from the associated countries and raising costs to employers in the Union.

It is almost certain that in the accession negotiations, the European Union will demand a long transition period for the free movement of labour. It is questionable whether this will be necessary in the short or in the long run. As mentioned earlier, the experience of the Spanish and Portuguese accessions suggests that accession gives such a stimulus to inward investment and general economic confidence in the new Member State that its nationals abroad tend to return home, creating net immigration rather than the expected emigration. Given the low level of average incomes on accession, this effect may well be less evident in the coming accession than in the Iberian case. However, accession will also lead to an increase in real wages in the associated countries, again reducing the incentive of workers to leave their home countries.

In the longer term, the present European Union will experience a major reduction in its active labour force as the population ages. Even increasing the age of retirement substantially will not significantly alter this fact. A steady flow of migrants from Central and Eastern Europe, with a generally high average level of education, is likely to provide an easily integrated source of labour. In this light, it would not be sensible to segregate the labour markets of the new Member States and the old EU-15 by insisting on a very long transition period.

It would appear, therefore, that both in the context of immigration and the free movement of labour, the European Union has less to fear from accession than many have suggested in the past. From an economic point of view, it is certainly to its advantage if the Union takes a liberal standpoint on these matters. Experience, however, suggests that it will not!

### 'Third-pillar' issues

Third-pillar issues are defined by article K1 of Title VI in the Union Treaty as:

- asylum policy
- the control of persons crossing the external borders of the Member States
- immigration policy
- combating drug addiction
- combating international fraud
- judicial cooperation in civil matters
- judicial cooperation in criminal matters
- customs cooperation
- police cooperation in certain defined areas.

The Treaty allows Member States to adopt joint positions and joint actions and to draw up conventions, where these are better done at the Union rather than at the Member State level (article K3). These matters are decided unanimously, though once a joint action has been unanimously decided, implementing measures can be decided by qualified majority.

Progress within the European Union has been very slow in all these areas. This is partly due to the decision-making procedure and partly to the complex nature of third-pillar issues. In spite of these internal difficulties, the Member States have shown considerable enthusiasm for cooperation with the associated countries. The reasons for such willingness to cooperate is fairly clear: these are all issues in which the Member States feel potentially threatened by enlargement.

Asylum policy, the protection of the external borders of the Union and immigration policy, including combating illegal immigration, are areas in which the associated countries, as new Member States, will have to take on major responsibilities because, with the exception of the Czech Republic, they will all contain part of the external frontier of the Union. The existing Member States have some reservations about the present capacity of the associated countries both to control their borders and to deal with asylum and immigration. The associated countries are also considered by many in the existing Union to be relatively safe centres for international criminals and for drug trafficking and financial crime, because of the inexperience of their police forces and the lack of investment in combating such phenomena. Improving the performance of police forces in the associated countries and developing cooperation with them is seen as a promising way to reduce crime throughout the continent.

Cooperation in the legal field is surely the most difficult of the third-pillar subjects, given the differences between existing Member States and between them and the associated countries. Progress here has probably been less than in any other area.

### The Berlin Declaration

The first serious step towards cooperation on third-pillar issues was taken by the European Council meeting in Corfu in mid-1994. The Council invited the next German Presidency to organise a conference on drugs and organised crime with the associated countries. This conference took place in September 1994 in Berlin with the participation of the justice and home affairs ministers of the EU Member States and the associated countries (at that time, only six). This conference concluded with a statement of objectives, the 'Berlin Declaration'. The Berlin Declaration emphasised that justice and home affairs issues were an essential part of the accession process. Cooperation was envisaged in the following areas, which were of considerable importance to both sides:

- illicit drug trade
- theft of and illegal trade in radioactive and nuclear material
- traffic in human beings
- illegal immigration networks
- illegal transfer of motor vehicles.

These points represented some of the key concerns of the German Presidency and the other Member States geographically close to Central Europe. The Berlin meeting suggested that these matters should be followed up in the relevant working groups, to which the associated countries were invited.

Since the Berlin Declaration which set the agenda, there have been meetings of the ministers of justice and home affairs enlarged to include the associated countries, many meetings of the third-pillar working groups and a report drawn up for the Commission on 'Preparing the associated countries of Central and Eastern Europe for membership of the European Union: justice and home affairs', the so-called Langdon Report.[4] Progress has not, however, been significant, though given the nature of the questions this is not surprising. The associated countries in general feel that while the meetings in the context of the structured dialogue are important, they tend to lack content and real discussion, because of their formal nature and generally short duration. On the

---

[4] European Commission (1996c).

other hand, the working groups are considered to have been of consider-able value.

In the context of accession, the following problems are important:

- it is difficult to determine exactly what the *acquis* in this area consists of
- cooperation between institutions in the third-pillar area is difficult to organise
- in purely practical terms, the associated countries are in need of assistance from the Union, both know-how and equipment, in order to perform better.

### The Community acquis

The third-pillar area is one where it is difficult to say exactly either what the *acquis communautaire* is, or what it is likely to be when accession takes place. Title VI of the Union Treaty obviously forms the basic *acquis* to which the new Member States will have to subscribe. This title sets down the scope of cooperation and the way in which the Union can act in these areas. Beyond this, there are several resolutions and joint actions on immigration and asylum and certain international conventions (the 1995 Convention on simplified extradition and Europol, for instance) which can be considered part of the formal *acquis*. Asylum and the question of visas are two areas where the *acquis* is somewhat clearer than in most other areas. The new Member States will certainly be expected to ratify the 1990 Dublin Convention on asylum if it is in force at accession and to deal with asylum questions cooperatively with the other Member States. They will also be expected to participate in the Europol Convention when it comes into force. On visas, the new Member States will also be required to agree to the specification of the list of third countries whose nationals require visas when entering the Union. In the judicial area there are also certain conventions which should be considered part of the *acquis* – the Rome and Brussels conventions, the criminal conventions of the Council of Europe and UN conventions on drugs.

Beyond this formal but rather sparse *acquis*, there are many other vitally important areas where it is far more difficult to identify measures which the associated countries will be expected to take over. In many of the areas mentioned in the Berlin Declaration, there is no identifiable Community *acquis*. To realise the work programme of the Berlin Declaration, good police cooperation is required. Yet this is an area where there are many documents and statements on the subject but these are mainly statements of how cooperation can work or descriptions of existing practice rather than real *acquis*. The same problem exists for the whole question of border controls. However, the associated countries on accession will be expected to be able to control their borders which are external borders of the Union as efficiently as the present Member States do themselves.

Without clear legal statements on the *acquis* in third-pillar areas, it is difficult for the associated countries to prepare for membership. Yet everyone knows that these are some of the subjects which the populations and the governments of the existing Member States will consider most important in accession negotiations. Some clarification of the *acquis* would therefore be useful. However, probably the most important help which could be given to the associated countries is the extension of cooperation between the third-pillar institutions of the Union (police, judiciary, etc.) and those of the associated countries.

### Cooperation and assistance

The main problem for the associated countries is that they do not have sufficient experience of Union procedures and techniques in the justice and home affairs area. There is a major revealed need for more cooperation and more technical assistance. As far as cooperation is concerned, third-pillar issues are those where cooperation is frequently most difficult even within the Union, simply because the main actors have little experience of international cooperation. Unlike business which tends to be international, or indeed the civil service, the police, immigration authorities, customs and the judiciary are essentially national in outlook, even when they deal with international problems. There are consequently relatively few specialists in these areas who are able to cooperate with their equivalents in the associated countries.

Assistance in these areas has also been relatively restricted, though the Member States have offered a good deal of training in their own training establishments. In the particular case of Germany's neighbours, substantial resources were made available for the improvement of border control infrastructure and information systems in the context of Germany's agreements with those countries. Small amounts of equipment were made available by PHARE and by some of the bilateral programmes (Sweden, United Kingdom, France and Germany, for instance) to equip the police in the fight against crime and drugs. A relatively small PHARE regional programme has tackled the drugs issue by providing training, information systems and drug control techniques. In the customs area, PHARE has provided significant support to cooperation and transit facilitation. Finally, small amounts of assistance have been provided by PHARE through the Council of Europe to support judicial cooperation, while the British Know-How Fund has a significant programme in the same area.

The size of the third-pillar problems facing the associated countries and the importance given to this area by the Member States suggest that more assistance could be directed to them. The assistance could usefully be given through international specialised organisations, or through national authorities in the Member States. This would ensure an increase in the overall level of cooperation between specialised authorities throughout the region.

### Conclusion

It would appear that third-pillar issues could become far more important in the accession process than one might expect from the *acquis* which exists in the area. While there is not an imminent threat of large-scale migration from East to West, nevertheless the fear of such movements has led to the issue becoming an important point of public discussion in the Union. The additional fears of international crime and international drugs trafficking mean that these problems also need to be given attention. Such matters even raise problems between existing Member States, as witnessed by the tension between the Netherlands and France over drugs: how much more attention are they likely to get in the accession process?

Even apart from the accession issues, there is much to be gained from a reinforcement of cooperation between the Union's Member States and the associated countries. These issues should therefore be given a higher priority in political discussion and, subject to the viability of the projects proposed, a more important place in bilateral and multilateral assistance programmes.

# 14    The political economy of enlargement

## Introduction

Enlargement of the European Union to Central and Eastern Europe will not be decided alone by a sober analysis of its political and economic benefits and costs. It will be decided by the balance of interests in the Union for and against enlargement, by the power of those interests to influence the political process and by the skill with which they operate on governments in the Union and in the associated countries.

The most important factors at work will be both economic and political. Many operators in both the Union and in the associated countries enjoy economic rents derived from market failure or through protection given to them by the commercial policy or the domestic policy of their country of operation. Others enjoy what might be called 'political rents' (which can often be expressed as tangible economic or prestige benefits) resulting from the influence they exert on the political process and which may be lost on enlargement.[1]

While almost all studies of the costs and benefits of enlargement show that it will be of undisputed benefit to both sides, these benefits are distributed fairly equally around the different interests in both parties. The losses are, as always, far more concentrated on particular groups in society or on certain regions.[2] There is therefore a high probability that the anti-enlargement forces will mount a far more effective campaign than those who are in favour of enlargement. In order to win this argument, the political will of those governments which are in favour of enlargement must be strong.

---

[1] For instance, powers conferred on certain institutions which will be transferred to Brussels, or civil servants who fear loss of influence.
[2] Neven (1995), pp. 19–60.

## The political economy of enlargement in the European Union

The actors in the Union who can affect the enlargement process include the Member State governments, who are both actors and decision-makers, regional administrations, employers, including sectorally organised employers' federations, industrial sectors such as agriculture or the steel industry, organised labour through the trades unions, and a multitude of other groups including non-governmental organisations (NGOs) of every hue. Some of these actors are afraid of losing economic rents, others of losing political influence. They will be most effective if they are a relatively small tight-knit group, representing a narrowly defined interest, liable to make major economic or political gains from lobbying but unlikely to cause significant costs to others if their lobbying is successful. Some lobbies will actively promote enlargement while lobbying for their own interests to be taken care of in specific deals during the negotiations; there will also be lobbies which are actively promoting enlargement because it coincides with their own economic or political interest.

### The economic lobbies in the Union

#### Business and sector lobbies

The analysis carried out in chapter 3 showed that there will be potentially significant business lobbies against trade liberalisation and enlargement; most of these will be situated in the Northern half of the Union. However the business community in the present Union should overall be in favour of widening the European Union.

One significant sectoral lobby will be agriculture. Agriculture corresponds to the criteria for an effective lobby and a look at the history of the European Community suggests that it has been the most successful one (see chapter 9). With agriculture being one of the main problems on the way to enlargement, the scope for successful lobbying will be large. Enlargement will be seen as a threat by small farmers in the Community, or by those who are inefficient. These farmers enjoy in general a considerable measure of support in the population, even though their numbers are now much reduced.

However, agriculture may have lost some of its lobbying power, because the pace of world liberalisation of trade in agricultural products has increased in spite of farmers' pressure and to some extent the farmers themselves have accepted the need of reform in the CAP. Agriculture is also going through a period of high world prices and relative profitability, which diminishes both the popularity of its cause and the lobbying enthusiasm of farmers. Agricultural interests will also probably be split over enlargement. The initial fears that the Union would be overwhelmed by exports from CEE agriculture have receded as it has become clear that the supply problems in the region are serious. The Union's efficient commercial agriculture may now well consider enlargement an opportunity rather than a threat, with the possibility of buying into CEE farming and the opportunity to sell know-how and technology. This would seem to be the case amongst powerful French agricultural interests, for instance, which are far less protectionist than their reputation.

Disarming opposition from the farming lobby may still be difficult. It will require a more rapid move from price support to direct income subsidies as proposed in the 'Agenda 2000' package. If such changes are clearly linked to enlargement rather than to the need to reach a sustainable agricultural policy in the light of changes in the industry and in world trade, lobbying will be aimed against enlargement. A disaffected agricultural lobby would be a powerful opponent of enlargement.

Other sectoral groups which might use their influence to oppose enlargement or to work out special deals for themselves are those which produce basic industrial products such as iron and steel, basic chemicals, textiles and certain other low value added products. The opposition from these groups will probably grow beyond today's level as enlargement comes nearer. The reaction of the different industries will, however, vary considerably. Medium-technology sectors which have high labour costs and low sunk costs, especially if they are located in the centre or east of the Community, will have the choice to move some capacity to Central Europe. For these businesses, enlargement will be a bonus as long as they are prepared to relocate. To some extent this relocation has begun, especially from Germany to the Czech Republic, Hungary and Poland. There has, for instance, been a very considerable increase in outward processing to Central Europe in the textile industry. The businesses maintain a small staff in the Union to carry out certain processes like ironing which take place immediately before sale, but produce their goods in the associated countries.[3] Naturally those businesses which are not prepared to relocate and which cannot make serious cost savings will almost certainly oppose enlargement, but it is

---

[3] Many of these employers use the generous labour laws in countries like Belgium which permit technical unemployment paid for by the state. Without such disguised wage subsidies, the employment loss in this sector in the Union would have been far greater.

unlikely that they will form a significant lobby because of their diverse interests and lack of geographical concentration. An exception could be the textile industry in Portugal, which will profit neither from the opportunities of new markets nor from the possibility of relocation. However, this industry appears to be far less agitated about enlargement than it was in the early 1990s.

The situation is different for basic industries with high sunk costs but relatively high labour costs. These include, for instance, the steel industry and the basic chemicals sectors. Over the past few years these industries have been at the forefront of demands for safeguards or anti-dumping action against the Central Europeans. The European Commission has itself been drawn in two directions, on the one hand wanting to protect the Union steel industry (safeguards against Czech imports, for instance) on the other wanting to help the Central Europeans restructure their industry with technical assistance and technology from the Union. In steel, at least, latest indications are that rather than oppose enlargement the Union steel industry prefers to extend its organisation to include CEE industry. This is extremely bad news for the European consumer of steel and for CEE industry; it will, however, neutralise the voice the steel lobby in the enlargement debate.

The likelihood then is that there may well be sectors which protest against enlargement, but they will probably not be as united in their opposition as they need to be to really affect the debate. Some of the historically most successful lobbyists, such as steel and textiles, may well not enter the argument. Opposition to enlargement also makes less business sense in a situation where world trade is being liberalised rapidly and tariffs and NTBs are coming down. Industry in the Community is exposed to growing world competition, a situation which will not change with or without enlargement.

Indeed, many prominent enterprises are likely to be very much in favour of enlargement. These are the businesses which have already made large investments in Central Europe and which will be happy to see their investments protected and increased through enlargement. Companies such as ABB, Pilkington, Volkswagen, Fiat, Lucchini, General Motors, ICL, Thomson, Philips, ING and many other giants of the European corporate scene are all major investors in the regions. More and more small companies, especially German, Austrian and Nordic businesses, are also investors. All of these form a powerful and relatively united lobby in favour of enlargement. As inward investment from the Union in Central Europe accelerates over the next five years, this lobby of major European firms will become more influential.

*Organised labour*

The very basic economics of integration would suggest that as the Union and Central Europe move towards enlargement, factor prices will tend to converge. Since 1989 there has been a considerable growth in trade and there has been a small but significant movement of capital towards Central Europe. There has also been a certain movement of labour from East to West even though the barriers to such movement are high. The result should be that the return to capital in the East could fall and the return to labour (though not to human capital!) in the West should also fall. It is this second effect which may cause major opposition to enlargement amongst organised labour.

To date, the trades unions have been relatively muted in their approach to enlargement, generally emphasising that levels of social provision must be increased in Central Europe and raising the question of 'social dumping'. As enlargement draws nearer, there is a danger that the trades unions will become far more vocal against enlargement, though the arguments will be couched in terms of level playing fields and properly protecting workers in Central Europe. This is probably one of the most dangerous lobbies against enlargement, and politicians in favour should move to address the questions, which the labour movement is asking.

The fundamental problems of employment creation and unemployment in the Union exist independently of enlargement. The arguments about the need to reduce the cost of labour (especially in those countries with a very wide, inefficient and expensive net of social protection) and to make the labour market more flexible have all been well rehearsed and some Member States are making serious attempts to tackle them. The need to improve the levels of education and to pay special attention to the training of the socially weaker groups in society is also important to achieve a lower core rate of unemployment. If governments do not tackle these problems properly, enlargement will undoubtedly be made more difficult.

For short-term political convenience, certain Member States may attempt to resist change and to shore up a difficult economic situation by increasing protection against third countries outside the Union (and perhaps, in a disguised way, within the Union). Belgium, for instance, as a true consensus country, finds it difficult to reform a situation where both labour costs and the tax system are desperately in need of attention.[4] To touch either would be to destabilise a country which is already teetering on the brink of dissolution. The additional weight of

[4] Konings and Roodhooft (1996).

competition from trade or labour migration from Central Europe can only make the situation of Belgium worse, if it is not prepared to undertake reform. In Germany, both government and the trades unions appear to recognise the problem of inflexibility and high labour costs, and the government appears prepared to take some of the necessary measures. But politics here, too, appears to be frustrating reform.

The proper response to this challenge is twofold; on the one hand politicians should explain the problem more honestly to voters and on the other they should take action to make the necessary adjustments in the labour market and should not attempt to hide behind a shield of protection, which in the long run will lead to a lowering of European living standards. Explaining the problem more honestly consists of underlining the fact that enlargement will lead to faster growth and more employment, if the necessary adjustments are made. There are, however, already signs that politicians will try to duck these responsibilities in favour of re-election. Two examples can be quoted from 1996. In spite of having already taken some measures going in the right direction, the German government has proposed a law which imposes German wages and conditions on all building sites in the Republic, even on non-German labour from the other Member States of the European Union. A second example can be found in a speech of the Belgian Foreign Minister, where he complained in the context of enlargement that 'countries with poor social security systems will not be inclined to uniformise standards in the field, as differences in terms of wages and social policy rather attract investors'.[5] The implication is that until wages and social policy are raised to Community levels, enlargement is not desirable.

The probability must be that this opposition to enlargement will be expressed in the form of demands for social and environmental 'standards' to be raised in the associated countries before they are allowed to join the Union. This could well be extremely damaging to the economies of the associated countries, and should be resisted. Pressure on the negotiations for membership will also almost certainly lead to the proposal for a long transition period to apply to the freedom of movement of workers, as was the case with Spain and Portugal.

### Budgetary winners and losers

The discussion of the budgetary impact of enlargement is already well under way. The objective facts and forecasts on the Union budget have been discussed above. As far as the political economy of the budget is

---

[5] From a speech given by Mr Eric Derycke, Belgian Minister for Foreign Affairs, at the Third Ghent Colloquium (8 March 1996).

concerned, the following conflicting objectives of the different players will have to be resolved:

- the main net contributors – Germany, Austria, Sweden, the Netherlands and the United Kingdom – want better burden-sharing between the Member States so that their payments are reduced
- the net beneficiaries want their net receipts from the Community budget, as a minimum, to remain constant in real terms and certainly do not wish to become net contributors
- the net contributors do not want enlargement to lead to an increase in the Community budget, at least as a proportion of Community GDP
- the net beneficiaries are not interested in the overall level of the Community budget as long as they remain net beneficiaries; however all Member States are trying to meet the Maastricht criteria for public deficits and will not want to have their gross contributions increased
- there are powerful lobbies of regions, companies and NGOs, who are receivers of Community budgetary funds who will not be prepared to see their receipts decline because of enlargement.

The budgetary questions will probably not be the crucial ones in the enlargement process, but they may be the most discussed and those where brinkmanship at European Councils will reach its most dramatic.

In terms of political economy, the main questions are whether Germany, and to a lesser extent the Netherlands, will accept an increase in their net contributions, whether the cohesion countries will accept reductions in their net transfers and whether a simpler and more transparent system of gross contributions, and perhaps net contributions, to the budget will be designed. The Commission, in 'Agenda 2000', rejects changes in the financing system of the European Union before 2006.

One of the most remarkable changes in attitude to enlargement has come in the Netherlands, where the impact of the growing net budgetary contribution has been an outcry for more fairness in the way the budgetary burden is borne and certainly so in the light of the potential costs of enlargement. This has affected that country's general enthusiasm for enlargement, though undoubtedly to some extent this is positioning before a negotiation. Germany which, over the years in an uncomplaining way, has borne a large net share of the budget, has suddenly discovered that, with the burden of reunification and the need to reduce its government deficit to under 3% of GDP, it can no longer continue to support the other Member States of the Union. The pressure from Germany for better burden-sharing is also intense.

On the other hand, the Member States which have become used to subsidy are not keen to lose it. The cohesion countries, which after enlargement will be middle-income states in the Union rather than the poorest, have only recently become vocal in the context of the budgetary implications of enlargement, but this will change as proposals for the reform of the Structural Funds after 1999 are made more detailed

It is too early to see the outcome of this discussion clearly. All one can do is to look at the interests of the different groups in the discussion and predict how important enlargement and, indeed, European integration is to each player. Germany is clearly in a weak position. Its government considers European integration and enlargement to be two of the main planks of policy. It is the most ferocious supporter of monetary union, of further political integration within the Union and of enlargement. It is likely that Germany's bluff will be called, especially by Spain and other cohesion countries, which have little political interest in enlargement.

Germany's defence will probably be to seek agreement on a fairer system of financing for the Union. There is little correlation between indicators of prosperity and budgetary contributions. Denmark is a very clear gainer even though it has a level of GDP *per capita* well above that of Germany. France, through the CAP, is only a very small net contributor, even though it has a level of GDP per head close to that of Germany. It should be possible for Germany to make some progress here as it would have the support of some of the cohesion countries as well as the Netherlands, Sweden and Austria.

The whole budgetary discussion should always be placed in the light of the relatively small sums which are being discussed. The total budget is well below the limit of 1.27% of Community GDP and the net German contribution to the 1995 budget was only approximately one-tenth of the German government transfer to the New Bundesländer in that year. Even the most pessimistic estimate of the budgetary consequences of enlargement are unlikely to take the Community budget much beyond 1.27% of GDP. And the probability must be that, with reform in some common policies, the current level can be maintained over the coming financial period, as proposed by 'Agenda 2000'.

### The political lobbies in the Union

Germany will continue to be in favour of enlargement, as will the Nordic countries (the Netherlands subject to some movement on the budget problem) and probably Austria. The United Kingdom will also continue to support enlargement as long as it does not give rise to demands for an end to the UK's budget 'rebate'. This support comes from a mixture of motives – geopolitical and security reasons dominate for Germany, trade and business considerations are important for the Netherlands.

The real opponents of integration are likely to be countries which fear enlargement as a threat to their specific vital interests, such as the particular case of Belgium and possibly Ireland. Other opposition, for instance from Spain, Greece or Portugal, is liable to be less deeply entrenched, though real, and linked to the budgetary debate. But these countries are never likely to be in favour of enlargement, and at best will be neutral.

Politically the most difficult area may well be the automatic diminution of power and influence that all countries will suffer as the membership of the Union grows perhaps first to 20 and then to 26 or 27. This will be especially felt by the small countries in the Union, which will be under intense political pressure to give up some of their acquired rights to power and influence.

The choice of associated countries to be given privileged treatment in the case that accession takes place in groups at different periods will also pose difficult problems. Each Member State which is interested in enlargement has its own privileged candidate. This was seen most clearly by the tactics used by Greece to get the negotiations with Cyprus onto the agenda of the Union. Germany has already stated its preferences through the statements of Chancellor Kohl, who clearly wanted Poland, Hungary and the Czech Republic to be treated as a priority. Germany may be rather less enthusiastic on the Baltic states, reflecting the tradition of German foreign policy deference to Russia. France has traditionally patroned Romania, though there are limits to this support, which depend on progress being made with democratic institutions and real economic reform. Austria has particular interests in Hungary for historical and business reasons, and the Nordic countries are strong in supporting the Baltic states. These preferences will play a role in the unwinding of the enlargement puzzle. The 'Agenda 2000' choice for negotiations of the Czech Republic, Estonia, Hungary, Poland and Slovenia will, however, probably survive the debate in the Council.

Finally, it must be remembered that enlargement is decided on the basis of unanimity and has to be approved by a simple majority of the European Parliament. This procedure gives an enormous potential for linking completely separate decisions in the Parliament or for wringing more influence for the Parliament out of the Council. Enlargement will therefore not be decided on the merits of the case alone but will be subject to the most outrageous linking of separate causes in the Council and the Parliament. Nothing in the European Union is simple!

## The political economy of enlargement in the associated countries

The political economy of enlargement in the associated countries is likely to be somewhat less complicated. The perceived balance of advantage appears to be clearly in favour of accession. All the associated countries have given European integration a major place in their foreign policies, and to some extent their future stability depends on the accession option being open. Put succinctly, the associated countries see no alternative to European integration.

The idea of accession is supported by the majority of voters in all the associated countries.[6] At the present time, however, their populations know relatively little about the Union, except that it is politically stable and rather rich. The serious press has made in many cases a significant effort to inform its readership, but this has not led to much quantitative improvement in the understanding of the electorate in general. Governments have generally not made a major effort to inform the public, often lacking the means to do so, but also, like governments in the Union itself, backing away from trying to explain matters which governments themselves find very complex. As in the Union after Maastricht, there is a danger that it is only when the full consequences of the accession negotiation deals are known that the voters in the associated countries will realise that there are drawbacks in Union membership.

As the necessary changes become clearer, the same problems will arise of groups in the population who feel that they will lose economic or political rents. In all the countries there remain many sectors which have low productivity and survive behind protective barriers of one sort or another. These barriers are sometimes simply knowledge barriers, with consumers being unaware of the existence of higher-quality products, sometimes they are the result of rather opaque public procurement procedures and of cosy relationships between central and local authorities and certain producers. As integration progresses, the impact of the more thorough opening of markets in Central Europe will be perceived by those who are going to lose rents, and opposition will grow. Where the affected enterprises are large state companies or large privatised companies, which are often managed by people close to government power, there will be strong opposition to some elements of membership.

[6] European Commission (1996d).

Some of these forces are already hard at work, and this has led to trade conflict in the association committees. Apart from managers or owners of enterprises in protected sectors, labour in these same sectors may well become an obstacle to accession, as they make common cause with employers to protect their jobs in situations where unemployment will still be high.

In some cases, those losing real power will be bureaucrats rather than enterprises. The situation with the Polish certification authorities, which refuse to accept Community certificates, is partly due to defence of bureaucratic power in the administration. This will become more and more common as negotiations point to concentrations of bureaucratic power disappearing as the associated countries hand over some sovereignty to the Community. Indeed, the loss of sovereignty to Brussels coming so soon after the associated countries regained their independence from the Soviet Union, may prove to be an emotive public concern. The associated countries have the feeling that for the first time many of them have real power to shape their futures in stable democracies. The significance of EU membership in terms of a loss of power to national decision-making has not yet completely penetrated all parts of the population and State institutions, but it will be difficult to accept. Indeed, ministers frequently only have a superficial idea of what membership of the Union really means in terms of the sharing of power between the nation and the Union. One of the great advantages of the structured dialogue is that it gives at least to certain ministers a feeling for this sharing of sovereignty. However, measured against the overall gains from membership, the question of the loss of sovereignty is unlikely to be a sticking point.

A particular problem of political economy will be the relation between the associated countries in the preparatory phase for accession. As the notion that not all associated countries will join the Union at the same time is more generally debated, so the relationship between the associated countries will change. One reaction is that each country will try to show that it is the best candidate for entry into the European Union. The case of the Czech Republic is interesting. Since the changes in 1989, the Czech Republic has followed a clear policy of attempting to demonstrate to the world that it is not like the other transforming countries but is a case apart. Its economic reforms were carried out rapidly and are considered to have been effective, in spite of the economic crisis in early 1997. The Czech Republic rushed to become the first OECD member from Central Europe, which it achieved in Autumn 1995. Again this reaffirmed in a significant way that the Czech Republic was a case apart., The Czech Republic has been extremely

careful to limit relations with the other associated countries to pure
trading relationships, and has refused any political associations (CEFTA
is a demonstration of this). The policy of showing that the Czech
Republic naturally belongs to the group of advanced West European
market economies and has little in common with Central Europe has
been consistently followed.

The other countries considered by many to be in the first group for
membership – Hungary and Poland – work more closely together, partly
because of the Czech policy. Communication between these two countries at all levels is far closer than with the Czech Republic, though each
maintains a careful monitoring of the other's performance, to avoid
being linked too closely if the other partner shows any sign of weakening
resolve on reform or integration. These two countries are, however,
wary about being in too close a relationship with the other associated
countries (with the exception of Slovenia), because they realise that they
may have the chance to enter the Union earlier as part of a small group
of advanced reform countries.

On the other hand, the associated countries which feel that they may
well be in the slower track for accession look for the maximum level of
contact with the candidates which are considered to be on the fast track,
while at the same time protesting at any initiatives from the Union side
to differentiate between the associated countries.

This distinctive behaviour is likely to continue as the preparation for
accession progresses and is liable to make the work of the Community
institutions more complex. It will also be a permanent hindrance to the
express aim of the Union to encourage closer trade and political
relationships between the associated countries before accession.

Finally, the associated countries will attempt to use their particular
relations with certain Member States to support their cause, and will
attempt to maintain good relations with all Member States. This will
certainly be the case for the three Baltic states, which will continue to
develop their good relations with the Nordic countries with a view to
their support for Baltic accession. But, here again, with perceived
differences in the rate of reform in the three countries, the most
advanced will try to maintain distance from the others in order to book a
place in the first group of countries for accession.

## Politics and economics of enlargement
## and third countries

The most important third country relationship affecting accession is
that with Russia and particularly the relations between Germany and

Russia. Russian foreign policy has become more assertive since mid-1994, and at the same time policy has become less predictable. A declaration in 1996 by the Presidents of Russia and Belarus that they intended to build a 'corridor' through Poland to join Belarus to Kaliningrad, without any consultation of the Polish government, is an interesting indication of the lack of predictability.

The main objective of Russian foreign policy appeared to be aimed at dissuading NATO from expanding its membership eastwards. Having lost this battle, Russia may begin to object to enlargement of the Union. The discussion about security in the Union suggests that at some time, the Union's military capability may not be entirely within the NATO framework. The first objective could be to eliminate any of the Baltic countries, and perhaps especially Estonia with its large Russian minority, from the first wave of enlargement. The Nordic countries, and particularly Finland, would however put up very strong resistance to this type of pressure and their power and influence in the final decisions on enlargement should not be overlooked.

The United States, though far from the scene, has always taken a considerable political and economic interest in Central Europe. The United States is still the principal foreign investor in several of the associated countries and, as was seen in the Bosnian crisis and the problems between Greece and Macedonia, is still a major political actor on Europe's doorstep. Politically the United States is in favour of European integration to include Central and Eastern Europe, because this will favour peace and stability in the region. However the United States has never adjusted totally to the post-Cold War period, and still sees Russia as its major partner in foreign policy. The decision to invite the Czech Republic, Hungary and Poland to join NATO taken at the Madrid meeting in June 1997 and the rejection of bids by the three Baltic countries should not however be taken as indicative of US resistance to the Baltic expansion of the European Union.

## Conclusion

A brief look at the political economy of enlargement indicates that the process may be far more complex than the 'objective' facts suggest. The relationship between the Member States of the Union, and indeed between the leading politicians of these countries, will play an important part in the decisions. Matters totally unconnected to enlargement will be entangled with the strict enlargement questions, so that at certain times Member States themselves will find it difficult to follow the arguments. Those who risk losing economic rents on both sides through enlargement will pick on any event or fact which seems to support their case, and use it for their own ends.

Those governments which favour enlargement must therefore prepare a strategy which will take account of these different opposition groups. Without a clear strategy over the medium term, the whole exercise could founder.

# 15 Strategies for accession

## Introduction

There have been many attempts to outline a strategy for accession. The European Union has made two attempts to design such a strategy. The first pre-accession strategy was agreed at the Essen European Council at the end of 1994. The most recent attempt is that of the European Commission in its July 1997 'Agenda 2000' package, which has, however, to be confirmed by the Council.

This chapter evaluates the Union's strategy, that of some of the associated countries, as well as the strategies designed by theorists. It ends with the identification of the key elements which a successful strategy should include in both the Union and the Central European associated countries.

## The Union's strategy

The Union's concrete actions in the context of accession began with the European Council at Copenhagen. This Council declared that the Union shared the objective of the associated countries to accede to the Union, under certain conditions. Since Copenhagen, therefore, the objective has been clear. The conditions which had to be met before enlargement could be realised did, it is true, rather limit the enthusiasm of the associated countries. But the conditions can be realistically fulfilled. Even the last condition which establishes that accession can take place only if the Union has the capacity to accept new members can be realistically assessed; it will depend on the conclusion of the Amsterdam Treaty and the implementation of a reform package such as that proposed by 'Agenda 2000'.

At Essen, the Union agreed a pre-accession strategy, clearly aimed at helping the associated countries meet the second, third and fourth criteria of Copenhagen – namely, the existence of a functioning market economy, the ability to withstand the competitive pressures inside the

Union and the ability to take on the obligations of membership of the Union (the *acquis communautaire*). The main failing of the Essen strategy was that it concentrated on what the associated countries have to do to meet the Copenhagen criteria, but did not specify the changes the Union will have to make to its policies in order to meet its stated objective of enlargement. Its most important element was certainly the emphasis which it put on the need for the associated countries to prepare carefully for their entry into the internal market, a process which will of necessity cover a number of years.

To judge from the statements made by leading politicians in the Union, a rapid timetable for accession is expected. When President Chirac spoke in late 1996 in Warsaw about Poland's entry into the Union being completed, though presumably not ratified, by the year 2000, he was clearly thinking of a timetable as follows:

1 The Amsterdam Treaty will create the framework within which enlargement can take place
2 Following the Commission's opinions, the key decisions on the opening of negotiations are taken at the Luxembourg European Council in December 1997
3 Negotiations are opened with the chosen associated countries in early 1998
4 The negotiations are concluded in 2000
5 The accession treaties are ratified by all national Parliaments and the European Parliament by 2002.

The second strategic document, 'Agenda 2000', appears to confirm this timetable. 'Agenda 2000' attempts to fill the gap left at Essen by concentrating on the reform of Union policies. It is, however, clear that the Commission regards its reform proposals as essential with or without enlargement.

'Agenda 2000' contains essentially seven parts:

- a first outline of the EU budget (the New Financial Framework) for the period 2000–6 in the light of enlargement
- an analysis of the CAP after enlargement, and proposals to reform it
- an analysis of the necessary reforms in the Community's Structural Funds
- an assessment of enlargement's impact on other EU policy areas
- the Opinions on the applications for membership of the ten associated countries
- an overall assessment of which countries should be invited to negotiate with the European Union
- an outline of a new pre-accession strategy (see chapter 5).

The Commission proposes the following key assumptions for the reform of Union policies to accommodate the challenge of enlargement:

- the Community budget should not exceed the own-resources ceiling of 1.27% of Community GDP in the period to 2006 (see chapter 11)
- expenditure on the Structural Funds should not exceed 0.46% of Community GDP over the same period; a reform of the Structural Funds must be carried out leading to greater prioritisation and a transition period for the entry of the new Member States into the system: transfers will be capped at 4% of the recipient country's GDP (see chapter 10)
- reform of the CAP must continue, with a progressive change from price support to direct income support (see chapter 9)
- reform of the Community institutions must be accelerated (see chapter 12)
- 'Agenda 2000' is based on the assumption that EMU starts on time and that the Amsterdam Treaty is signed and ratified.

The Commission's analyses of the progress made in each applicant state led it to recommend that the Union should open negotiations with the Czech Republic, Estonia, Hungary, Poland and Slovenia (as well as Cyprus). The following points are, however, worth noting:

- it is the Council not the Commission which will decide at the Luxembourg European Council in December 1997 with which countries to negotiate
- negotiations are likely to start in Spring 1998 but no one knows how long they will last; it is probable that the key problems will be left to the end, which may be in 1999 or later
- 'Agenda 2000' contains the basis of the Union's negotiating mandate with the associated countries; however, the mandate will be decided by the Council not by the Commission, and there may be important changes
- negotiations with the individual countries will be organised separately, but the Council will try to keep them roughly at the same pace; however, if they prove difficult with one country, accession may not take place simultaneously
- certain of the excluded countries may join the negotiations once their problems are resolved; this applies particularly to Slovakia, where once the political problems are resolved it has been made clear that it can join the first group of countries in the negotiation: this means that the Union has not really departed from its basic principle of non-differentiation between countries on other than objective measurable criteria.

'Agenda 2000' is a very important step forward in the accession process and, if followed, could lead to accession in the period 2002–5. The detail of the proposed reforms to the CAP, the Structural Funds and the Union budget as well as of the reinforced pre-accession strategy have been dealt with in earlier chapters. The strategy is quite correct that reform of these key policy areas is essential if enlargement is going to happen. It is also quite right to insist on keeping the list of countries with which the Union will negotiate open, so that when other countries are ready they, too, can join the negotiations. However, the Commission has purposely left some things unclear in order to reduce opposition from Member States – indeed, it is important to realise that 'Agenda 2000' is addressed above all to the 15 Member States and not to the candidate countries.

While the timetable for the opening of negotiations is more or less confirmed, there is no real indication of a date for accession. Reading between the lines it is obvious that 'Agenda 2000' has been constructed around an assumption of accession taking place at the beginning of 2003. What is required, however, by the associated countries and by business throughout the region, is a firmly stated date, which is the objective for accession. Clearly changes in policy in the associated countries could mean delay, if they are incompatible with membership of the Union. But there should be a date which ties the hands of the Union and gives some degree of certainty to economic operators.

'Agenda 2000' is also not very clear on many areas where tense negotiations are to be expected in the Council of Ministers in Brussels. An example is the lack of clarity on the transition processes in the Structural Funds, as some regions are graduated out to make room for the new Member States. This is obviously a key topic, but one which will be solved only at the last moment through horsetrading in the Council.

Perhaps more seriously, 'Agenda 2000' does not appear to be very generous to the new Member States. This is particularly the case in agriculture, where there is planned to be massive subsidy to agriculture in the existing Union after enlargement but only a low level for farmers in the new Member States. A similar argument could be made for the Structural Funds, where the Commission is relying on low levels of absorption in the new Member States in the first few years of member-ship to allow a longer graduating out period for existing beneficiary regions.

The pre-accession strategy, which has many important new elements (for instance, conditionality), suffers mainly from a low level of finance compared to the financial effort which is being asked for from the associated countries in implementing the Union *acquis*. It also is imprecise about the amount of control of assistance which will be transferred to the associated countries: one particular reading of the documents could lead to an understanding that control in Brussels will be reinforced. This would make it even harder for the new Member States to gain experience in managing Structural Funds prior to membership, and would indeed lead to low levels of absorption in the first few years.

Finally, while 'Agenda 2000' contains many elements of a reinforced policy for those countries not in the first round of negotiations, these elements are not presented as a strong package. The disappointed countries will suffer a major crisis of confidence politically and economically through rejection, and every effort should be made to underpin their reform enthusiasm and their economic stabilisation and development.

### The strategy of the associated countries

The associated countries have the advantage of the objective of their preparations being much clearer than for the Union; all associated countries want and need accession to the Union in the short term, defined as five or six years. The achievement of this objective is, of course, only to a certain extent in their own hands and the fifth condition of Copenhagen makes it clear that even if they achieve the other four conditions they might still not enter the Union.

Specific strategies to prepare for accession have been prepared, or are in the process of being prepared, by most countries. The core of most strategies is the adoption of the measures mentioned in the White Paper on the internal market prepared for the Cannes European Council in June 1995. Systems have been developed in most countries to make sure that new legislation conforms to EU law, and timetables have been drawn up for the adoption of the key pieces of legislation. In Poland, a national strategy for integration has been prepared which goes well beyond the approximation of laws to deal with policies and the need for policy changes.

This adoption of the *acquis communautaire* is likely to be far more complex than either the associated countries or the Union think. The process is not simply a legal one of approximating legislation. It is changing both the legal framework in which society and the economy operate and revolutionising the institutions of the state. Each new piece of legislation involves some change of policy, which will require a period of transition until citizens or economic operators have adapted to it.

Many of the associated countries will need to review their strategies, devoting more resources to them and tightening up timetables.

The economic analysis of the consequences of adopting the *acquis* in the associated countries has generally not progressed very far. This is, however, essential. The associated countries will need to discuss their negotiating position between themselves to make sure that there is some common position on the macropolitics of transition periods, even though in the detail different countries will take different positions. There will also need to be considerable lobbying of the Member States in order to get these positions accepted by the Union. These further steps are not, however, possible without an initial deep analysis of where the problems are likely to lie.

Few of the associated countries have yet developed plans to inform the public of the needs and implications of accession to the Union. This is partly due to a lack of appreciation in government of the fundamental nature of the changes which they are promoting, and therefore of the need to keep the public thoroughly informed. Certain groups need particular attention. The business community in each country, for instance, will need to be helped to understand and plan for the changes which will come before and at accession. Much of this work will fall to the government, due to the weakness of chambers of commerce or other business organisations.

A crucial problem for the associated countries is policy reform uncertainties in the Union. The lack of progress with reform, and therefore of credibility of the accession offer from the Union means that the associated countries also have to assume that there is a significant probability that they will not enter the Union in the near future. The lack of alternative anchors for domestic and foreign policy, however, make any planning for this circumstance impossible. The 'rejection' of Romania, Bulgaria, Slovakia, Latvia and Lithuania through negative Opinions of the Commission may also have a destabilising effect on policy-making.

The first test of the capacity of these administrations to handle the work needed to prepare accession came in 1996 as the European Commission prepared its Opinions on the membership applications. The preparation of the *avis* required good coordination and a considerable investment by the associated countries. This preparation was also used to obtain the first indications for the establishment of a negotiating position for the subsequent membership negotiations. In general, the majority of the associated countries handled the *avis* challenge well, but improvements in administrative capacity will remain important.

## Theoretical strategies

There have been several attempts to design ideal strategies for accession. These all assume that there is a clear objective of accession and they generally aim at optimising the benefits to the associated countries, subject to constraints imposed by the other objectives of associated country policy and by the policy stance of the European Union.

One of the key differences between the strategies presented is the timescale for the preparation of accession. The first author to systematically consider the route to accession, Richard Baldwin, dismisses rapid accession as a political non-starter and therefore concentrates on a strategy for accession over a period of 20 or 30 years. Others, like Jeffrey Sachs, consider rapid membership to be both desirable and possible. A second variable is the number of countries considered as potential members. Some of the strategies have been designed with only a sub-set of the associated countries in mind and in the case of Richard Baldwin's work countries are included well beyond the associated countries. Thirdly, some strategies deal with accession in stages where the associated countries would be politically integrated before they were economically integrated. For other authors, this is a worst-case scenario.

### *Slowly towards an integrated Europe*

The first strategy for enlargement was presented by Richard Baldwin in 1994 in his book *Towards an integrated Europe.*[1] Although Baldwin's main proposals have not been acted on and indeed his whole approach to enlargement has been rejected by most authors and most politicians, his ideas were already having an impact politically in 1994. Four points form the background to the strategy for accession put forward by Baldwin:

- it is necessary to include all the Eastern European nations in the strategy
- it is necessary to replace the 'hub and spoke' bilateralism of the Association Agreements
- there is a need for an intermediate step between the Association Agreements and membership
- membership will not come for two decades.

The first point has to a certain extent been resolved by developments since the publication of Baldwin's work: Association Agreements have been negotiated with the three Baltic countries and with Slovenia. Ukraine, Moldova and Belarus, all included in the analysis, are clearly

---

[1] Baldwin (1994).

not in the minds of EU politicians for membership of the European Union or even for the negotiation of an Association Agreement. This point is not essential for Baldwin's argument, but is useful for reinforcing the fact that the enlargement of the Union to the East does indeed require that EU strategy includes relations of the enlarged Union with the European CIS countries.

Much of the first part of Baldwin's work is taken up with the theoretical discussion of the negative trade and investment impact on the associated countries of bilateral Association Agreements with the Union. The theoretical justification for this argument is sound. Where the Union has bilateral agreements with individual countries in Central and Eastern Europe, there is every incentive for companies supplying their goods to markets in both to locate their production in the Union. Whereas from a location in the Union the whole region can be supplied under the free trade or preferential tariff regimes of the Association Agreements, a location in one of the associated countries will give free trade or preferential access only to trade with the Union, but not with the other CEE partners.

There are, however, at least four reasons which tend to neutralise this argument. The first is that there is progressive integration going on in CEE trade regimes as well. The creation of CEFTA is a step in this direction: CEFTA attempts to achieve the same degree of liberalisation between its members as is achieved through the Association Agreements with the Union. The Baltic FTA was expanded to cover agricultural products on 1 January 1997.

Secondly, the July 1997 agreement on the pan-European diagonal cumulation of rules of origin is a major step in overcoming Baldwin's objections. It goes a long way to reducing the negative impacts of hub and spoke bilateralism, allowing goods produced in one country but using inputs imported from the other associated countries to be exported to the Union and obtain origin, therefore benefiting from preferential tariffs.

Thirdly, the arguments become somewhat less relevant as the process of general world reduction in trade barriers continues under the auspices of the WTO. Already five of the associated countries are members of the WTO, and the other countries are in various stages of preparing to join it. As trade barriers come down so the significance of the hub and spoke argument is reduced. Naturally some tariffs between the associated countries are still very high, but they should progressively be reduced. And above all, the trade disciplines imposed on WTO members will apply to trade relations between the associated countries.

Finally, the best way to avoid the distortions which the hub and spoke argument raises is to integrate the countries as soon as possible into the Union. A long period of waiting at the Union's doorstep would clearly have major negative effects on the associated countries: early entry would avoid these costs.

Baldwin's third argument – that there is a need for an intermediate step in the accession process between association and membership – also becomes less relevant if accession comes quickly. Faced by a long wait for membership, Baldwin argues for the need to have intermediate steps on the way to accession which would include in the first place the creation of a common market, the essential part of which would be a customs union and secondly entry into the internal market of the Union. Baldwin's argument would be indeed convincing if membership was to be dragged out over 20 or 30 years. The association relationship would certainly not avoid general disillusionment with the Union in those countries over this period. The analysis of Baldwin showing the enormous distance which the associated countries have to travel to reach accession is in itself important, but this does not mean that the process has to be separated into different stages. This analysis may well be pertinent, however, if enlargement takes place in several groups. It is difficult to see how those not in the early enlargement phase can simply be kept in an Association Agreement phase over many years. This is one of the reasons that the Union has proposed a European Conference, which would include all the associated countries and the Union.

The fourth argument – that accession will take several decades to achieve – is the crucial one. Baldwin assumes that the resistance to accession from the economic and political operators in the Union will be so great that there is no chance of rapid accession, unless, as he puts it, there is 'early enlargement on the cheap'. There are two problems with this supposition. Firstly it assumes that the European Union is unable to overcome its internal problems. The earlier chapters in this book suggest, that, while some of these problems are difficult, there are ways in which they can be overcome. Secondly it assumes stability in political and economic relationships stretching over 20 or 30 years up to the point of accession. It is unlikely that such a scenario will be realised. Already the level of instability is high and apparently growing, as witnessed by the conflicts in ex-Yugoslavia and Chechnya, the complex political situation in some countries, especially where there are substantial minority problems, and the more assertive foreign policy of Russia. Such instability will have an important negative influence on the CEE countries if they cannot be tied very closely into the European Union. Early accession is a condition for the political stability which will be necessary if economic recovery is to progress.

On the basis of these assumptions, Baldwin proposes a long-term strategy to achieve accession. His proposal envisages two phases with two separate institutions on the way to accession. At each stage a critical point in the proposal is that the European Union must take the leadership and be involved as an equal partner in these institutions, because there is no natural leader on the side of the associated countries. The two stages are as follows:

- An Association of Association Agreements (AAA) would be created in order to rationalise piecemeal liberalisation. All the countries with Association Agreements would be members, as would all the Member States of the Union. The objective would be to create a zone of liberalised trade, in which the associated countries would mutually open their markets to each other. The result would be a pan-European FTA. The AAA authority would be created with four roles: surveillance, enforcement, coordination and assistance. It would be dominated, according to Baldwin, by the European Union, which would have the advantage of engaging the Union in the process of integration.
- An Organisation for European Integration (OEI) would be created for those associated countries which have progressed far along the accession path and can enter an intermediate stage where they have access to the internal market of the Union. Again, the European Union would be the dominant partner. Countries could enter the OEI when they are sufficiently advanced to merit it, and it would be a relatively small step from here to accession. Baldwin does not really address the problem of determining at which stage a country would progress from being a simple AAA member to joining the elite club of the OEI.

These proposals have not received the study they deserved for two main reasons: the long-time span is considered politically unfeasible, and few people really want to create new institutions, which by their very nature will be highly politicised bureaucracies. However much of Baldwin's analysis is very pertinent to the problems of integration, especially if, as seems likely, enlargement takes place in different tranches of countries rather than together as a large group.

*Commitments, speed and conditionality*

The opposite view in terms of timing is put by Alain de Crombrugghe, Zanny Minton-Beddoes and Jeffrey Sachs, in a proposal in 1996.[2]

---

[2]  De Crombrugghe, Minton-Beddoes and Sachs (1996).

The proposal has four main themes:

- the Union should give certainty to the associated countries that they can join the Union, because only through certainty can all the positive economic effects (investment and growth) coming from business optimism be created and maintained
- this certainty can be given only through an exact timetable for the opening of the negotiations and for accession; accession should be rapid
- conditions must be set for accession by the European Union, and these must be policed; without conditionality, there is no real incentive for the associated countries to pursue reform
- there must be commitment from the European Union that accession is certain if these conditions are met.

That certainty about accession would have an important impact on investment, including inward investment, is not in doubt. A positive cumulative process of higher investment leading to higher growth and higher investment with positive impacts on reform, social consensus and macroeconomic stability is clearly one certain result of rapid accession combined with intelligent macroeconomic policies. That destabilising failure of the accession process could lead to pessimism, low investment, falling growth rates, and falling investment afflicted by social unrest and instability is also a clear possibility.

That this certainty could be achieved by an unequivocal declaration of the date by which negotiations could start and accession be finalised is also sure. Since the appearance of de Crombrugghe et al.'s article a date has been more or less set for the opening of negotiations, but it is hardly unequivocal. The Madrid Council 'expressed the wish that the preliminary stage of the negotiations will coincide with the start of negotiations with Malta and Cyprus'. 'Agenda 2000' accepts the probable date of Spring 1998 for the opening of negotiations with the first group of countries. However there is no certainty about the rest of the timetable. The degree of certainty also decreases as one goes from the Visegrád countries towards the other associated countries. This is no doubt one of the factors which is determining that the bulk of foreign investment is going to these countries.

Conditionality is an important incentive to reform and the preparation of integration. The absence of conditionality has led to policy in the associated countries being without a firm anchor. Politicians have been able to choose roads that did not lead to the Union, because there was no penalty to be paid. To introduce conditionality is not, however, as simple as is suggested by de Crombrugghe et al. Basically, the authors suggest two sorts of conditions: verifiable quantitative macroeconomic conditions for inflation, the government deficit and other macroeconomic variables and semi-quantitative conditions on the adoption of the Community *acquis communautaire*. This conditionality would apply immediately and continue during the pre-accession phase, being verified annually by the Commission.

The first type of conditionality should have been applied after the Copenhagen Summit, once the Union had decided that its objective was accession. The European Commission has considerable experience in monitoring economic performance and could easily mount such a surveillance operation. The second sort of criterion is more complex in its specification, its verification and indeed in its logic. This is the conditionality proposed in the new 'Agenda 2000' pre-accession strategy. Given the different situations in the applicant states and their different needs, objectives for legal harmonisation must be set essentially by the associated country and agreed by the Union. There is also the fundamental equity point, which is that normally the *acquis* is the subject of negotiation prior to accession. For the first time, in the case of Central Europe, the Union is requiring countries to take over the *acquis* before the negotiations start. It would hardly be fair if conditionality was used by the Union to avoid problems in the negotiations. Greater commitment from the Union in terms of accession if these conditions are met would clearly have to be agreed; it would not be fair to force the associated countries into a massive programme of adjustment, controlled by strong conditionality if, at the end of the day, the Union were still to refuse accession.

The proposal which comes out of this analysis consists of several conditions for accession and proposals for the period after accession. The conditions include:

- a time commitment by the Union to start negotiations by 1998 and to agree enlargement in 2000 subject to the conditions being met; if only a sub-set meet the conditions by this date, a new timetable will be set for the other countries
- the applicants refrain from making any treaties with non-EU Member States not agreed to by the Union
- the applicants will adopt the *acquis communautaire*, except in certain opt-out areas (agriculture, Structural Funds, etc.) and ensure the proper functioning of the legal framework of the market economy; this will be monitored annually by the Commission
- microeconomic and macroeconomic indicators will be set for

the associated countries and monitored by the Commission; they will not, however, be required to meet the Maastricht conditions for membership of EMU before accession.

The proposals include the following:

- there should be a ten-year transition period upon membership
- the new members will participate in the same way as the existing Member States in the decision-making process in the Union; but they will not be able to change the conditions affecting the transition period and agreed before accession or to vote in the areas they are not involved in during the transition period – agriculture, the Structural Funds, the Social Chapter, for instance
- no trade barriers will exist between the old and new members
- agriculture remains protected with border controls for a transition period of ten years
- the associated countries will renounce all claims to Structural Funds spending during the transition phase, but their contributions will also be scaled down to take account of the fact that they participate neither in the CAP nor in the Structural Funds; the new members will participate in Community-wide infrastructure schemes
- the freedom of movement for labour will be waived in the transition period
- the new members will meet the criteria for Monetary Union within five years of membership; their performance will be monitored by the Commission during the transition period.

The emphasis of this proposal is on the speed of entry because it is speed and certainty which are required to accelerate economic growth and catch-up. This proposal for a rapid accession process has elements of partial or second-class membership (the exclusion of the associated countries from participation in and decision-making on the CAP and the Structural Funds). Certain other elements do appear to be built on false assumptions: for instance, participation in the Community-wide infrastructure projects suggests that finance will be forthcoming, which at the moment looks questionable, and both sides renouncing trade restrictions on accession would seem to ignore the fact that the first thing which accession does for a country is to eliminate any form of protection within the Union.

The key question which needs to be asked of this strategy is why it is necessary to introduce elements of partial membership if the conditions for accession are set in such a way that it likely that only the most advanced countries can join. Introducing partial membership for basic policies is an extremely dangerous step involving the break-up of the Union into clearly separate blocs. This is totally different to the flexible integration discussed in chapter 12. Flexible integration would ensure that all Member States sign up to the basic policies of the Union, including the CAP and the Structural Funds. Even in the areas which were not compulsory, all Member States would be implicated in the development of the rules and scope of the policies and the qualifications for membership. What is proposed here would clearly relegate the associated countries to second-class membership over a decade.

The strategy does not include very much about the system of support which will need to be developed for the countries which do not make the conditions for the first round of enlargement. To set a new timetable may not convince economic operators that the countries will have any more chance of entering the Union the second time round than the first; something more than a new timetable will be required.

The strategy also does not require too much change from the Union. Rather than forcing all change on the associated countries and allowing the Union to continue untroubled with some of its less effective policies until the end of the transition period, it would be important for the Union to use enlargement to make some of its policies more effective. In other words, the changes forced on the Union by enlargement are an important part of the positive balance of advantage which the Union will draw from it.

What is important in the work of de Crombrugghe *et al.* is the emphasis put on the speed and certainty of enlargement. Commitment from the Union is one important missing element which is making economic policy-making for the associated countries very difficult. If the commitment could be reinforced, perhaps through agreeing certain conditions which would be policed by the European Commission, this would make the coming years of reform and economic development considerably easier.

### Partial membership

The elements of partial membership cited by de Crombrugghe *et al.* in their proposals are part of a strategy which has been proposed at a high level in some Member State governments. The analysis which leads to partial membership is that the economic problems of accession for the Union are just too difficult, as supposed also by Baldwin. What the associated countries really want and need, says this argument, is not economic integration but political integration. What is more simple then than to propose that the associated countries are offered partial membership, so that the budgetary implications are close to zero at least for a long transition period? This idea can look back on a long pedigree, having been proposed as early as 1990 by Commissioner Andriessen. However, whereas such a proposal was looked on seriously by the associated countries (which at that time were not associated) in 1990, progress with reform and economic recovery has been so rapid in several countries that a second-rate accession, where the new members would practically take part only in those parts of Union policy where little progress has been made (CFSP, for instance) would today be unacceptable.

Partial membership has been proposed recently to overcome the budgetary consequences of enlargement and in some countries to avoid changes in Community policy which would be politically difficult to manage nationally. Partial membership above all excludes agricultural policy and any Structural Funds and in its extreme form participation in the internal market. The supposed benefits are on the political and security fronts, where the associated countries would be totally integrated. This would mean that they had an implicit security guarantee and that they participated in the major decisions made in the area of foreign policy. Even this advantage is now devalued for the three Visegrád countries which will be joining NATO.

As discussed above, the Union would be a major loser in any system of partial accession, because it would remove the stimulus to reform Union policies which would be given by a normal accession. But beyond this, with most decisions in the Union still in the economic, business or trade areas, the associated countries would be shut out of three-quarters of the Union's work. This really would be second-class membership, and would be seen as such by economic agents, who would probably not consider such an accession as giving them sufficient assurance about the stability of the political and business environments in the associated countries.

### Accession in waves

One of the reasons that the Union has been so reticent in giving commitments to the associated countries about accession is that it was considered probable that some of the countries would take much longer to advance with reforms than others. Implicit in both the strategies of Baldwin and de Crombrugghe *et al.* is that there is unlikely to be an enlargement with all 12 countries (including Cyprus and Malta) entering the Community at the same time. Obviously it makes a considerable difference to the strategy design if three countries or 12 countries join in the first wave of accession.

The Union itself has, however, steadfastly refused to contemplate any differentiation between candidate countries, except on performance measured by the Copenhagen criteria. Efforts were made, for instance, to make sure that the Bulgarian and Romanian Association Agreements with the Community were brought into line with those of the Visegrád countries in 1994. And at Madrid, the Union heads of government refused to contemplate treating the associated countries differently. The position of the Union has always been, and remains, that all the associated countries start from the same contractual relationship and if all reform to meet the Copenhagen criteria, all will enter the Union together. The Commission Opinions, while apparently departing from this situation and opting for differentiation in selecting five countries as ready for negotiations, nevertheless maintains this overall position. 'Agenda 2000' clearly makes the point that other countries can join the negotiations when they are ready.

The consequences of a division into accession leagues could have grave consequences for the countries concerned, and should be a major point of strategic thinking on the part of the Union.

### Elements of a strategy for achieving enlargement

The elements presented here clearly build on 'Agenda 2000' and some of the academic work discussed in this chapter. Any strategy must attempt to avoid the dangers of either renewed division in Europe or of destabilising Central Europe with all the dangers which history tells us about. It must also be conscious of the need to preserve the achievements of 40-odd years of European integration, which have led to peace and cooperation in Western and Southern Europe that nobody could have dreamed of in 1945.

#### Cornerstones of a programme

The cornerstones of an enlargement programme should include the characteristics listed in figure 15.1.

#### Commitment, timing and openness

The arguments advanced by de Crombrugghe, Minton-Beddoes and Sachs on commitment by the Union to enlargement are of the greatest importance. Policy credibility is vital for investment and therefore growth and employment. Credibility will be given by a firm commitment of the Union to accession. This commitment should include:

- an objective for the date of the first accessions

1  The Union must commit itself to enlargement, accession needs to be rapid and a timetable should be given. All associated countries should have the same starting point but negotiations should be opened only with those countries which have a chance of meeting the criteria and which will not pose unacceptable political risks for the future of the Union; clearer measurable criteria should be set with surveillance of performance.

2  Reform and economic development should continue to have priority in the new Member States; nothing should be done which will restrict investment and growth. European integration should not divert attention from other priorities such as economic reform, the promotion of enterprise and the development of trade with other parts of the world, but should be made compatible with these objectives.

3  The Member States must seriously tackle the market rigidities in the Union which are driving it into a major economic crisis with unacceptably high unemployment and the Union must tackle reform of the agricultural policy, the Structural Funds and the budget, which require clear medium-term objectives.

4  Partial accession should not be considered, but transition periods will be needed. The Union must be flexible in certain key areas on the adoption of the *acquis communautaire* and must allow reasonable transition periods to apply to the new Member States in these areas.

5  The associated countries must give great importance to the preparation of the negotiating position, which requires wider impact assessment of the Community *acquis*. They should accelerate the implementation of national strategies for the adoption of the *acquis*, reinforce the coordination mechanisms in government on European integration and accelerate the reform and training of the administration.

6  Domestically, the associated countries must raise the profile of European integration in the administration and amongst their populations. Externally they must adopt a strategy of lobbying Member States and interested influential groups.

7  The Union should develop a pre-accession structural programme, which would apply to all applicant countries, not simply those in the first wave of negotiations.

8  The Union should develop a new policy for those countries not meeting the criteria for the first round of accession.

9  A policy towards Russia and the Ukraine to accompany enlargement needs to be designed, which does not give Russia a veto right over enlargement, but which promotes regional cooperation and preserves important elements from the foreign policy and economic relations of the associated countries with respect to the NIS.

*Figure 15.1* Elements of a strategy for enlargement

- conditions and dates for a second round of enlargement if all the applicants are not included in the first round; 'Agenda 2000' proposes an alternative which is an annual report on the preparations in the associated countries for membership, with the possibility for a decision to open negotiations on an annual basis
- a pre-accession structural programme.

The economic arguments put forward by de Crombrugghe *et al.* in favour of rapid enlargement are certainly correct. The impact on investment and growth in the associated countries of real commitment from the Union to accession at an early date would be very large. It would assure investors at home and abroad that the legal and regulatory environment for business would be the same as in the present Union and that there would be no further risks of the old Union making use of commercial policy measures, such as anti-dumping, against CEE countries.

But the political and security arguments for rapid accession are also convincing. Accession to the Union will be an important cornerstone for political stability in the associated countries.

Rapid accession needs a timetable attached to it for two reasons: it will give the associated countries a fixed point around which to design the enormous changes which they need to make in their legislation, policies and institutions, and it gives the Union a similar discipline to that which the '1992' programme gave. Such a timetable also makes it easier for private sector agents to make company plans for the future, and has a positive impact on economic development.

The approach to differentiation between the applicant countries taken by the Commission in 'Agenda 2000' is certainly the right one. The Union's basic position, of giving all the applicant countries the same starting position but opening negotiations only with those countries which are objectively ready, combines fairness with efficiency. In effect, the door to negotiations is being kept open for those countries which can carry out economic, social and political reform. The question is whether the 'annual review of progress' approach realistically keeps the door open to new negotiations while negotiations with the first group of countries are already well under way.

The question of setting clear criteria against which to measure progress in the associated countries has been discussed many times. Two main sorts of criteria can be set, beyond the absolutes of the Copenhagen Summit, as suggested by de Crombrugghe *et al.* The first concern progress with economic and social reform, where objective, and often quantitative, indicators can be set. The second would reflect progress with the adoption of the *acquis communautaire*. An essential of both is that the conditions are established and agreed to by both sides and not unilaterally imposed by the EU, in ignorance of the particular situation of each country.

The first criteria are well known and understood in the world of macroeconomic policy. They concern objectives for inflation, the government deficit, reduction in the stock of government debt and, in certain circumstances, the balance on current account. In the case of the associated countries further criteria, of a more microeconomic type, could be set, relating to privatisation, the degree of state or private monopoly, and the level of state subsidies. None of these criteria alone would be sufficient to discriminate against an applicant, but performance across the criteria would. Interim targets could be set jointly by the Commission and the country concerned and the performance would be checked annually. If targets are missed, joint discussion would seek to analyse the causes and the interim targets for the following year would be correspondingly adjusted.

The second sort of criteria would be more complicated to set, and more difficult to monitor. Each year agreed areas of approximation of legislation could be tackled and, as with the macroeconomic objectives, interim objectives could be set and monitored. The associated countries would be in control of the agenda: they would have to decide the sequencing and the priorities. This is similar to what is proposed for the 'accession partnerships' in 'Agenda 2000', although these 'partnerships' appear to give control of the agenda to the EU side. There is, however, a danger here for those countries which are already negotiating with the Union. Conditionality set in the accession partnerships should not conflict with the negotiations, otherwise the accession partnerships will become phantom negotiations.

The importance of criteria is perhaps less to differentiate between candidates, than to give various performance anchors to domestic policy in the associated countries. Governments can sell bad-tasting medicine to the voters if it is part of a strategy leading to the goal of membership of the European Union. If there are no objectives set by the Union, the selling of such policies is more difficult.

One major objection can be raised: is it not too late in the process to invent new criteria? More detailed criteria and a system of surveillance will, however, serve two purposes:

- They will be required to guide policy in the associated countries between now and accession in, say, 2001–2. But they will also be necessary during the transition periods after accession to help the new members to stay on a convergence course with the Union in the areas covered by the transitional arrangements.

- If not all the associated countries are included in the first negotiations, the criteria will serve to prepare the remaining countries for a later accession.

*Reform and economic development should continue to have priority*
A purely legal approach to accession is inadequate. This is the weakness of an approach which considers the Cannes White Paper to be the check-list against which progress towards accession can be measured. The associated countries are relatively poor and face major financial problems in the area of pensions and other social provision, the construction of an adequate infrastructure and the restructuring of state enterprises. The only hope to really successfully tackle these problems is if high investment and economic growth can continue for many years. Every piece of legislation the associated countries take over from the Union is a decision on economic policy, which can have very far-reaching impacts on the reform process and on economic growth. In the design of approximation programmes, the impact of each piece of legislation on the economy and society of the associated countries should be considered. Any legislation which is going to hinder the political or economic reform process or restrict investment and growth should be relegated to later in the programme. Giving priority to economic growth and reform is not only important for the associated countries. It will be easier for the Union to integrate countries which are developing quickly and which are rapidly becoming more like the older Member States in terms of the market economy than if the countries are very poor and reform is beginning to buckle under the weight of poverty and deprivation.

Progress with pensions reform, with macroeconomic stabilisation, with investment and job creation and with the internationalisation of the economy and society need to go on independently of accession. Regional integration in West Central Europe should not be considered an alternative to full integration into international bodies, exploring for markets in South East Asia, the United States or Eastern Europe, or looking for foreign investment from Japan and South Korea. Czech, Hungarian and Polish membership of OECD is far more important to those countries than many think: it already gives them equality with the industrialised countries of Western Europe and North America, with potentially large benefits in terms of improving the investment climate.

In general, the measures taken to promote integration will also promote reform and economic development. But this will not always be the case, and the associated countries should not undertake immediate approximation in areas where action will hold back economic growth.

### The Union and its Member States must reform national and Union policies

The economic situation in the Union in 1997 is not propitious for an enlargement. It is characterised by slow economic growth and growing unemployment, which is already at a high level. Consumer and producer confidence is muted in most Member States. There will no doubt be some cyclical improvement, but the major problem is not cyclical but structural. Unless there is a determined effort by Member States to increase flexibility in the economy and to rationalise over-extended social protection systems leading to higher employment and renewed growth, the economic climate for enlargement will not be good.[3]

Enlargement itself will, as explained earlier, help to add dynamism to the West European economy through an increase in competition and an enlargement of the domestic market. But the fear is that the poor economic condition within the Union will be used by the opponents of enlargement as an argument against enlargement itself.

An early start also needs to made on the reform of Community policies prior to enlargement. These discussions will be exceedingly difficult and long. Ideally, clear ideas of medium-term reform would be formulated in time for the accession negotiations beginning in early 1998. However, this is unrealistic and it is probable that the key decisions on the CAP, the Structural Funds and the budget will be put off until 1999. This will make the negotiations extremely complicated and rather unfair for the associated countries. Further progress on reform of the Union's institutions will also be necessary prior to enlargement.

### Flexibility, partial accession and transitional periods

Ideas of a partial accession, such as those put forward by de Crombrugghe et al. should be rejected for two reasons: they will create a club of second-class members who will be considered as such by the old Member States and this will generate ill-feeling within the Union; secondly partial membership will cause major problems for the operation of the Union and its further integration. Partial membership, where the associate countries are excluded from basic Union policies, will mean that frontiers are permanent and the objective of a frontier-free European political and economic space will not be met. Knock-on effects from this exclusion will occur in other policies – for instance,

---

[3] Siebert (1997), pp. 37–54.

exclusion from the CAP will mean special rules being adopted for processed agricultural products and this will have further impacts on other industries. Experience has shown that there is no third way between membership and non-membership of the Union.

However, there will be a need for long transition periods in a few areas of policy. De Crombrugghe *et al.*'s idea of a general transition period is attractive because it is simple and is reminiscent of the Treaty of Rome provisions under which the common market was to be established over a period of 12 years. However, the needs of the transformation process in the associated countries in specific sectors will mean that the transition periods should be policy- or directive-specific rather than general. The transitions allowed should be as limited as possible, but must include those policy areas where rapid alignment would curb investment and economic growth. These include some areas of social and environment policy.

A distinction must be made between product and process regulations. Product-related regulations will in general have to be introduced early in order to allow the full integration of the associated countries in the internal market of the Union. Process-related regulation, defining how products are produced rather than their proper characteristics, need not be immediately implemented by the associated countries. Such process directives are concentrated in the social and environmental areas. That ultimately the new members will have to take on the whole *acquis* is clear, but transition periods must be available in those areas where the additional financial costs will put too heavy a burden on the economy.

### *The associated countries should accelerate their preparation for membership, while maintaining reform priorities*

The work to prepare a position for the negotiations expected to start in 1998 is progressing in all the associated countries. But much work remains to be done before such a negotiating position is arrived at. Detailed economic analysis of the impact of integration on investment and growth must be carried out, as well as estimates of the institutional capacity of each country to support accession.

Most of the associated countries have now adopted national strategies for the integration of their countries into the European Union, which go well beyond the needs of the *avis* or the definition of a negotiating position. These strategies are important but they should frequently be stricter, with timetables for the changes which are to be undertaken and also with clearer attribution of responsibilities.

In many associated countries there appears still to be a feeling that transition periods can be negotiated across wide swathes of the Community *acquis*. This will not be the case, and rapid progress needs to be made in the area of approximating product directives, in adopting European norms and standards, in the implementation of competition policy and the control of state aids and in some basic areas of the internal market such as banking, insurance and accountancy law.

The coordination mechanisms in many of the associated country governments also need to be reinforced. There is obviously no one recipe for coordination and within the Union the Member States have used different systems as they prepared to join, but in almost all cases there was strong centralised coordination exercised in a clearly identified part of the administration. The need for such coordination is even stronger in the associated countries. Coordination requires good officials in each ministry who are responsible for the work of their ministry on European integration and who are tied into the coordination process. In order to get highly qualified staff involved in this process, the importance of European integration must be regularly underlined at the highest level in the government and each minister must interest himself in the work of the responsible officials. Only if the government makes this subject a priority, will it be treated as such by the officials concerned.

The reform of the administration in most of the associated countries has lagged behind other areas of reform. The reasons are complex, but they are usually associated with poor remuneration and complex job-security rules in the state sector. The senior levels in the administration are also over-politicised, leading to an enormous loss of knowledge and talent with every change in government. Training in administration is of vital importance. Quality management techniques are frequently missing in the administration, and training specifically on European integration issues needs to be carried out much more widely.

*Domestic and foreign information and public relations programmes
in the associated countries need to be developed further*

Today accession to the European Union is a popular theme in Central Europe, partly because no one knows what it really means. In order to avoid a setback to efforts to join the Union inflicted by a popular backlash against accession when details become known, it is important to spend more time and money on explaining the facts and the implications of membership to the voters. This is a difficult lesson, which the Member States of the Union have not yet learned, but it is a vital part of any strategy. Specific parts of the electorate need specific information. This is particularly true of the business community, which will be directly affected by the changes made before and after accession.

So far, the information available to business has been insufficient and, when it exists, very general. With business organisations being weak in the region, it is important for governments (with help from Member States of the Union) to be active in supporting efforts to disseminate information and to provide advice to business. Similar efforts need to be made for the trades unions, farmers, local authorities and other groups. Work in the schools and universities also needs attention. Only if there is a very wide effort to disseminate information will governments carry their publics with them.

External ly, it will be very important for the associated countries to lobby the Member States but also industry, the trades unions and other organisations in the Union in order to keep up support for accession. It is the Member States in Council which will decide on the accession process. Keeping close to the most effective supporters and opponents of enlargement will therefore be part of any serious strategy. Germany will be of great importance, as will the Nordic countries, but it will be vital to maintain good relations, too, with countries such as Spain which are essentially neutral on enlargement as long as their allocation of Structural Funds is not affected.

Other lobbying activity will concentrate on large business groups which have invested heavily already in the associated countries and which can be expected to have considerable influence in the capitals of the Member States. But here, too, it will be important to maintain good relations with groups in the Union who might be considered to be potential opponents of accession – the trades unions, farmers, and so on.

### A pre-accession structural programme

The Union should develop a pre-accession programme with the associated countries, changing the PHARE resources into a pre-accession Structural Fund and if possible increasing those resources in the coming years. This is a very different proposal to that made by de Crombrugghe *et al.* to renounce budgetary transfers.

The argument that subsidies blunt the entrepreneurial spirit and lead to low efficiency and poor performance is correct: one only needs to look at the experience of highly subsidised regions like West Berlin, Northern Ireland, the Mezzogiorno or Greece to see how true this is. However a pre-accession programme should not subsidise enterprises but should concentrate on bringing the quality of the infrastructure in these countries up to the level of the Union.

Such a programme would need the following characteristics:
- it would cover all associated countries, irrespective of whether they all accede to the Union at the same time or not

- control of the programme would be in the hands of the associated countries not the Union, and it would be run as a Structural Fund; this would give the associated countries experience in managing funds, which they do not have with the current approach of the PHARE programme
- EIB loan finance and PHARE grants would be combined and the Union should invite the World Bank and the EBRD to participate
- the programme would concentrate on improving infrastructure in the region; 'infrastructure' would be defined widely to include physical infrastructure but also educational infrastructure and the development of human capital
- the programme would be co-financed, with a high maximum of 75%–85% of project value being available in loan or grant form from the Union or other backers
- the fund would not normally finance technical assistance, the latter being financed through national or bilateral funding; however, some funding for legal approximation and the development of networking between Member State institutions, NGOs, business organisations and trades unions would be retained.

The programme could be set up on a country-by-country basis or as a region-wide infrastructure programme. The region-wide programme would have the advantage that it could be designed as an integrated infrastructure network. It would, however, be more complex to start quickly and to organise and control afterwards. Whichever system was used, the programme would tackle the improvement of important national infrastructure as well as the Trans-European Networks (TENs). The latter should not dominate such a programme, however, for it should concentrate on the highest rate of return to investment, which will rarely be found in the TENs.

Agricultural infrastructure and infrastructure for business should also be included in the programme. The Fischler report to the Madrid European Council (see European Commission, 1995c) already gives a good idea of what would be required in the agricultural sector. Investment in human capital infrastructure should also be encouraged; here, the Irish experience should be highly relevant.

Obviously such a pre-accession programme could operate with any level of funding but the present level would be inadequate. It must be remembered that the additional cost of taking on the Union *acquis*, especially in the years before accession, may well amount to 6% or more of the associated countries' GDP annually. The Union should consider a considerable increase in funding, including loan finance from the EIB or through a special restructuring loan facility, as suggested by the Commission at the Essen Summit.

'Agenda 2000' proposes a strategy which includes many of these characteristics, but which is not sufficiently clear on the decentralisation of control to the associated countries and which is limited in the resources to be made available.

### Policy for associated countries not in the first wave

At the same time as the choice is made for the first-round negotiations, the Council should announce its policy towards the remaining applicants. The impact of an announcement of the countries not in the first wave without a simultaneous announcement of a new accompanying policy would have potentially disastrous impacts on their political, economic and social stability. It is therefore of great importance that the Union designs a clear policy towards these countries. 'Agenda 2000' already contains most of the elements of such a policy, but these need to be spelled out in a coherent fashion.

### Policy towards Russia and the Ukraine and regional cooperation

The objective of the enlargement process is to take a further step towards unifying Europe. It would be perverse if the result were to lead to a new division in the continent between an enlarged Union and Russia and the Ukraine. It would also be a severe disadvantage for the new Member States, which need close and peaceful relations with these large neighbours. Part of any enlargement strategy must therefore be to pursue a policy of closer cooperation with the Ukraine and Russia, developing the Union's PCAs and continuing the assistance effort.

The promotion of regional cooperation, which was an important part of the Essen pre-accession strategy, has advanced, but should go further. This is not simply because apparently the European Union is in favour of it. It is simply that it makes good sense to foster regional cooperation in trade and in terms of regional security. CEFTA has already made progress at the trade level. Greater cooperation between the countries on third-pillar issues would also be very important at a time when crime is become ever more international and the Union is putting so much importance on the issues of justice and home affairs.

Cooperation across the associated countries in the context of preparing the negotiations with the Union is a more delicate issue. It is certain, however, that coordination between the negotiating teams of the countries negotiating accession after 1998 would be very beneficial in obtaining better terms from the Union.

## Conclusion

Enlargement will not be a smooth process. It will undoubtedly bring great benefits to all participants, but for some it is potentially threatening. Like EMU, it will radically change the whole nature of the Union. The keys to past achievements were a strong leadership role played by the European Commission, the cyclical situation in an economic upswing and a delicate balancing of interest so that the gains were spread over the Union as a whole. These characteristics may not be all present for enlargement: the European Commission has been forced into a defensive position, the economic situation is characterised by grave structural problems in several of the Member States and it will be more difficult to spread the gains from enlargement to all members. These conditions make it all the more necessary for the Union to adopt a clear strategy for enlargement, but all the more difficult to do so.

# 16    Conclusions: transition, integration and cooperation

Enlargement is a win-win process. It is necessary in order to complete the reintegration of the European Continent and to ensure peace and stability. But in a much narrower view it will also bring economic benefits to the existing European Union and to the new Member States.

Integration is just one of the three processes which are transforming the CEE countries into normal middle-income European countries after 40 years of central planning and separation. The transformation processes themselves are not finished; much still has to be done in areas as different as privatisation and the development of civic society. Integration with the European Union normally, but not always, underpins these transformation processes. But the internationalisation of the associated countries must go well beyond their integration into the European structures. The development of cooperation with America, South-East Asia and other regions, and their integration into international institutions, is also vital to achieve 'normalisation' throughout the region.

Integration into the European Union is important for the associated countries politically and economically. Decisions taken by the Union affect the whole Continent. This is as true for decisions on foreign policy as it is for monetary union and economic policy. For the associated countries, it is important to have a voice in deciding these policies, and this participation can be achieved only through accession. In the economic area, the degree of integration of the associated countries with the economies of the Union is now so great that to be outside the Union and potentially subjected to commercial policy measures is dangerous.

For the European Union, enlargement offers the chance to cement peace, stability and freedom on the Continent. This was the spirit of 1989, which has become rather muted over the following years, as the European Union has experienced internal problems and as the costs of enlargement to certain groups in the Union have become apparent. But it also offers concrete economic gains. In a very basic way, these economies have become major export markets for EU-15 firms and are liable to remain so for many years. But enlargement also presents the chance to the Union to undertake reforms which are necessary if Europe wishes to remain a leading economic force in the next century.

Enlargement is therefore a win-win situation for the Union. It may also be a necessary step for its further development. The strains which can arise if enlargement does not take place are probably considerably greater than those which arise because it takes place. However the strains created by the enlargement process must be dealt with. Every reform creates problems for certain groups in society – sometimes professional (agriculture, for instance), sometimes geographical (such as the 'cohesion' countries). These problems are often dealt with inefficiently in the Union because of the possibility of any one country using the power decision by unanimity gives it to extort over-generous compensation for supposed losses out of its partners. It is to be hoped that enlargement does not lead to major losses of efficiency through negotiations within the EU-15, which would reduce the net gains to the Union.

There are, however, several years before the actual accession of the first CEE countries to the Union. During this period it will be the Association Agreements which determine the detail of the relationship between the associated countries and the Union. For those countries not included in the first wave of negotiations, or with whom negotiations are formally opened but not pursued rapidly, the Association Agreements will remain the key legal relationship with the Union for many years to come. Both parties to the agreements should consider whether improvements should not be made: the associated countries could consider liberalising trade in certain goods or services more quickly than programmed by the agreements, while the Union should make substantial changes to the commercial defence policy provisions.

But the political climate will be determined by the debate over enlargement. On the European Union side, enlargement appears to some simply to add to already insuperable problems. The real problems, however, are fear of the future, an inability to tackle real economic reform and an anxiety that the integration which the Union has achieved over four decades could easily be destroyed; and these problems have little to do with enlargement. This fear is illustrated by the remarkable change of attitude amongst the public between 1985 and 1995. With strong economic growth, the completion of the internal market in full swing and a rapid warming of relations with the Soviet Union, the late 1980s were a period of great optimism and support for the idea of European integration. Today, with high unemployment and no clear political will to tackle the problems, with national stabilisation policies being implemented in the name of Monetary Union rather than domestic mismanagement and with a continuation of the technocratic Maastricht style of operation in the Union, there is an indifference in the population about EU affairs and, in certain countries, a fairly clear rejection of deepening European integration.

European integration is not an end in itself, but a means to increase the welfare of the citizen. Many citizens and voters apparently just do not see the connection today. In the second half of the 1980s the positive effects of the completion of the internal market were obvious to most people, and there was little to restrict the independence of the Member States in important areas of action. The Maastricht Treaty, the push for Monetary Union and the agenda of the IGC appear, however, to have unsettled voters even in some of the most integrationist Member States like Belgium and the Netherlands. Further major changes such as enlargement may lead to even greater uncertainty amongst citizens of the existing Member States, coming on top of the other unresolved problems of the Union's agenda.

Even more significant are the unresolved economic problems in the Member States. The globalisation of the world economy requires changes in the way in which the economies and societies of the Member States operate. Yet the will to adapt amongst the population appears weak, and in some countries the very need to adapt does not seem to have been appreciated. At the political level, reform plans are therefore postponed. Even areas of obvious crisis, such as pensions, are not being tackled in many of the Member States, even though some associate countries have made good progress with reform. This inability to undertake fundamental reform has led to low economic growth rates and high unemployment rates in continental Europe. This in turn is leading to increased nationalism amongst populations, which see 'foreigners' as one of the causes of their economic problems. Enlargement, which will bring increased competition on certain parts of the labour market, is therefore likely to be opposed by many people, who fear for their jobs in the longer term. This is surely a serious risk to enlargement today.

Finally, amongst some political classes, enlargement raises the fear that the progress towards greater integration in the Union will be slowed down or stopped altogether. Perhaps the greatest step towards deeper integration will be taken totally independently of enlargement: it is difficult to imagine a more integrating step than monetary union. The success or failure of monetary union will, however, in no way be affected by enlargement. It is true that enlargement to the CEE countries will fundamentally change the Union, just as previous enlargements have done. However, just as each previous enlargement has introduced new and positive influences, so will this one.

On the side of the associated countries, the problem in general is not one of political motivation to join the Union – all surveys show a clear majority for accession. The real problem is the need for further change in societies which have experienced so much change and disruption in the last few years that they really need some time for consolidation. But these countries will not have the luxury of consolidation and policy stability for at least another decade or two. The associated countries have shown themselves capable of accepting and implementing change in a way which is inconceivable in the societies of Western Europe; nevertheless, the problem of passing and implementing so much new legislation in such a short time, while respecting the rules of the democratic process, is a major challenge. To persuade the electorates in the CEE countries that further change is necessary, two pre-conditions are required. The first is that economic growth is buoyant enough that the majority in society feel that they are better off and that the returns from change are reasonably fairly distributed. The second, in the context of accession, is that there is certainty at the end of the process of the harmonisation of legislation and its implementation that accession to the European Union will be on offer.

The first has been a continuing theme of this book. Both the associated countries themselves and the European Union will gain if the gap in income and wealth between the EU-15 and the associated countries is reduced as quickly as possible. For the associated countries, this means a renewed effort to accelerate reforms leading to liberalising trade and markets, building a strong privatised banking sector and attracting foreign investment. For the Union, which has gained already so much from trade with the associated countries, it means removing the final barriers to trade and thinking less about 'level playing fields' when it comes to accession negotiations. If long-term thinking could dominate in the Union, this position would be easy to adopt. Unfortunately, it is usually short-term political positions which triumph. It is strange that 'Agenda 2000', with all its positive proposals to promote integration, does not even mention further trade liberalisation on the side of the Union, though it does emphasise that the associated countries should avoid adopting trade decisions which negatively affect Union exporters. There is no mention of liberalising agricultural trade, understandably given the reform agenda which has to be tackled; but that there is no mention either of the EU voluntarily desisting from the use of commercial defence instruments against the associated countries is much more difficult to understand. The 'level playing field argument', which says that enterprises in the associated countries should have to bear the same burdens of regulation as those in the Union from the first day of accession, should also not be used to reduce growth in these countries. While in many areas it will be essential to take on EU regulation immediately, other areas will need to be tackled over sometimes quite long transition periods.

The second pre-condition, that there should be certainty about accession in return for these countries adopting EU regulation, is particularly vital and particularly difficult. Certainty is, however, not only important for the associated countries, but also for foreign enterprises investing in or trading with these countries. For the European Union, the difficulty is one of avoiding making accession promises so firm that the applicant countries feel able to reduce their integration efforts. The Union could, however, give indicative timetables for accession when negotiations are opened. It could also give an idea of the timetable for negotiations of those countries which are not in the first group with which the Union negotiates. It seems, however, unlikely that the Union will consider this option. The best way of creating certainty is then to open negotiations as quickly as possible and to pursue the negotiations with determination and speed.

In determining its negotiating position, the Union should also avoid creating the impression that accession is simply copying Union laws, policies and structures and that there is nothing worth retaining of the systems which exist in Central Europe. It would also be wrong if accession to the Union meant reintroducing controls on people or goods which no longer exist in Central and Eastern Europe: it would be inappropriate to create new trade barriers between those countries that join the Union, those which will negotiate in the future and those, like Russia and the Ukraine, which are unlikely to join. This also applies to visa regulations and the movement of persons. Considerable study should be given to these questions in the Union in order not to appear like a colonising power, but also in order not to break precious relationships built up over the years since 1989.

This implies that the realisation of enlargement also requires that the Union gives consideration to its policy towards Russia and the Ukraine. The fear of these countries that enlargement means an economic wall coming down across Europe dividing the enlarged rich Union from struggling economies in the East must be countered by a deepening of the economic and political relationship between the enlarged Union and Eastern Europe.

The Union has never opened negotiations with applicant countries in a more uncertain and unprepared situation. Since the negotiations with the United Kingdom, Ireland and Denmark it has not negotiated to add such a large population to the Union and it has not negotiated with economically so different countries. Enlargement to include the CEE countries will, however, lead to a stronger European Union, with more political influence in the world and, if reforms are carried through, a stronger economy. It will be a different European Union, one where flexibility beyond the core policies of the Union determines the development of new policies. It will also probably be a Union where centralisation of power to Brussels is effectively controlled by the growing influence of the regions and an increase in their own power. But this does not mean a weaker Union. The alternative, where enlargement does not take place, contains the risk of a break-up of the current Union and renewed chaos in Central Europe. The future of the Continent depends on the success of enlargement and for this reason it must be the central objective of European policy in the coming decade.

# Postscript

The Luxembourg European Council, which was held on 12–13 December 1997, decided to open negotiations for accession to the Union with the Czech Republic, Estonia, Hungary, Poland, Slovenia and Cyprus. The enlargement process will formally start in London at the end of March 1998.

The European Council went to considerable lengths to avoid creating a new division in Europe between these countries and those with which the Union will not start negotiations immediately (Bulgaria, Latvia, Lithuania, Romania and the Slovak Republic). These measures include:

- The creation of a European Conference which all EU Member States and all the applicant countries, including Turkey, will be invited to join. This Conference will discuss all matters relevant to its members and will meet once each year at head of state and government level and once at foreign minister level. Turkey immediately made it clear that it was not prepared to participate, though there is a possibility that this decision may be reversed in the future.

- A single framework for the negotiation process including the EU-15 and the ten applicant countries. It is in this framework that the enlargement process will start in March 1998. Within this framework foreign affairs ministers but also technical ministers can meet to discuss questions of common interest; it is therefore a continuation of the structured dialogue set up at Copenhagen and Essen. If Turkey decides not to participate in the European Conference, these two bodies become identical in membership.

- It made clear that any country can join the negotiation process when it meets the requirements. The annual Commission report on each applicant country will be used, among other indicators, to judge whether a country should be invited to join the process.

- It agreed that the screening of the *acquis communautaire* would begin not just with the six negotiating countries but also with the five countries not involved in the negotiations.

- The pre-accession strategy will apply equally to all the applicant countries of Central Europe and Cyprus.

The dangers involved in the Union negotiating with certain applicant countries and not with others are quite obvious – the rejection by the Union of immediate negotiations, coming after the rejection by NATO, could cause serious political problems in these countries as a major support of foreign policy is taken away. There is also a risk that these countries will give up their ambitions to join the European Union and begin a period of political and economic drift, which destabilises even some of the countries which are negotiating. If, however, these countries are bound tightly into the European Union through regular meetings at all levels, through the screening of the *acquis* and through continuing financial assistance, and if the access to negotiations remains open, the EUs strategy may well prove to be the correct one.

The Luxembourg summit was not successful however in even making a start on the reform of Community policies. The European Union is hopelessly divided on the reform of the Structural Funds, while the reform of the CAP is only just beginning to attract the notice of agriculture ministers. There appears to be more agreement on the need for budgetary restraint, though here, too, the Member States are only at the beginning of their work. This means that the decision to open negotiations has been taken without any strategy on the EU side. This is still the greatest risk to enlargement.

It now seems likely that the reform of EU policies will have to wait until 1999, when decisions will be forced on the Community, both by the need to agree a new financial guideline for the period 2000–6 and by the beginning of the next WTO Round. This will make the negotiations with the CEE countries rather complicated and longer than expected. If real negotiations on the complex parts of these policies cannot start until towards the end of 1999, the whole negotiation and ratification process is likely to delay accession to the EU until 2003–5.

Finally the European Council decided on an enhanced pre-accession strategy including accession partnerships with reinforced conditionality. It did not however decide on any level of assistance for the period after 2000, nor how assistance should be shared out between the applicant countries. The enlargement process will begin in Spring 1998. However the end of the enlargement process cannot be predicted, even for the first group of countries. Little more can be drawn from the conclusions of the Luxembourg European Council.

The next decade will again be filled by changes in the economics and geopolitics of the European Continent which will probably leave it very different from the Europe of today. Monetary Union and the impact this will have both on policy-making and economic development in Europe, the extension of NATO eastwards, the increasing speed of globalisation and the ongoing technological and telecommunications revolutions, the evolving reform policies in Russia and the Ukraine and growing international migration flows are but some of the developments which will compete for attention with the Union's Eastern enlargement. These developments will sometimes slow down and sometimes speed up enlargement. However, Europe has now the chance to repair at least one part of the terrible inheritance of the Second World War.

If enlargement is completed in the coming decade, it will be one of the great achievements of post-war European politics. But only the first easy step has been taken and what follows will be far more difficult. Success will demand commitment and flexibility on both sides. The Luxembourg European Council has shown that national interest will dominate the debate, but it may have started a process leading to another triumph, like German reunification, which will launch Europe into the twenty-first century.

# Bibliography

Abraham, F. and Konings, J. (1997). 'The integration of post-Communist countries with western Europe' (Leuven), mimeo

Altmann, F., Andreff, W. and Fink, G. (1996). 'The future expansion of the European Union in central Europe', *IEF Working Paper*, 8 (Vienna)

Anderson, K. and Tyers, R. (1995). 'Implications of the EC expansion for European agricultural policies, trade and welfare', in R. Baldwin *et al.*, *Expanding membership of the EU* (Cambridge: Cambridge University Press)

Backé, P. (1997). 'Interlinkages between European Monetary Union and a future EU enlargement to Central and Eastern Europe', Bank of Finland, *Review of Economies in Transition*, 2, 27–45

Balcerowicz, L. (1995). *Socialism, capitalism, tranformation* (Budapest: CEU Press)

Baldwin, R. (1994). *Towards an integrated Europe* (London: Cambridge University Press for the CEPR)

Baldwin, R., Francois, J. and Portes, R. (1997). 'The costs and benefits of Eastern enlargement: the impact on the EU and Central Europe', *Economic Policy*, 24, 125–76

Baldwin, R., Haaparanta, P. and Kiander, J. (1995). *Expanding membership of the European Community* (London: Cambridge University Press for the CEPR)

Bernard, P., van Sebroeck, H., Spinnewyn, H., Gilot, A. and Vandenhove, P. (1994). *Delocalisation des entreprises* (Brussels: Bureau de Plan Belge)

Besnainou, D. (1995). 'Les fonds structurels: quelle application aux PECO?', *Économie internationale, la revue du CEPII*, 2, 215–32

Blanchard, O., Dornbusch, R., Krugman, P., Layard, R. and Summers, L. (1991). *Reform in Eastern Europe* (Cambridge, MA: MIT Press)

Blanchard, O., Boycko, M., Dabrowski, M., Dornbusch, R., Layard, R. and Shleifer, A. (1993). *Post-Communist reform: pain and progress* (Cambridge, MA: MIT Press)

Blanchet, T., Piipponen, R. and Westman-Clement, M. (1994). *The agreement on the European Economic Area (EEA)* (Oxford: Oxford University Press)

Bofinger, P. (1995). 'The political economy of the eastern enlargement of the EU', CEPR, *Discussion Paper*, 1234

Boner, R. and Krueger, R. (1993). 'The basics of anti-trust policy', World Bank, *Technical Papers*, 160 (Washington, DC: World Bank)

Booss, D. and Forman, J. (1995). 'Enlargement: legal and procedural aspects', *Common Market Law Review*, 32, 95–130

Buckwell, A., Haynes, J., Danidova, S. and Kwiecinski, A. (1994). *Feasibility of an agricultural strategy to prepare the countries of Central and Eastern Europe for EU accession* (Brussels: European Commission) (December)

Cecchini, P. (1988). *The European challenge, 1992, the benefits of the internal market* (Brussels: European Commission)

Centre for Economic Policy Research (1992). *Is bigger better? The economics of EC enlargement* (London: Cambridge University Press for the CEPR)

Collins, S. and Rodrik, D. (1991). *Eastern Europe and the Soviet Union in the world economy* (Washington, DC: Institute for International Economics)

Csaba, L. (1995). 'The political economy of trade regimes in Central Europe', in Winters (1995), 64–88

Dahrendorf, R. (1990). *Reflections on the revolution in Europe* (London: Chatto & Windus)

De Crombrugghe, A. and Fakin, B. (1997). 'European policies and economic growth of new entrants', Natolin Conference (Warsaw) (June), mimeo

de Crombrugghe, A., Minton-Beddoes, Z. and Sachs, J. (1996). 'EU membership for Central Europe: commitments, speed and conditionality', *Cahiers de la Faculté des Sciences Economiques et Sociales*, Namur, 29

de la Serre, F. (1996). 'L'élargissement aux Peco: quelle différentiation', *Revue du Marché Commun*, 402 (November), 642–7

Delegation du Senat Français pour l'Union Européenne (1996). *Union Européenne : les consequences économique et budgetaire de l'élargissement à l'Est* (Paris) (February)

De Long, B. and Eichengreen, B. (1993). 'The Marshall Plan: history's most successful structural adjustment programme', in Dornbusch et al. (1993), 189–230

Deutsche Bundesbank (1996). *Zahlungsbilanz nach Regionen* (Frankfurt) (August)

Deutsches Institut für Wirtschaftsforschung (1996). *Die wirtschaftliche Integration des assoziierten Länder* (Berlin: DIW) (September)

(1997). 'Europäisches Union: Osterweiterung und Arbeitskräftemigration', *DIW Wochenbericht*, 5 (January), 89–96

Dewatripont, M. et al. (1995). *Flexible integration, towards a more effective and democratic Europe* (London: Cambridge University Press for the CEPR) (November)

Dönhoff, Gräfin M. (1988). *Kindheit in Ostpreußen* (Berlin: Siedler Verlag)

Dornbusch, R., Nölling, W. and Layard, R. (eds.) (1993). *Postwar economic reconstruction and lessons for the East today* (Cambridge MA: MIT Press)

Drábek, Z. and Smith, A. (1995). 'Trade performance and trade policy in Central and Eastern Europe', CEPR, *Discussion Paper*, 1182

Eatwell, J., Ellman, M., Karlsson, M., Nuti, D. and Shapiro, J. (1997). 'Solidarity in Europe: the political economy of EU enlargement to the East', mimeo

EBRD (1996). *Transition report* (London: European Bank for Reconstruction and Development)

(1997). *Transition report* (London: European Bank for Reconstruction and Development)

Economic Commission for Europe (ECE) (1995). *International migration in*

*Central and Eastern Europe and the Commonwealth of Independent States* (Geneva)

EDC (1997). *Compliance costing for approximation of EU environmental legislation in the CEEC* (Dublin, May)

Eichengreen, B. and Uzan, M. (1992). 'The Marshall Plan; economic effects and implications for Eastern Europe and the former USSR', *Economic Policy*, 14 (April), 14–75

Emerson, M. (1996). *Redrawing the map of Europe* (London: Centre for Economic Performance, London School of Economics) (November)

European Commission (annual publication). *Annual reports on the Community's anti-dumping and anti-subsidy activities* (Brussels)

(various years). European Council: *Conclusions of the Presidency, Bulletin of the European Union*:
Dublin (June 1990)
Lisbon (June 1992)
Edinburgh (December 1992)
Copenhagen (June 1993)
Essen (December 1994)
Cannes (June 1995)
Madrid (December 1995)
Amsterdam (June 1997)

(1993). *Towards a new association with the countries of Central and Eastern Europe* (Brussels)

(1994). *Competitiveness and cohesion: trends in the regions* (Brussels)

(1995a). *Agricultural situation and prospects in the Central and Eastern European countries* (11 vols., 2 on Bulgaria and a summary vol.) (Brussels)

(1995b). *Phare funding 1990–1994* (Brussels)

(1995c). The 'Fischler' Report to the Madrid European Council (Brussels)

(1995d). *White Paper on the preparation of the associated countries of Central and Eastern Europe for integration into the Internal Market of the Union* (Brussels, COM (95) 163) (May)

(1995e). *Thirteenth annual report from the Commission to the European Parliament on the Community's anti-dumping and anti-subsidy activities (1994)* (Brussels) (July)

(1996a). *Phare annual report 1995* (Brussels)

(1996b). *First report on economic and social cohesion* (Brussels)

(1996c). Document SEC (96) 86 (The Langdon Report) (Brussels)

(1996d). *Central and East European Barometer*, 6 (Brussels) (March)

(1997a). *'Agenda 2000', The challenge of enlargement* (Brussels, COM (97) 2000) (July)

(1997b). *Central and East European Barometer*, 7 (Brussels) (March)

(1997c). *New policy guidelines for the Phare Programme in the framework of pre-accession assistance*, Information note of the Commission (26 March 1997)

European Constitutional Group (1993). *A proposal for a European Constitution* (London: ECG) (December)

European Court of Auditors (1996). *Annual Report 1995, OJ* C340 (Luxembourg) (12 November)

European Policy Centre (1997). *Making sense of the Amsterdam Treaty* (Brussels)

Faini, R. and Portes, R. (1995). *European Union trade with Eastern Europe: adjustment and opportunities* (London: Cambridge University Press for the CEPR)

Fingleton, J., Fox, E., Neven, D. and Seabright, P. (1996). *Competition policy and the transformation of Central Europe* (London: Cambridge University Press for the CEPR)

Franzmeyer, F. and Weise, C. (eds.), (1996). *Polen und die Erweiterung der Europäischen* Union, Sonderheft 158 (Berlin: DIW)

Garton Ash, T. (1993). *In Europe's name: Germany and the divided continent* (London: Jonathan Cape)

Government of the Republic of Hungary (1995). *Hungarian National strategy for the implementation of the recommendations of the White Paper on the integration into the internal market of the EU* (Budapest: Government of Hungary) (December)

Grabbe, H. and Hughes, K. (1997). *Eastward enlargement of the European Union* (London: Royal Institute of International Affairs)

Gros, D. and Gonciarz, A. (1994). *A note on the trade potential of Central and Eastern Europe* (Brussels: CEPS)

Gros, D. and Steinherr, A. (1995). *Winds of change; economic transition in Central and Eastern Europe* (London: Longman)

Herrnfeld, H.-H. (1996). *European by law: legal reform and approximation of law in the Visegrád countries* (Gutersloh: Bertelsmann Foundation Publishers)

Hoekman, B. (1995). 'Trade laws and institutions: good practices and the World Trade Organisation', World Bank, *Discussion Paper*, 282

Holmes, P. (1995). 'Competition, integration and business interests: levelling or tilting the playing field' (Prague), mimeo

Huntington, S. (1993). 'The clash of civilisations', *Foreign* Affairs, 72 (3), 22–49

Inotai, A. (1995). 'From Association Agreements to full membership: the dynamics of relations between the Central and Eastern European Countries and the European Union', *Working Paper*, 52 (Budapest: Institute for World Economics)

Jackson, M. and Biesbrouck, W. (1995). 'Marketization, restructuring and competition in transition industries of Central and Eastern Europe', *LICOS Studies on the Transitions in Central and Eastern Europe*, vol. 3 (Leuven)

Johnson, S. and Loveman, G. (1995). *Starting over in Eastern Europe* (Cambridge, MA: Harvard Business School)

Kaliszuk, E. (1994). 'Analysis of the particular problems of dumping during the transition period, Poland', OECD, *Working Paper* (March)

Kaminski, B. (1997). 'Foreign trade policies and institutions: getting ready for accession', Natolin Conference (Warsaw) (June), mimeo

Kaminski, B., Kun Wang, Z. and Winters, L. (1996). 'Foreign trade in the transition: the international environment and domestic policy', *World Bank Studies of Economies in Transformation*, 20

Kirchner, C. (1997). 'Competence catalogues and the principle of subsidiarity in a European constitution', *Constitutional Political Economy*, 8, 71–87

Kirk, D. (1946). *Europe's population in the inter-war years* (Princeton)

Kirman, A. and Widgrén, M. (1995). 'Voting in the European Union –

European economic decision-making policy: progress or paralysis?', *Economic Policy*, 21 (October), 421–60

Konings, J. and Roodhooft, F. (1996). 'How elastic is the demand for labour in Belgian enterprises?', Departement toegepaste economische wetenschappen, *Onderzoeksrapport*, 9540

Körber Stiftung (1995). 'Europa – aber wo liegen die Grenzen?', *Bergedörfer Gesprächskreis*, 104

Kornai, J. (1992). *The socialist system: the political economy of communism* (Oxford: Oxford University Press)

Kwiecinski, A. (1995). *Structural funds in the European Union – possible benefits for Poland* (Warsaw: FAPA)

Lankes, H.-P. and Venables, T. (1996). 'Foreign direct investment in economic transition: the changing pattern of investment', *Economics of Transition*, 4/2, 331–48

Layard, R., Blanchard, O., Dornbusch, R. and Krugman, P. (1992). *East–west migration: the alternatives* (Cambridge, MA: MIT Press)

Lippert, B. and Schneider, H. (eds.) (1995). *Monitoring association and beyond. The European Union and the Visegrád States* (Bonn : Europa Union Verlag)

Mahe, L. P. (1994). *L'agriculture et l'enlargissement de l'Union européene aux pays d'Europe centrale et orientale: transition en vue de l'integration ou integration pour la transition?* (Brussels: European Commission)

Mahe, L., Cordier, J., Guyomard, H. and Roe, T. (1995). 'La PAC et l'élargissement', *Economie internationale, la revue du CEPII*, 2, 233–54

Mayhew, A. (1996a). 'Going beyond the Europe Agreements: the European Union's strategy for accession', in Franzmeyer and Weise (1996), 13–39

(1996b). 'L'assistance financière à l'Europe centrale et orientale; le programme Phare', *Revue d'études comparatives est–ouest*, 27/4, 135–58

Messerlin, P. (1995). 'CEEC's trade laws in the light of international experience', in Winters (1995), 40–63

Milward, A. (1984). *The reconstruction of Western Europe* (London: Methuen)

Molle, W. (1994). *The economics of European integration* (Aldershot: Dartmouth)

Monar, J. and Morgan, R. (eds.) (1994). *The third pillar of the European Union* (Bruges: College of Europe)

Nagarajan, N. (1994). 'Putting dumping in context: EU imports from Central and Eastern Europe' (Brussels: European Commission), mimeo

Nallet, H. and van Stolk, A. (1994). *Les relations de l'UE et des Pays d'Europe Centrale et Orientale dans le domaine agricole at agro-alimentaire* (Brussels: European Commission)

Neven, D. (1995). 'Trade liberalisation with Eastern nations: how sensitive?', in Faini and Portes (1995), 19–60

OECD (1993). *Integrating emerging market economies into the international trading system* (Paris: OECD)

(1994a). *Economic Survey, Poland* (Paris: OECD)

(1994b). *Analysis of the particular problems of dumping during the transition period, Poland*, working party of the Trade Committee on East–West trade (Paris: OECD) (March)

(1994c). 'Report to the working party no. 1 on competition and international trade: anti-dumping and competition policy', chapter 5, Competition and the EC anti-dumping regulations (Paris: OECD) (February)

(1997). *Agricultural policies in transition economies, monitoring and evaluation* (Paris: OECD)

Orłowski, W. (1997). 'Domestic and foreign savings in financing growth', Natolin Conference (Warsaw) (June), mimeo

Orłowski, W. and Mayhew, A. (1997). 'The impact of EU accession on enterprise adaptation and institutional development in the EU-associated countries in Central and Eastern Europe', study for the EBRD (London: European Bank for Reconstruction and Development), mimeo

Republic of Poland (1997). *National Strategy for Integration* (Warsaw: Government of Poland) (January)

Rollo, J. and Smith, A. (1993). 'The political economy of EC trade with Eastern Europe: why so sensitive?', *Economic Policy*, 16 (April)

Rudka, A. and Mizsei, K. (1995). *East Central Europe, between disintegration and reintegration; is CEFTA the solution?* (New York: Institute for East–West Studies)

Sachs, J. (1993). *Poland's jump to the market economy* (Cambridge MA: MIT Press)

Saint Aubin, B. (1995a). 'Le coût de l'élargissement', *Économie internationale, la revue du CEPII*, 2, 255–64

(1995b). *Le PAC et l'elargissement* (Brussels: CEPII)

Sapir, A. (1995). 'The Europe Agreements: implications for trade laws and institutions', in Winters (1995), 89–107

Senior, Nello S. and Smith, K. (forthcoming). 'The European Union and Eastern Europe: the implication of enlargement in stages', *EUI Working Paper* (Florence)

Siebert, H. (1997). 'Labour market rigidities: at the root of unemployment in Europe', *Journal of Economic Perspectives* (Summer), 37–54

Smith, A., Holmes, P., Sedelmeier, U., Smith, E., Wallace, H. and Young, A. (1996). 'The European Union and central and eastern Europe: core-accession strategies', Sussex European Institute, *Working Paper*, 15

Swain, N. (1992). *Hungary, the Rise and Fall of Feasible Socialism* (London: Verso)

Tangermann, S. and Josling, T. (1994). *Pre-accession agricultural policies for Central Europe and the European Union* (Brussels: European Commission) (December)

Tarditi, S., Senior-Nello, S. and Marsh, J. (1994). *Agricultural strategies for the enlargement of the European Union to Central and Eastern European countries* (Brussels: European Commission)

Treuhandanstalt and Bundesverband der deutschen Wirtschaft (1993). *Privatisieren* (Köln: Deutsche Instituts-Verlag)

Vandenbussche, H. (1995). 'How can the Japanese and Central European exporters to the European Union avoid anti-dumping duties?', *World Competition* (March)

Warsaw School of Economics (1994). *Transforming the Polish economy* (Warsaw: WSE)

Westendorp, C. (1995). *Report of the reflection group* (Brussels) (December)

Winckler, G. (1992). *Central and Eastern Europe, roads to growth* (Washington, DC: International Monetary Fund and Austrian National Bank)

Winters, L. A. (1995). *Foundations of an open economy, trade laws and institutions for Eastern Europe* (London: Cambridge University Press for the CEPR)

World Bank (1996). *World Development Report 1996: From Plan to Market* (Oxford: Oxford University Press)

   (1997a). *Country Economic Memorandum, Poland* (Washington, DC: World Bank (July)

   (1997b). *Country Economic Memorandum, Slovakia* (Washington, DC: World Bank (July)

# Index

(This index does not refer systematically to the EU Institutions or the individual Member States; these are referred to throughout the book. Use should also be made of the detailed 'Contents' listing at the front of the book.)